Adobe®
Photoshop® 6.0

Studio
TECHNIQUES

 Windows/Macintosh

Ben Willmore

Adobe Photoshop 6.0 Studio Techniques

Ben Willmore

Copyright © 2001 by Ben Willmore

This Adobe Press book is published by Peachpit Press. For information on Adobe Press books, contact:

Peachpit Press
1249 Eighth Street
Berkeley, CA 94710
(510) 524-2178
Fax: (510) 524-2221
http://www.peachpit.com

For the latest on Adobe Press books, go to http://www.adobe.com/adobepress

Editors: Wendy Katz, Wendy Sharp
Technical Editors: Victor Gavenda, Conrad Chavez
Production Coordinator: Kate Reber
Compositor: Maureen Forys, Happenstance Type-O-Rama
Contributing Editor: Regina Cleveland
Indexer: Emily Glossbrenner, FireCrystal Communications
Cover design: Mimi Heft
Cover illustration: Alicia Buelow

Notice of Rights

Notice of Liability

Trademarks

ISBN 0-201-71612-7

9 8 7 6 5 4 3 2

Printed and bound in the United States of America

Contents

About the Author

Ben Willmore is the founder of Digital Mastery, a Boulder, Colorado–based training and consulting firm that specializes in electronic publishing. Ben has always been known to be a little nutty about all things technical, even as a child. Not long after he traded in his tricycle for training wheels, he started building cameras out of do-it-yourself kits. In 1981, at the tender age of 14, he made his official debut into computer nerd-dom when he attended CompuCamp. That's where he discovered his first two loves, computers and graphic design, and where he learned how to use a graphics tablet to produce art on an Apple][computer—three full years before the Macintosh said its first "Hello."

Not surprisingly, he went on to become a graphic designer. In those days that meant knowing all about such primitive things as typesetting, keylining, and stat cameras. When the first tools of electronic publishing started showing up, Ben began his trend as an aggressive early adopter of new technologies. While most people in the business were holding back in a wait-and-see attitude, Ben was charging ahead and embracing the new tools like long-lost friends. His first serious push into the new arena was when he converted his college's daily newspaper from traditional techniques to electronic tools in the late '80s.

Ben became known as someone who likes to push his tools to the limit, causing many printing companies and service bureaus to ask "How'd you do that?" His obsession with the nuts and bolts of electronic publishing turned him into an unwitting one-man customer support center for all his friends and coworkers. It was this, he discovered, that was his third love—helping others truly understand graphics software. And so he decided to go out on his own and teach his favorite program (Photoshop) full time.

In 1994, he created what has become the hugely successful seminar, Photoshop Mastery (aka Master Photoshop in 3 Days). Since then he has taught over 10,000 Photoshop users, and travels all over the country presenting his seminars and speaking at publishing events such as PhotoshopWorld. He is an alpha and beta tester for Adobe Photoshop and writes a monthly column for *PEI* magazine and *Photoshop User* magazine. Ben can be reached at willmore@digitalmastery.com.

Author's Acknowledgments

Even though my name appears on the cover of this book, it was, of course, a collaborative effort, and would not have been possible without the help of the following people:

Regina "GNR's" Cleveland, the "Queen of Logistics" here at Digital Mastery, who (as usual) went way beyond the call of duty to get this book out the door. I don't think she's had a day off in well over a month and I doubt she's been getting too many hours of sleep, either. Without her, I would never have been able to get to the finish line. Now that the book is done, I'm sure she'll be happy to regain her weekends and will very soon be asking for a well-deserved vacation.

Marjorie Baer (Executive Editor) and her remarkable patience in allowing the book to continue over what felt like a millennium while I lived through everything from a threatening forest fire and a relentless travel schedule to a slew of commitments that always found a way to distract me from the business of writing.

Susan Walton, who put her trust in me when I was a first-time author.

The Watchful Wendys, Wendy Sharp and Wendy Katz, whose scrupulously careful editing and insightful suggestions made for a much better book.

Victor Gavenda and his persistent ability to go through the technical content with a fine-tooth comb and split hairs when necessary.

Kate Reber, who has rallied people in four time zones to keep this project on schedule and made it her business to see that it was done well.

Maureen Forys, for translating a bunch of words and pictures into great-looking pages.

Matt Wagner and Vivian Glyck, whose assistance has made this revision more rewarding.

Jay Nelson, who has helped me in more ways than I can imagine or remember. He's an amazing guy who always comes through in a pinch, and seems happiest when he's lending someone a hand.

Jerry Kennelly at Stockbyte and Stephanie Robey at PhotoSpin, whose generous contributions of stock imagery made it possible for us to include a bunch of great practice images on the CD at the back of the book.

My brother Nik, who was always at the ready with as much constructive criticism as I could handle, while others would simply say "Oh, that's nice."

To all of the gifted artists and organizations who contributed images to this book: your illuminating work transformed our bare pages into things of elegance, sparkle, and humor.

Don Barnett	David Plunkert
Howard Berman	Howard Schatz
David Bishop	Jeff Schewe
Robert Bowen	Naomi Shea
Robert Brünz	Michael Slack
Alicia Buelow	Bronson Smith
Jimmy Chen	Gordon Studer
Tom Nick Cocotos	Stephen Wishny
Bob Elsdale	Dutton Children's Books
Diane Fenster	Graphis Press
Louis Fishauf	HarperCollins Publishers
Ryszard Horowitz	Lowe & Partners/SMS
Chris Klimek	Rizzoli Publishers International Press
Maria Kostyk-Petro	
Nick Koudis	Schieffelin & Somerset
Eric Meola	Sony Electronics, Inc.
Beverly Ornstein	

And finally, I thank all the people who have attended my seminars over the past six years. You've given me a limitless supply of inspiration and feedback and have allowed me to follow my passion for knowledge and understanding.

Foreword

Learning to use Adobe Photoshop is similar to learning to play an electric guitar; with a little instruction and a little practice, you can create some very pleasant art. Or, if you're really motivated, you can lock yourself in a closet with it for 12 years and emerge playing some amazing "chops." Most of us fall somewhere in between, and all of us have more to learn.

But the thing is, while few people are frightened by a guitar, many people find Photoshop very intimidating. That's what is so great about Ben Willmore, the author of this book: he takes away your fear.

For the past several years, Ben has traveled across the United States, presenting his unique Photoshop seminar. Unique because it focuses on real-world jobs done every day by Photoshop users, and unique because Ben explains concepts and techniques in a way that everyone in the room can understand. Ben's examples are based on his professional production experience, so everything he teaches helps you create images that successfully reproduce on paper or the Web.

I attended his seminar and was especially impressed by his ability to avoid technical jargon, and by his uncanny knack for answering questions before they're asked. Ben is a rare teacher; even advanced users are satisfied, and rank beginners never feel lost. Like all great teachers, Ben uses metaphors, relating new ideas to concepts you're already comfortable with. In the pages of this book, you'll see Photoshop's most esoteric concepts clearly explained, while its major features are masterfully positioned into a framework of "how do I accomplish the task at hand?"

We each have different uses for Photoshop, and we each have different ways of learning. Fortunately for our increasingly overtaxed brains, less than half of Photoshop's features are used to accomplish most real-world tasks. And more fortunately for us, Ben Willmore has written this book.

Enjoy the time you share with Ben and Photoshop. I'm sure you'll find it a rare pleasure.

Jay J. Nelson
Editor
Design Tools Monthly
www.design-tools.com

Introduction

Orville Wright did not
have a pilot's license.
–Gordon Mackenzie

Courtesy of David Bishop, www.dbsf.com

Why *This* Book?

When I was writing the 5.0 version of this book, I took a hard look at the bookshelves at Barnes and Noble and asked myself the question, "Does the world really need another Photoshop book?" I believed that even though there were literally dozens of excellent publications available on the subject, there was still a need for a book that focused on truly *understanding* Photoshop, rather than just blindly following step-by-step techniques. Two years later, I'm happy to say that thousands upon thousands of readers have confirmed that belief and have flooded my In Basket with e-mails that share a common theme—"After reading your book, I finally GET Photoshop!" I want to thank each and every one of you who wrote expressing appreciation. And I especially want to thank the ones who took the time to offer their constructive criticism and suggestions. This book is better because of it.

Secure in the knowledge that I'm taking the right approach, I now want you to GET Photoshop 6.0. It's been touted as "the biggest upgrade in Photoshop's history," and is packed to the rafters with exciting new features. I was fortunate enough to Alpha test this version for over six months before it was released, and I can safely say (at risk of sounding like an Adobe salesman) that from the smallest touches to the largest features, it's obvious that Adobe has really been listening to their customers.

What's In This Book?

Well, first I'll tell you what's *not* in it. It's not a special-effects cookbook that concentrates on bizarre and exotic tricks and effects (although there are a few juicy ones in the "Creative Explorations" section). Nor does it tackle the artistic aesthetics of digital design. There's a truckload of books available on those subjects, which will most likely be sitting right next to this one at the bookstore.

My mission is to help you graduate from "I'm just going through the motions" to "At last, I *really* understand Photoshop." Once you've made that leap, you will experience an incredible ripple effect. Your efficiency level will skyrocket. Your costs will go down. Your creative genius will come out of the closet like gangbusters, and your clients (or boss) will be thrilled. Really! I've seen it happen more times than I can remember. And I still get a thrill whenever I see one of my students go through what I've come to think of as the "transformation."

The Latest From 6.0

Many of the enhancements are radical and practically shouting to be noticed, while others are more subtle and take quite a bit of ferreting to unearth. Photoshop's color management features have gone through a much-needed facelift, making them considerably more powerful and user-friendly. The new Type features make it so that Photoshop acts more like a page layout program, but it still lacks a spell checker or style sheets. Adobe has added vector support, which means that you can finally create non-jaggy type that remains that way even when saved and printed from another application. And if you have ever struggled with an image with abundant layers, you'll be ecstatic to know that layer management has improved dramatically. By increasing the number of layers you can use, and by allowing you to organize them into layer sets, you can now make a hundred-layer image appear to only have three layers! The new layer styles are layer effects on steroids, and the sky's the limit when it comes to what you can do with them using gradients, patterns, strokes, and more.

If you have just upgraded from 5.0, and skipped the 5.5 version, you'll discover that ImageReady, Adobe's advanced Web production tool, is now bundled with Photoshop. It includes built-in slicing tools, rollover styles, and weighted optimization controls, all of which will help you refine the visual results you can achieve on-screen, and significantly streamline your Web graphics production.

No Technical Mumbo Jumbo!

I hate technical mumbo jumbo! If words like gamma, bitmapped, clipping paths, algorithms, dither, posterize, and anti-aliasing drive you crazy, you'd better believe that they drive me even crazier. So, you'll find that I'm very big on stories and metaphors. I'll do whatever it takes to communicate the concept to you, without relying on ten-syllable words or terms that sound like they came from the inside of an engineer's head. And for those of you who can't live without the technical terms, you'll find all those icky words and their full definitions in "Ben's Techno-Babble Decoder Ring" at the end of most chapters.

Something for Everyone

This book has greatly expanded its scope from the 5.0 version to include a whole new section (four new chapters!) on Web graphics. So, whether you're preparing images for print, multimedia, or the Web, you'll find a wealth of information that will go far toward helping you produce a highly professional result. In terms of skill level, this book is written in such a way that users who are generally comfortable with their computer should be able to fully comprehend the information, no matter how advanced the topic. I've made the assumption that you've either installed Photoshop, or that you're using the *Photoshop User Guide* to do that. (There's no reason to duplicate that kind of information here.) And if you're an advanced user, don't worry. Just because the book is very understandable doesn't mean that we won't get into the real meat of Photoshop.

Mac and Windows: Equal Rights for All!

If are a Windows user and you read the last version of this book, you might have felt a bit left out because all the keyboard commands were given for the Macintosh, and Windows users were asked to make the translation. My intentions were good—I wanted the text to be clean and easy to read. But I've learned that good intentions don't cut it for everyone, and since more than half of the Photoshop universe resides on Windows, I've added the Windows keyboard commands. In all instances, both Mac and Windows keyboard commands are integrated into the text.

Get Inspiration from Others' Perspiration!

Even though I claim that this is not a special-effects cook-book, I've made sure that there's enough artistic inspira-tion in this book to help rev your creative engine. At the beginning and end of most chapters you can feast your eyes on samples from many of my favorite artists. It's true that they all have the "gift," but remember, nobody comes out of the womb understanding Photoshop, and each and every one of these digital masters had to take the time and effort to navigate Photoshop's learning curve, much the same as you are doing now.

Stuff on the CD at the Back of the Book

In an effort to keep the page count down, I've included some helpful bits of information on the CD at the back of the book. There you'll find supplements for several of the chapters, including additional image blending tech-niques; how to perform color correction in CMYK mode; and expanded coverage of Levels, Curves, and Selections. Each of these supplements is included in a PDF docu-ment, and Adobe Acrobat Reader has been included so that you can easily view all of these PDF files.

You'll also be able to demo a version of Photoshop 6 (in the event you don't already own a copy).

And to make it as easy as possible for you to follow along with my examples, we've provided many of the example images on the CD. For those of you who read the 5.0 ver-sion of this book and were disappointed by the number of images available, you'll be delighted to find dozens more images included. You can find these in a folder called Sample Images.

A book like this can't be put together without the help of some very helpful stock image companies. PhotoSpin and Stockbyte came to the plate with some great images. Stockbyte, in particular, was kind enough to allow me to use as many images as I wanted from their library, so while you're perusing the CD, check out their folder and see what else they have to offer.

Beyond the Book

I'd like to think that this one book can teach you everything you need to know about Photoshop, but the reality is that it would probably take 5,000 pages and a dozen authors to even begin to exhaust the potential that exists within this remarkable program. This book will give you what you need to master Photoshop's most essential features, and when you are ready for more, you are invited to visit the book's companion Web site, **www.digitalmastery.com/companionsite/**. There you will find a treasure trove of tips, corrections, magazine articles, and resources that will fortify you as you continue your adventures with Photoshop. You are also invited to subscribe to my free Tip of the Week at **www.digitalmastery.com/tips**. And of course, I would love to see you at one of my seminars. To find out if I'll be presenting a seminar in your area, please visit **www.digitalmastery.com.**

So, enough blabbing; let's get on with the "transformation." I'll make it as easy on you as I possibly can, but just remember the words of my favorite character, Miracle Max, from the movie *The Princess Bride*: You rush a miracle man, you get rotten miracles.

Part I **Working Foundations**

Courtesy of Diane Fenster, www.dianefenster.com

1 Tool and Palette Primer

Out of clutter,
find simplicity.
–Albert Einstein

Opening Photoshop for the first time and seeing all the tools and palettes competing for space on your screen can be a dizzying experience. You might find yourself thinking "that's great, but they forgot to leave room in there for me to work!" Some of the more fortunate Photoshoppers get to have a second monitor, just to hold all their palettes. The rest of us make do and find ways to keep our screens neat and tidy. You'll discover that finding places to put your tools and palettes is almost as important as knowing how to use them. This chapter is all about effectively managing your workspace and getting acquainted with the oodles of gadgets and gizmos found in the tools and palettes.

Preparing Your Workspace

Before we get into functionality, we'll talk about how to control that prodigious profusion of palettes. But first, a word of advice: no matter how many times you feel like nuking a palette when it's in your way, no matter how many times your screen turns into a blinding jumble of annoying little boxes, just remember that you can organize the clutter into an elegant arrangement in just a few seconds.

Controlling Those Palettes

The first order of business is to get you enough space to work effectively with your images. We'll accomplish this by organizing the palettes so that they don't obstruct your view of your document. I don't think you'll like the default position of the palettes—that is, unless you use a 36″ screen. The palettes take up too much valuable screen real estate (**Figure 1.1**).

Collapsing the Palettes

One way to quickly maximize your workspace is to collapse the palettes when you're not using them and move them to the bottom of your screen. To collapse a palette, double-click any of the name tabs at the top of the palette. To reposition a palette, click the little gray bar at the top of the palette and then drag it toward the bottom of your screen. When you move a palette close to the bottom of the screen, it should snap in place (**Figure 1.2**).

Note

To force a palette to snap to the edge of your screen, press the Shift key as you reposition the palette.

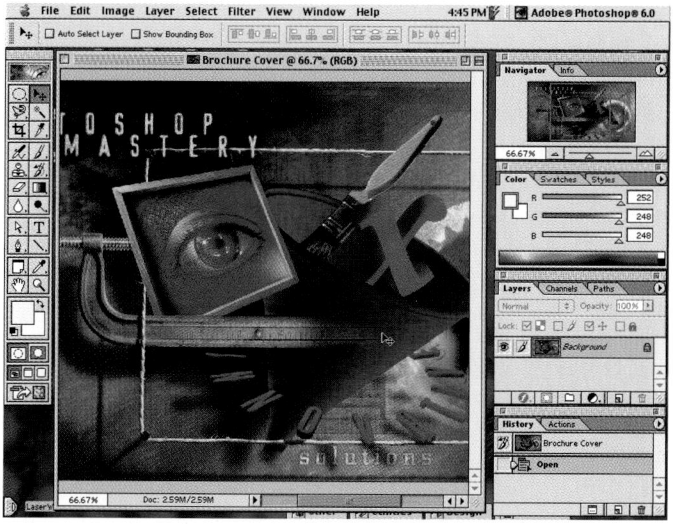

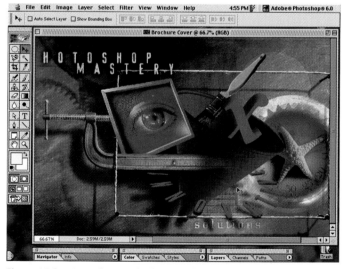

Figure 1.1 Photoshop's palettes take up a large portion of the screen.

Figure 1.2 Stowing palettes at the bottom of the screen. (Image courtesy of Chris Klimek)

Note

If you click on the Zoom tool and then turn on the Ignore Palettes button in the Options bar, Photoshop will ignore your palettes whether or not they're close to the right edge of your screen.

One thing you need to make sure of when repositioning your palettes is to not place any palettes too close to the right edge of your screen. This edge, affectionately known as palette alley, can cause you great pains when zooming in on your images (**Figure 1.3**). Here's why: If you have a palette too close to the right edge of your screen and you press Command-+ (Macintosh) or Ctrl-+ (Windows), Photoshop can't resize the document window to the width of your screen. Instead, it leaves palette alley open and doesn't allow the document window to intrude into this space. This means your efforts to reposition the palettes in order to save space were futile.

Figure 1.3 Palette alley stays clear whenever a palette is close to the right edge of your screen.

If you need access to any of these palettes, double-click the palette's name tab and the palette will instantly pop open (**Figure 1.4**). When you're done using the palette, just double-click its name tab to collapse it again.

Regrouping the Palettes

Another way to maximize your screen real estate is to change the way your palettes are grouped. For example, if your most frequently used palettes are the Color and History palettes, you can put them in one group so that you have one palette open at any given time instead of two. To regroup the palettes, drag the name tab of the palette you want to move (in this case, Color) on top of the palette grouping you want to move the palette into (History, in this case). You can then remove any palettes you don't want in this grouping by dragging the name tab of a palette onto an open area of the screen (**Figure 1.5**).

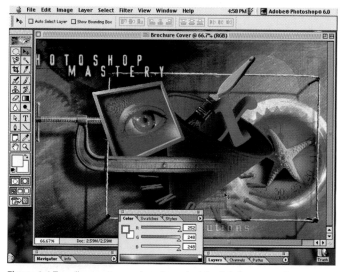

Figure 1.4 To collapse or expand a palette, double-click the name tab.

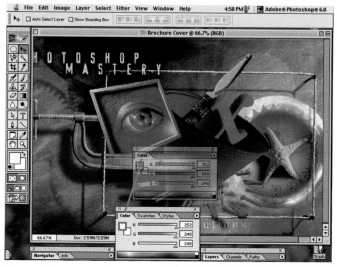

Figure 1.5 To separate a palette from a grouping, drag the name tab to an open area of your screen.

The Palette Well

If you have a screen that can display more than 800x600 pixels total, then you'll have another special place to store your palettes—Photoshop 6.0's new Palette well. If you look in the Options bar at the top of your screen, you should notice a dark gray area on the far right. That's a special spot where you can drag the name of a few palettes to store them until they're needed. Then, when you'd like to have access to one of those palettes, just click on the name of the palette, and it will drop down from the Palette well (**Figure 1.6**). After you're done using a palette, just click anywhere outside of the palette and it should collapse itself back into the Palette well.

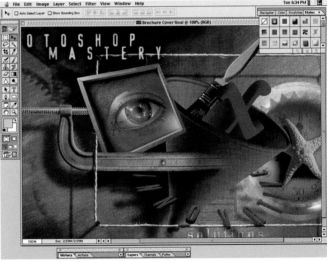

Figure 1.6 To temporarily expand a palette, click on the name of a palette in the Palette well.

Stacking Palettes

In Photoshop 6.0, you can now stack palettes one on top of another, and if you move the top palette (by dragging the gray bar at the top of the palette), the palettes that are stacked will move together. To stack two palettes, drag the name tab of one palette to the middle of another palette and then drag down until you see a black rectangle appear across the bottom of the palette you are dragging onto. You can drag to the top or bottom of a palette depending on how you'd like the palettes to be stacked. I like to stack the Character and Paragraph palettes together so I can keep all the type settings in one convenient area (**Figure 1.7**). After you have two palettes stacked together, you can drag other palettes into the grouping so that the top palette might be a group of three and the bottom a single palette.

Notes

If you really mess things up and your screen gets to looking like an Escher print, you can easily set all the palettes back to their default locations. To do this, choose Window > Reset Palette Locations.

If you turn off the Save Palette Locations checkbox in the File > Preferences > General dialog box, each time you launch Photoshop, the palettes will be at their default locations.

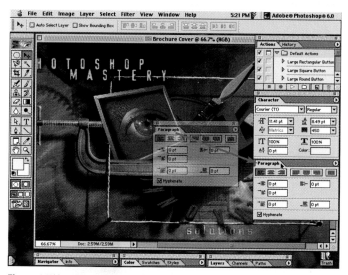

Figure 1.7 You can stack two palettes by dragging the name of one palette to the top or bottom of another.

If, after moving and regrouping your palettes, you find that a palette appears to be missing, don't panic. You can always find it in the Window menu. This menu lists all the palettes that are available (**Figure 1.8**).

Working with Screen Modes

Even with the palettes conveniently stowed at the bottom of your screen, your image still doesn't use all of the screen space available. You can use the three screen mode icons at the bottom of the Tools palette to easily solve this problem.

Standard Screen Mode

The first icon, Standard Screen Mode, is the default mode (**Figure 1.9**). You're probably used to working with this one. In this mode, the name of your document is at the

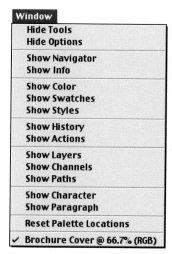

Figure 1.8 The Window menu lists all the palettes available in Photoshop.

top of the document window, and the scroll bars are on the side and bottom of that window.

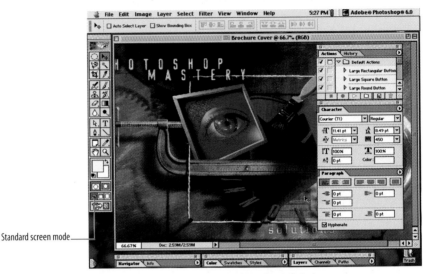

Standard screen mode

Figure 1.9 The first screen mode is Photoshop's default.

Full Screen Mode with Menu Bar

The second icon, Full Screen Mode With Menu Bar, lets the image flow all the way across your screen and slip right under the palettes (**Figure 1.10**). If you click this icon, the scroll bars will disappear, so you'll have to use the Hand tool to navigate around your document. But that's okay, because you can hold down the spacebar at any time to temporarily use the Hand tool. If you zoom out of a document so that it doesn't take up the entire screen, Photoshop will fill the area around the image with gray.

Full Screen Mode

The third screen mode icon, Full Screen Mode, is my favorite. In this mode, Photoshop turns off even the menu bar! Now your image can take over the entire screen (**Figure 1.11**). You can still use many of the menu commands, as long as you know their keyboard equivalents. If you zoom out while in this mode, Photoshop will fill the area around your image with black (I don't know how to change that one). I use this mode whenever I show images to clients. If you don't let them know you're in Photoshop, they might think you are in a cheap little slide-show program, and won't ask you to make changes on the spot. However, you won't be able to fool anyone if all those palettes are still on your screen. Just press Tab and they'll all disappear (**Figure 1.12**). Don't worry, you can get them back just as fast by pressing Tab again.

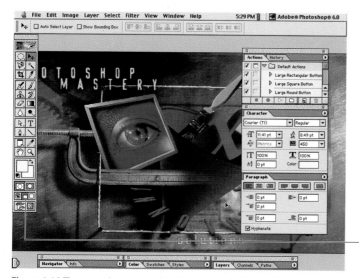

Full screen mode
with menu bar

Figure 1.10 The second screen mode allows you to use the entire screen.

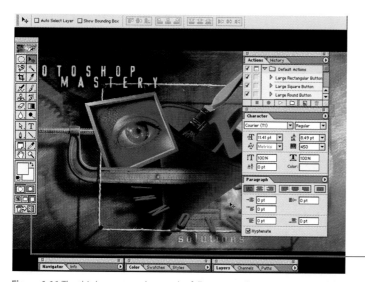

Full screen mode

Figure 1.11 The third screen mode uses the full screen and removes the menu bar.

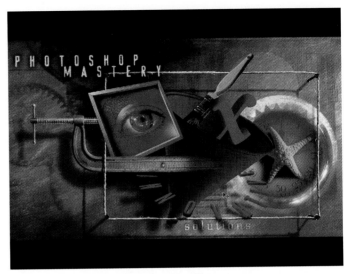

Figure 1.12 Press Tab to hide or show the palettes.

Screen Mode Shortcuts

I use the different screen modes every single day, but it's not very often that I actually click those three little toolbox icons. Instead, I use keyboard commands. Just press the F key on your keyboard to cycle through the different screen modes. You can even type F-F-Tab while an image is opening; that way, when it's done loading, Photoshop will switch to the third screen mode and rid your screen of all the palettes!

Now that you have your screen under control, we can start to explore some of the tools and palettes.

A Quick Tour of the Tools

There are more than 40 tools available in the Tools palette. Describing all of them in detail would take up a huge chunk of this chapter (which you probably don't have the patience for), so for now we'll take a look at the ones that you absolutely can't live without. Don't worry about missing out on anything—as you work your way through the book, you'll get acquainted with the rest of the tools. In the meantime, I'll introduce you to some tool names so that when I mention one, you'll know what to look for (**Figures 1.13 and 1.14**).

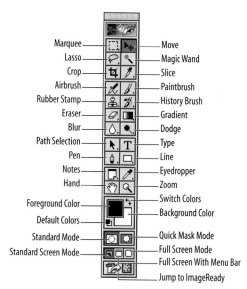

Figure 1.13 Photoshop's default Tools palette.

Marquee — Move
Lasso — Magic Wand
Crop — Slice
Airbrush — Paintbrush
Rubber Stamp — History Brush
Eraser — Gradient
Blur — Dodge
Path Selection — Type
Pen — Line
Notes — Eyedropper
Hand — Zoom
Foreground Color — Switch Colors
Default Colors — Background Color
Standard Mode — Quick Mask Mode
Standard Screen Mode — Full Screen Mode
Full Screen With Menu Bar
Jump to ImageReady

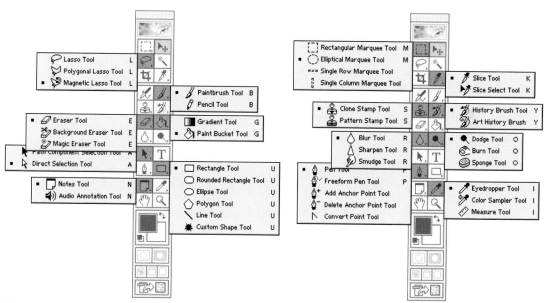

Figure 1.14 Photoshop's arsenal of tools.

The Options Bar

Most of the tools have settings associated with them. To access these settings, take a peek at the Options bar that extends across the top of your screen.

You'll be able to change the various settings more quickly if you know exactly how to navigate the Options bar. For example, all the painting and retouching tools have a percentage setting near the right side of the bar. There are quite a few ways to change this number. One is to highlight the number and then type a new one. You can also click the number and then use the up arrow and down arrow keys on your keyboard (add the Shift key to change the number by increments of 10). You can also click the arrow to the right of the number and drag across the slider that appears. All of the above options will work with any numeric entry in a palette (not just the Options bar), but there is a special method for changing the percentage setting for your painting tools. If none of the text fields in the Options bar are active for editing, then you can just type a number (not in a field, just type). If you type 1, then you'll end up with 10%, 23 will give you 23%, 0 will give you 100%, and so forth.

If there's more than one setting that lets you enter a number, press Return or Enter to highlight the first one, then tab your way through the others. Once a number is highlighted, you can change it by pressing the up arrow and down arrow keys or by typing a new number.

Navigating Your Document

Most of us struggle with monitors that are not large enough to view an entire document (except, of course, the more privileged Photoshoppers who have monitors that are practically as large as drive-in movie screens). To deal with this ever-present limitation, you must train yourself to be a quick and nimble navigator. Photoshop offers you a huge array of choices, and, as usual, you'll need to weed through them to find your favorite method. In this section, we'll cover the palettes and tools you need to maximize the speed with which you get around your document.

The Navigator Palette

If you do a lot of detail work where you need to zoom in on your image as if you're wearing glasses as thick as Coke bottles, you should love the Navigator palette (**Figure 1.15**). The Navigator palette floats above your document and allows you to quickly move around and zoom in and out of your image. A little red box indicates which area of the image you're currently viewing. By dragging this box around the miniature image of your document that appears in the Navigator palette, you can change which area you're viewing in the main image window. You can also just click outside the red box and the box will center itself on your cursor.

There are a number of ways to zoom in on your document by using this palette. Use the mountain icons to zoom in or out at preset increments (50%, 66.67%, 100%, 200%, and so on), or grab the slider between them to zoom to any level. You can change the number in the lower-left corner of the palette to zoom to an exact percentage. However, my favorite method is to drag across the image while holding down the Command key (Macintosh) Ctrl key(Windows) to zoom into a specific area.

Hand Tool

The Hand tool is definitely the most basic tool in Photoshop. By clicking and dragging with the Hand tool, you can scroll around the image. This tool is—excuse the pun—handy for scrolling around images that are too large to fit on your screen and for moving without the scroll bars. Since this tool is used so often, Adobe created a special way to get to it. While working with most of Photoshop's tools, if you press the spacebar, you will temporarily activate the Hand tool. When you release the spacebar, you'll be back in the tool you were using previously.

Zoom Tool

Whenever you click on your image by using the Zoom tool, you zoom in on the image to a preset level (just like the mountain icons in the Navigator palette). I almost never use the tool in this way because it takes too long to get where I want to be. Instead, I usually click and drag

Figure 1.15 The Navigator palette.

Note

If you don't like the color of the little red box, or if there's so much red in your image that the box becomes difficult to see, you can change the box color by choosing Palette Options from the side menu of the palette.

across the area I want to enlarge, and Photoshop immediately zooms me into that specific area.

In addition to zooming in, you also have options for quickly zooming out. Double-click the Hand tool icon in the Tools palette to fit the entire image on screen. You can also double-click the Zoom tool icon in the Tools palette to view your image at 100% magnification. (This will show you how large your image will appear when viewed in a Web browser or in any program designed for multimedia. It is not an indication of how large it will be when printed.) Option-clicking (Macintosh) or Alt-clicking (Windows) with the Zoom tool zooms you out at preset levels.

View Menu

If you're going to be doing a bunch of detail work in which you need to zoom in really close on your image, you might want to create two views of the same document (**Figures 1.16 and 1.17**). That way, you can have one of the views at 100% magnification to give you an overall view of your image, and you can set the second one to 500% magnification, for instance, to see all the fine details. To create a second view, choose View > New View. This will create a second window that looks like a separate document, but it's really just another view of the same document. You can make your edits in either window and both of them will show you the result of your manipulations.

From the View menu, you can also select from the Zoom In, Zoom Out, Fit On Screen, and Actual Pixels options. As you'll probably notice, each of these actions can also be accomplished by using the Zoom and Hand tools. The reason they're also listed under the View menu is to allow you to quickly use them with keyboard commands. Here are the View menu options:

▶ **Zoom In/Zoom Out**—Same as clicking with the Zoom tool. Uses the easy-to-remember keyboard shortcut Command-+ (Macintosh) or Ctrl-+ (Windows) to zoom in and Command-− (Macintosh) or Ctrl-− (Windows) to zoom out. Those are plus signs and minus signs, in case that's not completely clear.

Figure 1.16 100% magnification. (© 2000 Chris Klimek)

Figure 1.17 500% magnification.

▶ **Fit On Screen**—Same as double-clicking the Hand tool. Uses the shortcut Command-0 (Macintosh) or Ctrl-0 (Windows). That's a zero, not the letter O.

▶ **Actual Pixels**—Same as double-clicking the Zoom tool. Uses the shortcut Option-Command-0 (Macintosh) or Alt-Ctrl-0 (Windows). Again, that's zero, not the letter O.

▶ **Print Size**—Allows you to preview how large or small your image will appear when it's printed.

Just when you thought there couldn't possibly be any more ways to zoom in and out of your document, Adobe threw in just one more method for good measure. You can change the percentage that appears in the lower-left corner of your document window; just drag across it and enter a new percentage.

There are indeed many ways to zoom around in Photoshop. Now all you have to do is test out all the options, decide which one you prefer, and ignore the rest.

Picking Colors

My father's Webster's Dictionary—a 1940 model that's over half a foot thick—devoted four entire pages to describing one word: color. These pages are filled with lush descriptions of hue, tint, shade, saturation, vividness, brilliance, and much, much more. It's no wonder that choosing colors can be such a formidable task. Do you want Cobalt Blue or Persian Blue? Nile Green or Emerald? Carmine or Vermilion? Fortunately, Photoshop has done an excellent job of providing the tools you need to find the colors you want. Of course, each tool has advantages and disadvantages. You just have to play around with them and decide which one you prefer.

Foreground and Background Colors

The two square overlapping boxes that appear toward the bottom of your Tools palette are the foreground and background colors (**Figure 1.18**). The top box is the foreground color; it determines which color will be used when you use any of the painting tools. To change the foreground

---

Note

The Print Size option is almost never an accurate reflection of how large your image will print. It makes the assumption that your screen is currently using pixels that are .014 inches square (or 72 ppi). When the Macintosh was released back in 1984, it had a built-in screen that just happened to use pixels of that size. Now, there are so many different kinds of monitors that 72 ppi is no longer the standard. In fact, there *is* no standard. If you really want to see how large an image will print, then choose View > Show Rulers. You can set the ruler measurement system (inches, points, picas, and so on) by choosing Edit > Preferences > Units & Rulers. The keyboard command to show the rulers is Command-R (Macintosh) or Ctrl-R (Windows); to hide the rulers press the same shortcut again. Then choose View > Print Size and hold a real ruler up to your screen and you'll see how far off it is from reality.

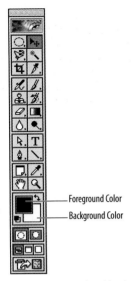

Foreground Color
Background Color

Figure 1.18 Foreground and background colors.

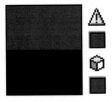

Figure 1.19 The warning triangle indicates a color that is not reproducible in CMYK mode. The cube symbol indicates that a color is not a Web-safe color and might appear dithered in a Web browser.

color, click it once (this will bring up a standard Color Picker). The bottom box is the background color; it's used when you're erasing the background image or when you increase the size of your document by using Image > Canvas Size. When you use the Gradient tool with default settings, your gradient will start with the foreground color and end with the background color. You can swap the foreground and background colors by clicking the small curved arrows next to them in the Tools palette. You can also reset the colors to their default settings (black/white) by clicking the small squares in the lower-left corner of that same area.

Color Picker Dialog Box

The Color Picker dialog box is available in many areas of Photoshop. The easiest way to get to it is to click your foreground or background color. There are many choices in this dialog box because there are many different ways to define a color. In this section, we'll cover all the various ways you can choose a color. I'll start off by showing you how to preview the color you're selecting.

Previewing a Color

While you're choosing a color, you can glance at the two color swatches to the right of the vertical gradient to compare the color you've chosen (the top swatch) to the color you had previously (the bottom swatch).

Be sure to watch for the out-of-gamut warning, which is indicated by a small triangle that appears next to these color swatches (**Figure 1.19**). This triangle warns you that the color you have chosen is not reproducible in CMYK mode, which means that it cannot be printed without shifting to a slightly different color. Fortunately, Photoshop provides you with a preview of what the color would have to shift to in order to be printable. You can find this preview in the small color swatch that appears directly below the triangle icon, and you can select this printable color by clicking the color swatch. Or, you can have Photoshop show you what all the colors would look like when printed by choosing View > Proof Colors while the Color Picker dialog box is open. That will change the look of every color that appears in the picker, but you will still have to click that little triangle symbol, because that's just a preview—it doesn't actually change the colors you're choosing.

Choosing Web-safe Colors

In Part Four of this book, you'll learn all about Web graphics, but for now, let's take a look at just one Web-related feature in the Color Picker dialog box. There is a set of special colors, known as Web-safe colors, that are used for large areas of solid color. By using a Web-safe color, you will prevent those areas from becoming dithered (that is, simulated by using a pattern of two solid colors; for example, adding a pattern of red dots to a yellow area to create orange). So, if you are choosing a color that will be used in a large area on a Web page, look for the Color Cube symbol (**Figure 1.19**). Web-safe colors are also known as colors that are within the color cube—that's why Adobe used a cube symbol for this feature. When you click the cube symbol, the color you have chosen will shift a little to become a Web-safe color.

Selecting with the Color Field

Usually, the simplest method for choosing a color is to eyeball it. In the Color Picker dialog box, you can click in the vertical gradient to select the general color you want to use. Then click and drag around the large square area at the left to choose a shade of that color.

Selecting by Hue, Saturation, and Brightness

You can also change what appears in the vertical gradient by clicking any of the radio buttons on the right side of the dialog box (**Figures 1.20 to 1.22**). In this dialog box, H = Hue, S = Saturation, and B = Brightness. You can use the numbers at the right of the dialog box to describe the color you've chosen (this can be a big help when you're describing a color to someone on the phone). So, if you know the exact color you need, just type its exact numbers into that area.

Note

CMYK colors are meant to be printed (which involves ink), whereas RGB colors (which involve light) are meant for multimedia. Due to impurities in CMYK inks, you can't accurately reproduce every color you see on your screen.

Warning

If your method for picking white is to drag to the upper-left corner of the color field, be sure to drag *beyond* the edge of the square; otherwise, you might not end up with a true white. Instead, you'll get a muddy-looking white or a light shade of gray.

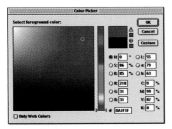

Figure 1.20 Hue.

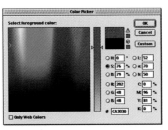

Figure 1.21 Saturation.

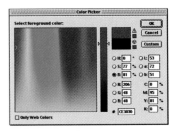

Figure 1.22 Brightness.

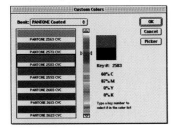

Figure 1.23 The Custom Color Picker.

> **Warning**
>
> Although the Custom Color Picker is great for users printing with CMYK inks, it's not so hot for those using true spot colors (metallic, fluorescent, and other colors that cannot be reproduced using CMYK inks). If you're going to be using true spot colors, see Chapter 9, "Channels."

Selecting Custom Colors

If you want to pick your colors from a swatch book (PAN-TONE, TruMatch, and so on), click the Custom button. This will bring up the Custom Color Picker (**Figure 1.23**). Choose the swatch book you want to use from the pop-up menu at the top of the dialog box, then scroll through the list to find the color you desire. You can also type in numbers to select a specific color (I know, there isn't the usual text field to enter them in, but just start typing), but make sure you type really fast. I'm not sure why it works this way, but this part of Photoshop gets impatient with slow typists. For example, if you slowly type the number 356, Photoshop might jump to a color number starting with 3 and then go to one that starts with 5. This is sort of annoying, but it shouldn't pose a problem as long as you type the number quickly. (You can purchase swatch books at an art supply store.)

Color Palette

You can think of the Color palette as a simplified version of the Color Picker dialog box. Just like in the Color Picker, you can pick colors by typing in numbers. However, you first need to choose the type of numbers you want to use from the side menu (**Figure 1.24**).

There's one special option that's not available in the Color Picker dialog box and can only be used in the Color palette. Web Color Sliders will allow you to choose colors that are made from red, green, and blue light, but it will also force the sliders to snap to the tic marks that appear along the slider bars. Those tic marks indicate Web-safe colors and makes this choice especially useful when creating Web graphics (**Figure 1.25**).

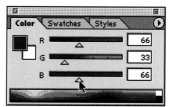

Figure 1.24 Choosing the slider type from the palette's menu.

Figure 1.25 When you choose Web Color Sliders, the sliders will snap to the tic marks on the slider bars that indicate where Web-safe colors are located.

You can also pick colors by clicking the color bar at the bottom of the palette (use Option-click on the Macintosh or Alt-click in Windows to change your background color). You can change the appearance of the color bar by choosing a color-range option near the bottom of the side menu of the palette. Here are the options:

▶ **RGB Spectrum**—Displays all the colors that are usable in RGB mode. Use this setting for multimedia and the Web.

▶ **CMYK Spectrum**—Shows all the colors that are usable in CMYK mode. Use this setting for images that will be reproduced on a printing press.

▶ **Grayscale Ramp**—Shows shades of gray from black to white. Use this setting any time you need shades of gray that do not contain a hint of color (also known as neutral grays).

▶ **Current Colors**—Displays a gradient using your foreground and background colors.

▶ **Make Ramp Web Safe**—Shows only the colors that are Web safe from the above choices.

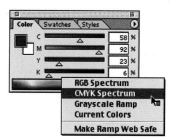

Figure 1.26 Changing the color bar's setting.

Eyedropper Tool

In addition to using the Color Picker and Color palette to select colors, you can use the Eyedropper tool. One advantage to the Eyedropper is that you can grab colors from any open Photoshop file. After selecting the Eyedropper, you can click any part of your image and bingo!—you've got a new foreground color. You can also Option-click

(Macintosh) or Alt-click (Windows) to change your background color. You don't have to click within the document you're currently editing; you can click any open image.

You can also change the Sample Size setting in the Options bar to choose how it looks at, or samples, the area you click (**Figures 1.27 to 1.30**). Here are your options:

▶ **Point Sample**—Picks up the exact color of the pixel you click.

▶ **3-by-3 Average**—Averages the area around your cursor using an area that's three pixels wide and three pixels tall.

▶ **5-by-5 Average**—Works the same way as 3-by-3 Average, but with a larger area.

In many cases, you'll find it helpful to use one of the Average settings. They prevent you from accidentally picking up an odd-colored speck in the area from which you're grabbing, thereby ensuring you don't select a color that isn't representative of the area you're choosing.

Figure 1.27 The Sample Size option determines the area the Eyedropper tool will average when you're choosing a color.

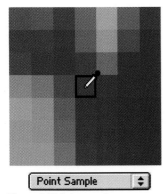

Figure 1.28 Point sample.

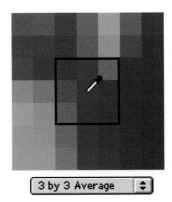

Figure 1.29 3-by-3 Average.

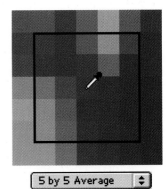

Figure 1.30 5-by-5 Average.

Swatches Palette

The Swatches palette is designed to store colors that you can use again and again. You can choose how you'd like to view the swatches by choosing either Small Thumbnail (**Figure 1.31**) or Small List (**Figure 1.32**) from the side menu of the Swatches palette. To paint with one of the colors stored in the Swatches palette, move your cursor over a swatch and click the mouse button. Your foreground color will change to the color you clicked. To change your background color, hold Option (Macintosh) or Alt (Windows) while clicking any swatch.

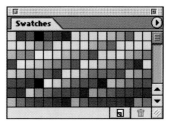

Figure 1.31 The Swatches palette using Small Thumbnail view.

To store your current foreground color in this palette, just click in the open space below the swatches. Photoshop will prompt you to name the color and then will add that color to the bottom of the palette. If there is no open space, resize the palette by dragging its lower-right corner. You can also click the New Swatch icon (it looks like a sheet of paper with the corner turned up) at the bottom of the Swatches palette. That will add a new swatch without asking for a name (hold Option on the Macintosh or Alt in Windows to be prompted for a name).

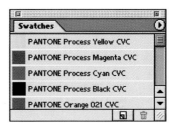

Figure 1.32 The Swatches palette using Small List view.

You can also remove a color from the Swatches palette by Command-clicking (Macintosh) or Ctrl-clicking (Windows) on the swatch. Shift-clicking lets you change the color of an existing swatch to match your foreground color. To reset the swatches to their default settings, choose Reset Swatches from the side menu of the palette.

After you've stored the colors you want, you can choose Save Swatches from the Swatches palette's side menu. This will bring up a standard Save dialog box to allow you to assign a name to your personal set of swatches (**Figure 1.33**). After saving a set of swatches, you can reload them by choosing Replace Swatches from the side menu.

Figure 1.33 The dialog box for saving swatches.

Photoshop comes with a bunch of preset swatch files you can load into the Swatches palette. These files are stored in the Color Swatches folder in your Presets folder, which resides in your Photoshop application folder. If you save your swatches file into this folder, it will show up along

Figure 1.34 Preset swatch files are listed at the bottom of the menu.

Figure 1.35 The Replace Swatches dialog box.

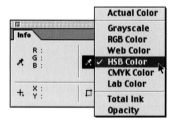

Figure 1.36 Changing how the Info palette measures color.

with other preset swatch files at the bottom of the side menu in the Swatches palette (**Figure 1.34**). When you choose one of those presets, Photoshop will prompt you with a dialog box that has two options (**Figure 1.35**). Append will add the swatches you are loading to the bottom of the swatches that are already there; OK will replace the current swatches with what you are loading. If you'd like to avoid this dialog box altogether, you can hold the Option key (Macintosh) or Alt key (Windows) when you choose one of the presets from the side menu, and Photoshop will replace the swatches automatically.

Info Palette

Although you can't actually choose a color by using the Info palette, you'll find it helpful for measuring the colors that already reside in your document. The top part of the Info palette measures the color that appears below your cursor.

You can change the measurement method used by the Info palette by clicking the tiny eyedropper icons within the palette (**Figure 1.36**). RGB is usually used for multimedia purposes; CMYK for publishing. Total Ink adds together the C, M, Y, and K numbers to indicate how much ink coverage will be used to reproduce the area under your cursor.

You can set up the Info palette to keep track of different areas of your image, so you can see what's happening when you make adjustments. You can do this by clicking your image using the Color Sampler tool. This will deposit a little crosshair on the area you click and will also add another readout to the Info palette (**Figure 1.37**). You can add up to four of these "samples" to your image. Then when you are adjusting the image using any of the choices under the Image > Adjust menu, the Info palette readouts will change into two readouts for each Color Sampler (**Figure 1.38**). The left number indicates what the color was before the adjustment; the right number indicates what the color will be after the adjustment. You can even add a color sample to your image while an adjustment dialog box is active by holding the Shift key and clicking on the image (the Color Sampler tool does not need to be active to do this).

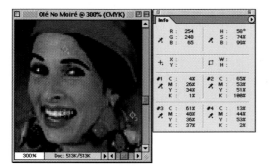

Figure 1.37 Color samples and Info palette readouts. (Original image © 1998 Adobe Systems, Inc.)

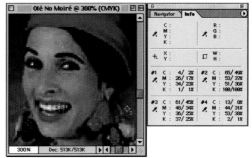

Figure 1.38 Info palette readouts while an adjustment dialog box is in use.

To remove a sample, hold the Option key (Macintosh) or Alt key (Windows), and click on it, or just drag it off the screen. Or, if you'd like to remove all the color samples, click the Clear button in the Options bar (it's available only when the Color Sampler tool is active). Occasionally you may want to hide the sample points when you're working on your image; you can do this by choosing Hide Color Samples from the side menu of the Info palette. We'll use these samples when you read about color correction in Chapter 8.

Basic Editing Tools

Like the majority of Photoshop's features, you'll find that there's more than meets the eye with the editing tools. For now, we'll cover their most obvious applications, but as you make your way through the rest of the book, keep in mind that these deceivingly simple tools can perform some remarkable tricks. For example, the painting and gradient tools can be used for more than just painting and adding color—they can also be used for making intricate selections, compositing photos, and creating cool fadeouts. You can use them to create an infinite number of dazzling effects.

Painting Tools

Although each of the painting tools gives you a slightly different end result, they all share the same basic settings; only a few settings are unique to each tool. Before we dive into their options, let's look at the basic difference between the Pencil, Paintbrush, and Airbrush tools.

To begin with, the Paintbrush and Airbrush tools always have soft edges, whereas the Pencil tool always has a hard edge (**Figures 1.39 to 1.41**).

Figure 1.39 Paint stroke created with the Airbrush tool.

Figure 1.40 Paint stroke created with the Paintbrush tool.

Figure 1.41 Paint stroke created with the Pencil tool.

You can change the softness of the Paintbrush and Airbrush tools by choosing different brushes from the Brushes palette.

Opacity

If you lower the Opacity setting of the Paintbrush tool (called Pressure for the Airbrush), you can paint across the image without worrying about overlapping your paint strokes (**Figure 1.42**). As long as you don't release the mouse button, the areas that you paint over multiple times won't get a second coat of paint. Using the Airbrush tool is a different story. When you paint over an area multiple times, the Airbrush adds another coat of paint each time you drag the tool across the area (**Figure 1.43**). The Pencil tool acts just like the Paintbrush when it's got a low opacity setting (one coat only).

Figure 1.42 A continuous stroke using the Paintbrush tool.

Figure 1.43 A continuous stroke using the Airbrush tool.

If you're not familiar with the concept of opaque versus transparent, take a look at **Figures 1.44 and 1.45**.

Figure 1.44 Opaque (left) versus transparent (right). (© 1998 PhotoSpin, www.photospin.com)

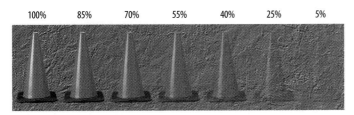

Figure 1.45 Varying opacity. (© 1998 PhotoSpin, www.photospin.com)

Now let's take a look at the options available to you when using the painting tools. The majority of these options will be shared among all three painting tools.

Blending Mode

The Mode pop-up menu in the Options bar is known as the blending mode menu. We'll be covering all the options under this menu in Chapter 12, "Enhancement," so right now I'll just explain a few basic uses (**Figures 1.46 to 1.48**). If you would like to change the basic color of an object, you can set the blending mode to Hue. If you're using a soft-edged brush, you can set the blending mode to Dissolve to force the edges of your brush to dissolve out. That's all for now; we'll explore the rest of this menu in Chapter 12.

Figure 1.46 Normal. (© 1998 PhotoSpin, www.photospin.com)

Figure 1.47 Hue.

Figure 1.48 Dissolve.

Fade

To change the Fade setting for the currently active painting or retouching tool, click on the Brush Dynamics button on the far right of the Options bar. With the Color option set to Fade, the painting tools will begin applying the foreground color, but will fade out to your background color. If you set the Opacity option to Fade, then your paint color will become more transparent as you paint. You can even make your brush become smaller by setting the Size option to Fade (**Figures 1.49 and 1.50**). The higher the fade number, the longer you have to paint before the paint fades all the way out. This number is not measured in pixels, inches, or any other measurement system you would recognize. In order to understand exactly how this setting is calculated, you must first understand how the brushes work, and we'll talk about that in the "Brushes Palette" section later in this chapter.

Figure 1.49 Setting the Fade option to become transparent.

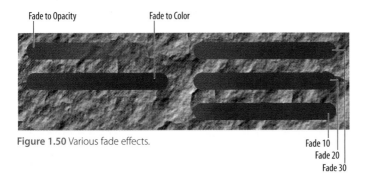

Figure 1.50 Various fade effects.

Wet Edges

The Wet Edges option will apply the full intensity of the paint only in the areas of your brush that are partially transparent. The center of the brush will look as if you lowered the Opacity setting to 51%. This can simulate the look of water color paints or magic markers (**Figure 1.51**).

Figure 1.51 The Wet Edges effect.

Stylus Options

The only time the Stylus options become available is when you have a pressure-sensitive graphics tablet installed; otherwise (and that will be the case on the majority of machines you use), they will be grayed out. These options allow you to control the size, opacity setting, and color of the paint while you're painting, without having to let go of the mouse button (**Figure 1.52**).

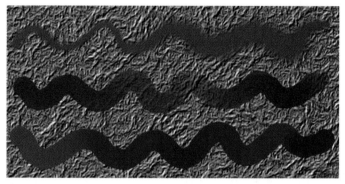

Figure 1.52 Various stylus options: pressure set to Size (top), Opacity (middle), or Color (bottom).

Graphics Tablets

Ever try signing your name with a mouse? It looks like you wrote it with your arm in a plaster cast. I can't begin to tell you how much more control you'll have over your images if you use a graphics tablet. I think it's cruel and unusual punishment to force Photoshop users to use a mouse. Those pesky mice make it hard to do just about everything in Photoshop, and they can even make your wrists hurt. In contrast, tablets are designed for precision and control. With a tablet, not only can you sign your name with a flourish, you can also trace the most intricate shapes and edges; you can place a magazine or book up to a half-inch thick on top of the tablet, and the pen will still be able to control your cursor. Try doing *that* with a mouse. If you haven't already taken the plunge, you really should think about getting into the market for one. When you do, get a Wacom brand tablet—they are simply the best I've found (and no, they didn't pay me to say that). Get one about the size of your mouse pad. You'll end up forking over less than $100 for the smallest one (4x5 inches) and around $300 for an average size tablet (6x9 inches).

Eraser Tool

If you use the Eraser tool while you're working on a background image (we'll talk about the background in Chapter 3, "Layer Primer"), it acts like one of the normal painting tools—except that it paints with the background color instead of the foreground color. It even lets you choose which type of painting tool it should mimic by allowing you to select an option from the pop-up menu in the Options bar (**Figure 1.54**).

Figure 1.54 Choosing Eraser tool behavior.

Figure 1.53 Shift-click to create straight lines.

However, when you use the Eraser tool on a non-background layer, it really erases the area. If you lower the opacity setting, it makes an area appear partially transparent. Bear in that mind that the same does not apply to the background image. You cannot "erase" the background.

Background Eraser Tool

Hiding under the normal Eraser tool is a special version known as the Background Eraser. Click and hold on the Eraser tool until you see a drop-down menu—the Background Eraser is the middle tool shown in that menu. When you move your cursor over an image, you'll notice that the Background Eraser gives you a round brush with a crosshair in the middle (**Figure 1.55**). When you click on the image, it will look at the color that is under the crosshair and delete it from within the circular cursor (**Figure 1.56**).

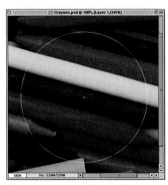
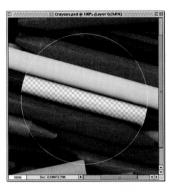

Figure 1.55 The Background Eraser will present you with a round cursor with a crosshair in the middle. (© 2000 Stockbyte, www.stockbyte.com)

Figure 1.56 The Background Eraser erases (from within the circular cursor) the color that's under the crosshair.

If you look up at the Options bar, you'll notice a lot of choices affecting how the Background Eraser will look at your image:

Tolerance—determines the range of colors that will be erased, based on the color that appears under the crosshair (high settings erase a large range of colors; low settings erase a narrow range of colors).

Protect Foreground Color checkbox—protects colors in the image that are similar to the current foreground color.

Sampling pop-up menu—determines how often Photoshop will look at the color under the crosshair and therefore which colors will be deleted. Continuous keeps a constant watch; Once only looks at the moment you click the mouse button; and Background swatch uses the current background color instead of looking at the image to determine what should be erased.

Limits pop-up menu—changes what the Background Eraser is capable of erasing. Discontiguous allows the Background Eraser to jump across areas that shouldn't be deleted to erase areas that don't touch the crosshair (**Figure 1.57**). Contiguous limits what can be erased to areas that actually touch the crosshair (**Figure 1.58**). Find Edges uses the Contiguous option, but will try to maintain crisp edges instead of allowing the edges to become partially transparent (**Figure 1.59**).

> **Note**
>
> If you want a transparent background that will still be transparent in other programs (for instance, if you're preparing an image for use in Adobe InDesign), be sure to check out Chapter 11, where we'll talk about clipping paths.

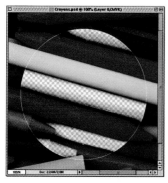

Figure 1.57 The Background Eraser using the Discontiguous option.

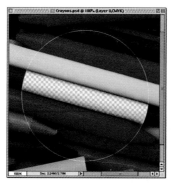

Figure 1.58 The Background Eraser using the Contiguous option.

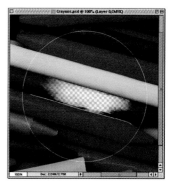

Figure 1.59 The Background Eraser using the Find Edges option.

Brushes Palette

When a painting or retouching tool is active, you'll see the currently active brush shown in the Options bar. If you click on the small triangle just to the right of that brush, the Brushes palette will appear as a drop-down palette (**Figure 1.60**). All of the painting and retouching tools available in the Tools palette use the Brushes palette to determine their brush size. Each individual tool remembers the last brush size you used with it, and will return to that same size the next time you select the tool. In other words, the brush size you choose doesn't stay consistent when you switch among the tools.

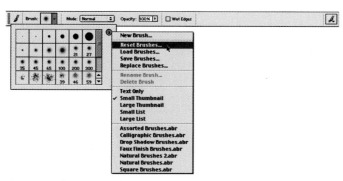

Figure 1.60 The Brushes palette.

You can change the active brush by clicking once on any brush that's available in the Brushes palette (double-clicking will allow you to rename the brush). If you choose a brush that's larger than the squares in the palette, a small version will be displayed (just to show you if it has a hard or soft edge), and a number will appear beneath the preview indicating exactly how wide the brush is.

For even more fun, keep an eye on the brush in the Options bar and then press the < or > key on your keyboard (without holding Shift). You can use these keys to cycle through all the brushes shown in the Brushes palette.

Brush Options

To change the settings for any brush, click on the brush preview in the Options bar (not the drop-down Brushes palette) to access the options for that brush. You can change the brush size, edge softness, and other settings (**Figure 1.61**). Here's an explanation of the settings:

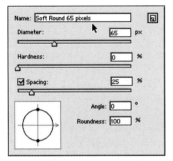

Figure 1.61 Click the brush preview in the Options bar to adjust its settings.

▶ **Diameter**—Determines the size of the brush (**Figure 1.62**).

▶ **Hardness**—Determines how quickly the edge fades out. Default brushes are either 100% soft or 0% soft (**Figure 1.63**).

▶ **Roundness**—Determines whether the brush shape will be round or oval (**Figure 1.64 and 1.65**).

▶ **Angle**—Rotates oval brushes but has no effect on round ones (**Figure 1.66**).

▶ **Spacing**—Determines the distance between the paint daubs that make up a brush stroke (**Figure 1.67**).

Figure 1.62 Diameter determines the size of the brush.

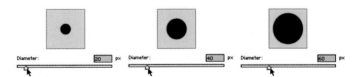

Figure 1.63 Hardness determines how soft the edge will be.

Figure 1.64 Roundness determines if the brush will be round or oval shaped.

Figure 1.66 Angle rotates oval brushes but has no effect on round ones.

Figure 1.65 Effects of the Roundness setting.

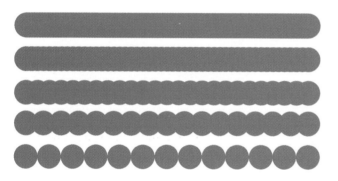

Figure 1.67 Spacing settings from top to bottom: 1%, 25%, 50%, 75%, 100%.

Notes

Instead of entering values for the Angle and Roundness settings, you can modify the diagram in the lower-left corner of the dialog box. Drag one of the two small circles to change the roundness setting; drag the tip of the arrow to change the angle.

Lower the Spacing setting when using large hard-edged brushes to prevent rough edges.

Saving Brushes

Once you have changed the settings of a brush, you have in essence created a new brush that is no longer related to the original one that you chose in the Brushes palette. But the changed brush won't show up in the Brushes palette unless you resave it by clicking on the New Brush icon in the upper right corner of the Brush Options drop-down palette. Once you have created a set of brushes you like, you can choose Save Brushes from the side menu of the palette to save the set in a file. If you ever need to get back to a saved set of brushes, choose Replace Brushes from the same menu. You can also choose Reset Brushes to get the brushes back to the default settings.

Preset Brushes

Photoshop comes with a variety of preset brushes. You can load these sets by choosing either Replace Brushes or

Note
Preset brushes are located in the Brushes folder within the Presets folder in your Photoshop program folder. If you want your own brushes to show up in the Brushes drop-down palette, you'll need to store them in the same location.

choosing a specific name that appears at the bottom of the Brushes palette side menu (**Figure 1.68**). These preset brushes are not like the normal brushes found in the default Brushes palette; they were created by converting pictures into brushes, and therefore don't necessarily offer the same options as normal brushes when you click the brush preview in the Options bar (**Figures 1.69 to 1.71**).

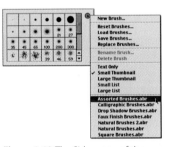

Figure 1.68 The Side menu of the brushes drop-down palette.

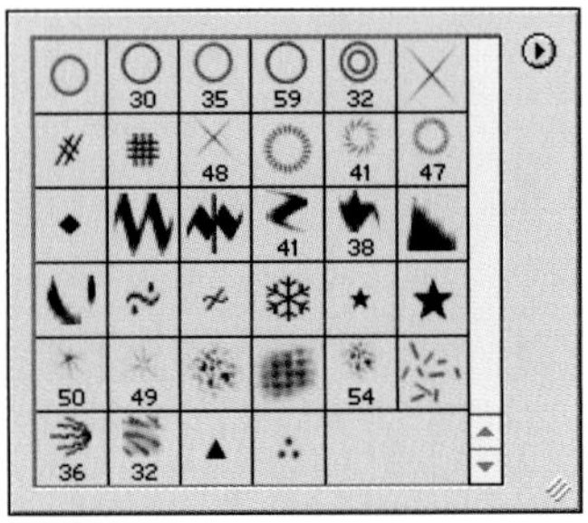

Figure 1.69 Assorted brushes.

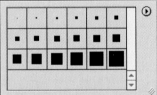

Figure 1.70 Square brushes.

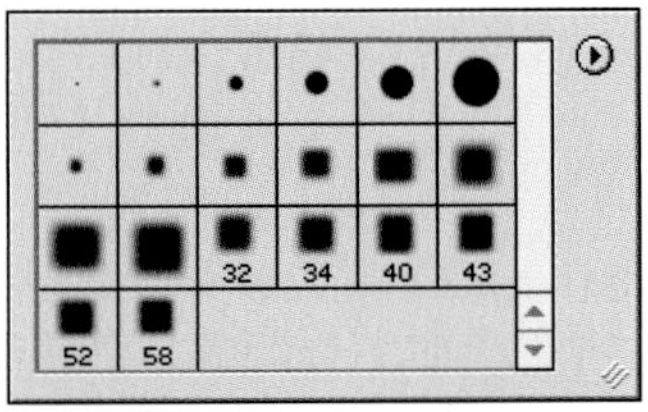

Figure 1.71 Drop shadow brushes.

If you click on one of these preset brushes in the Options bar, you'll find only two options available: Spacing and Anti-Aliased. The Spacing setting works just like it does with normal brushes. The Anti-Aliased setting softens the edge of the brush by one pixel, allowing it to blend into the image and appear smoother (**Figures 1.72 and 1.73**). Round brushes don't have an anti-aliased option available because the Hardness setting determines how much those brushes will blend into the underlying image.

Figure 1.72 Anti-aliased off.   **Figure 1.73** Anti-aliased on.

Custom Brushes

You can create your own custom brushes from any open image by selecting any area (selections are covered in Chapter 2, "Selection Primer") and choosing Define Brush from the Edit menu (**Figure 1.74**). This will copy the area that's selected, convert the copy to grayscale (if it was color to start with), and turn it into a custom brush.

Any shades of gray that appear in the brush will effectively lower the opacity of the brush when it's applied to the image (20% gray areas will look the same as painting with a normal brush set to 20% opacity). White areas will be ignored when creating custom brushes because that would lower the opacity of the brush to 0% in that area, so nothing would be applied when painting.

If the area you select is larger than the squares in the palette, you will see a small version of the brush with a number below it that indicates its size. You cannot create a multicolored brush because brushes always use the current foreground color to paint with.

Custom brushes are great. For instance, you can create cool textured brushes by clicking once with a normal brush, applying filters to the image, and then turning the filtered image into a custom brush. These custom brushes become more useful when you increase the spacing to a setting above 100% (**Figure 1.75**).

Figure 1.74 Defining a custom brush.

What's more, if you are using a pressure-sensitive tablet with a custom brush, you can get some interesting effects by simply increasing or decreasing the pressure of your pen (Figure 1.76).

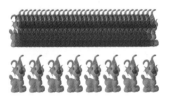

Figure 1.75 Painting with a custom brush. (© 1998 PhotoSpin, www.photospin.com)

Figure 1.76 Using a pressure-sensitive tablet with a custom brush.

Paint Bucket Tool

Use the Paint Bucket tool to fill areas with the foreground color. Each time you click on the image, Photoshop will fill areas that contain colors similar to the one you clicked. You can specify how sensitive the tool should be by changing its Tolerance setting (**Figures 1.77 to 1.79**). Higher Tolerance settings will fill a wider range of colors.

Figure 1.77 The Paint Bucket Options bar.

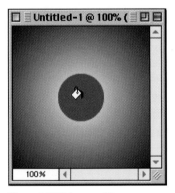

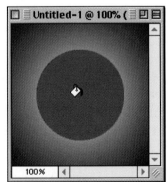

Figure 1.78 Tolerance: 32.

Figure 1.79 Tolerance: 75.

Shape Tools

In Photoshop 6.0, Adobe added some wonderful new tools for creating simple geometric shapes (**Figure 1.80**). These tools are much more powerful than what you'd expect at first glance. We'll look at the basics here, and then expand on them in later chapters.

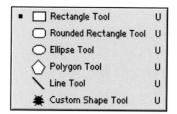

Figure 1.80 Press and hold one of the Geometric Shape tools to see a full list of the tools available.

Before you dive into the Shape tools, you need to think about what kind of result you want to achieve, because you have three ways of using these tools, each of which will lead you to a different outcome. You'll find the trio of choices in the far left of the Options bar (**Figure 1.81**). The first (leftmost) choice will create a special layer that's new to Photoshop. It's known as a Shape layer and it has some very special qualities:

▶ It will have crisp edges when printed on a Postscript printer (even if the pixels that make up the image are large enough to cause the rest of the image to appear jagged).

▶ You can scale it (up or down) without degrading its quality. This makes it ideal for creating button bars on Web sites where the client might decide to add more text to a button, which would require a larger button.

▶ You can add to or take away from it using the other Shape tools.

▶ It can be filled with a solid color, a gradient, pattern, or adjustment.

The second choice in the Options bar will deliver a path that will show up in the Paths palette. This can be useful when creating a Layer Clipping Path as we'll discuss in Chapter 11. The third choice in the Options bar will fill an area on the currently active layer using the current foreground color. I mainly use the Shape layer option because it seems to give me the most flexibility.

Once you've made your choice of what type of result you'd like, you can click and drag across an image to create a shape. If you'd like to have a little more control over the end result, you can click on the small triangle that appears to the right of the shape tools in the Options bar. That will present you with options that are specific to the particular shape you are creating (**Figure 1.81**).

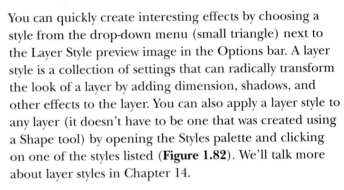

Figure 1.81 Click on the triangle next to the shape tools to see additional options for that particular tool.

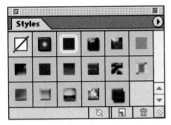

Figure 1.82 The Layer Styles palette.

You can quickly create interesting effects by choosing a style from the drop-down menu (small triangle) next to the Layer Style preview image in the Options bar. A layer style is a collection of settings that can radically transform the look of a layer by adding dimension, shadows, and other effects to the layer. You can also apply a layer style to any layer (it doesn't have to be one that was created using a Shape tool) by opening the Styles palette and clicking on one of the styles listed (**Figure 1.82**). We'll talk more about layer styles in Chapter 14.

Measure Tool

Figure 1.83 The Info palette indicates the angle of the Measure tool. (Courtesy of Derek Brigham)

The Measure tool allows you to measure the distance between two points or the angle of any area of the image, which can be helpful when you want to rotate or resize objects precisely. In order to see the angle and distance measurements, you must have the Info palette open. As you drag with the Measure tool, the Info palette indicates the angle (A) and length (D, for Distance) of the line you're creating (**Figure 1.83**). You can change the measurement system used to measure distance by clicking the small cross in the lower-left corner of the Info palette. After creating a line, you can click directly on the line and drag it to different positions. You can also click and drag one end of the line to change the angle or distance.

If you want to resize an image so that it fits perfectly between two objects, you can measure the distance between them with this tool and then choose Image > Image Size to scale the image to that exact width.

You can also use the Measure tool to determine the angle between two straight lines. If you Option-click (Macintosh) or Alt-click (Windows) the end of the line, you can pull out a second line and move it to any angle you desire. Now the angle (A) number in the Info palette displays the angle between those two lines.

Gradient Tool

At first, you might not see any reasons to get excited about using the Gradient tool. However, after we cover Layers (Chapter 3), Channels (Chapter 9), and compositing techniques (Chapter 11), you should find that the Gradient tool is not only worth getting excited about, it's downright indispensable. I want to make sure you know how to edit and apply gradients before we get to those chapters, so let's give it a shot.

First let's look at how to apply gradients to an image. To apply a gradient, simply click and drag across an image using the Gradient tool. You'll get different results depending on which type of gradient you've chosen in the Options bar (**Figure 1.84**).

Notes

To straighten a crooked document, first drag with the Measure tool along a line which should be horizontal or vertical; then choose Image > Rotate Canvas > Arbitrary and click OK. Photoshop calculates the exact angle needed to rotate the image.

To rotate a layer to a specific angle, first use the Measure tool to specify the angle you'd like to use, then choose Edit > Transform > Rotate. Photoshop enters the angle of the line you drew into the Options bar and rotates the active layer that amount.

Warning

Unless you select an area before applying a gradient, the gradient will fill the entire image.

Figure 1.84 The Gradient pop-out menu.

Here's an explanation of the gradient settings (**Figures 1.85 to 1.89**):

▶ **Linear**—Applies the gradient across the length of the line you make. If the line does not extend all the way across the image, Photoshop fills the rest of the image with solid colors (the colors you started and ended the gradient with).

▶ **Radial**—Creates a gradient that starts in the center of a circle and radiates to the outer edge. Where you first click determines the center of the circle; where you let go of the mouse button determines the outer edge of the circle. All areas outside this circle will be filled with a solid color (the color that the gradient ends with).

▶ **Angle**—Sweeps around a circle like a radar screen. Your first click determines the center of the sweep, then you drag to determine the starting angle.

▶ **Reflected**—Creates an effect similar to applying a linear gradient twice, back to back.

▶ **Diamond**—Similar to a radial gradient except it radiates out from the center of a square.

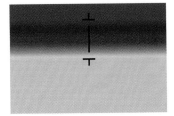

Figure 1.85 Linear gradient.

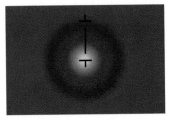

Figure 1.86 Radial gradient.

Figure 1.87 Angle gradient.

Figure 1.88 Reflected gradient.

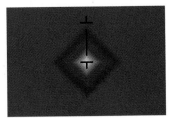

Figure 1.89 Diamond gradient.

Note

In Photoshop 6.0.1 you can press Enter to show or hide the preset gradients without accessing the Options bar.

Gradient Colors

You can choose from different preset color combinations by clicking on the small triangle that appears next to the gradient preview in the Options bar (**Figure 1.90**). You can also reverse the direction of the gradient by turning on the Reverse checkbox in the Options bar. Then, if you have a gradient that usually starts with blue and ends with red, it would instead start with red and end with blue (**Figures 1.91 and 1.92**). Some of the preset gradients will contain transparent areas. To disable transparency in a gradient, turn off the Transparency checkbox.

Figure 1.90 The Linear Gradient Options bar.

Figure 1.91 Reverse "off."

Figure 1.92 Reverse "on."

Dithered Gradients

When you print an image that contains a gradient, you'll sometimes notice banding across the gradient (also known as stair-stepping or posterization). To minimize this, be sure to turn on the Dither checkbox in the Options bar. This will add noise to the gradient in an attempt to prevent banding. You won't be able to see the effect of the Dither checkbox onscreen; it just makes the gradient look better when it's printed (**Figures 1.93 and 1.94**). If you find that you still see banding when you print the gradient, you can add some additional noise by choosing Filter > Noise > Add Noise (use a setting of 3 or less for most images).

Figure 1.93 Dither "off."

Figure 1.94 Dither "on."

Custom Gradients

The Gradient drop-down menu might not always contain the exact type of gradient you need. When that's the case, click directly on the gradient preview in the Options bar to create your own custom gradient. The Gradient Editor dialog box that appears has so many options that it can sometimes feel overwhelming, but if you take it one

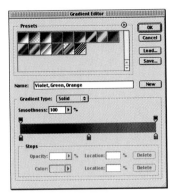

Figure 1.95 Click just below the gradient preview to add colors to the gradient.

step at a time, you shouldn't run into any problems (**Figure 1.95**).

The list at the top of the dialog box shows you all the gradients that usually appear in the Options bar. Click any one of them, and you'll be able to preview it at the bottom of the dialog box. Once you have chosen the gradient you want to edit, you can modify it by changing the gradient bar (or you can click New to make a copy and proceed from there). To add additional colors (up to a maximum of 32), click just below any part of the bar. This adds a color swatch to the bar and changes the colors that appear in the gradient.

You have three choices of what to put into your new color swatches. You'll find these choices on the drop-down menu to the right of the Color swatch at the bottom left of the dialog box. The Foreground and Background choices don't just grab your foreground or background colors at the time you create the gradient, as you might expect. Instead, they look at the foreground and background color when you apply the gradient. Therefore, each time you apply the gradient, you can get a different result by changing the foreground and background colors. If you don't want the gradient to contain your foreground or background colors, then choose User Color from the same menu and click on the Color swatch to access the Color Picker.

After you have added a swatch of color to the gradient bar, you can reposition it by dragging it from left to right, or by changing the number in the Location box below. I like to click the Location number and then use the up arrow and down arrow keys on my keyboard to slide the color swatch around. A little diamond shape, known as the midpoint, will appear between each of the color swatches; it indicates where the two colors will be mixed equally.

Transparent Gradients

You can also make areas of a gradient partially transparent by clicking just above the gradient preview. In this area, you cannot change the color of a gradient; you can only make the gradient more or less transparent. You can add and move the transparency swatches just as you would the color swatches below. Transparent areas are represented by the checkerboard pattern (**Figure 1.96**).

Notes Tool

In Photoshop 6.0 you can add text or audio annotations (also known as notes). When you use the Notes tool (which looks a bit like a Post-it Note), you can click and drag on your image to create a text box in which you can then type your note (**Figure 1.97**). Once you're done typing, you can close the note by clicking the tiny box in its upper left corner (Macintosh) or in its upper right corner (Windows) and all you'll see is a tiny icon that indicates there is a note in that spot. Then, when you want to read the note, just double-click on that icon and the note will expand. Each note can have a different color and author, which you specify in the Options bar. If you find the notes to be distracting, then you are welcome to choose View > Show > Annotations to hide the notes.

Hidden under the Notes tool is another tool that allows you to record audio annotations. You'll have to have the proper hardware to get this feature to work (microphone, etc.). With the audio annotation, you simply click on your image, and a Record dialog box will appear (**Figure 1.98**). Click the Record button and then start talking. Once you're done, click the Stop button and you're all set. Now anytime someone double-clicks that audio annotation, they will hear your notes. That's pretty slick, but be careful, because audio annotations can really increase the file size of an image.

If you no longer need to keep the annotations you've created and you'd like to reduce your file size, you can click the Clear All button in the Options bar (the Annotations tool must be active for this button to be available).

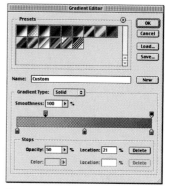

Figure 1.96 Editing the transparency of a gradient.

Figure 1.97 A text annotation. (© 2000 Stockbyte, www.stockbyte.com)

Figure 1.98 The Audio Annotation record dialog box.

PDF Annotations

What's really special about annotations is that you can save them (along with the image, of course) in a PDF file. You can give that file to anyone; they can read the annotations and see the image without having to use Photoshop. All they need is a free program called Acrobat Reader (available at www.adobe.com). Or, if they have the full version of Acrobat, they can add their own annotations to the PDF file. Then you can import them into the original Photoshop file by choosing File > Import > Annotations. This allows you to save an image in a universal file format, send it out for review to as many people as you like, and get back comments that you can re-import into the original high-resolution Photoshop file. It's a great way to communicate with clients.

Closing Thoughts

If you've made it through this entire chapter, you've just passed through Photoshop's welcoming committee of tools and palettes. By now your screen should look neat and tidy and you should be able to zoom in and out and scroll around your image with ease. You should also have a nodding acquaintance with a good number of the tools and palettes—at least familiar enough to know which ones you want to get more friendly with later.

Don't panic if some of this still seems like a blur. It will all begin to take shape once you spend some more time with the program. After a few intense Photoshop sessions, the things you learned in this chapter will become second nature to you. If any of the tools are completely new to you, you should probably play around with them before you move on to the next chapter.

But for now, let's get into the first installment of Ben's Techno-Babble Decoder Ring. And just for the fun of it, I'll throw in some keyboard commands that can really speed up your work.

Ben's Techno-Babble Decoder Ring

Anti-aliased—Smoothing the edge of an otherwise hard-edged object by adding partially transparent pixels. These pixels help to blend the edge of the object into the surrounding image, making it harder to see the edge of the pixels.

Posterization—The process of breaking up a smooth transition into visible steps of solid color. Often called stair-stepping, or banding, when referring to a gradient.

Dither—Simulating color by using a pattern of two solid colors (for example, adding a pattern of red dots to a yellow area to create orange). It also refers to adding a pattern of noise to a sharp transition to make the edge less noticeable.

Noise—A pattern of dots that resembles the static that appears on some televisions when no station is tuned in. This pattern is often used to break up crisp transitions between two colors by replacing a straight-line transition with one that has more of a random edge.

RGB—A model for creating color using red, green, and blue (RGB) light. You are able to see color because your eye contains cones in its retina that are sensitive to red, green, and blue. Scanners capture information by measuring how much RGB light is reflected off the original image. Computer monitors display information by shining RGB light into your eyes. All the colors you have ever seen with your eyes have been made from a combination of red, green, and blue light. It really is an RGB world out there.

CMYK—A model for reproducing RGB colors using cyan, magenta, yellow, and black (abbreviated "K" for Key) inks. Any time you print an image you will be using CMYK inks. Ideally, cyan ink would absorb only red light, magenta ink would absorb only green light, and yellow ink would absorb only blue light; you could therefore reproduce an RGB image by absorbing the light falling on a sheet of paper instead of creating the light directly. But due to impurities in these inks, CMYK inks (also known as process color) cannot reproduce all the colors that can be created using RGB light.

HSB—A method of manipulating RGB or CMYK colors by separating the color into components of hue, saturation, and brightness. Hue is the pure form of the color (red is the pure form of pink, maroon, and candy-apple red). Saturation is the intensity or vibrancy of the color (pink is a not very saturated red; candy-apple red is a very saturated red). Brightness is how bright or dark a color appears (pink is a bright, just not vibrant, tint of red; maroon is a dark shade of red). So, when talking about the hue of a color, you are not describing how bright and vibrant (saturated) the color appears. When talking about saturation of a color, you do not reveal its basic color (hue), or how bright or dark it appears (brightness). When talking about the brightness of a color, you are not describing the basic color (hue) or how vibrant it appears (saturation).

Lab—A scientific method of describing colors by separating them into three components called Lightness, A, and B. The Lightness component describes how bright or dark a color appears. The "A" component describes colors ranging from red to green. The "B" component describes colors ranging from blue to yellow. Lab color is the internal color model used in Photoshop for converting between different color modes (RGB to CMYK, etc.).

Keyboard Shortcuts

FUNCTION	MACINTOSH	WINDOWS
Zoom in	Command-+ (plus sign)	Ctrl-+
Zoom out	Command-– (minus sign)	Ctrl-–
Fit on Screen	Command-0	Ctrl-0
Temporarily use Zoom tool	Command-spacebar	Ctrl-spacebar
Zoom out by clicking	Option-Command-spacebar	Alt-Ctrl-spacebar
Show/Hide palettes	Tab	Tab
Cycle through screen modes	F	F
Hide or show menu bar when in full screen mode	Shift-F	Shift-F
Temporarily use Hand tool	Spacebar	Spacebar
Show/Hide rulers	Command-R	Ctrl-R
Select previous brush	, (comma)	, (comma)
Select next brush	. (period)	. (period)
Select first brush	Shift-, (<)	Shift-, (<)
Select last brush	Shift-. (>)	Shift-. (>)
Hand tool	H	H
Paintbrush tool	B	B
Eraser tool	E	E
Airbrush tool	J	J
Pencil tool	N	N
Reset Foreground/Background Colors	D	D
Exchange Foreground/ Background Colors	X	X

Courtesy of Robert Brünz, www.brunz.com

Courtesy of Robert Brünz, www.brunz.com

2 Selection Primer

I choose a block of marble and chop off whatever I don't need.
—François-Auguste Rodin, when asked how he managed to make his remarkable statues

Courtesy of Tom Nick Cocotos, www.cocotos.com

You've got to love the selection tools. I like to think of them as the chisels of Photoshop. With names such as Lasso, Magic Wand, Feather, and Transform, you get a sense that these aren't just everyday tools—they're the fine instruments of a digital sculptor. Selection tools can do so much more than just draw outlines: they can help you dig down into the guts of an image and perform wondrous transformations. What's more, you don't have to be a wizard to know how to use them. Selection tools take a little getting used to, but once you're familiar with them, they can help you tremendously.

Whatever you do, don't skip this chapter, because the selection tools are central to your success in Photoshop. They allow you to isolate areas of your image and define precisely where a filter, painting tool, or adjustment will change the image. Also, selections are not specific to a particular layer (we'll talk about layers in Chapter 3, "Layer Primer"). Instead, they're attached to the entire document. That means you can freely switch among the different layers without losing a selection. After you've mastered the basics, you'll be ready to jump into more advanced selections in Chapter 9, "Channels."

What Is a Selection?

Before you can edit an image, you must first select the area with which you want to work. People who paint cars for a living make "selections" very much like the ones used in Photoshop. If you've ever seen a car being painted, you know that painters carefully place masking tape and paper over the areas they don't want to paint (such as the windows, tires, door handles, and so on). That way, they can freely spray-paint the entire car, knowing that the taped areas are protected from "overspray." At its most basic level, a selection in Photoshop works much the same way. Actually, it works much better, because with one selection, you have a choice—you can paint the car and leave the masked areas untouched, or you can paint the masked areas and leave the car untouched.

When you select an area by using one of Photoshop's selection tools (Marquee, Lasso, Magic Wand, and so on), the border of the selection looks a lot like marching ants. Once you've made a selection, you can move, copy, paint, or apply numerous special effects to the selected area (**Figures 2.1 and 2.2**).

Figure 2.1 When no selection is present, you can edit the entire image. (© 1998 PhotoDisc)

Figure 2.2 When a selection is present, you can only change the selected area.

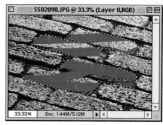

Figure 2.3 Normal selections have hard edges. (© 1998 PhotoDisc)

There are two types of selections in Photoshop: a normal selection and a feathered selection (**Figures 2.3 and 2.4**). A normal selection has a hard edge. That is, when you paint or apply a filter to an image, you can easily see where the effect stops and starts. On the other hand, feathered selections slowly fade out at their edges. This allows filters to seamlessly blend into an image without producing noticeable edges. An accurate selection makes all the difference when you're enhancing an image in Photoshop. To see just how important it can be, take a look at **Figures 2.5 to 2.7**.

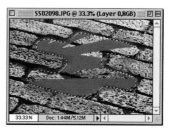

Figure 2.4 Feathered selections have soft edges.

Figure 2.5 The original image.
(© 1998 PhotoDisc)

Figure 2.6 An unprofessional selection.

Figure 2.7 A professional selection.

Basic Selection Tools

The Marquee, Lasso, Magic Wand, and Type Mask tools are the essential ingredients in your selection toolkit, and they're the ones you'll be using the most in your everyday work. It's a good indication that you've come to master these tools when you find yourself trying to use them in other software programs where they don't exist. When using other programs, I sometimes find myself muttering, "Why can't I just lasso this thing?"

The Marquee tool is the most basic of all the selection tools, and we'll cover it first. However, don't let this tool's simplicity fool you—it can perform a surprising number of tasks, so there's quite a bit to learn about it. If you hold your mouse button down while your cursor is over the Marquee tool icon, you'll get a variety of choices in a pop-up menu. We'll cover these choices one at a time, and I'll throw in some tricks along the way.

Rectangular Marquee Tool

The Rectangular Marquee tool is the first choice listed in the Marquee pop-up menu. It can select only rectangular shapes. With it, you create a rectangle by clicking and dragging across your document. The first click creates one corner, and the point at which you release the mouse button denotes the opposite corner (**Figure 2.8**). To start in the center and drag to an outer edge, instead of going corner to corner, press Option (Macintosh) or Alt (Windows) after you have started to drag (**Figure 2.9**). If you want to create a square, just hold down the Shift key after you start to drag. You can even combine the Option (Macintosh) or Alt (Windows) and Shift keys to create a square selection by dragging from the center to an outer edge.

Warning

If you press any combination of the Option (Macintosh) or Alt (Windows) and Shift keys before you begin a selection, they might not perform as you expect, because these keys are also used to manipulate existing selections.

Figure 2.8 A corner-to-corner selection. (© 1998 PhotoDisc)

Figure 2.9 A center-to-edge selection.

To discard the areas that appear outside the selection border, use the Rectangular Marquee tool and then choose Image > Crop.

If you hold down the spacebar and drag around your screen while you're making a selection (but don't release the mouse button), you'll move the selection instead of changing its shape. This can be a real lifesaver. If you botch up the start of a selection, this enables you to reposition it without having to start over. After you have moved the selection into the correct position, just let go of the spacebar to continue editing the selection. After you've finished making the selection, you no longer need to hold the spacebar to move it. To move a selection after it's created, select the Marquee tool and then click and drag from within the selection outline (**Figures 2.10 and 2.11**).

Figure 2.10 Original selection is misaligned. (© 1998 PhotoSpin, www.photospin.com)

Figure 2.11 Use the spacebar to reposition a selection while creating it.

Figure 2.12 The Elliptical Marquee tool in action (from center to edge). (1998 PhotoDisc)

Elliptical Marquee Tool

The second choice under the Marquee pop-up menu is the Elliptical Marquee tool. This tool works in the same way as the rectangular version, except it creates an ellipse (**Figure 2.12**). And it's a little bit trickier to define its size because you have to work from the "corner" of the ellipse, which doesn't really exist. (What were they thinking when they came up with this idea?) Actually, I find it much easier to choose View > Show Rulers and then drag out a few guides (you can get them by dragging from the rulers) and let the "corners" snap to them. Either that, or hold the spacebar to reposition the selection before you release the mouse button, just like I mentioned with the Rectangular Marquee tool.

Now let's look at the choices in the Marquee Options bar (**Figure 2.13**). When you click on any of the Marquee tools, their options will automatically be available in the Options bar at the top of your screen. The following list describes the options you'll find in this palette:

Figure 2.13 The Marquee Options bar.

▶ **Feather**—Allows you to fade out the edge between selected and unselected areas. I usually leave this option turned off, because I might forget that a feather setting had been typed in previously. This one little setting might mess up an otherwise great selection. Instead, I find it much easier to make a selection and then press Option-Command-D on the Macintosh or Alt-Ctrl-D in Windows (or just choose Select > Feather).

▶ **Anti-aliased**—This checkbox determines whether a one-pixel-wide border on the edge of a selection will blend with the image surrounding it. This provides nice, smooth transitions, and helps prevent areas from looking jagged (see **Figures 1.72 and 1.73** in the preceding chapter for examples). I recommend that you leave this checkbox on at all times, unless, of course, you have a great need for jaggies (sometimes they're preferred for multimedia applications).

▶ **Style menu**—Controls the shape and size of the next
selection made. When the Style pop-up menu is set to
Normal, your selections are not restricted in size or
shape (other than they have to be rectangles or ellipses).
After changing this menu to Constrained Aspect Ratio,
you'll be confronted with Width and Height settings
(**Figure 2.14**). By changing the numbers in these areas,
you can constrain the shape of the next selection to
the ratio between the Width and Height settings. For
example, if you change Width to 2 and leave Height at
1, your selections will always be twice as wide as they
are tall. This can be useful when you need to find out
how much of an image needs to be cropped when
printing it as an 8x10, for example.

Figure 2.14 The Constrained Aspect Ratio option.

I use the Fixed Size option much more often than the
Constrained Aspect Ratio option (**Figure 2.15**). Fixed Size
lets you type in an exact width and height; that way, any
time you click using either the Rectangular or Elliptical
Marquee tool, you'll get a selection exactly that size. What's
more, if you didn't get it in exactly the right spot, you can
just drag the selection around the screen before releasing
the mouse button. For instance, Macintosh desktop icons
are always 32 pixels wide and 32 pixels tall, so I use these
numbers when selecting something I want to use as an
icon. When entering a Width or Height setting, you can
specify a measurement system by adding a few letters after
the number you enter, otherwise Photoshop will default
to the measurement system used for the rulers.

Measurement System	Letters to use
Pixels	px
Inches	in
Centimeters	cm
Millimeters	mm
Picas	pica
Points	pt
Percentages	%

Figure 2.15 The Fixed Size option.

Single Row and Single Column Marquee Tools

The third and fourth choices under the Marquee tool
pop-up menu are the Single Row and Single Column
Marquee tools. These tools are limited in that they only
select a one-pixel-wide row or one-pixel-tall column. To be

honest, I hardly ever use them (maybe once or twice a year). However, they have gotten me out of few tight spots, such as when I had to clean up a few stray pixels from in between palettes when taking screen shots for this book.

Crop Tool

Two spaces below the Marquee tool, you'll find the Crop tool. While the Crop tool doesn't produce a selection, it does allow you to isolate a certain area of your image. Using this tool, you can crop an image as well as resize and rotate it at the same time (**Figures 2.16 and 2.17**).

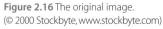

Figure 2.16 The original image. (© 2000 Stockbyte, www.stockbyte.com)

Figure 2.17 The original image cropped and rotated.

Figure 2.18 The cropping rectangle. (© 2000 Stockbyte, www.stockbyte.com)

When you click and drag over an image with the Crop tool selected, a dashed rectangle appears. When the Shield Cropped Area checkbox is turned on, the area outside of the cropping rectangle will be covered with the color indicated in the Options bar, and might appear to be partially transparent, depending on the Opacity setting (**Figure 2.18**). You can drag any one of the hollow squares on the edge of the rectangle to change its size. Also, you can hold down Shift while dragging a corner to constrain the rectangle's shape. Anything beyond the edge of the rectangle is discarded when the image is cropped (if you haven't turned on the Hide option).

To rotate the image, you can move your cursor just beyond one of the corner points and drag (look for an icon that looks like a curve with arrows on each end). You can also drag the crosshair in the center of the rectangle to change the point from which the rectangle will be rotated. To complete the cropping, press Return or Enter (or double-click within the cropping rectangle). Press Esc to cancel. If you're working on a layer (instead of the background) and the Delete option is chosen in the Options bar, then all information that appears outside of the cropping rectangle will be discarded. If the Hide option is chosen, then the area outside the cropping rectangle will not be discarded, but will instead remain as image data that extends beyond the bounds of the visible image. This option is very useful when you are creating animations in ImageReady and you'd like part of the image to start outside of the image area. We'll explore animation in Chapter 17.

Occasionally, you'll need to crop and resize an image at the same time. Maybe you need three images to be the exact same size, or perhaps you need your image to be a specific width. You can do this by specifying the exact Width, Height, and Resolution settings you desire before you create a cropping rectangle. Once you've created a cropping rectangle on your image, you'll notice that different options appear in the Options bar (**Figure 2.19**). By typing in both a Width and a Height setting, you constrain the shape of the rectangle that you draw. I occasionally leave one of these values empty so that I can still create any rectangle shape.

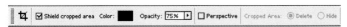

Figure 2.19 The Options bar after a cropping rectangle is added to the image.

The Perspective Crop choice in the Options bar is new to Photoshop 6.0 and very powerful (it becomes available once you've created a cropping rectangle). When that option is turned on, you will be able to move each corner of the cropping rectangle independently. This allows you to align the four corners with lines that would be level in real life, but may appear in perspective in a photograph (**Figure 2.20**). Once you have all four corners in place, you can press Return or Enter to crop the image and correct the perspective of the image in one step (**Figure 2.21**).

Figure 2.20 Getting the corners to line up with level lines. (© 1998 PhotoSpin, www.photospin.com)

Figure 2.21 Result of applying a perspective crop.

You don't have to crop the image while you are correcting its perspective. Once you have the corners in the correct location to establish the perspective of the image, move the side handles (not the corners) until the area you'd like to keep is within the cropping rectangle, and then press Enter (**Figures 2.22 and 2.23**).

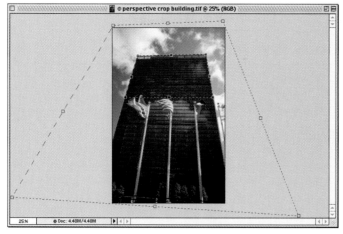

Figure 2.22 Establishing perspective and extending the cropping rectangle.

Figure 2.23 Result of correcting perspective.

Lasso Tool

The Lasso tool is the most versatile of the basic selection tools. By holding down the mouse button, you can use the Lasso to trace around the edge of an irregularly shaped object (**Figure 2.24**). When you release the button, the area will be selected. Be sure to create a closed shape by finishing the selection exactly where you started it; otherwise, Photoshop will complete the selection for you by adding a straight line between the beginning and end of the selection.

Sometimes you'll need to add a few straight segments in the middle of a freeform shape. You can do this by holding down Option (Macintosh) or Alt (Windows) and then releasing the mouse button (but not the Option or Alt key). Now, each time you click your mouse, Photoshop will connect the clicks with straight lines (**Figure 2.25**). To go back to creating a freeform shape, just start dragging and then release the Option key (Macintosh) or Alt key (Windows).

Notes

You can zoom in on your document to get a more precise view by typing Command-+ (Mac) or Ctrl-+ (Windows). You don't even have to let go of the mouse button—just press this key combination as you're dragging.

....

I suggest you zoom in on your image to make sure you're creating an accurate selection. If you can't see the entire image, you can hold the spacebar to access the Hand tool. You can do this without ever releasing the mouse button, which means you can alternate between scrolling and selecting until you've got the whole object.

Figure 2.24 The Lasso tool in action. (© 1998 PhotoSpin, www.photospin.com)

Figure 2.25 Using the Option or Alt key while clicking to create straight-line segments. (© 1998 PhotoSpin, www.photospin.com)

Polygonal Lasso Tool

You can use the Polygonal Lasso tool whenever you need to make a selection that consists mainly of straight lines. Using this tool, you just click multiple areas of the image, and Photoshop connects the dots for you (**Figure 2.26**). If you need to create a freeform selection, hold down Option (Macintosh) or Alt (Windows) and drag. To finish a selection, you can either click where the selection began or double-click when you add the final point.

Figure 2.26 The Polygonal Lasso tool in action. (© 1998 PhotoSpin, www.photospin.com)

Magnetic Lasso Tool

Whereas the Lasso and Polygonal Lasso tools are relatively straightforward, the Magnetic Lasso tool has a bunch of neat tricks up its sleeve. This tool can be a huge timesaver in that it allows you to trace around the edge of an object without having to be overly precise. You don't have to break a sweat making all of those tiny, painstaking movements with your mouse. Instead, you can make big sloppy selections, and the Magnetic Lasso will do the fine-tuning for you. What's more, if it doesn't do a great job in certain areas, you can hold down Option (Macintosh) or Alt (Windows) to use the freeform Lasso tool. However, before using the Magnetic Lasso tool, you'll want to change its settings in the Options bar (**Figure 2.27**). Let's take a look at these settings:

Figure 2.27 The Magnetic Lasso Options bar.

▶ **Feather and Anti-aliased**—These options work just as they would with any selection or painting tool.

▶ **Width**—Determines how far away from your cursor Photoshop will look for the edge of an object (just like a painting tool, it uses a circular area surrounding your cursor). You can see this area by pressing the Caps Lock key or by choosing File > Preferences > Displays & Cursors and setting the Other Tools option to Precise. You can quickly change the Lasso Width setting by typing] (right bracket) to increase the setting in increments of 1, or [(left bracket) to decrease the setting. If you're like me and really like keyboard commands, you can also press Shift-[to change this setting to the lowest possible value (1) or Shift-] for the highest possible value (40). You can even use these keyboard commands while you're dragging around the edge of an image.

▶ **Frequency**—Determines how often Photoshop will add anchor points (higher settings add more points). The complexity of the object you're tracing usually determines the proper Frequency setting; that is, as objects get more complex, you should use a higher setting (**Figures 2.28 and 2.29**).

Figure 2.28 A Frequency setting of 5. (© 2000 Stockbyte, www.stockbyte.com)

Figure 2.29 A Frequency setting of 99.

▶ **Edge Contrast**—I think this setting is the most important of the bunch. It determines how much contrast there must be between the object and the background in order for Photoshop to select the object. If the object you're attempting to select has well-defined edges, you should use a high setting (**Figure 2.30**). You can also use a large Lasso tool width. On the other hand, if the edges are not well defined, you should use a low setting and try to be very precise when dragging (**Figure 2.31**).

 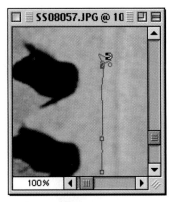

Figure 2.30 High edge contrast (20%). (© 1998 PhotoDisc)

Figure 2.31 Low edge contrast (7%). (© 1998 PhotoDisc)

If the Magnetic Lasso tool is not behaving itself, you can temporarily switch to the freeform Lasso tool by holding down Option (Macintosh) or Alt (Windows) as you drag. You can also periodically click to manually add anchor points to the selection edge. If you want to use the Polygonal Lasso tool, hold down Option (Macintosh) or Alt (Windows) and click in multiple areas of the image (instead of dragging). If you don't like the shape of the selection, you can press the Delete key to remove the last anchor point. (Pressing Delete multiple times deletes multiple points.) Once you have a satisfactory shape, finish the selection by pressing Return or Enter or by double-clicking. Remember, if you don't create a closed shape, Photoshop will finish it for you with a straight-line segment.

If you really get used to the features available with the Magnetic Lasso tool, you'll be able to create most of your basic selections with this tool alone. This will take some time, and you'll sometimes have to supplement its use by holding down Option (Macintosh) or Alt (Windows) to access the other Lasso tools for areas the magnetic one has trouble selecting.

Magic Wand Tool

The Magic Wand tool is great for selecting solid (or almost solid) colored areas, because it selects areas based on color—or shades of gray in grayscale mode—as shown in **Figure 2.32**. This is helpful when you want to change the color of an area or remove a simple background.

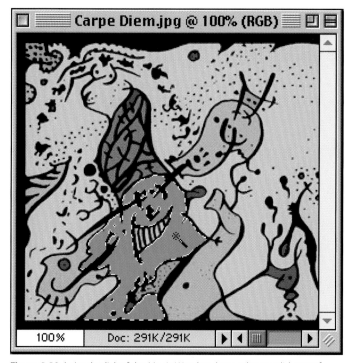

Figure 2.32 A simple click of the Magic Wand tool can select a solid area of color with ease. (© Nik Willmore…yes, he's my brother.)

You'll probably find it easier to understand how this works if you start by thinking about grayscale images, because they're less complex than color images. Grayscale images can contain up to 256 shades of gray. When you click one of these shades with the Magic Wand tool, it will select any shades that are within the Tolerance specified in the

Options bar. For instance, if you click shade 128 (Photoshop numbers the shades from 0 to 255) and the Tolerance is set to 10, you'll get a selection of shades that are 10 shades darker and 10 shades brighter than the one you clicked (**Figures 2.33 to 2.35**). When the Contiguous checkbox is turned on, the only shades that will be selected are those within an area that touches the spot you clicked— Photoshop can't jump across areas that are not within the tolerance.

Figure 2.33 Tolerance: 10.

Figure 2.34 Tolerance: 20.

Figure 2.35 Tolerance: 30.

Note

To quickly change the Tolerance setting, press Enter and then type the desired number and press Enter again. I know it sounds weird, but try it—it works!

Just in case you're not comfortable thinking in the 0-to-255 numbering system and would rather think about percentages, I've included a conversion table below. Otherwise, you can make this conversion by multiplying any percentage by 2.55 (1% in the 0 to 255 numbering system). Remember, the Magic Wand tool will select twice as much as the number you type in.

Color images are a little more complex. They're made from three components: red, green, and blue (that is, when you're working in RGB mode). The Magic Wand tool will analyze all the components (known as channels) in your file to determine which areas to select. For example, if you click a color made up of the components 32 red, 120 green, 212 blue (these numbers can be found in the Info palette) and you use a Tolerance setting of 10, Photoshop will look for colors between 22 and 42 in the red channel, 110 and 130 in the green channel, and 202 and 222 in the blue channel. The only colors that will be selected are ones that fall within all three ranges. Doesn't that sound complicated? Well, I have to confess, I don't usually think about the numbers, because they're something of a pain. Instead, I just experiment with the setting until I get a good result. Now, doesn't that sound a lot easier than dealing with all those numbers? If you really want to understand all about the color channels, take a look at Chapter 9, "Channels."

PERCENTAGE CONVERSIONS

Percentage	Tolerance Setting
0%	0
10%	26
20%	51
30%	77
40%	102
50%	128
60%	153
70%	179
80%	204
90%	230
100%	255

Type Tool

You can use Photoshop's Type tool to create a selection by turning on the Selection option in the Options bar (**Figure 2.36**). When you use that option, Photoshop will show you a preview of the selection (with a red overlay on the image, as shown in **Figure 2.37**) while you are editing the text, and then it will deliver a selection when you press Enter. We'll cover the options of this tool in Chapter 14, "Type and Background Effects."

Figure 2.37 The selection will be previewed using a red overlay on the non-selected areas.

Type selection option

Figure 2.36 The Selection option for the Type tool.

Refining a Selection

Selecting complex objects in Photoshop usually requires multiple selection tools. In order to combine these selection tools, you'll need to either use a few controls in the Options bar (**Figure 2.38**) or learn a few keyboard commands that will allow you to add, subtract, or intersect a selection.

Figure 2.38 These four choices in the Options bar allow you to create, add, subtract, or intersect a selection.

Adding to a Selection

To add to an existing selection, either click on the second icon on the far left of the Options bar (it looks like two little boxes overlapping each other), or hold down the Shift key when you start making the new selection. You must press the key *before* you start the selection; you can release it as soon as you've clicked the mouse button (**Figures 2.39 to 2.41**). If you press it too late, the original selection will be lost. Let's say, for example, you would like to select multiple round objects. One way would be to use the Elliptical

Marquee tool multiple times while holding down the Shift key. But you might find it easier to use the choice available in the Options bar because then you don't have to remember to keep any keys held down.

Figure 2.39 The original selection.
(© 1998 PhotoDisc)

Figure 2.40 Adding to the selection.

Figure 2.41 The end result.

Removing Part of a Selection

To remove areas from an existing selection, either click on the third icon on the far left of the Options bar (it looks like one little box is stacked on top of another), or hold down Option (Macintosh) or Alt (Windows) when you begin making the selection. If, for example, you want to create a half circle, you could start with an Elliptical Marquee tool selection and then switch over to the Rectangular Marquee tool and drag while holding down Option (Macintosh) or Alt (Windows) to remove half of the circle (**Figures 2.42 to 2.44**).

Figure 2.42 The original selection.
(© 1998 PhotoDisc)

Figure 2.43 Subtracting a second selection.

Figure 2.44 The end result.

Clicking while holding down Option (Macintosh) or Alt (Windows) is particularly helpful when you're using the Magic Wand tool to remove areas of a selection (**Figures 2.45 and 2.46**). With each click of the Magic Wand tool, you can use a different Tolerance setting.

Figure 2.45 The original selection.

Intersecting a Selection

To end up with only the overlapped portions of two selections, click on the third icon on the far left of the Options bar (it looks like two squares intersecting, with the overlap area colored in), or hold down Shift-Option (Mac) or Shift-Alt (Windows) while editing an existing selection. Sometimes I use the Magic Wand tool to select the background of an image and then choose Select > Inverse to get the object (or objects) of the selected image (**Figure 2.47**). However, when there are multiple objects in the image, as there are in **Figures 2.48 and 2.49**, I often have to restrict the selection to a specific area by dragging with the Lasso tool while holding down Shift-Option (Macintosh) or Shift-Alt (Windows).

Figure 2.46 Option-clicking (Macintosh) or Alt-clicking (Windows) with the Magic Wand tool.

Figure 2.47 Applying the Magic Wand tool to the background and then choosing Select > Inverse. (© 1998 PhotoSpin, www.photospin.com)

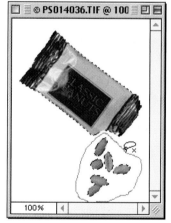

Figure 2.48 Dragging with Lasso tool while holding down Shift-Option (Macintosh) or Shift-Alt (Windows).

Figure 2.49 The end result.

The Select Menu

The Select menu offers you many choices that supplement the basic selection tools. Learning these features is well worth your time, because they'll help you save heaps of it in your everyday work. We'll look at these features in the same order they appear in the menu; then, later in this chapter, I'll show you how to replace many of these commands with an alternative that allows you to think visually instead of numerically.

Select All

Select > All selects the entire document. This can be useful when you need to trim off any "big data," or the part of an image that extends beyond the edge of the document (**Figure 2.50**). You can crop big data by choosing Select > All and then Image > Crop (**Figure 2.51**). Also, if you need to copy an entire image, you'll need to select everything, because without a selection, the Copy command will be grayed out.

Figure 2.50 An example of "big data" (these areas are not usually visible). (Original image © 1998 PhotoDisc)

Figure 2.51 Layers repositioned after the image has been cropped.

Deselect/Reselect

If you're done using a selection and would like to work on the entire image, choose Select > Deselect. If you don't have a selection, you can work on the entire image. Now, if you need to use the last active selection (and there isn't a

selection on your screen), you can choose Select >
Reselect. This is great when you need to use the same
selection over and over again. I use these two commands
all the time. However, I usually opt for the keyboard commands: Command-D (Mac) or Ctrl-D (Windows) for
Deselect, Shift-Command-D (Mac) or Shift-Ctrl-D
(Windows) for Reselect.

Inverse

As you might expect, the Inverse command selects the exact
opposite of what you originally selected. If, for example,
you have the background of an image selected, after choosing Select > Inverse, you'll have the subject of the image
selected instead (**Figures 2.52 and 2.53**). I use this command constantly, especially with the Magic Wand tool.
Sometimes it's just easier to select the areas that you don't
want and then choose Select > Inverse to select what you
really want to isolate. Sound backwards? It is, but it works
great.

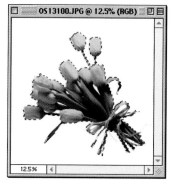

Figure 2.52 A Magic Wand tool selection. (© 1998 PhotoDisc)

Figure 2.53 The selection after using
the Select > Inverse command.

Color Range

You can think of the Select > Color Range command as the
Magic Wand tool on steroids. With Color Range, you can
click multiple areas and then change the Fuzziness setting
(how's that for a technical term?) to increase or reduce the
range of colors that will be selected (**Figure 2.54 and 2.55**).

Figure 2.54 The original image.
(© 1998 PhotoDisc)

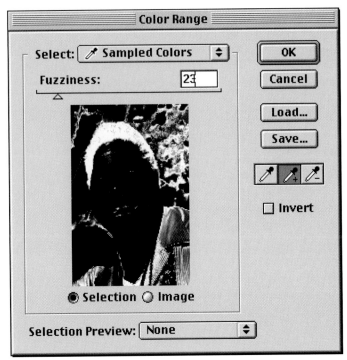

Figure 2.55 The same image in the Color Range dialog box after clicking on multiple areas within his hair.

As you click and play with the Fuzziness control, you'll see a preview of the selection in the middle of the Color Range dialog box. Areas that appear white are the areas that will be selected. The Selection and Image radio buttons allow you to switch between the selection preview and the main image. (I never actually use these two controls because I find it easier to switch to the image view at any time by just holding down Command on the Mac or Ctrl in Windows.) You can also see a preview of the selection within the main image window by changing the Selection Preview pop-up menu to Grayscale, Black or White Matte, or Quick Mask (**Figures 2.56 to 2.58**).

The Eyedropper tool on the right side of the dialog box allows you to add and subtract colors from the selection. Using the Eyedropper with the plus symbol next to it is really helpful, because it allows you to click the image multiple times. With each click, you tell Photoshop which colors you want it to search for. A low Fuzziness setting with many clicks usually produces the best results (**Figures 2.59 and 2.60**).

Figure 2.56 Choosing Grayscale will display the same preview that appears in the Color Range dialog box.

Figure 2.57 Choosing Black Matte or White Matte will fill the unselected areas with black or white.

Figure 2.58 Choosing Quick Mask uses the settings in the Quick Mask dialog box to create a preview on the image.

The selections you get from the Color Range command are not ordinary selections, in that they usually contain areas that are not completely selected. For instance, if you're trying to select the red areas in an image and there happens be a flesh tone in the same image, the fleshy areas will most likely become partially selected. If you then adjust the image, the red will be completely adjusted, and the flesh tones will only shift a little bit.

If a selection is already present when you choose Select > Color Range, the command will only analyze the colors within the selected area. This means you can run the command multiple times to isolate smaller and smaller areas. If you want to have the Color Range command add to the current selection, be sure to hold down the Shift key when choosing Select > Color Range.

Feather

Unlike the Feather option in the selection tools, this version only affects the selection that's currently active, and has no effect on future selections. You can't reduce the amount of feathering with this command once it's applied. Therefore, if you apply it once with a setting of 10 and then try it again on the same selection using a setting of 5, it will simply increase the amount again. It's just like blurring

Figure 2.59 An example of a single click with a high Fuzziness setting.

Figure 2.60 An example of five clicks with a low Fuzziness setting.

an image—each time you blur the image, it becomes more and more blurry.

I prefer using this command instead of entering Feather settings directly into the tool's Options bar (where they affect all "new" selections). If you enter these values directly, you might not remember the setting is turned on days later when you spend hours trying to select an intricate object. By leaving the tools set at 0, you can quickly press Option-Command-D (Macintosh) or Alt-Ctrl-D (Windows) to bring up the Feather dialog box and enter a number to feather the selection. Because this only affects the current selection, it can't mess up any future ones (**Figures 2.61 and 2.62**).

Figure 2.61 A watch pasted with a normal selection. (© 1998 PhotoDisc)

Figure 2.62 A watch copied using a feathered selection and then pasted into this document.

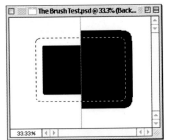

Figure 2.63 The left half of this split image shows where the selection would start to fade out and blend with the underlying image. The right half shows where the selection would stop affecting the image. Notice that the marching ants show up halfway between those two areas.

The problem with the Feather command is that there is no way to tell if a selection is feathered by just looking at the marching ants. Not only that, but most people think the marching ants indicate where the edge of a selection is, and that's simply not the case with a feathered selection. If you take a look at **Figure 2.63**, you'll find that the marching ants actually indicate where a feathered selection is halfway faded out.

Modify

The features in this little menu have helped get me out of many sticky situations. At first glance, it might not be obvious why you would ever use them, but I guarantee you that they'll come in very handy as you continue through the book. Here's a list of the commands found under the Select > Modify menu, as well as descriptions of what they do:

▶ **Border**—Selects a border of pixels centered on the current selection. If you use a setting of 10, the selection will be five pixels inside the selection and five pixels outside the selection. You can use this to remove pesky halos that appear when you copy an object from a light background and paste it onto a darker background (**Figures 2.64 and 2.65**).

▶ **Smooth**—Attempts to round off any sharp corners in a selection (**Figure 2.66**). This can be especially useful when you want to create a rounded-corner rectangle. It can also produce an interesting effect after you've used the Type Mask tool (**Figures 2.67 and 2.68**).

Figure 2.64 The original selection. (© 1998 PhotoDisc)

Figure 2.65 A 10-pixel border.

Figure 2.66 Smooth 16 pixels.

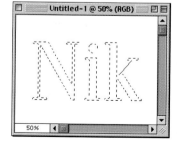

Figure 2.67 The original selection.

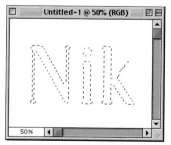

Figure 2.68 After applying a Smooth setting of 6.

> **Expand**—Enlarges the current selection while attempting to maintain its shape (**Figure 2.69**). This command works well with smooth, freeform selections, but it's not my first choice for straight-edged selections, because it usually slices off the corners.

> **Contract**—Reduces the size of the current selection while attempting to maintain its shape (**Figure 2.70**). The highest setting available is 16. If you need to use a higher setting, just use the command twice.

Figure 2.69 Expand 12 pixels.

Figure 2.70 Contract 12 pixels.

Grow

The Select > Grow command will search for colors that are similar to an area that has already been selected (**Figures 2.71 and 2.72**). In effect, it will spread your selection in every direction—but only into areas that are similar in color. It cannot jump across areas that are not similar to the ones selected. The Grow command uses the Tolerance setting that's specified in the Magic Wand Options bar to determine the range of colors it will look for.

Figure 2.71 The original selection. (© 1998 PhotoSpin, www.photospin.com)

Similar

The Select > Similar command works just like the Grow command except that it looks over the entire document for similar colors (**Figures 2.73 and 2.74**). Unlike the Grow command, the colors that Similar selects don't have to touch the previous selection. This can be very useful when you've selected one object out of a group of the same colored objects. For example, if you have a herd of gray

Figure 2.72 The selection after Select > Grow is used.

elephants standing in front of a lush green jungle, you can select the first elephant and then use Select > Similar to get the rest of the herd (provided, of course, that they're all a similar shade of gray). The same works for a field of flowers, and so on.

Figure 2.73 The original selection.

Figure 2.74 The selection after Select > Similar is used.

Transform Selection

After making a selection, you can scale, rotate, or distort it by choosing Select > Transform Selection. This command places handles around the image. By pulling on the handles and using a series of keyboard commands, you can distort the selection as much as you like. Let's take a look at the neat stuff you can do with Transform Selection:

▶ **Scale**—To scale a selection, pull on any of the handles. Pulling on a corner handle will change both the width and height at the same time. (Hold the Shift key to retain the proportions of the original selection.) Pulling on the side handles will change either the width of the selection or its height, but not both. This can be a great help when working with elliptical selections, because it lets you pull on the edges of the selection instead of its so-called "corners" (**Figures 2.75 and 2.76**).

▶ **Rotate**—To rotate the image, move your cursor a little bit beyond one of the corner points; the cursor should change into an arc with arrows on each end. You can control where the center point of the rotation will be by moving the crosshair that appears in the center of the selection (**Figures 2.77 to 2.79**).

Figure 2.75 The original selection.
(© 1998 PhotoSpin, www.photospin.com)

Figure 2.76 After choosing Select > Transform to scale the selection.

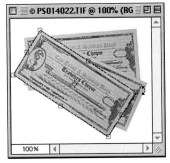

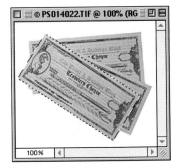

Figure 2.77 The original selection. (© 1998 PhotoSpin, www.photospin.com)

Figure 2.78 Rotating and scaling the selection.

Figure 2.79 The end result.

▶ **Distort**—To distort the shape of the selection, hold down Command (Macintosh) or Ctrl (Windows) and then drag one of the corner points. Using this technique, you can pull each corner independently (**Figures 2.80 to 2.82**).

You can also distort a selection so that it resembles the shape of a road vanishing into the distance. You do this by dragging one of the corners while holding down Shift-Option-Command on the Macintosh or Shift-Alt-Ctrl in Windows (**Figures 2.83 to 2.85**).

To move two diagonal corners at the same time, hold down Option-Command on the Macintosh or Alt-Ctrl in Windows while dragging one of the corner handles (**Figures 2.86 and 2.87**).

Finalize your distortions by pressing Enter (or by double-clicking inside the selection). Cancel them by pressing Esc.

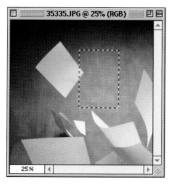

Figure 2.80 The original selection. (© 1998 PhotoDisc)

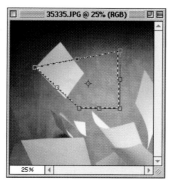

Figure 2.81 Dragging a corner while holding down Command (Macintosh) or Ctrl (Windows).

Figure 2.82 The selection after all four corners have been dragged.

Figure 2.83 The original selection. (© 1998 PhotoDisc)

Figure 2.84 Dragging a corner while holding down Shift-Option-Command (Macintosh) or Shift-Alt-Ctrl (Windows).

Figure 2.85 The end result.

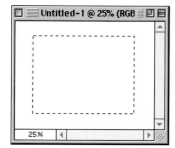

Figure 2.86 The original selection.

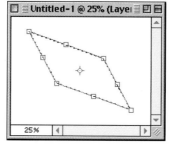

Figure 2.87 Dragging a corner handle while holding down Option-Command (Macintosh) or Alt-Ctrl (Windows).

Note
If you forget the keyboard commands that are required to distort a selection, you can instead choose Select > Transform Selection and then Control-click (Macintosh) or right-click (Windows) to choose the type of distortion you want to perform (**Figure 2.89**).

Free Transform
Scale
Rotate
Skew
Distort
Perspective
Rotate 180°
Rotate 90° CW
Rotate 90° CCW
Flip Horizontal
Flip Vertical

Figure 2.88 The menu that appears as a result of Control-clicking (Macintosh) or right-clicking (Windows) while you're transforming a selection.

Load Selection and Save Selection

If you've spent hours perfecting a selection and think you might need to use it again in the future, you can apply the Select > Save Selection command (**Figure 2.89**). This stores the selection as an alpha channel (you can think of channels as stored selections). Don't worry, you don't need to know anything about channels to use these commands—all you have to do is supply a name for the selection. If you want to find out more about channels, you can check out Chapter 9.

These saved selections remain in your document until you manually remove them using the Channels palette (see Chapter 9 to find out how to delete a channel). They won't be saved on your hard drive until you actually save the entire file. Only the Photoshop (.psd) or TIFF (.tif) file formats support saved selections.

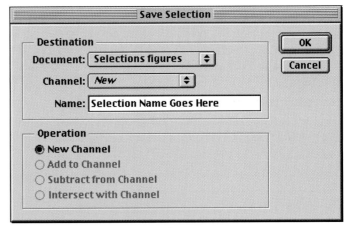

Figure 2.89 The Save Selection dialog box.

When you want to retrieve the saved selection, choose Select > Load Selection and pick the name of the selection from the Channel pop-up menu (**Figure 2.90**). When you use this command, it's just like re-creating the selection with the original selection tool you used, only a whole lot faster.

Load Selection

Source
Document: [**Selections figures** ‡]
Channel: [**Selection Name Goes Here** ‡]
☐ **Invert**

[**OK**]
[**Cancel**]

Operation
◉ **New Selection**
○ **Add to Selection**
○ **Subtract from Selection**
○ **Intersect with Selection**

Figure 2.90 The Load Selection dialog box.

Quick Mask Mode

Remember when we were talking about the marching ants and how they can't accurately show you what a feathered selection looks like? Well, Quick Mask mode can show you what a feathered selection *really* looks like, and can also help create basic selections. The Quick Mask icon is located directly below the foreground and background colors in your Tools palette (**Figure 2.91**). When the left icon is turned on, you are in Standard mode, which means you create selections using the normal selection tools, and they will show up as the familiar marching ants. The right icon enables Quick Mask mode, and that's where selections will show up as a translucent color overlay.

To see how it works, first make a selection using the Marquee tool, and then turn on Quick Mask mode by clicking on the right icon under the foreground and background colors (or just type Q to do the same thing). In Quick Mask mode, the selected area should look normal and all the non-selected areas should be covered with a translucent color (**Figure 2.92 and 2.93**).

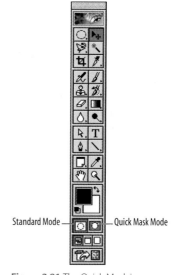

Standard Mode — Quick Mask Mode

Figure 2.91 The Quick Mask icons.

Figure 2.92 A selection shown in Standard mode. (© 2000 Stockbyte, www.stockbyte.com)

Figure 2.93 The same selection shown in Quick Mask mode.

Now that you're in Quick Mask mode, you no longer need to use selection tools to modify a selection. Instead, you use standard painting tools, and paint with black to take away from the selection, or white to add to it. When you're done modifying the selection, switch back to Standard mode and you'll be back to marching ants (**Figures 2.94 and 2.95**).

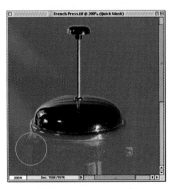

Figure 2.94 A selection modified in Quick Mask mode.

Figure 2.95 End result after switching back to Standard mode.

Now let's see what feathered selections look like in Quick Mask mode. Make another selection using the Marquee tool. Next, choose Select > Feather with a setting of 10, and then switch to Quick Mask mode and take a look (**Figures 2.96 and 2.97**). Feathered selections appear with blurry edges in Quick Mask mode. This happens because partially transparent areas (that is, ones that are more transparent than the rest of the mask) indicate areas that are partially selected (50% transparent means 50% selected).

The confusing part about this process is that when you look at the marching ants that appear after you switch back to Standard mode, they only show you where the selection is at least 50% selected. That isn't a very accurate picture of what it really looks like (**Figure 2.98**). But in Quick Mask mode, you can see exactly what is happening on its edge. So, if you want to create a feathered selection in Quick Mask mode, just choose a soft-edged brush to paint with. Or, if you already have a shape defined, then choose Filter > Blur > Gaussian Blur, which will give you the same result of feathering, but will show you a visual preview of the edge.

Figure 2.96 Normal. (© 2001 Stockbyte, www.stockbyte.com)

Figure 2.97 Feathered.

Figure 2.98 The marching ants show up where an area is at least 50% selected.

Shades of Gray

Try this out. Turn on Quick Mask mode—you don't need a selection to begin with. Type D to reset the foreground color to black, and then Option-Delete (Macintosh) or

Alt-Backspace (Windows) to fill the Quick Mask. Now paint within the Quick Mask with 20% gray (you can use the Color Picker palette to choose grays). Then turn off Quick Mask mode and paint in the selected area with bright red. Now choose Select > Deselect, lower the opacity of the painting tool to 80%, and paint with bright red. Your reds should look exactly the same. That's how Photoshop makes a selection fade out—simply by lowering the opacity of the tool you are using. This can sometimes be confusing, though, because the marching ants show up only where an image is at least 50% selected. So, try this one on for size. Turn on Quick Mask mode and paint with 49% gray, and then paint in another area with 51% gray. Then go back to Standard mode and paint across the area. Only the areas that are at least 50% gray show up as marching ants, but the other areas are still selected, even though the marching ants don't show up in those areas (**Figure 2.99**). Try turning on Quick Mask mode and then paint with 55% gray. Now go back to Standard mode and you'll even get a warning message, pictured in **Figure 2.100**.

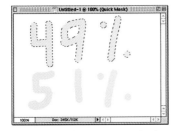

Figure 2.99 When painting in Quick Mask mode, only the areas that contain less than 50% gray will be visible when the selection is viewed as marching ants.

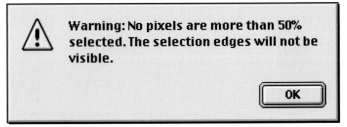

Figure 2.100 When you paint with shades brighter than 50% gray, a warning will appear when you go back to Standard mode.

We really haven't done anything fancy yet, so let's try something fun. To start with, you have to remember that when you work in Quick Mask mode, Photoshop treats the selection as if it is a grayscale image that you can paint on. That means you can use any tool that is available when working on grayscale images. So select an area using the Marquee tool, turn on Quick Mask mode, choose

Filter > Distort > Ripple, and mess with the settings until you've created something that looks a little kooky (**Figure 2.101**). Finally, go back to Standard mode and see what you've got. You can create infinite varieties of fascinating selections with this simple technique.

You can also "unfeather" a selection using Quick Mask mode (**Figure 2.102**). Remember, a feathered edge looks like a blurry edge in Quick Mask mode. All you have to do to remove that blurry look is to then choose Image > Adjust > Threshold. This will give the mask a very crisp, and therefore unfeathered, edge.

Figure 2.101 Applying the Ripple filter in Quick Mask mode.

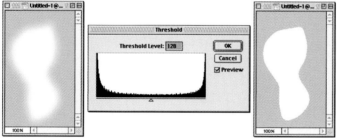

Figure 2.102 Unfeathering a selection using Threshold. Left: original image. Center: Threshold setting used. Right: result of applying Threshold.

Selections in Quick Mask mode

You can even use a selection to isolate a particular area of the Quick Mask, as shown in **Figure 2.103**. A selection in Quick Mask mode can help you create a selection that is only feathered on one side. To accomplish this, turn on Quick Mask mode, type D to reset the foreground color, and then type Option-Delete (Macintosh) or Alt-Backspace (Windows) to fill the Quick Mask. Next, choose the Marquee tool and select an area. Now use the Gradient tool set to Black, White and create a gradient within the selected area. Once you're done, switch off Quick Mask mode. Now to see exactly how this selection will affect the image, choose Image > Adjust > Levels and attempt to lighten that area by dragging the lower left slider.

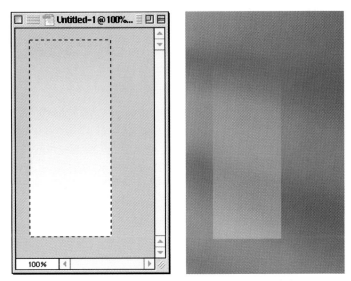

Figure 2.103 Using a selection in Quick Mask mode to restrict which areas can be edited.

Color

Photoshop also allows you to switch *where* the color shows up. You can specify whether you want the selected or unselected areas to show up. To change this setting, double-click on the Quick Mask icon and change the Color Indicates setting (**Figures 2.104 and 2.105**). Photoshop uses the term Masked Areas to describe areas that are not selected.

Figure 2.104 Changing the Color Indicates setting changes where the color overlay appears.

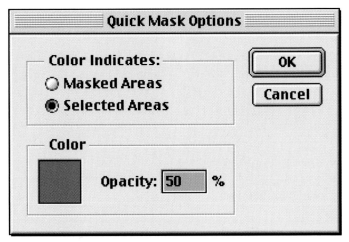

Figure 2.105 Quick Mask Options settings used.

The Opacity setting determines how much you will be able to see through the Quick Mask.

Closing Thoughts

After a few practice rounds with the various tools we covered in this chapter, you should be selecting like a pro. We'll go over more advanced methods of creating selections in Chapter 9, "Channels." But until then, it really is worth your while to build up your selection skills because you will be using them every day in Photoshop. And now it's time for another dose of Ben's Techno-Babble Decoder Ring.

Ben's Techno-Babble Decoder Ring

Feather—The process of converting a hard-edged selection into one that blends into the underlying image as you move closer to its edge.

Marching Ants—Term used to describe the edge of a selection. Used because the edges appear as very small moving specks (similar to ants).

Marquee—Like the rectangular marquees (signs) used at movie theaters to display the movies that are currently showing. In Photoshop, the Marquee tool is used to create rectangular (or elliptical) selections, and the resulting marching ants even resemble the flashing lights that used to be found surrounding movie marquees.

Big data—Any area of a layer that extends outside of the physical dimensions of the document.

Cropping—The process of reducing the dimensions of an image by removing unneeded space from the edge of the document. Also used to remove big data.

> **Note**
>
> On the CD accompanying this book, you'll find a PDF file that supplements this chapter. The file, called "extras.pdf," contains the following topics related to selections:
> - Copying selections between documents
> - Nudging a selection
> - Pasting control
> - Hiding edges
> - Fill and stroke
> - Printing a portion of an image

Keyboard Shortcuts

Function	Macintosh	Windows
Select All	Command-A	Ctrl-A
Deselect	Command-D	Ctrl-D
Reselect	Shift-Command-D	Shift-Ctrl-D
Select Inverse	Shift-Command-I	Shift-Ctrl-I
Feather	Option-Command-D	Alt-Ctrl-D
Marquee Tool	M	M
Lasso Tool	L	L
Fill Selection	Shift-Delete	Shift-Backspace
Magic Wand Tool	W	W
Fill with Foreground	Option-Delete	Alt-Backspace
Fill with Background	Command-Delete	Ctrl-Backspace

Courtesy of Tom Nick Cocotos, www.cocotos.com

Courtesy of Tom Nick Cocotos, www.cocotos.com

Courtesy of Jeff Schewe, www.schewephoto.com

3 Layers Primer

*The first rule to tinkering
is to save all the parts.*
—Paul Erlich

© Bob Elsdale, www.bobelsdale.com, Mac Side Up, a children's picture book
ISBN 0-525-46467-0, published by Dutton Children's books, New York

Our capacity to take things for granted seems to have no bounds. How often do you sit back and think, "Wow, life has really changed since the days when Smith Corona ruled and an Apple was just something you ate for lunch"? Probably seldom. However, if you think about it, you'll realize that colossal changes have taken place. We attained a unique kind of digital freedom when we evolved from the primordial ooze of manual typewriters, stat cameras, and typesetters. For graphic artists, this change has been nothing short of revolutionary.

In its own way, Photoshop's introduction of the Layers palette has had an equally profound impact on the graphic arts community. Before the Layers palette, we were forced to be very precise and final in our thoughts, because having to redo the work was incredibly time-consuming. The Layers palette released us from the shackles of single-layer images and gave us the ability to really let loose and explore our creative ideas.

How Do Layers Work?

At first glance, layers might seem complex, but the idea behind them is rather simple. You isolate different parts of your image onto independent layers (**Figure 3.1**). These layers act as if they are separate documents stacked one on top of the other. By putting each image on its own layer, you can freely change your document's look and layout without committing to the changes. If you paint, apply a filter, or make an adjustment, it only affects the layer on which you're working. If you get into a snarl over a particularly troublesome layer, you can throw it away and start over. The rest of your document will remain untouched.

Figure 3.1 Layers isolate different parts of the image.

You can make the layers relate to each other in interesting ways, such as by poking holes in them to reveal an underlying image. I'll show you some great techniques using this concept in Chapter 12, "Enhancement."

But first, you need to pick up on the basics—the founda-tions—of layers. If you've used layers for a while, you might find some of this chapter a bit too basic. On the other hand, you might find some juicy new tidbits.

Meeting the Layers

Before we jump in and start creating a bunch of layers, you should get familiar with their place of residence: the Layers palette (**Figure 3.2**). You're going to be spending a lot of time with this palette, so take a moment now to get on friendly terms with it. It's not terribly complicated, and after you've used it a few times, you should know it like the back of your hand.

As you make your way through this chapter, you'll learn about the Layers palette and the fundamental tasks associated with it. Also, I'll throw in a few layer styles just for the heck of it. Now, assuming that you've done your part and introduced yourself to the Layers palette, let's get on with the business of creating and manipulating layers in Photoshop.

Creating Layers

Photoshop will automatically create the majority of layers for you. A new layer is added anytime you copy and paste an image or drag a layer between documents (we'll talk about this later in the chapter). If you're starting from scratch, however, you can click the New Layer icon at the bottom of the Layers palette to create a new, empty layer.

Give it a try: Create a new document, and then use the Layers palette to create a new layer. Pick a bright color to paint with, and then use one of the shape tools to draw a big circle (**Figure 3.3**). Now create another layer, and draw a square on it, using a different color (**Figure 3.4**). Finally, create a third layer, and draw a triangle on it (**Figure 3.5**). You can use this simple document you've just created to try out the concepts in the following sec-tions that describe the features of the Layers palette (**Figure 3.6**).

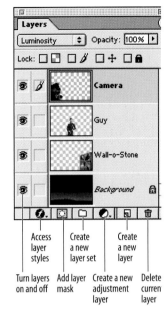

Figure 3.2 The Layers palette.

Note

I often create a new layer before using any of the painting tools or the Gradient tool. Because these tools apply changes directly to the active layer, the changes are difficult to modify once they've been applied. I like working with a safety net, so before using these tools, I create a new layer where I can easily edit the changes without disturbing the underlying image.

Figure 3.3 A new layer.

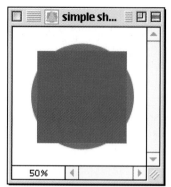

Figure 3.4 The second layer.

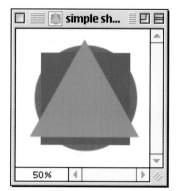

Figure 3.5 The third layer.

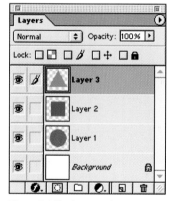

Figure 3.6 The Layers palette view.

Active Layer

You can only edit one layer at a time. Remember, Photoshop thinks of the layers as if they were separate documents. The layer you're currently working on is highlighted in the Layers palette. You should also see a little paintbrush icon next to it—that's just another indication that the layer is active for editing. To change the active layer, just click the name of another layer. Only one layer can be active at a time.

Stacking Order

You can change the stacking order of the layers by dragging the name of one layer above or below the name of another layer in the Layers palette. The topmost layers can often obstruct your view of the underlying images. You can change this by reordering the layers so that small images are near the top of the stack and the larger ones are near the bottom (**Figures 3.7 to 3.10**).

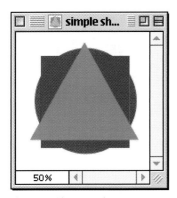

Figure 3.7 The original image.

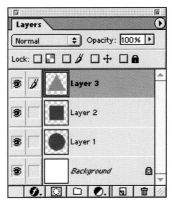

Figure 3.8 The original Layers palette.

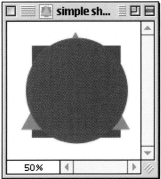

Figure 3.9 The changed stacking order.

Figure 3.10 The revised Layers palette.

Background Image

Photoshop will not permit you to drag a layer below the background, because it doesn't think of the background as a layer. If you liken the layers to the individual pages in a pad of tracing paper, you could think of the pad's cardboard backing as the background layer. The background is always opaque and cannot be moved. In some circumstances, though, you might want to delete the background. For example, when you output images to videotape, they can't be overlaid onto video if the background layer is present.

However, most of the time, keeping the background or not is just a personal preference. You don't have to have a background in your document. If you want to convert the

Notes

There is no need to hold down the Option or Alt key when double-clicking the background. In fact, doing so will cause Photoshop 6.0 to assign the background a generic name like "Layer 0."

If your document doesn't have a background (because you accidentally deleted or renamed the background), you can convert one of the existing layers into a background by choosing Layer > New > Layer from Background. Just changing the layer's name back to "Background" will not do the job. In earlier versions of Photoshop you could get a new Background layer by choosing Layer > New > Background.

background into a normal layer, just change its name (the background image must be named "Background," otherwise it becomes a normal layer). To change the name of a layer, hold down the Option key (Macintosh) or Alt key (Windows) while you double-click the layer's name in the Layers palette.

The Eyeballs: What They See Is What You Get

The eyeballs in the Layers palette aren't just cute, they determine which layers will be visible in your document as well as which ones will print. The eyeballs turn on and off in a toggle effect when you click them: Now you see them, now you don't.

If you turn off all the eyeballs in the Layers palette, Photoshop will fill your screen with a checkerboard. This checkerboard indicates that there's nothing visible in the document. (If Photoshop filled your screen with white instead, you might assume that there was a layer visible that was filled with white.) You can think of the checkerboard as the areas of the document that are transparent. When you view a single layer, the checkerboard indicates the transparent areas of that layer. As you turn on the other layers in the document, the checkerboard is replaced with the information about the other layers. When multiple layers are visible, the checkerboard indicates where the underlying image will not be obstructed by the elements on the visible layers (**Figures 3.11 to 3.14**).

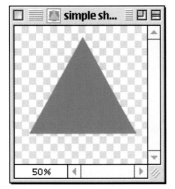

Figure 3.11 The checkerboard indicates a transparent area.

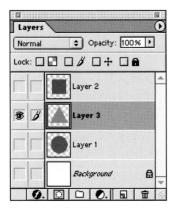

Figure 3.12 The Layers palette view.

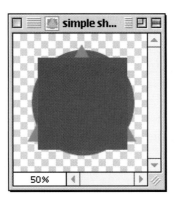

Figure 3.13 As more layers become visible, the transparent areas become smaller.

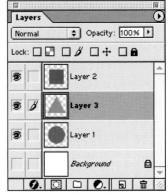

Figure 3.14 The Layers palette view.

Opacity

The Opacity setting at the top of the Layers palette controls the opacity of the active layer. When this setting is lowered, the entire layer becomes partially transparent (transparent is the exact opposite of opaque). If you want to lower the opacity in a specific area instead of the entire layer, you can lower the opacity of the Eraser tool and then brush across the area of the layer you want to become more transparent—that is, unless the background is active. If you use the Eraser tool on the background, it will simply paint with your background color instead of truly deleting areas (remember, the background is always opaque).

Try this: Open the document you created earlier in this chapter. Create a new layer, and then use any painting tool to brush across the layer. Now, lower the Opacity setting in the Layers palette to 70% (**Figures 3.15 to 3.17**).

Notes

To quickly turn off all the eyeballs in the Layers palette and view only the layer you're interested in, simply Option-click (Mac) or Alt-click (Windows) one of the eyeball icons. You can turn all the eyeball icons back on by Option-clicking (Mac) or Alt-clicking (Windows) the same eyeball a second time.

....

To quickly change the opacity of a layer, switch to the Move tool (typing V will switch you to the Move tool) and then use the number keys on your keyboard (1 = 10%, 3 = 30%, 56 = 56%, and so on).

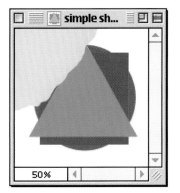

Figure 3.15 Layer at 100% opacity.

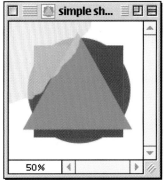

Figure 3.16 Layer at 70% opacity.

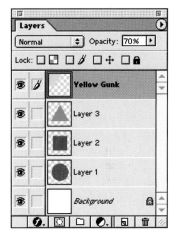

Figure 3.17 Lowering the opacity of a layer affects the entire layer.

Now let's compare this effect with what happens when you lower the Opacity setting of the Paintbrush tool. Create another new layer; however, this time leave the layer's Opacity setting at 100%. Now choose the Paintbrush tool, change the tool's Opacity setting to 70% (in the Options bar), and then brush across the layer. The paint should look exactly the same as the paint that appears in the other layer (**Figures 3.18 and 3.19**).

Note

You can figure out the exact opacity of an area by Option-clicking (Mac) or Alt-clicking (Windows) its eyeball icon and then opening the Info palette. Click the eyedropper icon in the Info palette, and choose Opacity; you'll get a separate readout that indicates how opaque the area is below your cursor.

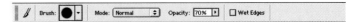

Figure 3.18 The Paintbrush Options view.

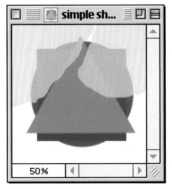

Figure 3.19 Painting with a low Opacity setting.

Finally, create one more new layer, and paint across it with the tool's Opacity setting at 100%. Now, brush across an area with the Eraser tool using an Opacity setting of 30% (**Figures 3.20 and 3.21**).

Figure 3.20 The Eraser Options view.

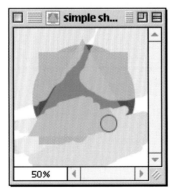

Figure 3.21 Using the Eraser tool with a low Opacity setting will also make areas of a layer transparent.

All of these options do the same thing to your image. You just have to think a bit: Do you want to apply the Opacity setting to the entire layer? If so, use the Layers palette's Opacity setting. Do you want to apply the Opacity setting to only part of the layer? If so, use the Opacity setting in the tool's Options bar. Do you want to change the opacity of an area you've already painted across? If so, use the Eraser tool with an Opacity setting.

Photoshop always (well, almost always) offers you more than one way of doing things. It reminds me of my favorite hardware store, McGuckins. It's the kind of place that takes your breath away—it has everything! If you just want a screwdriver, you'll probably find an entire aisle full of screwdrivers, each one designed for a specific use. Photoshop has the same approach; you just have to play around with it to figure out which tool best suits your needs.

Moving Layers

If you want to move everything that's on a particular layer, first make that layer active by clicking its name; then use the Move tool to drag it around the screen (**Figure 3.22**). If you drag the layer onto another document window, Photoshop will copy the layer into that document. If you want to move just a small area of the layer, you can make a selection and then drag from within the selected area using the Move tool.

Trimming the Fat

If you use the Move tool to reposition a layer, and a portion of the layer starts to extend beyond the edge of your document, Photoshop will remember the information beyond the edge (**Figure 3.23**). Therefore, if you move the layer away from the edge, Photoshop is able to bring back the information that was not visible. You can save a lot of memory by getting Photoshop to clip off all the information beyond the edge of the document (**Figure 3.24**). Here's a little trick for trimming off that fat (or big data, as Adobe calls it). Just choose Select > All and then choose Image > Crop—no more wasted memory.

Notes

If you've made a portion of a layer partially transparent with the Eraser or Paintbrush tool set to a low opacity, you can bring the layer back to 100% opacity by duplicating it multiple times. Keep in mind that it might take quite a few duplicates to get the layer back to full opacity. Once the image is completely opaque, just merge all the duplicate layers together.

When I need to precisely position a layer, I usually lower the Opacity setting just enough so that I can see the underlying layers. You can do this quickly by using the number keys on your keyboard (0 to 9) when using the Move tool. After positioning the layer, just press 0 to bring the layer back to 100% opacity.

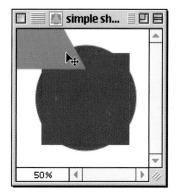

Figure 3.22 Using the Move tool to reposition a layer.

Figure 3.23 The original image. (© 1998 PhotoDisc)

Figure 3.24 After the image is cropped.

Copying Between Documents

When you use the Move tool, you can do more than just drag a layer around the document on which you're working. You can also drag a layer on top of another document (**Figure 3.25**). This copies the entire layer into the second document. The copied layer will be positioned directly above the active layer. This is similar to copying and pasting, but it takes up a lot less memory because Photoshop doesn't store the image on the Clipboard. You can achieve the same result by dragging the name of a layer from the Layers palette onto another document window.

When you drag layers between documents, occasionally an image will appear as if it has not only been copied but also scaled at the same time. That's not what's really happening. Instead, you're viewing the two images at different magnifications (**Figure 3.26**). Look at the tops of the documents; if the percentages do not match, the image size will appear to change when you drag the image between the documents. If you view both images with the same magnification, this won't happen. It doesn't change how large the image is; it simply gives you a preview of how large it will look. It's just like putting your hand under a magnifying glass. Your hand looks larger, but when you pull your hand out, it looks normal again.

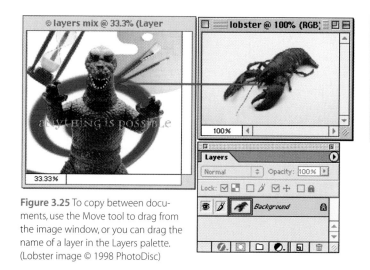

Figure 3.25 To copy between documents, use the Move tool to drag from the image window, or you can drag the name of a layer in the Layers palette. (Lobster image © 1998 PhotoDisc)

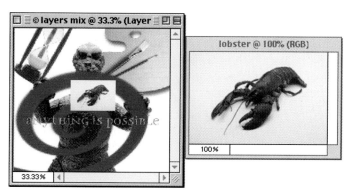

Figure 3.26 Images viewed at different magnifications.

Duplicating Layers

If you have a picture of Elvis, and you want to make Elvis twins, just drag the name of the layer onto the new-layer icon at the bottom of the Layers palette. This icon has two purposes: It will duplicate a layer if you drag one on top if it, or it will create a new empty layer if you just click it.

Deleting Layers

If you've created a document that looks a little cluttered, you can delete a layer by dragging its name onto the trash icon at the bottom of the Layers palette. Or, if you have a long distance to drag to get your layer in the trash, try Option-clicking (Macintosh) or Alt-clicking (Windows) the trash icon instead (the Option or Alt key prevents a warning dialog box from appearing). However, this icon does not work like the trash on a Mac or the recycle bin in Windows. Once you put something in it, you can't get it back (that is, not without resorting to the History palette).

Leapin' Layers! More Tools and Toys

Photoshop packs a large array of layer-manipulation controls. These controls allow you to go way beyond just creating, duplicating, and deleting layers. You'll be able to distort, adjust, and add wild effects after you wade through all these options.

Transforming Layers

To rotate, scale, or distort a layer, choose one of the options in the Edit > Transform menu; then pull the handles to distort the image. This will distort the current layer as well as any other layers linked to it (**Figures 3.27 and 3.28**). When you like the way your image looks, press the Enter key to commit to the change (press Esc to abort). If you want to know more about the transformation controls, see Chapter 2, "Selection Primer."

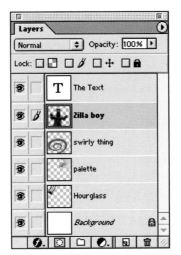

Figure 3.27 The Layers palette view.

Figure 3.28 Transforming a layer.

Linking Layers

If you need to move or transform more than one layer at a time, just click to the left of one of the preview thumbnails in the Layers palette. When you do, a link (chain) symbol will appear (**Figure 3.29**). This indicates that the active layer is now linked to all the layers that have the link symbol next to them. When you use the Move tool or choose Edit > Transform, the current layer and all the layers linked to it will change. This feature doesn't allow you to do anything other than move or transform layers (for example, you can't apply a filter to multiple layers).

When layers are linked, you can choose one of the options from the Layer > Align Linked menu, or the Move tool Options bar, to change their position relative to each other. For example, you can align the top edges of the linked layers, or you can center them horizontally.

Locking Up

The checkboxes at the top of the Layers palette allow you to lock the transparency, image, and position of an individual layer (**Figure 3.30**). Once a layer has been locked, changes that can be performed on that layer are limited.

Lock Transparency

The Lock Transparency checkbox (which looks like a checkerboard) at the top of the Layers palette gets in my way most often (because I forget it's turned on). Lock Transparency prevents you from changing the transparency of areas. Each layer has its own Lock Transparency setting. Therefore, if you turn on the Lock Transparency checkbox for one layer and then switch to another layer, the Layers palette will display the setting for the second layer, which might be different than the first one.

Try using the Eraser tool when Lock Transparency is turned on—it will mess with your mind! Because the Eraser tool usually makes areas transparent (by completely deleting them), it will start painting instead when Lock Transparency is turned on. It will fill with the current background color any areas you drag over. However, if you paint across an

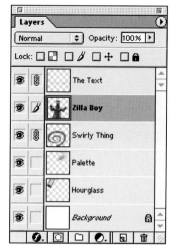

Figure 3.29 The chain icon indicates linked layers.

Note

When dragging linked layers between documents, be sure to drag from the image window instead of the Layers palette; otherwise, only one layer will be moved.

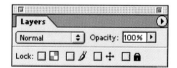

Figure 3.30 The Lock checkboxes.

Note

Lock Transparency was known as Preserve Transparency in previous versions of Photoshop.

area that's transparent, it doesn't change the image at all (because the transparent areas are being preserved). You can see how it can get in your way if you forget you turned it on.

Try this: Open a photo, and delete areas around it using the Eraser tool. To accomplish this, you'll have to change the name of the background first (you can't poke a hole in the background, but you can on a layer); then make sure Lock Transparency is turned off. Otherwise, you can't make areas transparent. Now choose Filter > Blur > Gaussian Blur and use a really high setting. You'll notice that the edge of the image fades out and blends with the transparent areas surrounding it (**Figure 3.31**). Now, choose Edit > Undo and try doing the same thing with the Lock Transparency option turned on (**Figure 3.32**). Notice that the edge cannot fade out because Photoshop will not change the transparency with this option turned on.

Figure 3.31 Lock Transparency is off.   **Figure 3.32** Lock Transparency is on.

Here is another example: Create a new layer, and scribble across it with any painting tool, making sure the Lock Transparency option is turned off. Next, drag across the image with the Gradient tool. The gradient should fill the entire screen (**Figure 3.33**). Now, choose Edit > Undo, and try doing the same thing with the Lock Transparency option turned on (**Figure 3.34**). Because Photoshop can't change the transparency of the layer, it cannot fill the transparent areas and therefore is limited to changing the areas that are opaque to begin with.

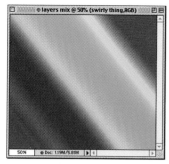

Figure 3.33 Lock Transparency is off.

Figure 3.34 Lock Transparency on.

When you're trying to use any of the techniques in this book, be sure to keep an eye on that little Lock Transparency checkbox. If it's turned on when you don't want it to be, it might screw up the entire effect you're trying to achieve. Therefore, unless I specifically tell you to turn it on (check it), you should assume that it should be left off (that's the default setting). If I ever tell you to turn it on, I'll let you know when to turn it back off again (uncheck it) so that you don't get messed up when trying to reproduce a technique from this book. Now, turn off that pesky (but useful) checkbox, and let's continue exploring Photoshop.

Lock Image

The Lock Image checkbox (which looks like a paintbrush) at the top of the Layers palette prevents you from changing the pixels that make up a layer. That means you won't be able to paint, erase, apply an adjustment or filter, or do anything else that would change the look of that layer. Just as with Lock Transparency, each layer has its own Lock Image setting. I use this checkbox after I've finished color-correcting and retouching a layer so I don't accidentally change it later on.

Lock Position

The Lock Position checkbox (which looks like the Move tool) at the top of the Layers palette prevents you from moving the active layer. I check this checkbox to prevent someone else from accidentally moving an element that I've taken great care to position correctly.

Lock All

The Lock All checkbox (which looks like a padlock) at the top of the Layers palette locks the transparency, image and position of the current layer.

Layer Styles

A bunch of really neat options are available under the Layer > Layer Style menu (**Figure 3.35**). To experiment with these options, first create a new, empty layer, and paint on it with any of the painting tools. Then apply one of the effects found in the Layer > Layer Style menu: Drop Shadow, Inner Shadow, Inner Glow, Outer Glow, Bevel and Emboss, etc. (**Figures 3.36 to 3.38**). You can use the default settings for now. After applying an effect, use the Eraser tool to remove some of the paint on that layer. Did you notice that the layer effect updates to reflect the changes you make to the layer? Layer styles create in one simple step the same results that would usually require multiple layers and a lot of memory.

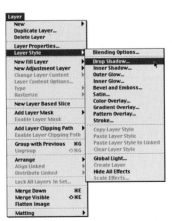

Figure 3.35 The Layer > Layer Style menu.

Figure 3.36 The original image.

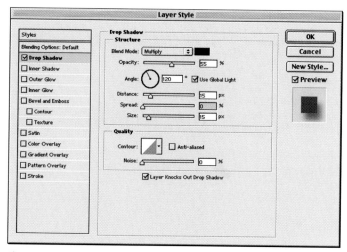

Figure 3.38 Drop Shadow style is shown in the upper-right corner of the document.

Figure 3.37 The Layer Style dialog box with the Drop Shadow panel.

In fact, you can choose Layer > Layer Style > Create Layer to have Photoshop create the layers that would usually be needed to create the effect. For example, you might want to choose Create Layers when you're going to give your file to someone who is using an older version of Photoshop. (Photoshop 5.5 supports some, but not all, of the styles in Photoshop 6.0.) Let's take a look at what different layer styles do to your image (**Figures 3.39 to 3.42**).

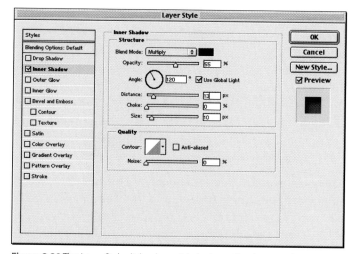

Figure 3.40 Inner Shadow style is shown in the upper-right corner of the document.

Figure 3.39 The Layer Style dialog box with the Inner Shadow panel.

Figure 3.41 Outer Glow style is shown in the upper-right corner of the document.

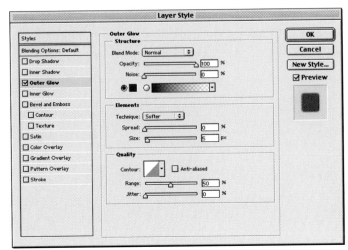

Figure 3.42 The Layer Style dialog box with the Outer Glow panel.

Adjustment Layers

When you choose an option available in the Image > Adjust menu, it only affects the layer that's currently active. (Remember, Photoshop treats each layer as if it were a separate document.) However, there's a special type of layer that will allow you to apply these adjustments to multiple layers. This is known as an *adjustment layer*.

To create an adjustment layer, choose Layer > New Adjustment Layer, or choose the type of adjustment you'd like from the Adjustment Layer pop-up menu at the bottom of the Layers palette (it looks like a circle filled with half black and half white). After you choose which type of adjustment you want to use (we'll discuss adjustment settings in the Production Essentials section of this book), the changes will modify all the layers that are underneath the adjustment layer. You can move the adjustment layer up or down in the layers stack to affect more or fewer layers.

These changes are not permanent; at any time you can simply turn off the eyeball icon on the adjustment layer and the image will return to normal. You can also lessen the effect of the adjustment layer by lowering its Opacity setting. To change the adjustment settings, simply double-click the Adjustment Layer icon on the left side of the adjustment layer (**Figures 3.43 to 3.47**).

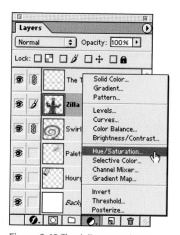

Figure 3.43 The Adjustment Layer pop-up menu.

Figure 3.44 The Hue/Saturation adjustment layer at the top of the Layers palette.

Figure 3.45 Hue/Saturation affects all layers.

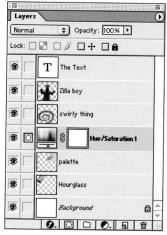

Figure 3.46 Changing the stacking order of the Hue/Saturation adjustment layer.

Figure 3.47 The adjustment layer applies to all layers below it but not to the layers above it.

Fill Layers

Adobe added a few new types of layers in Photoshop 6.0. The options in the Layer > New Fill Layer menu allow you to add solid color, gradient, and pattern content to a layer. This is especially useful when combined with Photoshop 6.0's new Layer Clipping Paths as described in Chapter 11. If you don't want a fill layer to fill your entire document, then make a selection before creating one. After a fill layer has been created, you can reset your foreground color by typing **D**. Then you can use the Eraser tool to hide the area and the Paintbrush tool to make areas visible again.

Solid Color Layer

Choosing Layer > New Fill Layer > Solid Color will create a layer that contains a solid color. After you've created one of these layers, you can double-click the left-most thumbnail of the layer in the Layers palette to edit the color.

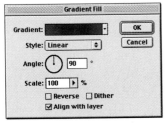

Figure 3.48 The Gradient Fill dialog box.

Gradient Layer

Choosing Layer > New Fill Layer > Gradient will allow you to create a new layer that contains a gradient (**Figure 3.48**). The gradient is always editable by double-clicking the left-most thumbnail in the Layers palette. If the Align with layer checkbox is turned on, then the start and end points of the gradient are determined by the contents of the layer instead of the document's overall size.

Pattern Layer

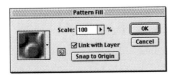

Figure 3.49 The Pattern Fill dialog box.

Choosing Layer > New Fill Layer > Pattern allows you to create a new layer that contains a repeating pattern (**Figure 3.49**). I like to use this type of layer to add a brushed-aluminum look to a background. Then, if I ever decide to change the pattern, it's as simple as double-clicking the thumbnail in the Layers palette and choosing New Pattern from the drop-down menu.

The Blending Mode Menu

The Blending Mode menu at the top of the Layers palette is immensely useful. It allows the information on one layer to blend with the underlying image in interesting and useful ways. Using this menu, you can quickly change the color of objects, colorize grayscale images, add reflections to metallic objects, and much more. This is an advanced feature, so you'll have to wait until you get to Chapter 11 to find out more about it.

Automatic Selections

To select everything on a particular layer, just Command-click (Mac) or Ctrl-click (Windows) the name of the layer. You can hold down the Shift key to add to a selection that already exists, or use the Option key (Macintosh) or Alt key (Windows) to take away from the current selection (**Figures 3.50 to 3.53**).

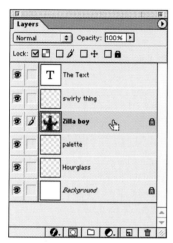

Figure 3.50 Command-click (Mac) or Ctrl-click (Windows) a layer to select all the objects on that layer.

Figure 3.51 The result of Command-clicking (Mac) or Ctrl-clicking (Windows).

Figure 3.52 Refining the selection with the Lasso tool, while holding down Option (Mac) or Alt (Windows) to take away from the selection.

Figure 3.53 The result of copying the selected area of Godzilla and pasting it on a layer above the swirl (look at his neck).

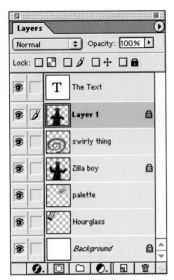

Figure 3.54 Result of using Layer > New Layer via Copy and moving the new layer over the swirly layer.

Via Copy

The Layers menu offers you a wide variety of options for copying, merging, and manipulating layers. Let's look at one of these choices. If you select an area of your image and then choose Layer > New Layer via Copy, the area you've selected will be copied from the layer you were working on and moved to a brand-new layer in the same position (**Figure 3.54**). This is particularly handy when you want to move just a portion of a layer so that you can place it on top of another layer.

All Layers

When you're editing on a layer, some of the editing tools might not work the way you expect them to. This happens because most of the tools act as if each layer is a separate document—they ignore all layers except the active one. That is, unless the tool has the All Layers checkbox turned on in the Options bar of the tool you're using. This checkbox allows the tools to act as if all the layers have been combined into one layer (**Figures 3.55 to 3.57**).

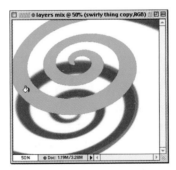

Figure 3.55 Using the Paint Bucket tool to add color with the All Layers option turned off.

Figure 3.56 Using the Paint Bucket tool with All Layers turned on.

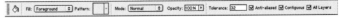

Figure 3.57 The All Layers checkbox in the Paint Bucket Options bar.

Shortcuts

You'll be doing a lot of switching between layers, and this can get a bit tedious. Therefore, I'll show you some quick shortcuts. First, you can Command-click (Mac) or Ctrl-click (Windows) anywhere in the image window when using the Move tool to activate the layer directly below your cursor. Then you can find out which layer you're working on by glancing at the Layers palette. You won't always need the layer below your cursor, so instead of Command-clicking (Mac) or Ctrl-clicking (Windows), try Control-clicking (Mac) or right-clicking (Windows). This will bring up a menu of all the layers that contain pixels directly below your cursor; you just choose the name of the layer you want to work on and Photoshop will switch to that layer.

Remember that you can get to the Move tool temporarily at any time by holding down the Command key (Mac) or Ctrl key (Windows). Therefore, if you hold down Command and Control (Mac) or Ctrl and right-click (Windows) at the same time, no matter what tool you are using, Photoshop will present you with the pop-up menu.

Layer Sets

Have you ever had one of those mega-complicated images with dozens of layers? If so, you are probably familiar with the agony of having to fumble through an endless sea of layers, hoping you won't drown before you find the right one. If this describes you, you'll be ecstatic to know that Adobe has finally thrown in a desperately needed lifesaver. In Photoshop 6.0, you can group a bunch of layers into a set. A set looks like a folder in the Layers palette. You can view all the layers in the set, or just the set name.

To create a set, click the Layer Set icon at the bottom of the Layers palette (it looks like a folder). A folder appears in the list of layers. You can move any number of layers into the set by dragging and dropping them onto the folder icon. The set will have a small arrow just to its left that allows you to collapse the set down to its name or expand the set to show

Note
You can also create a layer set by linking multiple layers togeter and then choosing New Set From Linked from the side menu of the Layers palette.

you all the layers it contains (**Figure 3.58 and 3.59**). This can greatly simplify the Layers palette, making a document of 100-plus layers look as if it's made of only five layers.

Layer sets can also be useful when you want to reorganize the layers in your image. If one of the layers within a set is active, then using the Move tool will only affect that layer (unless it's linked to other layers). If the layer *set* is active, then using the Move tool will move all the layers within that set. You can also move multiple layers up or down in the layers stack by first putting them into a set and then dragging the name of the set up or down in the layers stack.

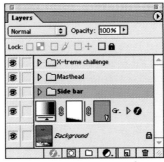

Figure 3.58 Collapsed layer sets.

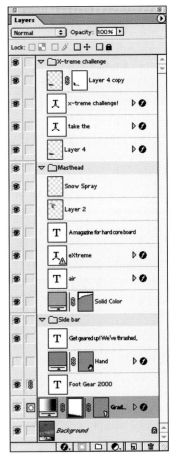

Figure 3.59 Expanded layer sets.

No Thumbnail Mode

If, after organizing your image into layer sets, you still find that the Layers palette is a mess, then you might want to simplify the way Photoshop displays layers. If you choose Palette Options from the side menu of the Layers palette, you'll find the option that allows you to turn off the layer thumbnails. Once you've done that, you should find that the list of layers takes up a lot less space, but you still have the full functionality of all of Photoshop's features (**Figures 3.60 and 3.61**).

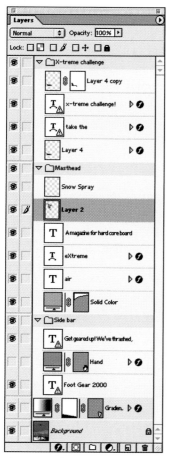

Figure 3.60 The Layers palette using the default thumbnail size.

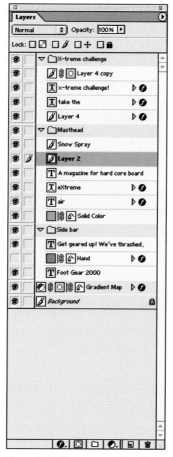

Figure 3.61 The Layers palette after setting the thumbnails setting to none.

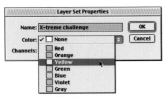

Figure 3.62 The Layer Properties dialog box.

Figure 3.63 Each layer can be color-coded using one of seven colors.

> ## Warning
>
> Once you've merged two layers, it's awfully hard to get them apart—the only way is to use the History palette. However, even with the History palette, you might lose all the changes you've made since you merged the layers.

Color Coding

If you work within a large group of Photoshop users, it can be useful to assign colors to layers to indicate their current status. Maybe some text needs to be proofed, maybe the client approved a certain part of the image, or perhaps an area needs to be sent off for color correction. All you have to do is hold down the Option key (Macintosh) or Alt key (Windows) and double-click the name of a layer. That will bring up the Layer Properties dialog box, where you can color-code a layer or layer set. (**Figures 3.62 and 3.63**).

Merging Layers

When you create a complicated image that contains dozens of layers, your project can start hogging memory, which in turn makes it difficult to manage all the layers. Every time you create a new layer and add something to it, Photoshop gobbles up more memory. Photoshop not only has to think about what's on that layer, it also has to remember what's below the layer (even if that information is completely covered by the information on the layers above).

Whenever possible, I try to simplify my image by merging layers together. This combines the layers into a single layer and thus saves memory (because Photoshop no longer has to remember the parts of those layers that were previously being covered). The side menu on the Layers palette gives you several ways to do this:

▶ **Merge Down**—Merges the active layer into the layer directly below it.

▶ **Merge Visible**—Merges all the layers that are currently visible in the main image window.

▶ **Merge Linked**—Merges all the layers that have the link symbol next to them, along with the active layer.

▶ **Flatten Image**—Merges all visible layers into the background, discards hidden layers, and fills empty areas with white.

If you want to know how much extra memory the layers take up as you're modifying your image, choose Document Sizes from the menu to the right of the numbers that appear at the bottom-center of your document (**Figure 3.64**). The number on the left should stay relatively consistent (unless you scale or crop the image); it indicates how much memory your image would use if all the layers were merged together. The number on the right indicates how much memory the image is using with all the layers included. This number changes as you add and modify your layers. Keep an eye on it so that you can see how memory-intensive the different layers are.

Figure 3.64 Memory-usage indicator.

The number on the right might get huge if you're using a lot of layers; however, keep in mind that you'll know exactly how large the image will be when you're all done by glancing at the left number.

Done Playing Around?

You've spent hours toiling away on your image, and now you're ready to save your file so it can go on to its next stop (which might be a printing company or one of your clients, or perhaps it's going to be posted to the Web). Then again, maybe it's not going anywhere—you just want to rest your eyes, take a break, and work on it later. Wherever the image ends up, you need to make sure to save it in a format you can work with in Photoshop (complete with layers, paths, channels, and so on). Then you can save it in another format that's appropriate for its destination.

It would be wonderful if all software programs could work with the same format, but alas, they can't. Therefore, it's worth your while to get familiar with the various file formats available in Photoshop.

Saving Layered Files

If you're not too familiar with file formats, you might wonder why there are so many options in the Save dialog box. It's like anything else with Photoshop—you just have to think about the end use. If you're going to use the file in Photoshop and keep the layers, you'll want to save it in the

Photoshop file format (also known as PSD). Photoshop, TIFF, and PDF are the only formats that recognize layers.

I mainly use the Photoshop format, as previous versions of Photoshop cannot extract the layers from a TIFF or PDF file. Unfortunately, most other programs cannot open files saved in the Photoshop file format, so it's a good habit to save the original image in Photoshop's native PSD format and then make a copy of the image without layers and save it in another format—JPEG or TIFF, for example.

Most formats other than Photoshop's native PSD format (EPS, JPEG, and so on) can't handle multiple layers, so you'll have to merge all the layers into the background of your image. You can do this quickly by choosing Flatten Image from the side menu of the Layers palette. Flatten Image combines all your layers, and any areas that were transparent are filled with white. The transparent areas are filled in because the other file formats don't know what to do with them. I usually save two versions of my files—one in the Photoshop file format (so I can get back to the layers) and one in TIFF or EPS format (to use in my page-layout program) or GIF or JPEG format (for the Web).

Closing Thoughts

Layers play such a huge role in Photoshop that to deny yourself any crucial information about them is asking for trouble. With every new release, Adobe likes to pack more and more functions into the Layers palette. So as time goes on, understanding them will become even more crucial. This is definitely a chapter you should feel comfortable with before you move on to the more advanced areas of Photoshop.

Ben's Techno-Babble Decoder Ring

Lock Transparency—A function in Photoshop that temporarily "freezes" the transparency of a layer. While Lock Transparency is in effect, you cannot increase or decrease how transparent an area will appear.

Opacity—The Opacity setting determines how opaque (the opposite of transparent) the information on a layer will appear. An Opacity setting of 100% will not allow you to see the underlying image. A setting below 100% will allow the underlying image to partially show through the current layer.

Keyboard Shortcuts

Function	Macintosh	Windows
Show/Hide Layers Palette	F7	F7
New Layer	Shift-Command-N	Shift-Ctrl-N
New Layer Via Copy	Command-J	Ctrl-J
New Layer Via Cut	Shift-Command-J	Shift-Ctrl-J
Toggle Lock Transparency	/	/
Make Top Layer Active	Shift-Option-]	Shift-Alt-]
Make Next Layer Active	Option-]	Alt-]
Make Previous Layer Active	Option-[	Alt-[
Make Bottom Layer Active	Shift-Option-[	Shift-Alt-[
Move Layer Up	Option-Command-]	Alt-Ctrl-]
Move Layer Down	Option-Command-[	Alt-Ctrl-[
Merge Down	Command-E	Ctrl-E
Merge Visible	Shift-Command-E	Shift-Ctrl-E

Courtesy of Gordon Studer, www.gordonstuder.com

Courtesy of David Bishop, www.dbsf.com

Part II Production Essentials

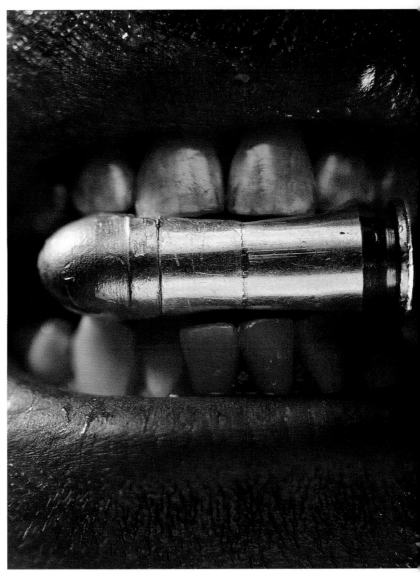

4 Resolution Solutions

© Bob Elsdale, www.bobelsdale.com

The difference between failure and success is doing a thing nearly right, and doing it exactly right.
–Edward C. Simmons

When it comes to resolution, we all want the same thing: we want to know what it takes to achieve the best possible image. But most people seem to be confused about resolution. What is it? What setting should I use? Why does it matter? These are some of the most common questions I get, and since resolution has such a dramatic effect on your final result, I think it's worth your while to take a bit of time to understand what it's actually all about. We'll start by demystifying all the stuffy techno-jargon (spi, ppi, dpi, etc.) and get down to what's really important about resolution. Then, once we know what we're talking about, we'll get to specific recommendations for optimal resolution settings.

For those of you who have no desire to pop the hood and learn the finer points, you have my permission to cheat and skip ahead to the section called "Optimal Settings." There you will find tables with my recommended settings. I won't think any less of you for taking a shortcut. The rest of you curious ones stick with me—we're going to shed some much-needed light on this subject.

The idea behind resolution is actually pretty straightforward. Resolution tells your scanner how many pixels to capture as it scans your image, and therefore how much space it will take up on your screen. Then, when you print the image, the resolution setting determines how large those pixels should be when you print them. It really is that simple.

If it's that simple, then why is everyone confused about it? Well, you have a lot of variables to deal with. For starters, there are several different methods by which to use your image (such as the Internet, inkjet printer, laser printer, dye-sub printer, and printing press), and each has different resolution requirements. There are also a bunch of terms that people like to throw around: ppi, dpi, lpi, spi, and so on. And to confuse matters more, people misuse those terms on a regular basis. So let's clear those muddy waters so that you can make the right decision the next time you're faced with that perennial question, "What resolution should I use?"

Scanning

When you scan an image, the resolution setting determines the width and height of the image, measured in pixels. In scanning, resolution is measured in *samples per inch*, or spi. The term makes sense because your scanner is sampling the image—seeing what it looks like—a set number of times in an inch. Scan a 3-by-5-inch original at a resolution of 100 spi, and you will end up with exactly 300 by 500 pixels. Or scan the same image at 72 spi, and you'll get 216 by 360 pixels total (3 inches x 72 samples per inch = 216, and 5 inches x 72 samples per inch = 360). Simple math will determine how many pixels you end up with.

But if that's the case, then it would seem that you could call that pixels per inch (ppi), because that's what you're ending up with, right? Almost, but not exactly. There is something called *pixels per inch,* but it has nothing to do with scanning. Instead, it indicates how large the pixels will be when you print the image. If you reproduce your image at 100% of its original size, then the spi and ppi settings are identical. But what if you scale your image up to twice its original size? In that case, you might take 200 samples per inch when the image is scanned, and then print the image at 100 pixels per inch. To understand this better, think back to that 3-by-5-inch image. If you scan it at a resolution of 200 samples per inch, then you'll end up with 600 by 1000 pixels. Then if you print those same pixels, but only print 100 of them per inch, wouldn't you end up with a 6-by-10-inch printed image? Again, it's simple math (600 pixels divided by 100 per inch = 6 inches). So, you could think of the spi setting as the scanning resolution and the ppi setting as the image's resolution. They are directly related to each other, but not the same.

In addition to understanding how resolution works, you also need to know that scanner manufacturers are doing their part to throw a curveball into the equation: some scanners offer a scale setting and others don't. This can put a lot of unnecessary guesswork into the process. If your scanner has a scale setting, then it will do a lot of work behind the scenes and make your life much easier.

Scanners with a scale setting use the resolution setting to determine how large you'd like the pixels to be when they are printed (also known as the ppi setting). Then, to determine how many pixels need to be captured from the original, the scanner takes the resolution setting (let's say you entered 100) and multiplies it by the scale setting you entered (let's say you used 200%). This determines the scanning resolution, which is also known as the spi setting. In the above example, your scanner would take 100 pixels per inch and multiply it by 200% to end up with a scanning resolution of 200 samples per inch. Let's look at what you'll have to do if your scanner doesn't offer a scale setting, and then you'll see why I like scanners that offer one.

With no scale setting, you are forced to calculate the scanning resolution yourself. To make that calculation, you have to do two things. First, take the image resolution you want to end up with; for now, let's say you need 300 pixels per inch. (I'll show you how to figure out what image resolution you want once we start talking about viewing the image onscreen and printing it.) Then multiply the resolution by how much you'd like to scale your image; in this case, let's make it 33%. If you want the image to be half its original size, then multiply the resolution by .5 or (50%); for one-third of its original size, multiply it by .3333 (or 33%). Then use the result as your scanning resolution. In this case, 300 multiplied by .3333 gives me a scanning resolution of 100. But I'm not done yet. If I open that scanned image in Photoshop and choose Image > Image Size, the size and resolution won't be what I really want. Remember, I want an image that is 33% of its original size with a resolution of 300. But I've done nothing to inform my scanner, or Photoshop, of my intentions. That means Photoshop only has the information my scanner supplied, which is that the image was scanned with a resolution of 100, with no scaling (remember, for this example the scanner does not have a scale setting).

That means we have one important step left. If you look at the top of the Image Size dialog box, you'll see how many pixels make up the image. That should be the exact amount we need, but the resolution setting is not what we want it to be (**Figure 4.1**). To fix that, uncheck the Resample Image checkbox, and then enter the resolution you want (300 in this case) as shown in **Figure 4.2**. Photoshop will use simple math (width in pixels divided by resolution setting) to figure out how large the image will be when printed. As you'll find out later in this chapter, resampling is similar to rescanning an image with a different resolution setting. In our example, we have the proper amount of information, but the pixels would be too large when printed, so we don't need to resample the image. Alas, the world would be a better place if scanner manufacturers would just include a scale setting, but sadly, many don't.

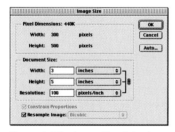

Figure 4.1 The Image Size dialog box indicates the settings that were used when the image was scanned.

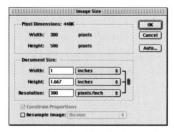

Figure 4.2 Unchecking the Resample Image checkbox allows you to change how large the image will be when printed, without changing the number of pixels that make up the image.

Display Onscreen

When you view an image onscreen in Photoshop, you don't see how large your image will be when it's printed. In fact, the resolution setting attached to the image is not taken into account. That's because the program displaying your image (whether Photoshop or a Web browser) does not control the size of the pixels that make up your screen—your operating system decides that. The setting in your Monitors or Display control panel (which is part of your operating system) determines how many pixels you see onscreen, and therefore their size.

Check it out for yourself: On a Mac, choose Apple Menu > Control Panels > Monitors; in Windows, choose Start > Settings > Control Panel > Display. This setting is known as monitor resolution because it determines the size of the pixels that make up your screen. Let's say your image has a resolution of 300 pixels per inch. In order to display an image using 300 pixels in each inch, a 15-inch monitor would have to be capable of displaying at least 3600 by 2700 pixels! (I doubt your monitor can go that high. In fact, most 15-inch monitors display only 1024 by 768 pixels.) When an image is displayed on a computer monitor, the width and height of the image in pixels determines how large the image will appear to be on screen. Photoshop doesn't care whether the resolution of your image is 300 or 72, because it can't change the size of the pixels that make up your screen.

But what happens when you view your image at 200% or 50% in Photoshop? When you zoom in to 200% view, Photoshop can't make the pixels 200% of their current size. Instead, it uses a 2-by-2 pixel area of your screen to show one pixel of your image. That way the image looks twice as big, even though you really haven't changed the size of the screen pixels. Zoom out to 50%, and Photoshop does the opposite—it averages a 2-by-2 area of your image to determine the color of a single screen pixel (this makes the image look half size when you haven't changed the size of the pixels that make up your screen). That also means you aren't seeing all the information in your file any time you view it at less than 100%.

Since the scanning resolution determines how many pixels you'll get out of every inch of the original, then the higher the scanning resolution, the more pixels you'll have in the width of your image. If you scan with a resolution setting that's too high, you might end up with so many pixels that the image will overflow your screen. In that case, it's not the resolution setting attached to the file that matters (the one that shows up in the Image Size dialog box), but the width and height in pixels.

Printed Images

So far, we've talked about scanning resolution (spi) and image resolution (ppi), but you might find that many people use the term *dots per inch*, or dpi to describe resolution.

Don't let them confuse you! Dpi has nothing to do with scanning or displaying an image. Instead, it describes the *size* of the dots that your printer uses to output an image. There is an important difference between dots and pixels, which explains why images are measured in pixels per inch instead of dots per inch. Dots can only have one of two states—on or off. A photograph printed on a desktop printer might *look* as if it contains shades of gray, but if you were to look at it under a magnifying glass, you'd see that it's really made up of pure black dots (**Figure 4.3**). A color printer is no different; it has four colors of ink (cyan, magenta, yellow, and black), but it still prints with solid dots of those colors (**Figure 4.4**). In order to simulate a shade of gray (or a shade of color, for that matter), the printer uses a pattern of black, or solid-colored, dots (different types of printers will use different kinds of patterns, as you'll see later in this chapter). Packing black dots together in a very dense pattern will create an area that looks like a dark shade of gray, and spacing them out will create what looks like a lighter shade. As long as the colored dots your printer uses are small enough that your eye can't focus on them individually, your brain is fooled into thinking that you are seeing shades of gray or shades of color (**Figure 4.5**), when you are really looking at solid black (or colored) dots.

Figure 4.5 If the dots your printer uses are small enough that your eye can't focus on them, then your brain will be fooled into thinking that you're looking at shades of gray, when in reality those shades are a pattern of solid black dots.

Figure 4.3 When you look at a printed image, your eye sees shades of gray, when in reality your image is printed using solid black dots. (©1998 PhotoSpin, www.photospin.com)

Figure 4.4 Color images are printed using solid cyan, magenta, yellow, and black dots.

Note

Printer resolution isn't always measured in dots per inch (dpi). A dye-sub printer produces output that resembles a photographic print because it can create true shades of gray. Since dye-sub printers don't use pure black and pure white dots, their resolution is measured in pixels per inch (ppi).

Your printer needs to use more than one dot to create the pattern necessary to simulate a shade of gray, which means the pixels that make up your image should always be larger than the dots your printer uses to output them. In essence that means the resolution of your image (ppi) should always be *lower* than the resolution of your printer (dpi).

A popular misconception is that higher image resolution settings are better, but that's simply not true. Your printer can handle only so much information, and when you feed it too much, your file size ends up being considerably larger than is needed, and the image will take a long time to print. What's happening is that the printer will discard all the extra information that it can't reproduce, and in doing so will also cause the quality of your image to suffer. As it attempts to discard the extra information, it will take the sharpening that was originally applied to your image and just average it out.

When the image resolution setting is too low, the pixels will be so big that you can easily see their edges, which will make the image appear pixilated (just like when you try to print an image from the Web). If you want the highest quality possible from your output device, then you need a resolution setting that is optimal for whatever kind of output device you use.

There are a few special instances when the resolution of your image (ppi) should match the resolution of your printer (dpi). For example, when your image is made out of pure black and pure white pixels (logos, text, and so on), it is a good idea to make those pixels the same size as the dots your printer will use to output the image. That way you'll get the highest-quality, most jaggy-free image possible. Another instance is when your output device can truly deliver shades of gray instead of simulating them with pure black dots. That is the case with dye-sub printers and 35 mm slides.

To recap:

▶ **Samples Per Inch (spi)** is how many pixels your scanner will create out of each inch of the original image.

▶ **Pixels Per Inch (ppi)** is how large the pixels of an image will be when printed.

▶ **Dots Per Inch (dpi)** describes the size of the dots your printer uses to reproduce your image.

It's nice to be familiar with these terms, but don't feel that you have to be an expert in defining them. So many peo- ... ately (even scanner man- ... as dpi) that it's usually ... just think about the ... ion might be mea- ... resolution. Image ... but I just say my ... at way anyone who ... ean. The one situa- ... hen describing the ... because everyone ... be easily confused.

... setting. This setting ... or, and all it means is ... width and height of ... . That's just a fancy ... by height in pixels, ... by-1200-pixel image ... is a 2 megapixel image (1600 multiplied by 1200 equals 1,920,000 pixels, which is approximately 2 million pixels).

When you open an image from a digital camera in Photoshop, Photoshop has to assign the image a resolution setting (ppi). It has no idea what you're going to use the image for, so it assigns 72, which is what an average com- puter monitor displays in each inch. If you print an image that has a resolution of 72 pixels per inch, it will most likely look pixelated (**Figure 4.6**). You can always change the image's resolution by choosing Image > Image Size. To do that, just uncheck the Resample Image check box in the Image Size dialog box, and then enter a new resolution set- ting. Photoshop will do some simple math (width in pixels divided by resolution = width in inches) to figure out how large the image will become with that setting (**Figure 4.7**).

Figure 4.6 An image with a resolution of 72 will usually look pixelated when printed.

Figure 4.7 If you change the resolu- tion of the image when the Resample Image checkbox is unchecked, Photo- shop will change the *size* of the pixels without changing *how many* pixels there are in the width and height of the image (in this case, the resolution was changed from 72 to 300).

If your digital camera doesn't record enough information for the print size and resolution you need, then you can use Photoshop to resample the image. Let's look at that term for a moment. Your scanner's resolution setting is expressed in samples per inch, and now you have a chance to resample your image. That would be like scanning an image, printing the scanned file, and then rescanning the printout with a different resolution setting. You'd end up with a different amount of information in the final file, but it would be based on the first file, not the original image. Lowering the resolution with resampling doesn't harm your image much because you're asking Photoshop to give you less information than that which your file already contains (**Figures 4.8 and 4.9**). But if you increase the resolution with resampling, then you're asking Photoshop to make up some extra information based on what's in your file (**Figures 4.10 and 4.11**). It does that with math. In essence it averages the brightness of two pixels to determine the shade to use when it makes a new pixel. The math it's using is known as interpolation. Some people will say they resampled an image and others will say they interpolated it, but they are both talking about the same thing.

Figure 4.8 Original image scanned with a resolution of 72PPI.
(© 2000 Stockbyte, www.stockbyte.com)

Figure 4.9 Image after resampling to a resolution of 300 ppi.

Figure 4.10 Original image scanned with a resolution of 600 ppi.

Figure 4.11 Image after resampling to a resolution of 300 ppi.

Optimal Settings

The type of output device you use will determine the correct resolution setting for scanning or printing your image. Below you'll find the correct resolution settings for the most common types of output devices. You can use lower resolution settings than the ones listed below; but if you do, you will be sacrificing quality for the convenience of a smaller file size.

Internet/Multimedia

A Web browser can't change the size of the pixels that make up your screen (only your operating system can do that), so the browser completely ignores the file's resolution setting and just looks at its width and height in pixels. That means that a 100-by-100-pixel image will look the same in a Web browser whether its resolution setting is 300 or 72.

Figure 4.12 For multimedia, think of the width and height in pixels instead of the resolution setting.

The following table indicates how much information can be displayed on most common monitors. If you create an image that contains more information than the monitor can display at one time, the edges of the image will be clipped off. To view the entire image, you will need to scroll. Or, if your image doesn't contain enough information to fill the monitor, there will be extra black space around the image.

Table 4.1 Monitor Settings and Usage

Resolution	% Used
640 by 480	7.5%
800 by 600	51.3%
1024 by 768	26.6%

Data on the percentage of Web users on each type of monitor was obtained from WebSnapshot.com

When I create graphics destined for the Internet, I always think about what type of monitor will be most commonly used to view my site. I work on a monitor that displays

1280 by 1024 pixels; most people use a monitor set to 800 by 600 pixels. To get a better sense of what my site will look like to the part of the world using smaller monitors, I change my monitor settings to 800 by 600 in the Monitors (Macintosh) or Display (Windows) control panel, open a Web browser, and take a screen shot. Then I open that screen shot in Photoshop and design my Web site within it. That way, I know exactly what it will look like on a smaller monitor, but I'm not forced to use the same settings. I also like to add guides to indicate where the edge of a 640-by-480 monitor would be, so that I can always keep in mind what my site will look like on the smallest monitor that might be used (**Figure 4.13**).

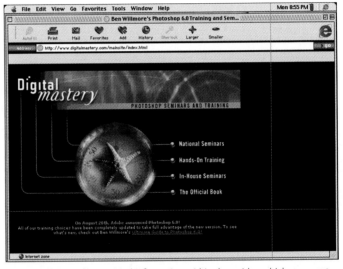

Figure 4.13 Try to keep critical information within the guides, which represent the smallest screen that will be used to view your site.

If you were to measure how large the pixels appear on most monitors, you'd find that between 72 and 96 pixels are visible in each inch. That means that in order to reproduce an image close to its original size, you have to use a scanning resolution between 72 and 96. If you want the image to be larger or smaller, then open the screen shot of the Web browser, make a selection to indicate how much space you'd like your image to take up, and look in Photoshop's Info palette to determine the width and height in pixels. Once you've found that out, you can divide the desired width (in pixels) by the physical width of the original (in inches), and the result will be the scanning resolution needed to end up with the desired size.

Or, if you don't like dealing with rulers and math, try this: Scan the image with a really high scanning resolution (such as 300). Then zoom out on your image by typing Command-minus (Macintosh) or Ctrl-minus (Windows) until the image becomes the size you'd like it to be in a Web browser. Note the percentage that appears in the bottom left of the document window. Now, choose Image > Image Size, check the Resample Image checkbox, change the Width pop-up menu to Percent, and then enter the number at which you were viewing your image. After you've completed those steps, your image should be the desired size when you view it at 100%.

If you're scanning an image to be used for multimedia (such as CD-ROMs or games) and you'd like to scan an image so it will completely fill the screen, try the following technique: Divide the width of the monitor, measured in pixels (see **Table 4.1**), by the width of the original image, measured in inches. The result is the exact scanning resolution needed to capture enough information to fill that specific screen size.

Halftones (Laser Printers, Printing Presses)

Most popular printer types (such as laser printers, imagesetters, printing presses, and thermal wax printers) cannot truly reproduce shades of gray. They either leave the paper white or turn it pure black. To simulate shades of gray (or tints of color), they use something called a halftone. Halftones fool your eyes into thinking they see grays when they're really looking at pure black and pure white (or pure color). The halftone does this by substituting small black circles for the shades of gray, using larger circles for dark shades and smaller ones for the light shades (**Figure 4.14**).

A setting called lines per inch, or simply lpi, determines the spacing of the circles used to simulate shades of gray. It's not called circles per inch, because you don't always use a grid of circles (you can use ovals, diamonds and other shapes). As the circles get packed closer together

Figure 4.14 Halftones use different-sized circles to simulate shades of gray or tints of color. (© 1998 PhotoSpin, www.photospin.com)

(higher lpi settings), the amount of detail your printer is capable of reproducing also increases (**Figures 4.15-4.17**). Higher lpi settings are usually more desirable because of the increased detail that results. However, as you pack more circles into each inch, the circles get smaller and are more difficult to reproduce on a printing press (the smallest circles start to disappear). Therefore, the printing process usually dictates the highest lpi setting that can be used. The following table shows the most common settings used and the defaults that are built into laser printers. The default settings are used whenever you print from a program that is not designed for publishing (such as spreadsheets or databases).

Table 4.2 Common LPI Settings

LPI	GENERAL USE
85	Newspaper advertisements
100	Newspaper editorial section
133	Magazines and brochures
150	High-end magazines and high-quality brochures
175	Annual reports and high-end brochures
53	300 dpi laser printers
106	600 dpi laser printers
212	1200 dpi laser printers

Figure 4.15 The image at 53 lpi.

Figure 4.16 The image at 85 lpi.

Figure 4.17 The image at 150 lpi.

Whenever you scan an image that will be printed with a halftone, you'll need to know the lpi setting before you scan the image, because it dictates how much detail you're going to get out of your printer. Once you know the lpi setting, multiply it by 1.5 if you would like your image to appear as sharp as possible, or multiply it by 2 if you want it to look a little soft. Then use the result as your scanning resolution. Use the soft setting for portraits (unless you really don't like the person); otherwise, every pore on his or her face might show.

You can use Photoshop as a calculator by choosing Image > Image Size and then clicking the Auto button. Next, enter the lpi setting you are going to be using, and then choose Good if you want detail (lpi x 1.5) or Best if you want your image to appear soft (lpi x 2). Once you click OK, the resolution setting will show you the scanning setting necessary to achieve the result you desire.

The lpi setting we have been talking about is not directly related to your printer's dpi setting. You can have a 600 dpi printer and print with any number of lpi settings. But it is the lpi setting that determines how much detail you will get in the end. You can specify an lpi setting to print with in the Page Setup dialog box of most publishing-oriented programs. Programs that are not designed for high-end publishing (like spreadsheet and database programs) will use the default setting that's built into your desktop printer.

Inkjet Printers

Most inkjet printers do not use halftones to simulate shades of gray; instead they use what appear to be random dots. To simulate grays, they pack these same-sized dots close together for dark shades or space them farther apart for light shades (**Figure 4.18**). That's why if you look closely at the output from an inkjet printer, it might look noisy (like a TV set that doesn't have a station tuned in).

To find out the scanning setting needed for images that will be output on an inkjet printer, just divide the resolution of the printer by 3 (or multiply it by .33). Example: inkjet printer resolution = 720 dpi, 720 x .33 = 238 ppi scanning resolution.

> **Note**
> The inkjet settings given here are what the inkjet printer manufacturers recommend. I find that you can usually get away with lower settings as long as your image does not contain high-contrast straight lines. So if you have an image of a sailboat (the mast is a high-contrast line), for example, then use the settings above; otherwise, experiment with lower settings.

Figure 4.18 Inkjet printers use same-sized dots to simulate shades of gray or tints of color.

Note
To find out more about line art scanning, see Chapter 5.

Figure 4.19 Line art images contain only pure black and pure white.

Figure 4.20 Dye-sub printers can truly reproduce the shades of gray and colors that appear in your images.

Line Art

Images that contain only pure black and pure white—no grays—are known as *line art* (**Figure 4.19**). The most common types of line art are logos and text.

To get the highest-quality line art (regardless of what type of printer you are using), you'll need the pixels in your image to be the same size as the dots your printer uses. To accomplish that, find out the resolution of your printer (measured in dpi), and type that number into your scanning software where it asks for a resolution setting. The highest setting you should ever need is 1200. Settings above 1200 create overly large file sizes without noticeable improvement in quality.

Dye-Sub Printers

Unlike lasers and inkjets, dye-sub printers are capable of reproducing 256 shades of gray and/or 16.7 million colors. The output from a dye-sub printer looks just like a real photo (**Figure 4.20**). To get the highest quality from a dye-sub printer, you need the pixels in your image to be the same size as the dots the printer uses. To accomplish this, find out the resolution of the printer, and use that number for the resolution setting in your scanning software.

35 mm Slides

When you want to output an image to a 35 mm slide (**Figure 4.21**), you use a device called a film recorder. The type of film recorder used determines the amount of information needed in your image. The resolution of a film recorder is measured in K (usually 2K or 4K). The K stands for 1,024 and indicates how many pixels can be reproduced in the width of a slide. So a 2K film recorder can reproduce 2048 pixels (2 x 1024) in the width of a slide. The ratio between the width and height of a 35 mm slide is 3:2.

Use the following technique to determine the scanning resolution needed to capture the exact amount of information that a 35 mm slide requires. First, determine how many pixels your film recorder can reproduce in the width of a slide (**Table 4.3**), and then divide this number by the width of your original image measured in inches. The result is the exact scanning resolution necessary to capture the proper amount of information.

Figure 4.21 For slides, think of the width and height in pixels instead of the resolution setting. (© 1998 PhotoDisc)

Table 4.3 Film Recorder Specifications

Film Recorder	Width and Height (in Pixels)	File Size (in Photoshop)
2K	2048 by 1365	8 MB
4K	4096 by 2731	32 MB
6K	6144 by 4096	72 MB

If you find it too difficult to determine the width of your original (because it's so darned small), then try this approach. In your scanning software, crop your image and adjust the resolution and scale settings until your software indicates that the file size will be the same as what's listed on the right side of the table above. No matter what your scanning settings are, if your file size ends up being correct, then you should have the proper amount of information for that type of slide.

Post-scan Adjustments

If you don't know the final output size ahead of time, you can use the information in the previous sections to determine the highest resolution setting you are likely to need, and then think of the largest possible size you'd ever need for that image. If you use that information to figure out the scanning resolution, then you can always scale things down in the Image Size dialog box. As long as the Resample Image checkbox is checked and you are lowering the resolution or size of the image, you won't be degrading the image's quality much. Every time I resample an image (making it larger or smaller), I apply the Unsharp Mask filter so that I'll end up with a nice, sharp image. We'll talk about that filter in Chapter 6.

Note
You can access most scanners from the File > Import menu. If your scanner does not appear in this menu, then you must install the proper Import plug-in, which should be on the disks that came with your scanner.

Scaling Images in Other Programs

When you scale an image in a page layout or illustration program, you are effectively changing the image's resolution. Unlike Photoshop, these programs cannot change the number of pixels in an image and therefore can only change the pixels' size. (Remember, pixel size is also called resolution and is measured in pixels per inch.) Scaling an image to 50% of its original size in a page layout program will shove twice as many pixels into each inch, effectively doubling the image's resolution.

If you are not sure how large your image will need to be, then scan the image for the largest possible size you think you might need. After you have scaled the image in your page layout program, write down the final size from the Measurements palette. Then, to ensure the highest quality, open the image in Photoshop and use the Image Size dialog box to scale the image to its final size. Finally, reload the image into the page layout program at 100% scale.

Closing Thoughts

There are so many misconceptions about resolution that it's very easy to get mixed signals about how to deal with it. Many people just scan their images with a generic resolution setting of 300 ppi and wonder why the results are so often disappointing. But by understanding how each device deals with resolution, and by giving the device the exact setting that is needed for your result, you'll be able to have smaller files that actually look better when printed. I hope this chapter has shed some light on the subject for you. I suggest you use it as a reference whenever you are dealing with an unfamiliar output device. The key is to get resolution to work for you rather than against you.

Ben's Techno-Babble Decoder Ring

Samples Per Inch (spi)—Determines the area a scanner will measure to determine the color of a single pixel. You can figure out the samples per inch setting that you need by multiplying the desired image resolution (ppi) by the amount the image will be scaled. Example: desired resolution 300 ppi, scale 200%; 300 x 200% = 600 spi.

Pixels Per Inch (ppi)—Determines how small the pixels in an image will be when printed. A setting of 150 ppi means that pixels will be $1/150$ of an inch when printed. The higher the setting, the smaller the pixels.

Dots Per Inch (dpi)—Determines the size of the dots an output device will use when printing an image. A 300 dpi laser printer uses black dots that are $1/300$ of an inch. This term is often used incorrectly to describe the resolution of an image (which should be measured in ppi).

Lines Per Inch (lpi)—Determines the spacing of halftone dots, and therefore their maximum size. The higher the lpi setting, the more apparent detail you can reproduce.

Imagesetter—A type of high-end output device that is used to output images onto photographic paper or film. Imagesetters are capable of outputting only pure black and pure white dots. The minimum resolution of an imagesetter is 2540 dpi.

Thermal Wax—A type of CMYK output device that bonds a waxy substance to a special type of paper. If you scratch the output of a thermal wax printer with your fingernail, you will usually be able to scratch off some of the waxy substance.

Inkjet—A type of output device that sprays CMYK inks onto special paper. Upon close inspection, the output of an inkjet printer typically appears noisy because the printer uses a diffusion dither pattern to simulate shades of gray.

Dye-Sub—A type of output device that produces a continuous-tone result by heating CMY dyes until they turn into a gas (without first becoming a liquid). The output of a dye-sub printer has a continuous-tone glossy look that resembles a photographic print.

5 Line Art Scanning

Courtesy of Alicia Buelow, www.aliciabuelow.com

Only those who have the patience to do simple things perfectly will acquire the skill to do difficult things easily.
—Johann Schiller

Scanning line art is a wonderful opportunity to learn how to do a relatively simple thing perfectly. Line art images consist of black lines on a white background. You see examples of line art every day in the text, logos, and signatures that are all around us. You'd think that scanning this type of image would be simple; after all, it's only pure black and white, right? Well, in order to really get control over your line art images, you'll need to go through a few hoops in Photoshop, but with a little effort, you can achieve stunning results.

Note

Not all scanners use the same names for their scanning modes: line art mode might be parading around under a different name, such as text mode.

Almost all scanners have a line art mode that gives you a pure black and pure white end result. However, don't be fooled by your scanner. Scanning in line art mode produces an image that doesn't contain anywhere near the amount of detail found in the original.

If you scan an image in line art mode, it will automatically end up in bitmap mode after it's loaded into Photoshop. That's practically useless, because Photoshop is not able to enhance images that are in bitmap mode. (For example, you can't use most of the editing tools, rotate the image in precise increments, or apply filters.) This is why so many people end up with line art reproductions that have jagged edges, broken lines, and dense areas that are all clogged up.

But that's not going to happen to *you*. You're going to ignore your scanner's advice and scan in grayscale mode instead of line art mode. After the image is scanned in grayscale mode, you can take full advantage of Photoshop's enhancement controls. With very little practice and a handful of tricks you learn in this chapter, you'll be able to create beautiful line art reproductions as they were intended to be—with crisp edges and sharp detail.

When you're all done producing your line art and are pleased with the result, you should convert your image into bitmap mode. This will keep your file size small and prevent you from accidentally adding shades of gray to the image. After all, true line art contains only pure black and pure white, and no shades of gray. By converting your image to bitmap mode in the end, you'll guarantee that it won't be contaminated with grays. (Shades of gray are reproduced using a pattern of black circles, known as a halftone, that would make their edges appear fuzzy.)

Avoiding the Jaggies

The most common complaint I hear about line art is that it has jagged edges. This happens when the pixels in the image are so large that you can easily see them when the image is printed. Thankfully, avoiding the "jaggies" is the easiest part of dealing with line art.

Resolution Is the Key

Photoshop gives users the ability to try a lot of wild things with images. But the one thing all users have in common is the desire to get the highest quality possible. And when you're working with pure black and white line art, that means you'll want each pixel in your image to be the exact same size as the smallest dot your printer can reproduce.

The size of the pixels in your document is determined by the resolution setting of your file. This is known as pixels per inch or ppi. The resolution of your printer dictates the smallest dot it can reproduce. This is known as dots per inch, or dpi. You'll want to find out the resolution of your printer and use that setting when scanning your image. This makes your pixels the same size as the smallest dot your printer can reproduce, thus giving you the best possible results.

Unfortunately, most people think higher settings produce better results, but that's not necessarily the case. If your end result is a dot matrix restaurant receipt printer, and you feed it an image with 300 pixels per inch, there's no way it can print dots that small. So it must distill the image and discard the extra information—and that's when your image will suffer. You're much better off using the correct resolution setting in the first place.

Printing companies and service bureaus have expensive output devices that offer resolutions of at least 2,540 dots per inch. After experimenting, I've found that it doesn't really help to use resolution settings above 1,200 for line art. Files with resolutions above 1,200 don't seem to produce better detail; they just give you huge file sizes and therefore slow down your computer. **Figures 5.1 to 5.6** show the effect of resolution on file size and quality.

> **Note**
>
> When scanning a line art image for onscreen display (for multimedia, the Web, and so on), it will usually look better if you leave it in grayscale mode. I know, I know, that really isn't true line art, but i t will look better on screen. Why? Because the pixels that make up your screen are quite large (between 72 ppi and 96 ppi), so it's easy to see the jagged edges of the pixels that make up your image. By including shades of gray, the edges of the image will fade out and have a smoother look. When scanning for onscreen use, use a resolution setting of 85.

Figure 5.1 Resolution: 150 ppi
File size: 38K

Figure 5.2 Resolution: 300 ppi
File size: 153K

Figure 5.3 Resolution: 600 ppi
File size: 230K

Figure 5.4 Resolution: 800 ppi
File size: 306K

Figure 5.5 Resolution: 1,200 ppi
File size: 459K

Figure 5.6 Resolution: 2,400 ppi
File size: 1.4MB

Photoshop Can Fake It

If your scanner is not capable of using a resolution setting
as high as you need, you can have Photoshop increase the
resolution of the image and add the extra information your
scanner couldn't deliver. To do this, scan with the highest

resolution setting available, and then choose Image > Image Size. Select the Resample Image checkbox, set the pop-up menu to Bicubic (that's the kind of math Photoshop will use to add information to your image), type in the resolution of your printer in the Resolution field, and then click OK. Remember, your image must be in grayscale mode; otherwise, this step will not improve image quality. This step is unique to line art images; if you were to increase the resolution of a photographic quality image, the result would appear blurry. In the case of line art, the extra information will not harm the image, because we're going to convert it to a pure black and white bitmap, which is incapable of appearing blurry.

Straightening the Image

If the image you've scanned needs to be straightened, you can use the Measure tool (it looks like a ruler and is grouped with the Eyedropper tool in Photoshop 6). Draw a line across an area that should be perfectly vertical or horizontal. If there's more than one area of the image that should be straightened, you can click the middle of the measurement line and drag it around your screen to make sure it matches all the affected areas. If you need to adjust the angle of the measurement line, just drag one of its ends. When you're certain the line is at the proper angle, check to make sure the background color is set to white and then choose Image > Rotate Canvas > Arbitrary. Photoshop has a great feature that automatically calculates how much the image needs to be rotated, so all you have to do is click OK (**Figure 5.7**). Once you're done, you can choose any tool other than the measurement tool to hide the measurement line.

Improving Definition

When you convert an image to bitmap mode (which we'll do at the end of this chapter), any areas that are darker than 50% gray will become pure black. This usually causes detail in the darkest, most densely packed areas to clog up

Notes

When you scan grayscale images that have already been printed using a halftone screen, you'll often get an unwanted repetitive pattern. You might get a better result by scanning the preprinted image as line art (even though it's a grayscale photo). This method will try to capture the halftone look instead of converting the image into a grayscale file. Using the line art technique described in this chapter, you can scan grayscale images that were printed with a halftone screen of 85 lines per inch or below. If an image was printed with a halftone screen above 85 lines per inch, the image should be scanned as a normal grayscale image instead of using the line art technique.

....

Straighten a scan while it's still in grayscale mode. If your image is in bitmap mode, it can only be rotated in 90-degree increments.

....

Whenever possible, avoid straightening scans in other software programs, such as your page layout program. If scans are straightened in other programs, the screen redraw will take longer and printing time will increase. Also, the quality of the art will suffer, and you'll not have a true image preview.

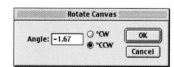

Figure 5.7 Photoshop automatically calculates the rotation amount needed and puts it in the dialog box.

and become a black blob. You can prevent this from happening by sharpening the image. Sharpening will add more contrast to those densely packed areas and produce better detail. However, before you sharpen an image, you'll want to take a snapshot of the unsharpened image so you can use it later to enhance the result.

Taking a Snapshot

Figure 5.8 After creating a new snapshot, click to the left of the snapshot icon to set the History brush to that snapshot.

Choose New Snapshot from the side menu of the History palette to record what the image looks like before you sharpen it. Name the snapshot something like "Before Sharpening" so you can remember what it contains. The snapshot you create will appear near the top of the History palette (**Figure 5.8**). Click the column just to the left of the snapshot thumbnail icon to tell Photoshop to use this version of the image when using the History brush.

Sharpening the Image

Now that you've created a snapshot version of the image, it's safe to proceed with the sharpening process. Double-click the Zoom tool in the Tools palette to view the image at 100% magnification; otherwise, the onscreen preview of the sharpening filter will not be accurate. Choose Filter > Sharpen > Unsharp Mask, and set the amount to 500, the radius to 1.2, and the threshold to 2. This is usually a good starting point because it will make the detail in the dark areas become more defined. You can increase the radius setting to open up and display more shadow detail. Radius settings between 1 and 5 usually produce the best results (**Figure 5.9**). A Threshold setting of 0 will sharpen all shades in the image, including the lightest grays. I usually keep the Threshold setting at 2, unless the paper texture starts to show up. (Light gray areas are often dirt, or texture picked up from the paper.) A setting around 7 will usually suppress the paper texture. If the image contains very fine detail, you might need to use a lower threshold setting. High threshold settings will only sharpen the darker thick lines in the image.

> **Note**
>
> The Unsharp Mask filter is used here because it's the only sharpening filter that gives you enough control over the end result. The other filters don't ask you for any settings.

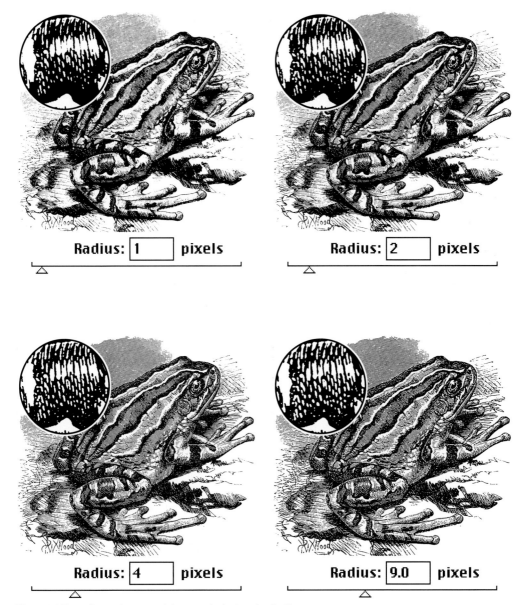

Figure 5.9 The radius setting controls how much shadow detail will appear.

Converting to Line Art

When you print an image that contains shades of gray, your printer uses a halftone screen, which prevents your grayscale image from having crisp edges. In order for you to get nice, crisp edges, the image must only contain pure black and pure white—that's true line art. So, how do you get there?

Adding a Threshold Adjustment Layer

You can use the Threshold command to rid the image of all shades of gray, leaving only pure black and pure white. By doing this on an adjustment layer instead of applying Threshold directly to the image, you'll be able to easily make changes after the image is black and white. To achieve an accurate preview when using Threshold, you must view the image at 100% magnification. Double-click the Zoom tool in the Tools palette to quickly zoom to 100%. Create a new Threshold adjustment layer by choosing Layer > New Adjustment Layer > Threshold. Adjust the slider until the lines in the image have the proper thickness and detail appears where it's most important in the image. You can compare the adjustment to the grayscale version of the image by turning the Preview option off and on (to toggle between the grayscale and black-and-white versions of the image).

The Threshold dialog box forces anything darker than the threshold number to black, and anything lighter than the threshold number to white (**Figures 5.10 to 5.15**). Refer to the table in Chapter 6, "Optimizing Grayscale Images," to see what the threshold numbers mean.

Figures 5.16 to 5.19 show the quality improvement that is possible by scanning in grayscale instead of line art mode. Even more detail could be brought out of **Figure 5.19** by using the enhancement techniques that were applied to **Figure 5.20**.

Figure 5.10 The lines appear to be breaking up.

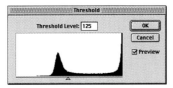

Figure 5.11 The threshold setting is too low.

Figure 5.12 This image shows good highlight detail without plugging up the shadow detail.

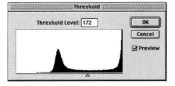

Figure 5.13 Proper threshold setting.

Figure 5.14 This image has no shadow detail and the lines are too thick.

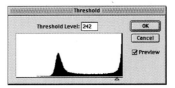

Figure 5.15 The threshold setting is too high.

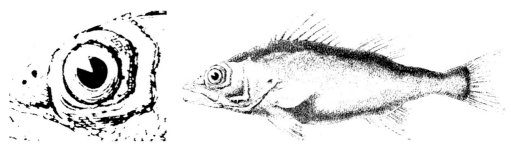

Figure 5.16 Raw line art scan (same as scanning in grayscale and using the default threshold setting).

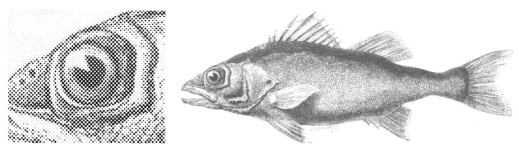

Figure 5.17 Raw grayscale scan (lines are not crisp, and the file size is very large).

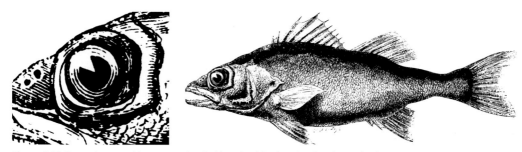

Figure 5.18 Grayscale scan with a proper threshold setting (shadow detail is plugged up).

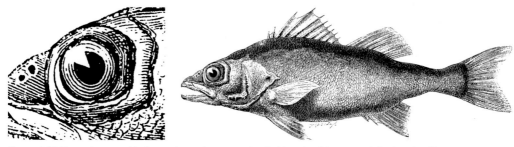

Figure 5.19 Grayscale scan with sharpening and a proper threshold setting (shows good shadow detail).

Refining Areas

To retain additional detail, you must enhance the gray-scale image that's below the adjustment layer. To do so, click the name of the layer that contains the original image. There are many ways to enhance the image, including the following:

▶ **Increase shadow detail**—Brush across the image with the Sharpen tool to bring out detail in shadow areas.

▶ **Fix broken lines**—Brush across the image with the Burn tool (with the Range option set to Shadows) to clean up broken lines or to make lines thicker. If the Burn tool doesn't change the image enough, use the History brush with the Mode option set to Multiply or Darken to increase the line thickness. Lower the Opacity setting if the changes are too extreme.

▶ **Reduce line thickness**—Brush across the image with the Dodge tool (with the Range option set to Highlights or Midtones) to reduce the thickness of lines. If the Dodge tool doesn't change the image enough, use the History brush with the Mode option set to Screen or Lighten to make the lines thinner. Lower the Opacity setting if the changes are too extreme.

▶ If the Dodge and Burn tools don't change the image enough, use the History brush with the Mode option set to Hard Light to make lines thinner. Lower the Opacity setting if the changes are too extreme.

▶ **Control text thickness**—If you're scanning text at large point sizes, you can make the text thicker by choosing Filter > Other > Minimum, or thinner by choosing Filter > Other > Maximum. If the adjectives used in these menu options seem contrary to common sense, well, they are. Just remember to apply reverse logic when dealing with text thickness.

Figure 5.20 shows examples of these settings.

The history brush using
Multiply blending mode.

The Dodge tool with
100% exposure setting.

The history brush using
Lighten blending mode.

The history brush using
Screen blending mode
at 45% opacity.

Figure 5.20 Refining the image.

Minimizing File Size

Nobody likes dealing with big, bloated files. They're
greedy resource hogs that slow down your system and
wreak havoc on your ability to work quickly and efficiently.
Any extra white space around the image is a file-fattening
waste, because it's not necessary for printing the image.
One way to simplify the image is to choose Flatten Image
from the side menu of the Layers palette and then use the
Eraser tool to clean up any stray pixels in the white area
surrounding the image. Finally, to discard any extra space,

choose Image > Trim, turn on all the checkboxes at the bottom and then choose whichever top choice would make Photoshop find a white pixel (**Figure 5.21**).

Converting to Bitmap

Your image is now pure black and white, but the file itself is still in grayscale mode. The image must be converted to bitmap mode to save disk space and make sure that any final editing doesn't produce unwanted shades of gray. Convert the image from grayscale to bitmap by choosing Image > Mode > Bitmap. This brings up the Bitmap dialog box (**Figure 5.22**). Make sure the input and output resolution numbers match, and use the 50% threshold method, which will ensure that shades of gray are converted into smooth lines and won't look noisy.

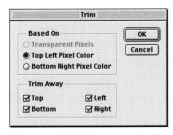

Figure 5.21 The Trim command will discard any extra space in your image.

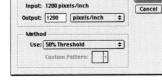

Figure 5.22 The Bitmap dialog box.

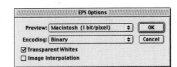

Figure 5.23 The EPS Options dialog box.

Choosing a File Format

If your image is destined to be printed, then you'll want to use the EPS or TIFF file formats. The EPS file format allows you to specify whether the white areas should be solid or transparent (**Figure 5.23**).

Line art images that are destined for the Web should be saved in the GIF file format.

Closing Thoughts

Lately I've been noticing that a lot of the line art out there is inferior to what I used to see only a few years ago. Check

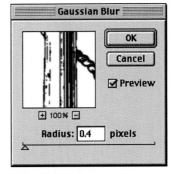

Figure 5.24 The Gaussian Blur dialog box.

it out for yourself! Pick up any magazine (even the high-end ones sometimes have this problem) and look through it for line art images. If your experience is anything like mine, you'll probably see some really mediocre stuff—edges are jagged, lines are broken up, and patterns look clogged. My theory is that people stopped sending out for line art scans and started performing them in-house.

That's fine, but only if you're not sacrificing quality for convenience. After reading this chapter, I hope you'll agree with me that you can have both. As long as you know how to get a good scan that captures the right amount of detail, and then know how to enhance the scanned image in Photoshop, there's no reason why you can't end up with exquisite line art.

And as a side note, I want you to know that just because you can achieve high-quality results using these techniques doesn't mean you will want to use them for every line art scan. I occasionally have to scan dozens of images for a single project. In that case, I might decide that speed is more important than quality, and just scan in line art mode to begin with. But if I'm scanning my own signature, a high-quality etching, or a logo I'll be using over and over again, then I will definitely spend the extra time to get a high-quality result.

Ben's Techno-Babble Decoder Ring

Bitmap—A confusing term, because Photoshop uses it in an unusual way. Technically "bitmap" means a grid of pixels. That means that any image you ever see in Photoshop that contains pixels is technically a bitmap image. That's why the native format for transporting pixel-based images on the Windows platform is called a BMP file. That stands for Windows Bitmap. Adobe has decided to reserve the term to describe images that contain only pure black and pure white (no grays or color). The reason can be attributed to Apple. The Macintosh was one of the first personal computers that was designed to deal with pixel-based images, and in its first incarnation it contained a black and white screen (no grays). "Bitmap" got associated with any pixel-based image on that first Mac model, and that's how the dual meaning came about.

Line Art—Any artwork that consists of pure black lines on a pure white background. Line art images always contain extremely crisp edges and no shades of gray or color.

Threshold—An adjustment that converts all shades of gray to pure black or pure white. Any shades of gray brighter than the threshold value will become white, and any shades darker than the threshold value will become black.

Resample—The process of changing the total number of pixels in an image without cropping or adding empty space.

Courtesy of Alicia Buelow, www.aliciabuelow.com

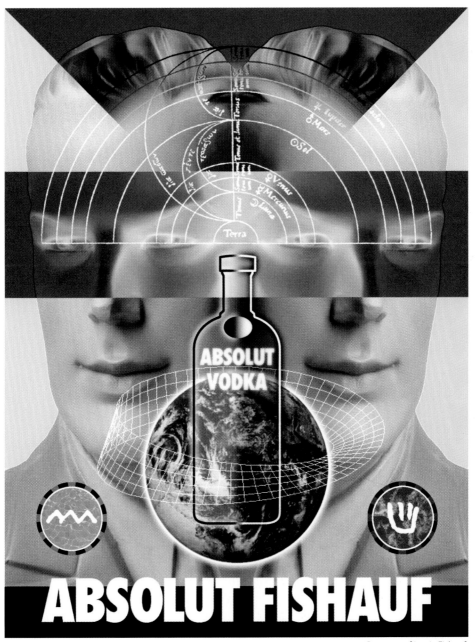

Courtesy of Louis Fishauf

Optimizing Grayscale Images

If you go through life
convinced that your way
is always best, all the
new ideas in the world
will pass you by.
–Akio Morita,
Founder of Sony

Nude Study #1108 from NUDE BODY NUDE by Howard Schatz
© 2000 Schatz/Ornstein (HarperCollins Publishers, 2000)

When inexperienced users first try to adjust a grayscale image, they usually look for something familiar and easy, and the Brightness and Contrast dialog box is frequently where they end up. With a mere flick of the mouse, they can dramatically improve their image. Big results, little effort. At first glance, the Brightness and Contrast dialog box seems to hold great promise. But does it *really* do the job?

If you were to compare images adjusted with Brightness and Contrast with the images you see in high-end magazines and brochures, you'd notice that the quality of the Brightness and Contrast images is inferior. Why? Because the Brightness and Contrast dialog box adjusts the entire image an equal amount. So, if you decide to increase the overall brightness of an image until an area that was 10% gray becomes white, then areas that are black will also be changed the same amount, and become 90% gray. Using controls like these, it is extremely hard to achieve professional quality. When you correct one problem, you usually introduce another.

Common adjustment complaints include:

▶ Images appear flat (lacking contrast)

▶ Images print overly dark

▶ Blown-out detail in the highlights (bright white areas in the middle of people's foreheads)

▶ Lack of detail in the shadows

All of these problems—and others—can be solved in one dialog box.

Levels Is the Solution

The Levels dialog box (choose Image > Adjust > Levels) is the cure for most common complaints about image quality (**Figure 6.1**). It offers you far more control and feedback than Brightness and Contrast. Instead of having only two sliders to adjust, Levels offers you five, as well as a bar chart that indicates exactly what is happening to the image. And unlike the sliders in Brightness and Contrast, the Levels sliders don't change the entire image in equal amounts.

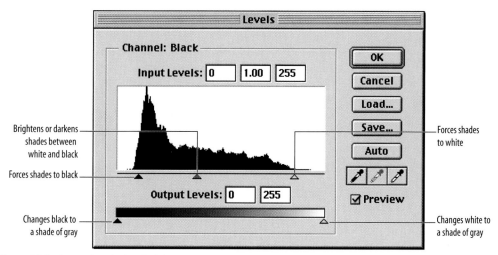

Figure 6.1 Understanding the Levels sliders.

It might take several pages to describe all the controls in the Levels dialog box, but once you know how to use them it will take you less than a minute to optimize an image. Just remember to apply all of the controls in Levels, because each builds on the last. You can liken the steps in Levels to the ingredients in crème brulée—leave one out and you might end up with pudding instead of perfection.

The Histogram Is Your Guide

You can use the bar chart (histogram) at the top of the Levels dialog box to determine if the adjustments you're making are going to harm the image or improve it. The histogram indicates which shades of gray your image uses and how much space those shades take up—that is, how much they are used in the image. If you find a gap in the histogram, you can look at the gradient directly below it to see which shade of gray is missing from your image.

By looking directly below the first bar that appears on the left end of the histogram, you can determine the darkest shade of gray in the image. If there were anything darker than that, then there would have to be some bars above those shades in the histogram. By looking directly below the last bar that appears on the right end of the histogram, you can determine the brightest shade of gray in the

Note

The height of the bars in a histogram suggest, visually, how much space the shades take up in an image. The height doesn't indicate an exact number of pixels; instead, it measures how much space the shade takes up—how much it's used—compared to the other shades in the image. It's as if everyone in a room stood up and you compared how tall each person was without using a ruler. You wouldn't know exactly how tall anyone was, but you'd have an idea of how tall each person was compared to the others (**Figure 6.2**).

Warning

In previous versions of Photoshop, you had to choose File > Preferences > Image Cache and turn off the Use Cache For Histograms checkbox in order to get an accurate histogram. If you left this setting turned on (which was the default setting in previous versions), then the histogram would be accurate only when you viewed your image at 100% magnification. This setting was designed to speed up the creation of histograms, but it also made them less accurate. Adobe changed the default in Photoshop 6.0, which forces the histogram to always be accurate.

image. So if you look at **Figure 6.3,** you might notice the image contains no pure blacks or pure whites. The darkest shade of gray is about 95%, and the brightest shade is about 6%.

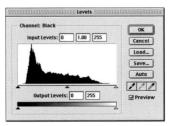 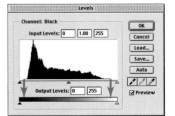

Figure 6.2 This histogram indicates that the shades between around 90% and 75% take up a lot of space (tall bars) and the shades between around 5% and 15% take up little space (short bars).

Figure 6.3 Look at the gradient bar directly below the ends of the histogram to determine the brightest and darkest shades present in the image.

Evaluate and Adjust Contrast

The brightest and darkest areas of your computer monitor are nowhere near as bright or dark as the objects you'll find in the real world. It's even more extreme when you look at the brightest and darkest areas of a printed brochure— the paper is actually pretty dull and the ink isn't all that dark. Because of this, you'll need to use the full range of shades from black to white in order to make your photos look as close to reality as possible.

By adjusting the upper right and upper left sliders in the Levels dialog box, you can dramatically improve the contrast of an image and make it appear more lifelike. When you move the upper left slider in the Levels dialog box, you force the shade of gray directly below it (and any shade darker than it) to black. So moving that slider until it touches the first bar on the histogram forces the darkest shade of gray in the image to black, which should give you nice dark shadows.

When you move the upper right slider, you will force the shade that appears directly below the slider (see the gradient), and any shade brighter than it, to white. So, as above (for dark colors), moving the right slider until it touches the last bar on the histogram forces the brightest shade of gray to white, which should give you nice white highlights.

By adjusting both sliders, your image will be using the full range of shades available to a grayscale image (**Figure 6.4**). If you move the sliders past the beginning and end of the histogram, you will get even more contrast, but you risk losing important detail in the process.

Hidden Features to the Rescue

To achieve maximum contrast without sacrificing detail, Adobe created a hidden feature in the Levels dialog box. It's known as Threshold mode because it acts like the Threshold dialog box. This feature allows you to see exactly which areas are becoming black or white, and it's the key to ensuring that you don't sacrifice detail. To get to the hidden feature, hold down the Option key (Macintosh) or Alt key (Windows) when you move the upper right or upper left sliders in the Levels dialog box.

When you move the upper left slider with Threshold mode turned on, your image should turn white until the slider touches the first bar on the histogram; then small black areas should start to appear. These are the areas that will become pure black. You want to make sure you don't force a large concentrated area to black, so move the slider until only small areas appear. You also want to make sure the areas that are becoming black still contain detail. Detail will show up looking like noise (not the kind you hear—the kind you see on television when you don't have an antenna hooked up), so make sure those small areas also look noisy. You'll need to repeat this process with the upper right slider to make sure you get optimal contrast (**Figures 6.5 to 6.14**).

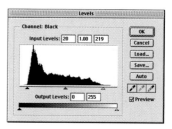

Figure 6.4 The shades that are beyond the upper right and left triangles will become pure black and pure white.

Notes

In earlier versions of Photoshop, you had to have the Preview checkbox turned off in order to use Threshold mode. Also, it would only work on about 10% of all machines running the Windows operating system.

....

The middle slider will move when you adjust the upper right or upper left slider. This happens because Photoshop is attempting to keep the middle slider in the same position relative to the other two sliders. So if the middle slider was centered between the other two, it will remain centered when you move one of the outer sliders.

Figure 6.5 Original.
(© 1998 PhotoDisc)

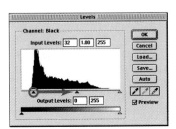

Figure 6.6 Way too far.

Figure 6.7 Large areas lose detail and become pure black.

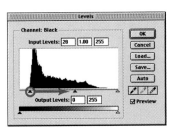

Figure 6.8 Just right.

Figure 6.9 Small areas become black, but still contain detail (noise).

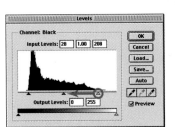

Figure 6.10 Way too far.

Figure 6.11 Large areas lose detail and become pure white.

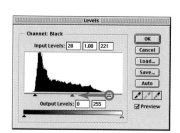

Figure 6.12 Just right.

Figure 6.13 Small areas become white, but still contain detail (noise).

Figure 6.14 Final result

The Histogram Gives You Feedback

Once you have applied an adjustment to your image, you can see an updated histogram by choosing Image > Adjust > Levels again. You should notice that after adjusting the upper right and upper left sliders, the histogram will stretch all the way across the area available. It's just like stretching out a Slinky (you remember, "it walks down stairs alone or in pairs"). As you pull on the ends of the Slinky, the loops stretch out and start to create gaps. The same thing happens to a histogram—because Photoshop can't add more bars to the histogram, it can only spread

Notes

If you find evenly spaced spikes in the histogram of an unadjusted image, it usually indicates a noisy scan (**Figure 6.17**). I know, noise is something you hear, not see. Well, just think of the static you see when you don't have an antenna attached to your television—that's visual noise.

....

Spikes that show up after an image has been adjusted with Levels do not indicate noise. It's as if you took your trusty Slinky and tried to squish it down to a centimeter wide—something would have to budge. The only way I can do it is to bend the Slinky into a "V" shape where the loops start piling up, one on top of the other. Otherwise, the loops just line up in a nice row and limit how much I can compress the Slinky. Well, the same thing happens with the histogram. Let's say you try to squish 20 bars into a space that is only 15 pixels wide on the histogram. Five of the bars have to disappear. They are going to just pile on top of the bars next to them and make those bars about twice as tall. When this happens, you get evenly spaced spikes across part of the histogram.

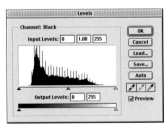

Figure 6.17 Noise.

out the ones that were already there. And remember, gaps in the histogram mean that certain shades of gray are missing from the image. So the more you adjust an image using Levels, the more you increase the possibility that you'll lose some of the smooth transitions between bright and dark areas (**Figure 6.15**).

If you see large spikes on either end of the histogram, as shown in **Figure 6.16**, it's an indication that you've lost detail. That's because you forced quite a bit of space to white or black using Levels. But you'd know you did that, because you were using the hidden feature, right? Or maybe you couldn't control yourself and were using that Brightness and Contrast dialog box, where you can't tell if you damage the image! You might also get spikes on the ends of the histogram if you scan an image with a brightness setting that is way too high or low.

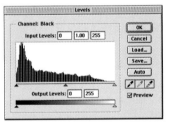 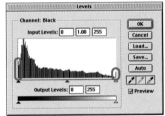

Figure 6.15 After adjusting the top two sliders, your image should use the full range of shades available.

Figure 6.16 Spikes on the end of a histogram usually indicate lost detail.

Improve Brightness

After you have achieved good contrast, your image might look too dark. The middle slider in the Levels dialog box can fix that. (Techies love to call this slider the gamma setting, but us plain folks call it the Midpoint.) If you move the middle slider to the left, the image will become brighter without messing up the dark areas of your image. Black areas will stay nice and black. Or you can move the middle slider to the right to darken the image without messing up the bright areas of the image. White areas will stay bright white.

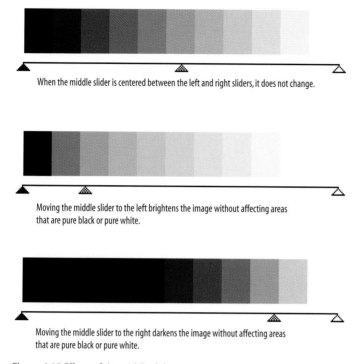

When the middle slider is centered between the left and right sliders, it does not change.

Moving the middle slider to the left brightens the image without affecting areas that are pure black or pure white.

Moving the middle slider to the right darkens the image without affecting areas that are pure black or pure white.

Figure 6.18 Effects of the middle slider.

If you want to know what this adjustment is doing, just look directly below the middle slider; the shade of gray there will become 50% gray. If you look at an updated histogram of the image, it will look like you stretched out a Slinky, then grabbed one side and pulled it to the middle. Some bars will get scrunched (is that a technical term?) together, while others get spread apart.

Setting Up Your Images for Final Output

If your images are going to be printed, especially with ink on paper, chances are that they will end up looking a lot darker than they did when you viewed them on screen. This is known as dot gain. Fortunately, Photoshop allows you to compensate for it. You can tell Photoshop ahead of time how you intend to output your images, and it will adjust the onscreen appearance of your image to look as dark as it should be after it's printed.

DOT GAIN SETTINGS

Newspapers	34%
Magazines and brochures	24%
High-end brochures	22%

Notes

If the dot-gain setting you need isn't listed in the Working Spaces area, you'll need a custom setting. Turn on the Advanced Mode checkbox at the top of the dialog box and then choose Custom Dot Gain from the Gray pop-up menu. To get a traditional dot-gain measurement (in which you only measure 50% gray), just add 50 to the dot gain setting you need, and enter the result in the 50% field.

In previous versions of Photoshop, the grayscale dot-gain setting was specified in the Edit > Color Settings > CMYK Setup dialog box. To have Photoshop simulate a printing press, you also would have had to turn on the Black Ink setting in the File > Color Settings > Grayscale dialog box.

If your image will only be displayed on screen (and not printed), then change the Gray pop-up menu to Gray Gamma 1.8 (for Macintosh) or Gray Gamma 2.2 (for Windows). You can even choose Gray Gamma 2.2 if you're on a Mac and want to see what it would look like in Windows. (Images displayed in Windows usually appear darker than they do on a Mac.)

If your images are destined for multimedia output (Web, video, animation, etc.) then you can skip over the next few steps and go directly to the Sharpening section later in this chapter.

To select or enter dot-gain settings, choose Edit > Color Settings. In the Working Spaces area, you'll use the Gray pop-up menu, as shown in **Figure 6.19**. You'll definitely want to ask your printing company about what settings to use; otherwise, you'll just be guessing and you might not like your end result. But just in case you're working at midnight or don't have time to ask your printing company, I'll give you a table of generic settings.

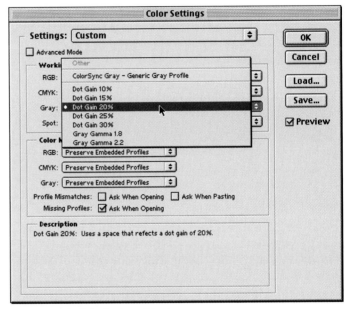

Figure 6.19 The Color Settings dialog box.

Prepare for a Printing Press

Take a close look at the black and white image in **Figure 4.16** on page 138, and imagine that you took that image to Kinko's and made a copy of it. Then you took the copy and copied it again at your local library. Then you took the library copy and ran it through the Xerox machine in your office. Then you held the version that had been copied three times up next to the original. Would you expect them to look the same? Of course not. In fact, the tiny dots that are in the brightest part of the image have begun to disappear, and become pure white, because every time you make a copy, you lose some quality. Well, the same thing happens when you hand over your image to a printing company. When you give your printing company your original output, they will have to make three copies of it before it makes it to the end of the printing process. They start by converting the original into a piece of metal called a printing plate to make the first copy. Then they put the plate on a big, round roller on the printing press and flood it with water and ink. The ink will stick to the plate only where your images and text should be; the water will make sure it doesn't stick to the other areas. Next to that roller is another one known as a blanket; it's just covered with rubber. The plate will come into contact with the blanket so the ink on the plate will transfer over to the blanket—that's your second copy. Finally, the blanket will transfer the ink onto a sheet of paper to create the last copy (**Figure 6.20**). Each time a copy is made, you lose some of the smallest dots in the image. Until you know how to compensate for this, you're likely to end up with pictures of people with big white spots in the middle of their foreheads.

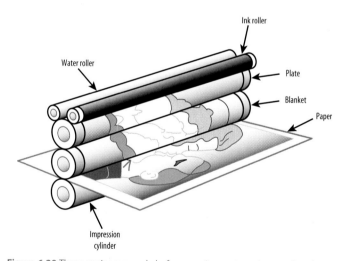

Figure 6.20 Three copies are made before your image turns into a printed page.

Before I show you how to compensate for the loss of detail in the bright areas of your image, let's look at what happens to the darkest areas, since we'll have to deal with them as well. When you print with ink on paper, the ink always gets absorbed into the paper and spreads out—just like when you spill coffee on your *Morning News*. This will cause the darkest areas of an image (97%, 98%, 99%) to become pure black. If you don't adjust for this, you will lose detail in the shadows of your image.

Most printing companies create a simple test strip that they print on the edge of your job, in the area that will be cropped after it's printed. This test strip contains shades of gray from 1% to about 5% to determine the lightest shade of gray that doesn't disappear on press and become pure white. Of course, the folks in the printing industry don't just use plain English to describe it; instead, they invented the term "minimum highlight dot reproducible on press." The test strip area also contains shades of gray from 99% to about 75% so they can see the darkest shade of gray that doesn't become pure black. For that one, they came up with the term "maximum shadow dot reproducible on press." If you ask your printing company, they can usually tell you exactly which settings to use. I know you don't always know who will print your images or don't have the time to ask, so I'll give you some generic numbers to use. But first, let's find out how we adjust for minimum highlight and maximum shadow dots.

Here's where you come in, and also where we get back to Levels. By moving the lower right slider in the Levels dialog box, you will change white to the shade of gray the slider is pointing to. You want to move this slider until it points to the minimum highlight dot—that is, the lightest shade of gray that will not disappear and become white on press.

You don't want to just eyeball this setting, so instead of just looking at the shades of gray, we'll use the Output Level numbers in the Levels dialog box. There is one problem with these numbers: they range from 0–255 instead of 0–100%! This is because you can have up to 256 shades of gray in a grayscale image and Photoshop wants you to be able to control them all. When you're using this numbering system, think about light instead of ink. If you have no light (0), then it would be pitch black; if you have as much light as possible (255), you could call that white. So that you won't need a calculator, I'll give you a conversion table.

Percentage Conversion Table

%	Value	%	Value	%	Value
100%	0	66%	87	32%	173
99%	3	65%	89	31%	176
98%	5	64%	92	30%	179
97%	8	63%	94	29%	181
96%	10	62%	97	28%	184
95%	13	61%	100	27%	186
94%	15	60%	102	26%	189
93%	18	59%	105	25%	191
92%	20	58%	107	24%	194
91%	23	57%	110	23%	196
90%	26	56%	112	22%	199
89%	28	55%	115	21%	202
88%	31	54%	117	20%	204
87%	33	53%	120	19%	207
86%	36	52%	122	18%	209
85%	38	51%	125	17%	211
84%	41	50%	128	16%	214
83%	44	49%	130	15%	217
82%	46	48%	133	14%	219
81%	49	47%	135	13%	222
80%	51	46%	138	12%	224
79%	54	45%	140	11%	227
78%	56	44%	143	10%	229
77%	59	43%	145	9%	232
76%	61	42%	148	8%	235
75%	64	41%	150	7%	237
74%	66	40%	153	6%	240
73%	69	39%	156	5%	242
72%	71	38%	158	4%	245
71%	74	37%	161	3%	247
70%	77	36%	163	2%	250
69%	79	35%	166	1%	252
68%	82	34%	168	0%	255
67%	84	33%	171		

COMMON MINIMUM HIGHLIGHT SETTINGS

Newspapers	5%
Magazines & brochures	3%
High-end brochures	3%

COMMON MAXIMUM SHADOW SETTINGS

Newspapers	75%
Magazines & brochures	90%
High-end brochures	95%

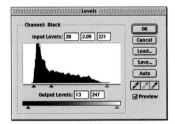

Figure 6.21 The bottom sliders reduce image contrast to compensate for the limitations of the printing press.

By moving the lower left slider in the Levels dialog box, you will change black to the shade of gray the slider is pointing to (**Figure 6.21**). You want to move this slider until it points to the darkest shade of gray that will not plug up and become black (known as the maximum shadow dot).

At first glance this stuff might seem complicated, but it is really quite simple. All you do is use the numbers from the tables, or ask your printing company for settings; then look them up in the Conversion Table. If you always print on the same kind of paper, you'll always use the same numbers, so you'll end up remembering them.

A Quick Levels Recap

There are several steps to using Levels to adjust grayscale images, but, as I've said, they're all quick and easy once you get used to them. Here's a brief recap of the role of each of the sliders in the Levels dialog box:

1. Move the upper left slider until it touches the first bar on the histogram to force the darkest area of the image to black. Use the hidden Threshold feature to go as far as possible without damaging the image (**Figure 6.22**).

2. Move the upper right slider until it touches the last bar on the histogram to force the brightest area of the image to white. Again, use the hidden feature to go as far as possible without damaging the image (**Figure 6.23**).

3. Move the middle slider to the left until the image looks nice and bright (**Figure 6.24**).

4. Move the lower left slider to make sure the shadows won't plug up and become pure black on the printing press. Use the tables I've provided for settings or ask your printer for more precise ones (**Figure 6.25**).

5. Move the lower right slider to make sure you don't lose detail in the highlights when the smallest dots in your image disappear on the printing press. Use the tables for settings or ask your printer for more precise ones (**Figure 6.26**). I usually adjust all five sliders before clicking OK to apply them.

Figure 6.22 Result of adjusting upper left slider.

Figure 6.23 Result of adjusting upper right slider.

Figure 6.24 Result of adjusting middle slider.

Figure 6.25 Result of adjusting lower left slider.

Figure 6.26 Result of adjusting lower right slider.

Note

If you own a 30-bit or higher scanner and your scanning software contains a histogram and has the same adjustment controls available, you can make adjustments within your scanning software. Most scanners can deliver a histogram without gaps because they can look back to the image and pick up extra shades of gray that would fill the gaps. For this to work, you have to own a 30-bit scanner or above. These days, almost all scanners are 30-bit or higher. If your scanner is more than five years old, there is a chance you might own a 24-bit model. If you are using one of those 24-bit scanners, there is no advantage to making the adjustments within your scanning software.

Post-adjustment Analysis

Any time you adjust an image, you run the risk of introducing some artifacts that might not be all that pleasant. So let's take a look at what can happen to your image after applying Levels. But don't worry—remember, in Photoshop there is usually at least one "fix" for just about every artifact.

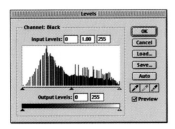

Figure 6.27 Gaps in a histogram indicate posterization.

Notes

To see an updated histogram after adjusting the image, you must first apply the adjustment, and then reopen the Levels dialog box.

....

I don't use this technique on every image, just on those that have extremely noticeable posterization.

Recognizing Posterization

When you look at an updated histogram, you might see wide gaps in the histogram—this indicates *posterization* (**Figure 6.27**). Posterization is when you should have a smooth transition between areas and instead you see a drastic jump between a bright and dark area. Some call this banding or stair-stepping. As long as the gaps in the histogram are smaller than three pixels wide, you probably won't notice it at all in the image.

Adjusting the image usually causes these gaps. As you adjust the image, the bars on the histogram spread out and gaps start to appear (remember that Slinky). The more extreme the adjustment you make, the wider the gaps. And if you see those huge gaps in the histogram, it'll probably mean that the posterization is noticeable enough that you'll want to fix it (it usually shows up in the dark areas of the image).

Eliminating Posterization

Here's a trick that can minimize the posterization. I should warn you that you have to apply this technique manually to each area that is posterized. Although it might take you a little bit of time, the results will be worth it.

To begin, select the Magic Wand tool, set the Tolerance to zero, and click on an area that looks posterized. Next, choose Select > Modify > Border, and use a setting of 2 for slight posterization or 4 for a moderate amount of posterization. Now apply Filter > Blur > Gaussian Blur until the area looks smooth (**Figures 6.28 and 6.29**). Repeat this process on all of the posterized areas until you're satisfied with the results.

Sharpening

By now your image should have great contrast, and it should reproduce nicely on a printing press. But I gotta tell you: almost all images that are scanned need to be artificially sharpened. First I'll show you the controls available when sharpening; then I'll show you exactly how I go about sharpening an image.

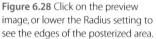

Figure 6.28 Click on the preview image, or lower the Radius setting to see the edges of the posterized area.

Figure 6.29 Increase the Radius setting until the posterized area appears smooth.

To sharpen an image, choose Filter > Sharpen. Photoshop will present you with a pop-out menu of choices. The top three might sound friendly (Sharpen, Sharpen More, Sharpen Edges), but you need to use the bottom one (Unsharp Mask). It's the only choice that allows you to control exactly how much the image will be sharpened. You can think of the other choices as being simple presets that just enter different numbers into the Unsharp Mask filter.

The reason it has the scary name is because way back before people used desktop computers, they sharpened images in a photographic darkroom. They would have to go through a process that involved a blurry (unsharp) version of the image. This would take well over an hour (don't worry, in Photoshop it only takes seconds) and would not be much fun. The process they'd go through in the darkroom was known as making an Unsharp Mask, so Adobe just borrowed that term.

The Unsharp Mask filter increases the contrast where two shades of gray touch in the image, making their edges more prominent and therefore easier to see. To easily view the effect of the Unsharp Mask filter (**Figure 6.30**), I'll demonstrate a document that contains only three shades of gray (20%, 30%, and 50%), as shown in **Figures 6.31 to 6.34**. When you choose Unsharp Mask, you'll be presented with three sliders: Amount, Radius, and Threshold.

> ▸ **Amount**—How much the contrast will be increased and, therefore, how obvious the sharpening will be.

> ▸ **Radius**—How wide a halo will be used. If you use too much, it will be obvious.

Note

To see the effects accurately when you're applying Unsharp Mask, you must view your image at 100% magnification. A quick way to view an image at 100% is to double-click the Zoom tool.

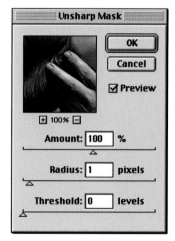

Figure 6.30 The Unsharp Mask dialog box.

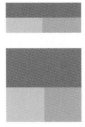

Figure 6.31 The simple document.

▶ **Threshold**—How different two touching shades have to be in order for sharpening to kick in. With Threshold set at 0, everything will get sharpened. As you increase this setting, only the areas that are drastically different will be sharpened.

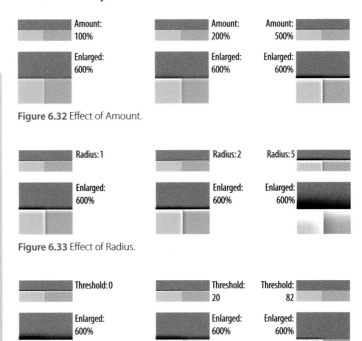

Figure 6.32 Effect of Amount.

Figure 6.33 Effect of Radius.

Figure 6.34 Effect of Threshold.

Now that we've explored all the options that are available with the Unsharp Mask filter, let's get down to business and find out how to apply them to an image.

Each time you apply the Unsharp Mask filter, it will remember the last settings you used. Because this filter is used on a wide variety of images (remember we used it for line art scanning), the first thing we'll need to do is make sure it isn't using an extreme setting. So choose Filter > Sharpen > Unsharp Mask and type in the generic numbers of Amount=100, Radius=1, Threshold=0, just to make sure you're in the normal range.

Now, I know you're not going to want to hear this, but I'll mention it anyway. If you are going to print this image, you should sharpen it until it looks just a little bit over-sharp.

Figure 6.35   A = 100, R = 1, T = 0   A = 150, R = 1, T = 0   A = 200, R = 1, T = 0

Adjust the Amount setting until the image looks nice and sharp. You'll know this setting is too high when the white halos become overly dominant or when the fine detail starts to break apart into pure black and pure white.

Figure 6.36   A = 150, R = 1.2, T = 0   A = 150, R = 2, T = 0   A = 150, R = 5, T = 0

If the Amount setting doesn't make the image look sharp enough, adjust Radius a small amount (1.1, 1.2, 1.3). I always use a very low setting. Go ahead and try any setting above 2—your image will look ridiculous.

Figure 6.37   A = 150, R = 1.1, T = 3   A= 150, R = 1.1, T = 7   A = 150, R = 1.1, T = 15

If your image contains skin tones or other areas that should look very smooth, increase the Threshold slider until those areas do look smooth. I usually use Threshold settings between 0 and 9.

Note

On the CD accompanying this book, you'll find a PDF file that supplements this chapter. The file, called "extras.pdf," contains the following topics:

▶ Using the Levels dialog box Save and Load buttons

▶ Using the Levels dialog box and eyedroppers

▶ Using the Levels dialog box Auto button

▶ Determining if rescanning your image using different Brightness and Contrast settings would improve the image.

Closing Thoughts

We've covered two main dialog boxes, Levels and Unsharp Mask. Remember, after you've practiced a few times, the whole process takes about a minute. When you feel that you have mastered Levels, you will be ready to take on the ultimate adjustment tool—Curves. Curves is equipped to do the same basic corrections as Levels, but can also do much, much more. In general, with grayscale images I always start out using Levels, and then move on to Curves to fix any problems that Levels can't handle; I also use Curves to work with color. It's like graduating from a Chevette to a Ferrari. The Ferrari takes more skill and coordination to master, but you get one hell of a ride. But that's another chapter.

Ben's Techno-Babble Decoder Ring

Unsharp Mask—A term used to describe the traditional process of sharpening an image by combining a blurry (unsharp) version of the image with a normal version. The idea behind Unsharp Mask is to increase contrast and therefore detail.

Minimum Highlight Dot—The smallest halftone dot that is reproducible using a particular printing process. This is usually measured as a percentage and reflects the lowest percentage of ink that will not lose detail when printed.

Maximum Shadow Dot—The largest halftone dot that will not combine with the surrounding halftone dots to become pure black. This is usually measured as a percentage and reflects the highest percentage of ink that could be used without losing detail when printed. The type of paper usually determines what the Maximum Shadow Dot setting will be.

30-bit—Designates how many colors a scanner can capture (10 bits of red + 10 bits of green + 10 bits of blue = 30 bits total). So 10 bits per channel (RGB) is the same as 30 bits total. 10 bits=2 to the tenth power, which equals 1024. So a 30-bit scanner can capture 1.1 billion colors (1024x1024x1024=1.1 billion), whereas a 24-bit scanner can only capture 16.7 million colors. When scanning in grayscale, a 24-bit scanner captures 256 grays and a 30-bit scanner captures 1024 grays.

Keyboard Shortcuts

Function	Macintosh	Windows
Levels	Command-L	Ctrl-L
Auto Levels	Shift-Command-L	Shift-Ctrl-L
Re-apply Previous Setting	Option-Command-L	Alt-Ctrl-L

Courtesy of David Plunkert, www.spurdesign.com

7 Understanding Curves

*Have patience.
All things are difficult
before they become easy.*
—Saadi

Courtesy of Michael Slack, www.slackart.com

If I were going to be dropped on a deserted island and could bring only one thing with me, I might choose a Swiss Army Knife. With that knife, I could cut firewood, spear fish, and clean my teeth (remember the toothpick?). Much like a Swiss Army Knife, Image > Adjust > Curves can be used for just about anything. In fact, if I had to pick one adjustment tool to use all the time, it would definitely be Curves. By mastering the Curves dialog box, you have so much control over your images that you might wonder why you would ever need to use the Levels or Brightness And Contrast dialog box. Let's take a look at some of the things you can do with the Curves dialog box. You can:

▸ Pull out far more detail than it's possible to see with the sharpening filters (**Figures 7.1 to 7.3**).

▸ Lighten or darken areas without making selections (**Figures 7.4 and 7.5**).

▸ Turn ordinary text into extraordinary text (**Figures 7.6 and 7.7**).

▸ Color-correct your images without guesswork. (**Figures 7.8 and 7.9**).

Figure 7.1 The original image. (© 1998 PhotoDisc)

Figure 7.2 After applying the Unsharp Mask filter.

Figure 7.3 After a simple Curves adjustment.

Figure 7.4 The original image. (© 1998 PhotoSpin, www.photospin.com)

Figure 7.5 After a simple Curves adjustment.

Magical Magical

Figure 7.6 The original text effect.

Figure 7.7 After a simple Curves adjustment.

Figure 7.8 The original image. (© 1998 Corel Corporation)

Figure 7.9 After a simple Curves adjustment.

None of these changes could be made by using Levels or Brightness/Contrast (that is, not without making complicated selections or losing control over the result). Now you can see why you'll want to master Curves!

Using Curves, you can perform all the adjustments available in the Levels, Brightness/Contrast, and Threshold dialog boxes, and much, much more. In fact, you can adjust each of the 256 shades of gray in your image. (**Figure 7.10**).

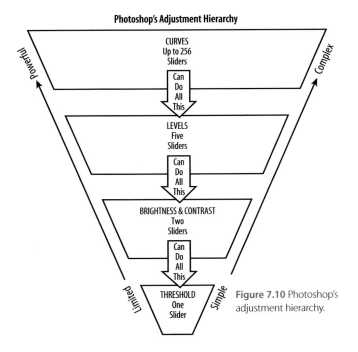

Figure 7.10 Photoshop's adjustment hierarchy.

With Power Comes Complexity

I find that the majority of Photoshop users never truly master (or even become comfortable with) Curves, just as some people never drive cars with manual transmissions. Perhaps the first time they tried to drive with a clutch, they drove up a really steep hill and encountered a stop sign at the top. Then, maybe a big garbage truck pulled up behind them within what seemed like an inch of their bumper.

If you've ever driven a car with a clutch, you know what I'm getting at. When you're not comfortable with something and are forced to use it in a challenging situation, the tendency is to give up. However, if you've spent enough time getting comfortable with a manual transmission, you don't even think about it when you're driving. Curves works the same way. If you just play around with it, you might get scared off, but if you hang in there, it becomes easier to use, and you'll find yourself doing some amazing things to your images. This chapter might seem long-winded, but the truth is that until you truly "get" Curves, you will be a prisoner of Photoshop's less powerful tools. So, fasten your seatbelt, adjust your rearview mirror, and settle in for the ride.

But First, a Test!

Before we delve into Curves, I want to test your present knowledge of the Curves dialog box. Don't worry, though, because the lower your score, the more you should enjoy this chapter.

Look at the curve shown in **Figure 7.11** and see if you can answer the following questions:

▶ Which areas of the image will lose detail from this adjustment?

▶ Which areas of the image will become brighter?

▶ What happened to 62% gray?

▶ What happened to the image's contrast?

If you truly understand the Curves dialog box, then you found these questions extremely easy to answer. However, if you hesitated before answering any of them or couldn't answer them at all, then this chapter was designed for you.

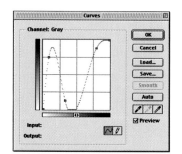

Figure 7.11 Can you figure out exactly what this curve will do to an image?

The Idea Behind Curves

Because the Curves dialog box allows you to adjust every shade of gray in an image (256 in all), it works quite a bit differently from the other adjustment tools. To get a clearer picture of what Curves does, let's construct our own Curves dialog box from scratch, using something you're already familiar with: the plain old vanilla bar chart. You know what I'm talking about—those wretched bar charts that can't be avoided in magazines, brochures, television, and pretty much everywhere you look. Now we can finally put one to good use by using it to help us understand Curves.

What if you created a bar chart that indicates how much light your monitor uses to display each color in an image? This bar chart would be just like any other that you've seen, where taller bars mean more light and shorter bars mean less. You could show the shade of gray you are using below each bar, and then draw a line from the top of each bar over to the left so you could label how much light is being used for each shade. I think you'd end up with something that looks like **Figure 7.12.** Or you could just as easily change the chart to indicate how much ink your printer would use to reproduce the image. Now that we're talking about ink, short bars would mean less ink, which would produce a light shade of gray, and tall bars would mean a lot of ink and would produce a dark shade of gray. To make the change, all we'd have to do is flip all the shades at the bottom of the graph so the dark ones are below the tall bars and the bright ones are below the short bars. The result would look like **Figure 7.13,** right?

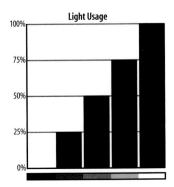

Figure 7.12 This bar chart indicates the amount of light used to display the shades of gray shown at the bottom.

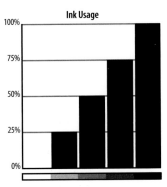

Figure 7.13 Flip the shades at the bottom, and you've got a graph that represents ink usage.

Okay, now that you've got the root concept, let's expand on that to accommodate the real world. Our basic bar chart might work for a simple logo with just a few shades of gray (one bar representing each shade), but most of your images will contain many more than that. So, we just increase the number of bars (**Figure 7.14**), right? Well, sort of. The fact is, your image can contain up to 256 shades of gray. But if we jam 256 bars (one for each shade) into our chart, then they won't look like bars anymore, they'll just turns into a big mass (**Figure 7.15**). You can't see the individual bars because there isn't any space between them.

All the same, our images contain up to 256 shades of gray, so we really need that many bars in our chart. Now that they're all smashed together, we don't have room to label each bar, so why don't we just overlay a grid (**Figure 7.16**) and label that instead? If that grid isn't detailed enough for you, we could add a more detailed grid, such as the one shown in **Figure 7.17**.

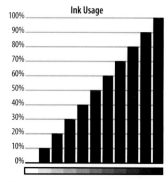

Figure 7.14 Add more bars for additional accuracy.

Figure 7.15 The 256 bars take up so much space that the chart no longer looks like a bar chart.

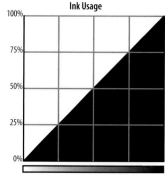

Figure 7.16 A grid can help you figure out how much ink is used.

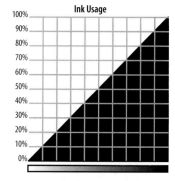

Figure 7.17 The more detailed grid allows you to be even more accurate.

If you've followed along and this makes sense to you, then you have grasped the principle behind Curves. We have just a bit more to go. Stick with me, and trust me—all these details are well worth slogging through because they'll help you get a much deeper understanding of Curves.

The sample chart we've created isn't really all that useful...yet. It's not telling you anything you can't find in the

Info or Color palettes. For example, if you really want to know how much ink (or light) you'd use to reproduce a shade of gray, you could just open the Info palette by choosing Window > Show Info (**Figure 7.18**), and then move your pointer over the image; the Info palette would indicate how much ink would be used in that area. The Color palette (Window > Show Color) is set up similarly and will tell you how much ink or light makes up a shade of gray (**Figure 7.19**). The main difference between the two methods is that the Info palette gives you information about your image—specifically, what's under the pointer. The Color palette isn't image specific but gives you generic information about how much ink or light makes up a shade of gray.

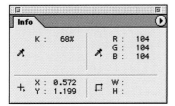

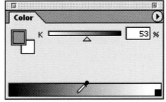

Figure 7.18 The Info Palette indicates how much ink would be used to reproduce the color that is under the pointer.

Figure 7.19 The Color palette indicates how much ink would be used to reproduce your current foreground color.

The Curves dialog box, meanwhile, is really just a simple bar chart—with a lot of bars that are very close together—that shows how much ink or light will be used in your image. The gradient at the bottom shows all the shades of gray you could possibly have, and the chart above shows how much ink or light will be used to create each shade. But the wonderful thing about the Curves dialog box is that it doesn't just sit there like a static bar chart that only gives you information. It's interactive—you can use it to change the amount of ink (or light) used to reproduce your image (**Figure 7.20**).

Think of our Ink Usage bar graph: As the shades of gray get steadily darker, each shade uses slightly more ink, resulting in a straight diagonal line. But in the Curves graph, you can move points on the line. For example, you can flatten the

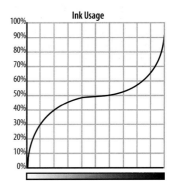

Figure 7.20 Changing the shape of the line in the Curves graph changes how much ink is used throughout the image.

line so that in your modified image, many shades of gray are represented by a single shade. Or you can make a dramatic change to the line, dragging a point up or down so that a shade changes to become much darker or lighter.

The Gradients Are Your Guide

Go ahead and pick any shade of gray from the gradient, and then look above it to figure out how much ink would be used to create it (**Figure 7.21**). You can use the grid to help you calculate the exact amount of ink used (about 23% in this case). But wouldn't you rather see what 23% looks like? Suppose we replace those percentage numbers with another gradient that shows how bright each area would be (**Figure 7.22**). Just to make sure you don't get the two gradients confused, read the next two sentences twice: The bottom gradient represents the shades of gray you are changing. The side gradient indicates how bright or dark a shade will be if you move the line to a certain height (**Figure 7.23**).

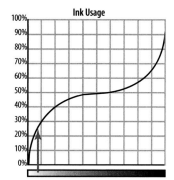

Figure 7.21 Use the grid to help determine how much ink is used in an area.

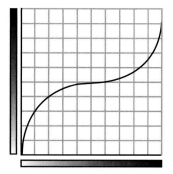

Figure 7.22 The gradient on the left indicates how dark an area will become if the curve is moved to a certain height.

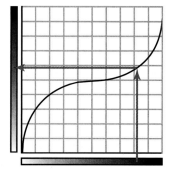

Figure 7.23 The bottom gradient scale is what you're changing. The left gradient scale is what you changed it to.

Congratulations. You've survived Ben's Bar Charts 101. Now you're ready to graduate from charts and take flight with the full-fledged Curves dialog box (**Figure 7.24**). Does it look familiar? It should. You might notice that the Curves dialog box is a bit smaller than the bar chart we were using. To get a larger grid, click the Zoom box

(Macintosh) or Minimize/Maximize box (Windows) on the far right of the title bar of the Curves dialog box. Each time you click this symbol, it toggles between a grid that's 171 pixels wide and one that's 256 pixels wide (**Figure 7.25**). I generally use the large grid because it shows all the grays you can have in your image, which makes it easier to be precise. In fact, if you use the small version, you can't control every shade of gray (your image contains 256 shades of gray, and the smaller grid is only 171 pixels wide). I only use the 171-pixel version when working on a small screen, because then the large version covers up too much of the image.

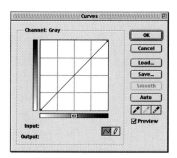

Figure 7.24 The grid in the small version of the Curves dialog box is only 171 pixels wide.

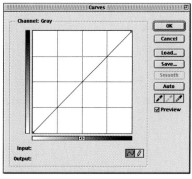

Figure 7.25 The grid in the large version of the Curves dialog box is 256 pixels wide.

Ben, Are We There Yet?

I know what you're thinking. "I wanna play with Curves, now!" Be calm, you're *almost* ready. There are just a couple of thoughts I need to plant in your brain first.

If you go back to when we first started to create the bar chart, you'll remember that we started measuring how much light our monitor was using to display things. Then we flip-flopped and measured how much ink we'd use for printing. The same thinking applies to the Curves dialog box. Remember how we accomplished that switch earlier in the chapter—didn't we just reverse the shades of gray at the bottom of the chart? Hold that thought, and look at the middle of the gradient at the bottom of the Curves dialog box. Clicking those arrows reverses the gradient, which toggles the chart's context between light and ink. (**Figures 7.26 and 7.27**).

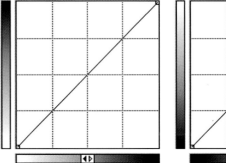 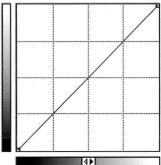

Figure 7.26 When black is at the top, you are using ink (remember, up means more).

Figure 7.27 When white is at the top, you are using light (again, up means more).

The *mode* of your image determines what you'll start with. Photoshop assumes that images that are in grayscale, CMYK, or Lab mode will be printed, and therefore it defaults to using the gradient that represents ink. Since your monitor displays everything using red, green, and blue light, images in RGB mode will cause Photoshop to use the gradient that represents light.

Photoshop doesn't care which system you use. It can easily translate between the two, because light is the exact opposite of ink. When you switch from one scale to the other, not only do the light and dark ends of the gradients get swapped, but the curve flips upside down. Be sure to look out for which mode I use throughout the examples in this chapter—otherwise you might end up getting the exact opposite result! I'll stick to the default settings unless there's a good reason to change them, and when I do, I'll clue you in.

Remember, the side gradient indicates what you'll end up with if you move a point on the curve to a certain height. You can always glance at the side to find out how much light or ink you're using. Just remember that up means more of something and that you can either use light or ink.

Next comes the grid. Remember how we ended up with one that is more detailed than the one we started with? Well, you can toggle between those two grids by Option-clicking (Macintosh) or Alt-clicking (Windows) anywhere within the grid area. It's up to you which grid you use. It doesn't affect the result you'll get in Curves; it's just a personal preference (**Figure 7.28**).

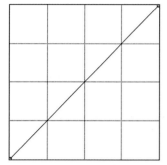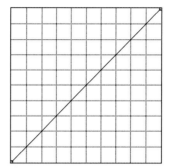

Figure 7.28 Option-click (Macintosh) or Alt-click (Windows) anywhere on the grid to toggle between a 25% increment grid (left) and a 10% increment grid (right).

Take Curves for a Test Drive

Okay, start your engines. We're going to stop babbling and start driving! Go ahead, open an image, choose Image > Adjust > Curves, and start messing with the curve. Just click anywhere on the curve to add a point, and then drag it around to change the shape of the curve. If you want to get rid of a point, drag it off the edge of the grid. You can also click a point and then use the arrow keys on your keyboard to nudge it around the grid. You can even add the Shift key to the arrow keys to nudge it in larger increments.

Now, here's the final piece of the Curves puzzle. To understand what you're doing, you must compare the curve you're making to the original line. After all, how can you know how much of a change you've made unless you know where you started? I usually just grab a pencil and hold it up to the screen to represent the original line (**Figure 7.29**). Now let's see what we can do with all this.

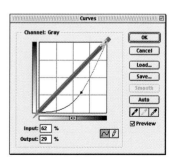

Figure 7.29 Use a pencil to represent the original line.

Improving Dark Images

Try this: Open any grayscale image you think is too dark (I'll show you how to work with color in a minute), as shown in **Figure 7.30**. Next, choose Image > Adjust > Curves, and add a point by clicking the middle of the line. Pull the line straight down, and see what happens to your image. Compare the curve with the gradient at the left of the Curves dialog box (**Figure 7.31 and 7.32**). The farther you move the curve down, the less ink you use and therefore the brighter the image becomes. If part of the curve bottoms out, the shade represented by that area becomes pure white because there will be no ink used when the image is printed.

Figure 7.30 Start with a dark grayscale image. (© 2001 Stockbyte, www.stockbyte.com)

Figure 7.31 Move the curve down to reduce how much ink is used.

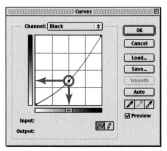

Figure 7.32 Comparing the curve with the gradients.

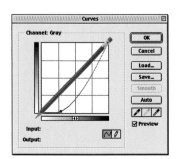

Figure 7.33 To figure out how much ink you've removed, look below where the line used to be.

Any part of a curve that's below the original line indicates an area that is using less ink, which means that it has been brightened. Look at the gradient directly below those areas to determine which shades of the image were brightened (**Figure 7.32**). The farther the line is moved down from its original position, the brighter the image will become (**Figure 7.33**).

Previewing the Changes

You can compare the original and changed versions of the image by checking and unchecking the Preview checkbox. As long as the checkbox is unchecked, you'll see what the image looked like before the adjustment. When you click to check it, you'll see the changes you just made.

Color Is Different

The concepts and adjustments we talk about with Curves apply equally to grayscale and color images. But when you work on a color image, you have to be more careful; otherwise you might end up shifting the colors, rather than just the brightness, of your image. There are two ways to apply Curves to your image, and therefore two methods for limiting its effect on the brightness of a color image. First, you can apply a curve to the currently active layer by choosing Image > Adjust > Curves. Immediately after applying Curves, you can choose Edit > Fade and set the Mode pop-up menu to Luminosity (**Figure 7.34**). The Fade command will limit the last change you made (Curves in our case) to only changing the brightness (luminosity is just another word for brightness) of the image—it will not be able to shift the colors or change how saturated they are.

Your other choice would be to apply a curve to more than one layer by choosing Layer > New Adjustment Layer > Curves. Then, when prompted (**Figure 7.35**), you would set the Mode pop-up menu to Luminosity. An adjustment layer will affect all the layers below it but none of the layers above it. It's also a nonpermanent change, because you can click twice on the adjustment-layer thumbnail in that layer to reopen the Curves dialog box and make changes. That means that any Curves techniques you use for adjusting grayscale images will work on color images if you use the Luminosity blending mode (**Figures 7.36 to 7.38**).

Note

In previous versions of Photoshop (before 6.0), the Fade option was located on the Filter menu instead of the Edit menu.

Figure 7.34 Choose Edit > Fade Curves to limit your changes to the brightness of your image.

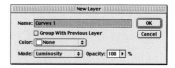

Figure 7.35 When creating an adjustment layer, change the Mode menu selection to Luminosity.

Note

If you're using the adjustment layer icon from the bottom of the Layers palette, be sure to hold down Option (Mac) or Alt (Windows) to choose a blending mode.

Figure 7.36 Original image. (©1998 PhotoSpin, www.photospin.com)

Figure 7.37 After brightening the image with Curves, the color and saturation change.

Figure 7.38 Using the Luminosity blending mode prevents adjustments from shifting the colors in the image.

Ghosting an Image

Curves can also be helpful when you plan to add text to a photograph. When you place text on top of a photo, it's often difficult to read because there isn't much contrast between the text and the image. However, if you lighten the photo, the text will be easier to read (**Figure 7.39**). This is known as *ghosting,* or *screening back,* an image.

Figure 7.39 Ghosted image. (© 2001 Stockbyte, www.stockbyte.com)

Try this: Open any color photo (make sure it's in RGB mode); then use the Marquee tool to select about half the image. Choose Image > Adjust > Curves, and click the control point in the lower-left corner of the grid area to select it (use the upper-right point for CMYK images). Now move that point up (down, in CMYK mode) using the up arrow on your keyboard. You have just lightened (or *ghosted)* the dark part of the image. This technique is often used to lighten a photo so that any text placed on top of it is easier to read.

Compare the line you just made with the original (remember to use your pencil). See how the dark areas of the image have changed a large amount, and the bright areas have not changed as drastically (**Figure 7.40**).

Using Curves to screen back an area of an image provides professional-looking results. Resist the temptation to resort to this commonly-used quick-and-dirty method: Create a

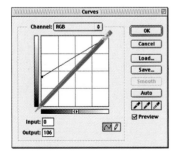

Figure 7.40 This curve brightens the dark areas of the image more than the bright areas.

new layer above the image, make a rectangular selection on the new layer and fill it with white; reduce the opacity of the new layer until it forms a ghostly box. Cheating like this tends to change all the shades in the image an equal amount and could easily blow out the detail in the highlights of the image.

Increasing Contrast and Detail

So far, we've learned that moving the curve up or down will increase or decrease the amount of ink used to make the image. Now let's look at how changing the angle of the curve can help us. What if you had an image of a polar bear, and the brightest part of the bear was white and the darkest was only 25% gray? Would it be easy to see the detail in the polar bear? I don't think so (**Figure 7.41**).

Figure 7.41 You can't see much detail in the polar bears because the brightness is limited to 0%–25%.

Now think about how that image would change if we applied the curve shown in **Figure 7.42**. If you look closely at this curve, you'll notice that areas that are white in the original image wouldn't change at all and areas that used to be 25% gray would end up being around 75% gray. Wouldn't that make it much easier to see the detail in the polar bear? In an overexposed image like this one, you have to make the curve steeper in the lighter part of the curve. (We already learned that in an underexposed image, like the one in **Figure 7.30**, you have to make the dark part of the curve steeper to bring out the detail.) You always have to compare the curve with the original line to determine how much of a change you've made. If you make the curve just a little steeper than the original, then you'll add just a little contrast to that area. Remember to look at the gradient below to figure out which shades of gray you are changing.

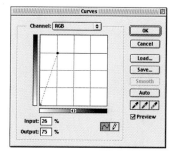

Figure 7.42 This curve adds more contrast, making it easier to see the detail in the polar bears.

Open any grayscale image, and choose Image > Adjust > Curves. Move your pointer over the image, and then click and drag across the area where you want to exaggerate the detail. You'll notice that a circle appears in the Curves dialog box. Photoshop is simply looking at the bottom gradient to find the shade of gray under your pointer; it then puts a circle on the curve directly above that shade. This

Figure 7.43 After making the curve steeper, it's easier to see the detail in the bears.

Note
You can reset the Curves dialog box back to the default line by pressing and holding Option (Macintosh) or Alt (Windows) and then clicking the Reset button.

circle indicates the area of the curve that needs to be changed in order to affect the area you're dragging across. Add control points on either side of this area of the curve. Next, move the top point you just added up, towards the top of the chart, and move the bottom point down, towards the bottom of the chart. The area you dragged across should appear to have more detail (**Figures 7.44 to 7.46**).

Figure 7.44 Original image. (© 2001 Stockbyte, www.stockbyte.com)

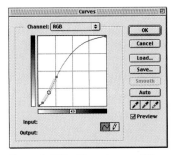

Figure 7.45 Find the range you'd like to change, and then make the curve steeper in that area.

Figure 7.46 After making the curve steeper.

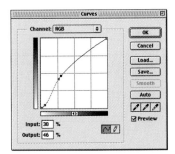

Figure 7.47 Fix the rest of the curve so you don't exaggerate the contrast in other areas.

Note
If you're trying to exaggerate the detail in the darkest areas of an image, you'll have to be very careful not to force areas to pure black (if an area becomes pure black, then it will contain absolutely no detail). You can do this by making sure no part of the curve bottoms out, or by being careful only to brighten areas.

You might also need to fix the rest of the curve to make sure that the contrast in those areas doesn't change radically. You can do this by adding another point and moving it so that the majority of the curve looks normal—that is, diagonal (**Figure 7.47**).

Decreasing Contrast and Detail

Any part of the curve that's flatter (more horizontal) than the original line indicates an area where the contrast has been reduced (shades of gray become more similar). Look at the gradient directly below these areas to determine which shades of the image were changed. The flatter the line becomes, the less contrast you'll see in that area of the image. When you lower the amount of contrast in an image, it becomes harder to see detail. This can be useful if you *want* detail to be less visible. If the curve becomes completely horizontal in an area, you've lost all detail there (**Figures 7.48 to 7.50**). Remember, it's a bar chart—the same height means the same brightness.

Figure 7.48 Original image. (© 2001 Stockbyte, www.stockbyte.com)

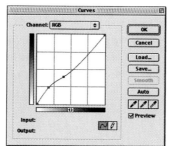

Figure 7.49 Curve used to reduce apparent detail in stonework.

Figure 7.50 Result of applying curve to reduce apparent detail.

Let's Analyze a Classic Tip

Have you ever heard the tip "make an S curve"? Well, let's explore exactly what an S curve does (**Figure 7.51**).

Remember, to find out what a curve is doing to your image, you should compare the curve with the original line. Look at the areas of the curve that are steeper than the original line—namely, the middle of the curve. The shades represented by these steeper areas appear to have more detail. Whenever you pull detail out of one part of an image, you'll also lose detail in another part. Therefore, look at either end of the curve, at the areas of the curve that are flatter than the original line (more horizontal). These areas appear to have less detail. Thus, an S curve attempts to exaggerate detail in the middle grays of the image. However, it also gives you less detail in the highlights and shadows.

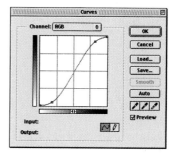

Figure 7.51 A classic S curve.

Checking Ink Ranges

Look at **Figure 7.52** and concentrate on the gradient at the left side of the Curves dialog box. This gradient indicates how dark an area will become if you move the curve to a particular height. Pick a shade of gray from that gradient (such as 90%); then look directly to the right of it to determine if you'll have any areas that shade of gray. Pick another shade and do the same thing. If the curve starts in the lower-left corner and ends in the upper-right corner, each one of the shades should be used somewhere in the image. However, there might be a few shades that are used in more than one area of the curve.

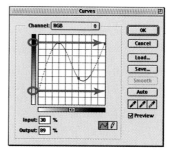

Figure 7.52 After this adjustment, the image won't contain any areas darker than 90% or brighter than 18%.

Inverting Your Image

Think of a stock-market chart that indicates what's happening to the market over a month's time. If you're like most investors, whenever the market's going up, you're happy. However, you're always carefully watching that chart to see if the market starts to dip. If it does, that's when you start to panic. You can think of curves in the same way. As long as the curve is rising, you're fine; however, if the curve starts to fall, you should expect unusual results. Look at **Figure 7.53**, and try to figure out what's happening in the area that's going downhill. The dark areas of the image (around 75%) became bright, and the bright areas (around 25%) became dark. That means you've inverted that part of the image. You'll usually want to minimize or avoid this situation unless you're going for a special effect (**Figures 7.54 and 7.55**).

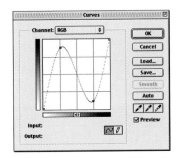

Figure 7.53 Areas between 25% and 75% have been inverted.

Figure 7.54 Original image. (© 2001 Stockbyte, www.stockbyte.com)

Figure 7.55 Result of applying the curve shown in Figure 7.53.

Freeform Curves

To bend the curve, you're not limited to adding and moving points. Another way to define a curve is to click the pencil icon at the bottom of the Curves dialog box and draw a freeform shape (**Figure 7.56**). However, the shape you draw has to resemble a line moving from left to right. Go ahead, just try to draw a circle. You can't do it. That's because the Curves dialog box is just like a bar chart, and you can't have two bars for a single shade. Just for giggles, draw a really wild-looking line across the grid area, and then look at your image. Drawing your own line with the Pencil tool is usually better for special effects than for simple image adjustments.

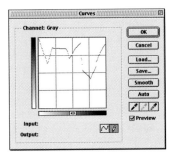

Figure 7.56 A curve created with the Pencil tool.

Let's take a quick look at some of the things you can do when working with a freeform curve:

▶ **Smooth**—After creating a curve with the Pencil tool, you can click the Smooth button to smooth out the shape you drew (**Figure 7.57**). Go ahead and click it multiple times to keep smoothing the curve.

▶ **Convert to Points**—To convert any line drawn with the Pencil tool into a normal curve, click the curve icon (**Figure 7.58**).

▶ **Straight Lines**—You can also draw straight lines with the Pencil tool (**Figure 7.59**). Just Shift-click across the graph area, and Photoshop will connect the dots to create a straight line.

▶ **Posterize**—By drawing a stair-step shape with the Pencil tool, you can accomplish the same effect as if you had used the Posterize command (**Figure 7.60**).

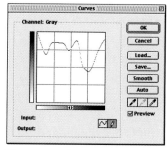

Figure 7.57 A freeform curve after Smooth is applied.

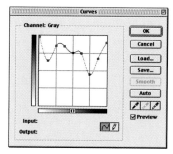

Figure 7.58 The result of converting a freeform curve into a normal curve.

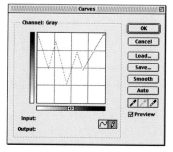

Figure 7.59 Straight lines drawn by Shift-clicking with the Pencil tool.

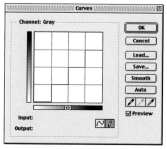

Figure 7.60 Drawing stair-steps is the same as choosing Image > Adjust > Posterize.

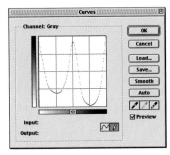

Figure 7.61 Freeform curve used to create chrome effect.

To try this out, open the image called "chrome.jpg" from the CD, and then play around with the pencil tool in the Curves dialog box. Try making a huge M or W, and experiment with different shapes. You should be able to transform the 3D type into some cool-looking chrome text if you experiment long enough (**Figures 7.61 to 7.63**).

Chrome Chrome

Figure 7.62 Image from the CD.

Figure 7.63 Result of applying the curve in Figure 7.61.

Notes

Clicking the Save button brings up a standard Save dialog box, which allows you to save the current settings for future use. The file that's created contains the Input and Output settings for each of the points used on the current curve. To reuse a saved setting, click the Load button.

....

When you're changing the Input and Output numbers, press the up or down arrow key to change a number by 1, or press Shift-up arrow or Shift-down arrow to change a number by 10.

Input and Output Numbers

The Input and Output numbers at the bottom of the Curves dialog box allow you to be very precise when adjusting an image. Input is the shade of gray being changed; Output is what it will become. When the points on the curve appear as hollow squares, the Input and Output numbers relate to your pointer. The Input number tells you which shade of gray is directly below your pointer. The Output number will tell you what the shade of gray (height of the bar chart) would be if you moved the curve to the height of your pointer.

Try it. First, click the curve icon (not the pencil), and then make sure that none of the points on the curve are solid. Do this by moving your pointer around until it looks like a white arrow, and then click the mouse. Now move your pointer around the grid area. You'll notice the Input and Output numbers changing. All they're doing is telling you which shades of gray are directly below and to the left of your pointer (**Figure 7.64**). If you trace over the shape of a curve, the Input and Output numbers will show you exactly what the curve is doing to all the shades of gray in your image.

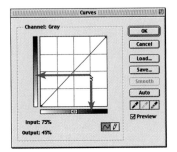

Figure 7.64 Input and Output numbers indicate the location of your pointer relative to the two gradients in the Curves dialog box.

Two Numbering Systems

Two different numbering systems can be used in the Curves dialog box. You can switch between the 0–100%

system and the 0–255 numbering system (which we used in Levels) by switching between light and ink (remember the little arrows that appear in the middle of the bottom gradient). Go ahead and give it a try (**Figure 7.65**).

Figure 7.65 Click the arrow symbol to switch numbering systems.

If you're working on an image that's in RGB mode, Photoshop assumes you're going to use the image on screen instead of printing it. Therefore, when you open Curves, it uses Input and Output numbers ranging from 0 to 255. These numbers represent the amount of light your monitor will use to display the image onscreen (0 = no light, or black; 255 = maximum light, or white). Using this numbering system allows you to have control over each shade.

If you're working on an image that's in grayscale or CMYK mode, Photoshop assumes you'll be printing the image. Therefore, when you open Curves, it uses numbers ranging from 0% to 100%. These numbers represent the amount of ink used to reproduce each level of gray in the image (0% = no ink; 100% = solid ink).

When you click the arrows that switch between the two different numbering systems, Photoshop also reverses the gradients at the bottom and left of the graph. It does this to keep the zero point of each numbering system in the lower-left corner of the graph, which effectively changes between light and ink. You don't have to remember or understand why this happens—it's just nice to know there's a reason behind it.

When you switch the numbering system, this also changes the gradient on the left side of the Curves dialog box. Therefore, if you're using the 0–255 numbering system, you have to move a curve up to brighten the image and down to darken it (the exact opposite of what you do in the 0–100% numbering system). I always look at the gradient on the left to remind me; if black is at the top (the 0–100% system), you're using ink, and moving a curve up will darken the image. If white is at the top of the gradient (the 0–255 system), you're using light, and moving a curve up will brighten the image.

Entering Numbers

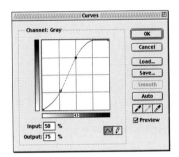

Figure 7.66 To alter the position of a point on the curve, just change one of the numbers.

After you've created a point, it will appear as a solid square. This represents the point that's currently being edited. The Input and Output numbers at the bottom of the dialog box indicate the change this point will make to an image. The Input number represents the shade of gray that's being changed. The Output number indicates what's happening to the shade of gray, the value that you're changing it to. As long as the point appears as a solid square, you can type numbers into the Input and Output fields to change the location of the point (**Figure 7.66**).

Those numbers can be very useful. We'll end up depending on them once we get into the chapter on color correction. But for now, let's see how they can be useful when attempting to change the brightness of an image. Remember that you can click on your image and a circle will appear in the Curves dialog box that indicates what part of the curve would affect the shade in that area? Well, you can also Command-click (Macintosh) or Ctrl-click (Windows) on your image and Photoshop will add a point where that circle would show up. So, what if you'd like two areas of your image to have the same brightness level? Command-click or Ctrl-click one of them to lock in its brightness level. Then, before you release the mouse button, glance at the numbers at the bottom of the Curves dialog box to see exactly how bright that area is. Command-click or Ctrl-click the second area, and change the Output number to match that of the first object (**Figure 7.67**). The bar chart will be the same height in both areas, which means that both areas will end up with the same brightness. But you have to be careful when doing this, because the bar chart will flatten out between those two points. When that happens, there won't be any detail in those shades, so other parts of your image might seem to disappear (**Figure 7.68 and 7.69**).

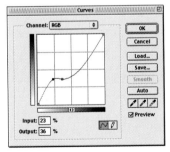

Figure 7.67 When two points are at the same height, those two areas will have the same brightness level.

Figure 7.68 Original image. (© 2001 Stockbyte, www.stockbyte.com)

Figure 7.69 Result of making the far and close buildings the same brightness levels.

The Info Palette

The Info palette can also show you how Curves affects your image (**Figure 7.70**). When you move your pointer over the image, the Info palette indicates what's happening to that area of the image. (If you want a more precise cursor, press the Caps Lock key to change your cursor from the default eyedropper to the crosshairs.) The first number in the Info palette tells you how dark the area is before using Curves. The second number tells you how dark it will be after Curves is applied.

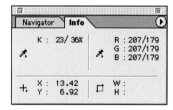

Figure 7.70 The first number is what you have before using Curves; the second is what you get after using Curves.

A Quick Recap

Now, to verify that you're ready to move on, you should make sure you understand the general concepts. Take a look at the curve in **Figure 7.71** and see if you can answer the following questions:

▶ Which areas of the image will lose detail with this adjustment?

▶ Which areas of the image will become brighter?

▶ What happened to 62% gray?

▶ What happened to the image's contrast?

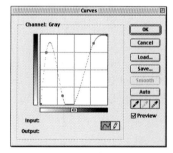

Figure 7.71 Can you figure out what this curve will do to an image?

Just in case you couldn't answer all these questions, let's recap what we've covered:

▶ Angle = Contrast = Detail.

▶ Up means darken in the 0–100% system.

▶ Down means darken in the 0–255 system.

▶ Up means brighten in the 0–255 system.

▶ Down means brighten in the 0–100% system.

Note

On the CD accompanying this book, you'll find a PDF file that supplements this chapter. The file, called "extras.pdf," contains information about applying what you know about the Curves dialog box to Levels.

Closing Thoughts

My hope is that after you've read this chapter you'll have come to the conclusion that Curves really isn't such a brain twister. And if you come out of it thinking of ways you might use Curves in the future, even better. The Curves dialog box is one of a handful of Photoshop features that separate the experts from everyone else. But there's no reason why you can't propel yourself into the expert category. Once you get comfortable with Curves (okay, it might take a while), you'll be able to do so much more than you can do with any other dialog box. So hang in there and stick with it. The initial learning curve might be somewhat daunting, but the fringe benefits are dynamite.

Ben's Techno-Babble Decoder Ring

Contrast—The range between the brightest and darkest areas of an image.

S curve—A generic curve used to exaggerate the detail in midtones of an image by suppressing the detail in the highlights and shadows.

Keyboard Shortcuts

FUNCTION	MACINTOSH	WINDOWS
Curves	Command-M	Ctrl-M
Move point up	Up arrow	Up arrow
Move point down	Down arrow	Down arrow
Move point left	Left arrow	Left arrow
Move point right	Right arrow	Right arrow
Select next point	Command-Control-Tab	Ctrl-Tab
Select previous point	Shift-Command-Control-Tab	Shift-Ctrl-Tab
Deselect all points	Command-D	Ctrl-D

Color Correction

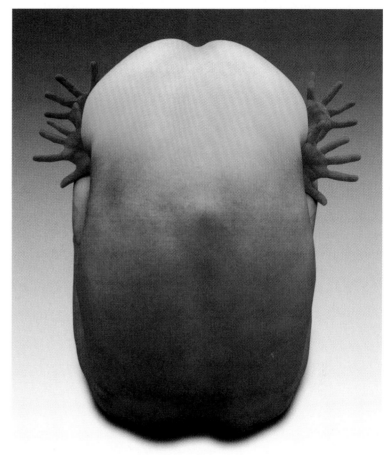

The camera, you know,
will never capture you.
Photography, in my
experience, has the
miraculous power
of transferring wine
into water.
—Oscar Wilde in "Lillie"

Knot #82 from BODY KNOTS by Howard Schatz
© 1999 Schatz/Ornstein (Rizzoli Publishers International Press, 1998)

This chapter might seem somewhat long and loaded with nitty-gritty details, but with color correction, the devil really *is* in the details. I find that most books that include color correction just jump in and start adjusting photos. That's okay, but it doesn't really leave you equipped to understand what is happening to your images. Instead, you get only a few clues about how to fix it. In fact, the more you understand, the more you can control, and the less fixing you'll have to do; this is one of those instances where knowing the mechanics of the process will really pay off later.

The fundamental rule of good color management is to take care of any potential color problems as early as possible in the image creation process—during the initial photography, developing, scanning, and on up the chain. In this chapter I'll give you a precise, step-by-step technique that will safely guide you through color correction, and on the way I hope you'll learn, finally, what's really happening to your images. Just remember, getting good at color correction is like a toddler learning to take his first steps. Your legs might feel a little wobbly at first, but if you keep putting one foot in front of the other, it will start to feel natural, and finally it will become second nature.

The Genesis of Color

Let's start at the beginning. What is color, anyway? Isn't it just the appearance of the light entering your eye? Then let's take a look at how your eye perceives color. There are two types of light-sensitive areas at the back of your eye. One kind only works in low light situations and isn't sensitive to color. The other only works when there is a lot of light entering the eye. That's the kind that allows us to see color. These light-sensitive areas perceive color as a combination of red, green, and blue light. Everything you've ever seen with your eyes has been a combination of those colors of light. Then how can you see purple, yellow, orange, etc.? Well, think about shining light through a prism. All of those rainbow colors (**Figure 8.1**) are just a

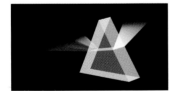

Figure 8.1 A prism will transform white light into a full spectrum of colors.

combination of red, green, and blue light. To see what I mean, launch Photoshop and click on your foreground color. Then, in the RGB area, type in 255 for Red, zero for Green, and zero for Blue. That should give you a nice vivid red. Now click on the type field that's labeled H (for Hue), and press Shift-up arrow multiple times until Photoshop makes it through all the colors in the rainbow. As you're doing that, watch the RGB numbers and you'll see how your eye can perceive the full spectrum of colors as a combination of red, green, and blue light. You might have also noticed that only one or two colors (in RGB) were needed to create the entire spectrum of the rainbow. What do you think would happen if we end up using all three colors? Well, try it out. Go back to the Color Picker and type in 255R, 255G, and 0B, use the up arrow to slowly increase the amount of blue light, and watch what happens. In fact, just try using equal amounts of each color and you'll find that you get gray. That means that you get less vivid colors by using all three colors (**Figure 8.2**). So how do you think you'd darken those colors? If you're using light (RGB), you'd just use less of it. Try it for yourself: just use the Color Picker, pick a bright color, and then lower the B (brightness) setting and watch what happens to the RGB numbers (**Figure 8.3**).

In a nutshell, here's what I'm saying: When you look at an apple, light falls on it, and two things happen: the apple absorbs some of the light, but it also reflects some of the light back into your eyes, and you see that light as a different color than the light that originally hit the apple. Your eyes interpret it as a blending of red, green, and blue, and it's the unique combination of those colors that determines its coloration, vividness, and brightness.

Let's review. Your eye is sensitive to red, green, and blue light. You only need one or two of these to get vivid colors—the third just makes it less vivid (moves it more towards a gray). In fact, equal amounts of all three colors of light give you pure gray. Lower numbers mean less light, which deliver darker colors. You wouldn't believe how many people think they know color correction without knowing these simple facts. Without them, it's next to impossible to know what

> **Note**
> If you happen to be color blind, that means you can only perceive one or two of the RGB colors entering your eye, and therefore cannot see a full rainbow of colors.

Figure 8.2 Colors become less vivid when you use all three colors.

Figure 8.3 Darker colors are created by lowering the RGB numbers.

you're doing when working with color in Photoshop. In fact, you'd most likely end up completely trusting your screen and randomly moving sliders until your image looked acceptable. But you're not going to do that. Instead, as I promised, you're going to learn a step-by-step precision technique that removes all guesswork.

The Digital Version of Color

Now let's see how all of this colorful information relates to digital imaging. To display color, your computer monitor uses tiny bars of red, green, and blue light, all smashed together. They are so small your eye can't focus on any one of them individually, but together they create the spectrum of colors you see on your screen (**Figure 8.4**). That's why your monitor can display a wide range of colors using only three colors of light. A scanner works the same way. It's just like our apple example—the scanner shines light on something and measures how much RGB light bounces off. Then that data is used to determine how much RGB light your monitor should use to display that color and, therefore, how much RGB light will enter your eye. See how it really is an RGB world out there?

Figure 8.4 If you look closely at your monitor, you'll that see everything it displays is made from red, green, and blue light.

Printing Your Image

But what happens when your image escapes from your computer and goes out to a printer? First off, you can't print your images using red, green, and blue ink—it just won't work. Think about it…as your eye sees it, the light hitting a sheet of paper is made out of RGB components. If you print with red ink, the ink would absorb all the green and blue light that is hitting the paper and allow only the red light to reflect off and enter your eye. Green ink would absorb all the red and blue light, and blue ink would absorb all the red and green light (**Figure 8.5**). So if you were to use two colors (red and green), you would end up seeing pure black, because you would have absorbed all the light falling on the paper.

Figure 8.5 Combining red and green ink results in black.

We still want to be able to reproduce our RGB images; we just need to take a different approach to printing in order to do so. We need to find three colors of ink to use: one that absorbs only red light, one that absorbs only blue light, and one that absorbs only green light. To find out exactly which colors are needed, take a peek at **Figure 8.6.**

Think of the three circles as the output from three separate flashlights: one that has a red bulb, one a green bulb, and one a blue bulb. Look in the middle, where they all overlap—and remember that when you combine RGB light in equal proportions, you get gray (and that white is the brightest shade of gray you can get). Now let's find out which colors we need to use when printing an image. Look at the area where the blue and green flashlights overlap (but the red one does not); that's the color of ink you need to control red light. Then look at the area where the red and blue flashlights overlap; that's the color of ink needed to control green light. Finally, look at the area where the red and green flashlights overlap; that's the color of ink you'd need to control blue light.

▶ Cyan ink absorbs red light.

▶ Magenta ink absorbs green light.

▶ Yellow ink absorbs blue light.

That's why the Info palette is set up the way it is; one side talks about light (RGB) and the other talks about ink (CMYK). These models are the exact opposites of each other. In fact, it's just like a seesaw; if one side is high, the other side has to be low. So, if you increase the amount of red light being used, you are simultaneously reducing the amount of cyan ink needed to reproduce that color (**Figure 8.8**). 100% cyan shouldn't let any red reflect off the paper. 90% cyan will let 10% of the red light bounce off the sheet and into your eye.

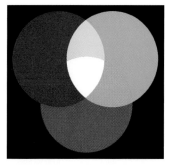

Figure 8.6 Imagine that these three circles were created from three flashlights: one red, one green, and one blue.

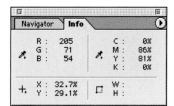

Figure 8.7 The RGB and CYMK numbers are directly across from each other, making it easy to remember which color of ink absorbs which color of light.

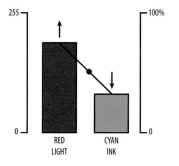

Figure 8.8 The relationship between RGB and CMY is like a seesaw. When you increase red light, you are, in effect, reducing cyan ink.

213

Notes

Using CMYK inks to reproduce a wide range of colors is also known as process color printing.

The exact RGB number you'll end up with when creating 100% cyan ink will depend on the setting in the Color Settings dialog box, so your numbers might end up being a little different than mine. But no matter what those settings are, you'll notice that cyan ink messes with green and blue light, when it shouldn't.

CMY Text

Figure 8.9 Misregistration can cause a mess when using CMY to create black text.

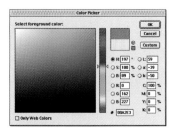

Figure 8.10 Impurities in cyan ink cause it to absorb more than just red light.

Black Ink Saves the Day (and some money, too)

If cyan ink absorbs red light, magenta absorbs green light, and yellow absorbs blue light, then combining all three colors of ink should give you solid black. So why do we use black ink in CMYK mode? There are a lot of reasons to use black ink. If you used three colors of ink to make black text, what would happen if those colors didn't line up perfectly on the printing press (**Figure 8.9**)? And doesn't a single ink cost less than three? So wouldn't it be cheaper to use it for your black text? You could also use it in the dark parts of your images to replace equal amounts of red, green, and blue, because, after all, isn't that how you make gray?

These are all good arguments for using black ink. But the main reason we do so is because we haven't figured out how to make perfect inks. We try to make a cyan that only messes with red light, but the impurities in the ink also cause it to absorb some green and blue light. Check it out for yourself. Open the Color Picker and choose 100% cyan, 0% magenta, 0% yellow, and 0% black. Then look at the RGB numbers. You should end up with 0 for red (because cyan absorbs red light), 255 for green and 255 for blue. But you didn't, did ya? (**Figure 8.10**.) Now click OK and open the Color Picker again. This time let's see what cyan *should* look like. To see the ideal cyan, type in 0 for red and 255 for both green and blue. Now you should be able to compare the cyan we really use to the ideal one by looking in the upper right of the Color Picker. Look at the difference in color! (I'd love to show you this in the book, but I can't; everything printed here is using those impure inks.) Did you also notice a little triangle that showed up next to the color you chose? That's because CMYK inks can't reproduce all the colors you can create in RGB mode. This, too, is due to the impurities in the inks. The color that shows up next to that warning symbol is what Photoshop thinks is the closest reproducible color. If you want to use that color, just click on the warning symbol and then you'll know you have a reproducible color.

Now go ahead try the same test for magenta and yellow ink to find out how impure they really are. (You'll find that yellow is the best of the lot.) With those impurities, 100% cyan, 100% magenta, and 100% yellow together just produce a muddy looking dark brown color (**Figure 8.11**). So, we end up using black ink to create deep, rich black shadows that we couldn't get with CMY.

Figure 8.11 100% of cyan, magenta, and yellow don't produce a dark enough "black," so black ink is added to the mix to ensure a good result.

You can see just how far off these inks are when you create gray in CMYK mode. Do this by opening the color palette (Window > Show Color), choosing Grayscale Ramp from the side menu of the palette, and then choosing CMYK Sliders from the same menu. Now click and drag across the gradient that appears at the bottom of the palette, and watch the CMYK numbers (**Figure 8.12**). See if you can figure out a consistent formula for creating gray. It might not be as easy as in RGB mode, but there is still a relatively simple formula—you just need equal amounts of magenta and yellow and more cyan. If the inks were perfect, it would be just like RGB mode where you simply use equal amounts of each color to create gray.

If you'd like to see a dramatic example of the limitations of CMYK, just visit your local bookstore. Walk down the magazine aisle, grab a few of your favorites and look for deep, true-blue skies. You just won't find any. You'll most likely find one of two things: a bright cyan sky (which usually looks pretty good) or a dark purple sky (which usually looks terrible). If you're having trouble finding the purple version, then you must be looking at well known, high-end magazines. Instead, find one you've never heard of—about collecting Barbies or something. That's where you'll usually see the bad versions. Not that I have anything against Barbie, of course.

Welcome Warnings

Go into Photoshop's Color Picker, choose the brightest pure blue color you can find, and then click on that warning symbol (**Figure 8.13**) to see what you'd get if you converted it to CMYK mode. You'll find that it's simply not possible to create a deep blue in CMYK mode (**Figure 8.14**). In the Channels chapter, I'll show you how to add a custom color of ink to create a true blue, but then you'll be paying for a fifth color of ink, which will make your printing job

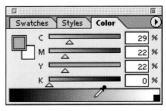

Figure 8.12 To create gray in CMYK mode, you need equal amounts of magenta and yellow, and more cyan.

Figure 8.13 This symbol indicates that the currently chosen color cannot be reproduced with CMYK inks.

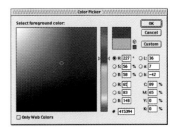

Figure 8.14 After clicking the warning symbol, you'll get the printable version of the color.

more expensive. If that's not in your budget, be sure to check out the CD at the back of this book, because that's where I'll show you how to shift the color of your sky to a bright cyan color commonly used in high-quality books and magazines. The whole point of this example is that you have to be very careful when working in RGB mode, otherwise you might get a big surprise when you convert to CMYK mode and find that your beautiful colors have turned to mush.

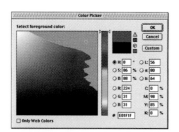

Figure 8.15 The View > Gamut Warning command will cover all the non-reproducible colors with gray.

The little warning symbol is a great help when *choosing* colors, but how can you know that you're not screwing up your image when you are adjusting it with Hue/Saturation, Levels, or Curves? Thankfully, there are a couple of ways to approach this dilemma. One is to choose View > Gamut Warning; then Photoshop will cover all the non-reproducible colors with gray (**Figure 8.15**). This might seem useful, but it really isn't. The problem is that there is no indication of *how much* those colors will shift. Most of those areas will probably change just a little bit, which usually isn't a cause for alarm, but the gray "blanket" looks pretty drastic and may worry you. Instead, when I make adjustments to my image, I prefer to use the View > Proof Colors command. When you turn that on, Photoshop will show you what your image will look like after you convert it to CMYK mode. That way you can adjust away and you will always be aware of what your results will be after converting the image. However, this feature does slow down the screen display, so I only turn it on when I'm worried about creating non-reproducible colors. That way I won't get any nasty surprises when I convert to CMYK mode.

Notes

The View > Proof Colors command relies on the choices you've specified in the Edit > Color Settings dialog box. If you end up changing those settings before you convert to CMYK mode, then the Proof Colors command won't accurately reflect your end results. I'll walk you through what's needed in the Color Settings dialog box later in this chapter.

. . . .

View > Proof Colors was called View > Preview > CMYK in older versions of Photoshop.

By now, you might be thinking "why the heck doesn't he just shut up about color and teach me color correction!" I want you to really understand all the color problems you might encounter in Photoshop. Otherwise I'd just be teaching you how to click buttons and then you'd find yourself up against a brick wall when you encounter any out-of-the-ordinary problems. And then you'd really hate me.

RGB: Don't Leave Home Without It

Hands down, I choose to work in RGB mode and convert to CMYK later. Even though you have to be a bit more careful working in RGB, I've found that the benefits far outweigh the bit of extra effort you need put out to work in that mode. I switch to CMYK when I consider my image complete, or when I need to do one of the few things that isn't possible in RGB mode—like creating a black-only shadow (although I'll show you how to get around that in the Channels chapter).

Let me show you why RGB should be your mode of choice, and then I promise we'll get on with actual color correction. Open a color image, choose Image > Duplicate, and then change the mode of the duplicate—you want one to be in RGB and the other in CMYK mode. Move them so you can easily see both at the same time and they don't overlap.

Better Adjustments

In the RGB image, try this: Choose Image > Adjust > Desaturate. That will pull all the color out of your image. Try the same command on the CMYK image and see what you get. The RGB image should look fine, but the CMYK one will look more brown. Most adjustments in Photoshop will give you better results if applied in RGB mode, for which many of Photoshop's adjustments are optimized.

More Filters

Now, click on the RGB image to make it active and then look through all the choices that appear in the filter menu. Every single filter works in RGB mode—over 100 in all. Try the same thing with the CMYK image (**Figure 8.16**). Dozens of filters are gone!

Better Filters

Click back on your RGB image, choose Filter > Stylize > Emboss, and use the default settings. The Emboss effect looks pretty good; subtle and attractive. But now try the

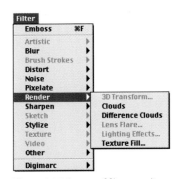

Figure 8.16 Dozens of filters are disabled when working in CMYK mode.

Note

The majority of Photoshop's filters don't deal properly with black ink. They often end up using just as much black as the other colors of ink, when black should only be used in the shadow areas of the image. This often results in overly dark images.

same commands on the CMYK image (**Figures 8.17 and 8.18**). Yuck! So, I repeat: most of the filters work better in RGB mode.

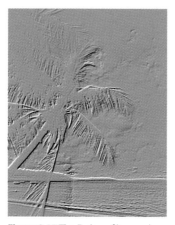 

Figure 8.17 The Emboss filter works as expected in RGB mode.

Figure 8.18 Embossing an image in CMYK mode produces a dark brown result.

Better Fadeouts

Grab the CD from the back of this book and open the file called "green glow.psd." I created this image using the most vivid green that was reproducible in CMYK mode—100% cyan and yellow. Click on your foreground color, type in the same numbers I used to create the green, and then compare that to the glow you see. I think we can do much better than that! Let's find out how.

Before we mess with this image, choose Image > Duplicate so we have two versions. Go to the duplicate image and convert it to RGB (choose Don't Flatten when prompted, so we still have the layers in RGB mode). Ahh, much better. You see? Your image blending will look superior if you do all your layers work in RGB mode. Then, convert it back to CMYK mode, but be sure to flatten the layers together—otherwise, Photoshop will re-blend all the layers in the less-than-ideal CMYK mode. Go ahead and convert the image to CMYK mode, choosing Flatten Image when prompted (**Figures 8.19 and 8.20**).

Figure 8.19 Layer blending in CMYK mode often produces less-than-ideal results.

Figure 8.20 You'll get better results if you flatten your image before converting to CMYK mode.

Better Blending

Photoshop offers dozens of Blending Modes (found at the top of the Layers palette and elsewhere) that are extremely powerful. You won't be surprised to hear that I find that the majority of them work better in RGB mode. Just open the file called "button.psd" from the CD at the back of the book. Convert it to CMYK mode without flattening it. Then choose Undo and try it again, but this time flatten the image during the conversion. See the difference (**Figures 8.21 and 8.22**)! If the blending is finalized in RGB mode, it will look better. That's why it's pretty important to flatten your image when converting to CMYK mode.

Figure 8.21 Flatten your images before converting to maintain the look of your image.

Figure 8.22 Failing to flatten your images can cause color and brightness to shift.

Figure 8.23 When bigger isn't better. CMYK files are always larger than RGB files.

Smaller files

Open any RGB image and take a look at the number that appears near the lower left. Convert the image to CMYK mode and watch that number change. The number indicates the approximate file size of your image. CMYK files are always larger than RGB files (**Figure 8.23**).

Easier Corrections

Color correction is simply easier in RGB mode. Remember when we were talking about how screwed up the inks are in CMYK mode? That makes color correction in CMYK much more complex.

More Flexibility

If you color-correct your image in CMYK mode, then you'd better be prepared to use it for just one purpose—a magazine, newspaper, brochure, etc. The adjustments will have been made with that specific output in mind, with settings tailored to the particular medium (for example, newspapers use less ink than brochures). With RGB color correction, the corrected image can be used for any output and resolution, and there is no need to change any of the steps you go through. That's not the case in CMYK mode!

RGB Recap

Does all this stuff make sense? If so, then you can see why it's a good idea to work in RGB mode. I'm not saying that CMYK mode is bad. But since your image is captured in RGB, displayed in RGB, and perceived by your eyes as RGB, while the inks used for CMYK mode are less than ideal, then doesn't it make sense to work in RGB mode for as long as possible? (The only time I perform color correction in CMYK mode is when someone gives me an image that's already in CMYK mode.)

There are plenty of people out there who work exclusively in CMYK, and who refuse to work in RGB or acknowledge its benefits. When you run across one of those people, listen to everything they say—take notes, even—and then use any techniques they mention, *after* you convert to

CMYK mode. They've got a lot of good ideas and expertise, but don't ignore RGB altogether.

If you've read this far, you already know all of the concepts that you'll need to perform color correction. You just have to find out how to organize the information and apply it to an image. So, let's jump in and start applying our knowledge.

Use *Gray* to Fix Color?!?

Do you remember how to make gray in RGB mode? Equal amounts of red, green, and blue, right? Let's open an image and see if we can find an area that should be gray. Then we can look in the Info palette to see if it really *is* gray in Photoshop—all without trusting your monitor or eyes! Open the image on the CD that's called "make gray.jpg." The wall behind the firefighting equipment should be gray. If the RGB numbers in the Info palette aren't equal—no matter what it looks like on your monitor—it's not gray. If it's not gray, then it must be contaminated with color (**Figure 8.24**). But would that color contaminate only the gray area? I doubt it. Then why not use the wall as an area to measure what's wrong with the entire image, so we can fix it? Let's give it a try.

How could those contaminating colors get in there? Here are a few potential culprits: indoor, artificial lighting (you *know* how "off" that can be); temperature of the chemicals used to develop the film being too hot or too cool; inappropriate filters used in a photographic enlarger when your prints are being made; and aging bulbs in a scanner that might shift the colors during the scanning process. We're going to use the Curves dialog box to make our adjustment. But don't worry, you don't have to remember much about the last chapter to do this. Here's what you need to know:

▶ Clicking on the curve will add a point.

▶ The Input number indicates what you are changing.

▶ The Output number determines what you'll end up with in the area you are changing.

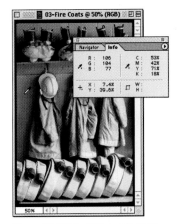

Figure 8.24 If the RGB numbers are not equal, then that area is not gray.

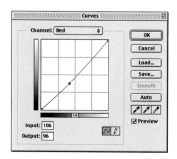

Figure 8.25 The numbers you enter will move the point to the correct position.

Figure 8.26 When you're done, the area should be gray. The left numbers indicate what was originally in the image; the right numbers indicate the result of our adjustment.

Put your cursor on the gray wall. Now glance over at the Info palette and write down the RGB numbers. In order to make that wall area a *real* gray, we'll need to make those RGB numbers equal. But we don't want to change the *brightness* of the wall. To make sure that doesn't happen, let's just average the RGB numbers so we maintain about the same amount of light as is currently there, using a balanced amount of red, green, and blue. You can use a calculator to average the numbers. Now that we know what we're starting with (from the Info Palette) and what we want to end up with (from the calculator), we can adjust our image.

If you choose Image > Adjust > Curves and leave the menu at the top set to RGB, you'll end up changing red, green, and blue in equal amounts, which would just change the brightness of the image. (That's what we did in the last chapter.) What you want to do is start by choosing Red from the pop-up menu at the top of the Curves dialog box. Next, click anywhere on the curve to add a point. Then let's make sure that point is in the right place to make the change we need (**Figure 8.25**). Click on the Input number and type in the red value you wrote down from the Info palette. That should move the point horizontally until it's above the shade we need to change. Your image might look pretty weird now, but pay no attention to that until we're done with everything. Now click on the output number and enter what we got when we averaged the Info palette numbers. That should move the point up or down until it's at the correct height to make the change we need. Now choose Green from that menu and do the same thing all over again—just add a point and then enter the Info palette number for green (the one you wrote down) for Input and the other number (the averaged one) for Output. Finally, choose Blue from the menu, add a point, and type in the correct Input and Output numbers. It's now safe to peek at your image (**Figure 8.26**). The wall should be gray! If it's not, and you're quite sure you followed the steps correctly, your monitor is way out of whack and may need calibration.

But now, look back at the three curves we applied to this image (**Figures 8.27 to 8.29**). We measured what was wrong with the image in the gray areas, but our adjustment changed the entire image. That's logical enough, because whatever is wrong with the gray areas is also affecting the rest of the image. But when you look at those curves, does it look like we *really* changed the whole image? Almost—but not quite. We didn't change the brightest and darkest areas. So, we really haven't finished our color correction until we've adjusted the whole thing. But at least we saw that our concept of measuring and adjusting gray works. Now let's see how we can expand on this technique to improve an image even more.

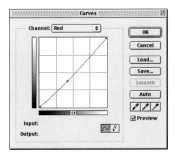

Figure 8.27 The red curve.

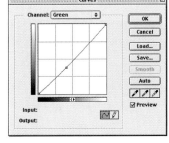

Figure 8.28 The green curve.

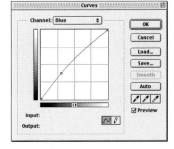

Figure 8.29 The blue curve.

Professional Color Correction

We will look at the process of professional color correction in six parts: achieving good contrast, balancing colors, fine-tuning skin tones, saturation, sharpening, and converting to CMYK. You don't always have to perform all six parts, but the more you do, the better your result will be.

Achieve Good Contrast

No matter how you reproduce an image, you'll never be able to achieve as much contrast as was present when the photograph was taken. The brightest white your computer monitor can produce is nowhere near as bright as the one you'll see in real life. And the paper you print on isn't even as white as your computer screen. The same problem exists with the dark area of your image; your monitor can get only so dark, and ink on paper is not very dark; again, they pale in comparison to shades you can see in the real world. Given all this, you will usually want to use the full range of available contrast to get your image as close to reality as possible.

Before you attempt to pull out the full contrast of your image, you'll want to discard any information that won't be used in the end result. If you are going to use only a small portion of your image, or it contains a black border, crop the image first (**Figure 8.30**). There are many ways to crop an image (Crop tool, Image > Crop, Image > Canvas Size, and so on), but I usually just make a selection using the Marquee tool and then choose Image > Crop (**Figure 8.31**).

Figure 8.30 Original image contains lots of space that won't be used, and has white around its edge. (© 1998 PhotoDisc)

Figure 8.31 Crop the image so it contains only the information you want to use.

To make sure that your image doesn't look flat and lifeless, let's optimize the contrast. To do this, you'll need to have the full range from white to black. If you click on your foreground color and choose white, you'll notice that the RGB numbers change to 255R, 255G, and 255B. Conversely, if you choose black, you'd see 0R, 0G, and 0B. Well, then, wouldn't it make sense that in order to get the full range from white to black, you'd also have to have a full range of red, green, and blue? You can get the most out of your image by choosing Image > Adjust > Levels (**Figure 8.32**) and adjusting the sliders for each individual color (that is, don't use the default combined RGB choice from the menu; that will limit the amount of contrast you can get before you damage the image). Change the pop-up menu at the top of the dialog box to Red. Now you can start messing with the sliders: pull in the upper left and upper right sliders until they touch the beginning and end of the histogram. That will make sure your image contains the full range of red light and get us on our way to optimal contrast.

Notes

Some histograms already extend all the way across the area available and therefore already have good contrast and don't need to be adjusted with Levels.

For information about how to work with the Levels dialog box, see Chapter 6, "Optimizing Grayscale Images."

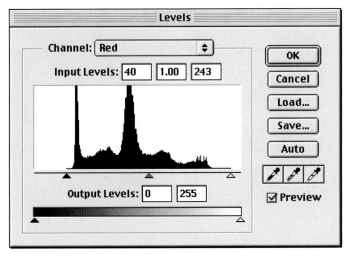

Figure 8.32 Choose Red from the Channel pop-up menu, then move in the upper right and upper left sliders until they touch the histogram.

After you have adjusted the Red channel, you can perform the same type of adjustment to the Green and Blue channels. Occasionally you'll find a histogram that contains a few stray pixels that aren't really connected to the main histogram, as shown in **Figure 8.33.** When this happens, you can ignore them and go right to the first connected part of the histogram. But you don't want to damage your image, so make sure the only pixels you pass by are those that really look like they don't belong.

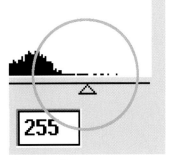

Figure 8.33 If you encounter any stray pixels that are a few pixels away from the main part of the histogram, pass them by.

The process you've gone through up to this point should give you the full range from 0 to 255 with all three colors. If that's the case, then it's possible to have true white and black in the image (compare **Figures 8.34** and **8.35**). If you found yourself moving some of the sliders further than others, then the colors will have also changed because you created a different blend of red, green, and blue. 98% of the time, this technique will improve your image. But that doesn't guarantee that gray areas are not contaminated with color. And if a gray area has the potential of containing color, then the entire image might be contaminated with an unwanted color cast.

Figure 8.34 Before adjusting contrast by using Levels.

Figure 8.35 Result of achieving good contrast.

Balance Your Colors

To eliminate any color casts that are in your image, you'll need to look for color contamination in gray areas of your image and then use that information to help correct the whole image. There are three standard areas of your image that should usually be a shade of gray. The first one is the brightest area of the image, which is usually known as the highlight. The second is the darkest area of the image, which is usually known as the shadow. (On most photos, the highlight and shadow areas shouldn't contain color.) The third area is a gray object in the scene. We'll first locate these areas, and then we'll set up Photoshop to monitor what happens to them as we adjust the image. (That way you don't have to write everything down.)

You'll use the Color Sampler tool to place "sample points" (that look like little numbered crosshairs) on each area of the image that is going to be adjusted. The Color Sampler tool is hidden in with the Eyedropper tool. Set its sample size setting to 3 by 3 Average (**Figure 8.36**) so that it won't get messed up if we place it on top of a speck of noise. Instead, it will average a small area to determine what color it is. Now let's find those areas and place some samples.

Notes

To remove sample points, Option-click (Macintosh) or Alt-click (Windows) the points, or drag them to the edge of the screen, still using the Color Sampler tool.

....

The highlight is an area that should contain detail, so don't pick the brightest part of a metallic object, a light bulb, or a reflection on the edge of a glass object; those areas are known as specular highlights and should not contain detail.

....

You can use the up and down arrow keys to change the Threshold setting.

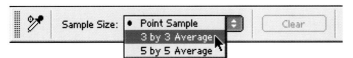

Figure 8.36 Before using the Color Sampler tool, set its Sample Size setting to 3 by 3 Average.

Locate Highlight

First let's locate the highlight. This is the brightest area that should still contain detail. You'll often find it in a white shirt collar or button, a Styrofoam cup, the whites of someone's eyes, or a sheet of paper. In **Figure 8.35** on the previous page, the brightest white falls on the handlebar grip next to the boy's left hand.

I hate having to guess at anything when I'm working on my images, so here's how I find the brightest area. Choose Image > Adjust > Threshold and move the slider all the way to the right; then slowly move it toward the left (**Figure 8.37**). You don't want to find the very brightest speck (that could be a scratch), so be sure to look for a general area at least five or six pixels in size. Once you've found the correct area, hold down the Shift key and click on that part of your image to add a color sample to that area. (You only have to hold Shift if you're still in an adjustment dialog box like Threshold.) Click Cancel to get out of Threshold, and then open the Info palette to see what is in that area (**Figure 8.38**).

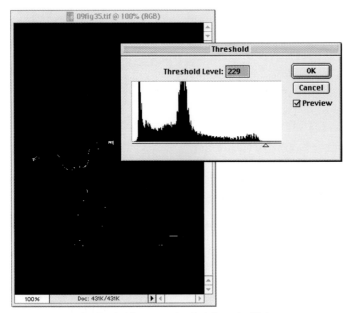

Figure 8.38 After using the Color Sampler tool, you should see an additional color readout in the Info palette.

Figure 8.37 Use the Threshold command to find elusive highlights.

Locate Shadow

When I mention the shadow, I don't mean a traditional shadow like the kind cast from an object; instead, I'm talking about the darkest area of an image. All images have a shadow area, but it can sometimes be hard to locate because there may be multiple candidates.

You can use the same trick I described for finding the highlight: the trusty Threshold dialog box. This time, you start with the slider all the way to the left. This will show you where the darkest area of the image is hiding. You don't want to find the darkest speck (that could be dust), so be sure to look for a general area at least five or six pixels in size.

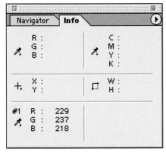

Figure 8.39 After adding a second sample point, you should see two readouts at the bottom of the Info palette.

Once you've located the shadow, Shift-click on that area to place a sample point on top of it, and then click Cancel to get out of the Threshold dialog box. Now you should see two extra readouts at the bottom of the Info palette, one for the highlight and one for the shadow, as shown in **Figure 8.39**.

Locate Gray

Now we're looking for any area that should be gray in the final image—not bluish gray or pinkish gray, but pure gray (also known as neutral gray). You might have to really hunt for a gray; it is not always obvious. It could be a sweatshirt, a white shirt, or the edge of a book. If you have any doubt at all that the area you have chosen should be gray, then you most likely picked the wrong spot. But don't try too hard; not every image contains a true gray. For example, you might not be able to find one in a photograph of a forest. If you can't find one, then (of course) don't adjust it.

On the other hand, you might run across an image that has dozens of gray areas to choose from. In that case, try to pick one that is not overly bright or dark, because we are already adjusting the highlight and shadow of the image. The closer we get to a middle gray, the more effective your adjustment will be.

Once again, when you find what you want, slap a sample point on it, and notice that you get yet another readout from the Info palette (refer to **Figure 8.40**). But this time, since we're not using the Threshold dialog box, there is no need to Shift-click on the image, although you do have to be using the Color Sampler tool.

What We're Shootin' For

The color correction technique we're going through will work for any kind of output (monitor, inkjet, slide, etc.), but we'll base this setting on a printing press. Why? Because the setting for print works great for the Internet, video, and everything else, so if we get it right, we know our adjustments will work universally.

In the sections above, you located the highlight, shadow, and (if any) gray areas. Now we want to make sure they don't have a color cast. To do this, you'll need to adjust their RGB numbers so that they are equal in each of those areas. Refer to the three Sampler readouts at the bottom of the Info palette. If the RGB numbers are equal, then the image doesn't have a color cast (I really doubt that's the case).

Figure 8.40 A neutral gray is any area that should appear as just plain gray, with no hint of color. After you use the Color Sampler tool to click on a neutral gray, you should find three readouts in the Info palette.

We also want to make the brightest area of the image as bright as possible, and the darkest area as dark as possible, all without losing detail. The combination of all of these adjustments will allow us to use the full range of our limited output device (monitor, printer, etc.).

You don't want the highlight to become pure white because it would look too bright. You want to reserve pure white for those areas that shine light directly into the camera lens (light bulbs, shiny reflections, etc.). That means you want the highlight to be just a tad bit darker than white.

If you remember back to the chapter on grayscale images (Chapter 6), I mentioned that the lightest percentage of ink you can use on a printing press is usually 3% (5% for some newspapers). That means we don't want to use less than 3% of any ink in the brightest part of our image; otherwise, we might lose detail. But we're adjusting our image in RGB mode, and when you do that, you'll be using a numbering system that ranges from 0–255, not 0–100%. So let's figure out how to create a minimum of 3% ink in RGB mode. Click on your foreground color to open the Color Picker. Then, set the saturation setting (S) to 0 and the brightness setting (B) to 100%, and click on the brightness radio button (B). Slowly move down the slider that is attached to the vertical bar (which should contain grays) until the magenta (M) and yellow (Y) readouts indicate at least 3%. Cyan (C) will be higher, but don't worry about that. At this point, the numbers will show you exactly what RGB values are needed to produce that much ink—in this case, 240R 240G 240B (**Figure 8.41**).

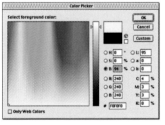

Figure 8.41 A good highlight value is 240R 240G 240B.

Now, on to the dark side. We're going to make the darkest area of your image pure black (0R 0G 0B) in order to use the full range your computer monitor is capable of displaying. Black wouldn't be a good choice if you are really outputting to a printing press (you'd lose a lot of detail), but we'll set it up so that Photoshop will adjust your image automatically if you have to convert to CMYK mode. That way we'll be guaranteed that no detail will be lost no matter what the output. Remember, we're trying to perform color correction where the end result can be used for any purpose.

The setting for the neutral gray area varies depending on how bright the area is. To determine the exact setting needed, all you have to do is analyze the numbers that appear in the Info palette (the third readout was for the gray area). We'll use the same technique as we did when we were first learning the general concepts of color correction. Remember when we just averaged the red, green, and blue numbers that showed up in the Info palette? Just do the same thing here.

Making the Adjustment

Now it's finally time to make our color-balancing adjustments. First we'll adjust the highlight, shadow, and gray areas, and then we'll take a look at our image and see if any other areas need tweaking. To start out, create a new adjustment layer by choosing Layer > New Adjustment Layer > Curves.

Since we are attempting to balance the red, green, and blue light in three areas, you need to work on the individual color channels by changing the pop-up menu at the top of the Curves dialog box. You'll add a total of three adjustment points to the curve: one for the highlight, one for the shadow, and one for gray. For each new point you create, you'll take a number from the Info palette to determine the proper Input setting, and then use your predetermined Output settings for highlight and shadow (240 and 0, respectively) and the averaged setting you determined for the gray area.

Let's start with the highlight adjustment. Look over to the first set of numbers at the bottom of the Info palette; they should be for the highlight of the image (**Figure 8.42**). You will see that each of the RGB readouts show two numbers separated by a slash. The number on the left is what was in the image before the adjustment; the number on the right is what you will end up with after the adjustment. (The two numbers are identical because you haven't made any changes yet.)

To change the amount of red being used for the highlight, be sure the pop-up menu at the top of the Curves dialog

Notes

Since grays in RGB mode contain equal amounts of all three colors, the color that is the farthest off is the one that is creating the majority of the color cast. When I don't have a calculator around, I just average the two numbers that are closest together and then set all three RGB numbers to that setting. It's not quite as precise as averaging all three numbers (the brightness of that area might change a little), but it's easier to do in your head.

In earlier versions of Photoshop (pre-6.0), you created an adjustment layer by choosing Layer > New > Adjustment Layer and then choosing Curves from the dialog box that appeared.

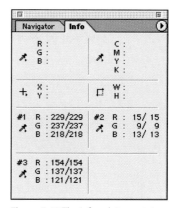

Figure 8.42 The Info palette contains all the Input settings you'll need when using the Curves dialog box to adjust your image.

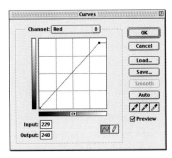

Figure 8.43 Adjust the upper right point until the Input number matches what is in the Info palette and the output number reads 240.

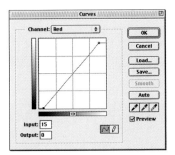

Figure 8.44 Adjust the lower left point until the Input number matches what is in the Info palette and the output number reads 0.

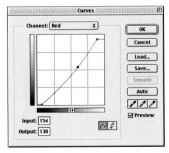

Figure 8.45 Add a point to the middle of the curve to adjust the neutral gray setting.

box is set to Red. Now look at the brightest area of the gradient at the bottom of the Curves dialog box. Go straight up from there and you should find a point on the curve (**Figure 8.43**). That point affects the brightest part of the image (also known as the highlight). Go ahead and click on it to make the numbers at the bottom of the dialog box available for editing. The Input number determines what you're changing, so look in the Info palette to see how much red light we have in the brightest part of the photo. That will be the first readout; use that number for the Input value at the bottom of the Curves dialog box. When you enter a number there, you're really moving the point you clicked on so that it's directly above the shade of red that you need to change. Now enter 240 for the output number (because that value will make it so that we end up with 3% of each ink in CMYK mode). That should move the point down a bit to the brightest part of the image that is not white. Congratulations—you've got the highlight adjusted! But don't click OK yet, because we're going to do all these adjustments at once (highlight, shadow, gray).

To adjust the shadow area, click on the point that is directly above the darkest part of the gradient. Now click on the Input field and grab the number from readout #2 at the bottom of the Info palette. (Remember that we're still working on red, so be sure to grab the right number.) We want that area to become black, so enter 0 for the output number and notice that the point you were working on moved to make that change happen (**Figure 8.44**).

Now we'll adjust the gray area. With the last two adjustments, Photoshop already had the points that we needed, but this time we're going to have to add one. Click anywhere along the curve to add a point—but not near the points that are already there, because you might move them by accident. Other than that, it doesn't really matter where you add a point because the Input and Output numbers you use will determine where that point ends up. Now set the Input number to what you find in the Info palette (the red readout for sample point #3). To figure out the Output setting, use the number you got when you averaged the RGB numbers that were in the Info palette (**Figure 8.45**).

After you have three points on the curve for red, do the same thing for green and blue. For each of those colors, you'll get your Input numbers from the Info palette. (Again, make sure you grab the right numbers—red readouts for red adjustments, green for green, blue for blue.) The output numbers will be exactly the same as what you used when you adjusted the red stuff (highlight=240, shadow=0, gray=average of Info palette numbers). When you have completed this step, your image should be free of any color casts. Compare **Figures 8.46 and 8.47**.

Figure 8.46 Before color correction, the image contains a slight red cast (look at the road surface).

Figure 8.47 After correction, the cast has been removed.

We have now attempted to adjust three areas of our image—highlight, shadow, gray—to eliminate any color cast from the whole image. This technique is almost always the best place to start, and the one that will be satisfactory for many images. Of course, there are always exceptions; we can't always adjust all three areas. (Remember the sunset picture, and the ones where there isn't a true gray.) And even if you can adjust all three areas, sometimes you'll need to tweak any skin tones, because if they are at all off, people will notice right away.

Adjust Skin Tones

You might be thinking that I'm going to give you some kind of magic formula for creating great skin tones (kind of like what I did with grays), but if I give you just one formula, then every skin tone in nature's vast diversity would look identical in your images! I'd much rather show you how to get a unique formula for each color of skin you might run across—Asian skin, olive skin, sunburnt skin, fair skin, and all the different shades of black skin. Even better, we can do all that without trusting your monitor at all. (Of course they will still look good on your screen, but unless you've calibrated your screen using a hardware device, then you shouldn't make critical decisions based on your screen image.)

You know how you can buy images from companies like Stockbyte and PhotoSpin—there are literally dozens of companies that sell royalty-free stock photography. If you call one of those companies and ask them for a catalog of their images, they'll be more than happy to send you a really thick book chock-full of images (it will either be free, or they might charge you for shipping and handling). At the back of that book will be a CD that contains tiny versions of those images, complete with the stock photo company's logo slapped in the middle of it so you'd never use it for a real project. But we don't care about that, because right now we're after something else—most of them contain a veritable treasure trove of flesh that you can transform into your own personal stockpile of skin tones! So, flip through one of those wonderful catalogs, pick the person who has the skin tone that best matches your needs, and then open the corresponding image from the CD at the back of the catalog. Next, use the Eyedropper tool and click on an area of the skin that is a medium brightness (**Figure 8.48**). Now click on your foreground color to see the RGB formula needed to create that exact color!

Figure 8.48 Reference photo from a stock photo catalog. (© 2001 StockByte, www.stockbyte.com

Now let's figure out how to use that information to improve another image. Open the one you need to correct and add a color sampler to the area that contains the troublesome skin. Be sure to click in an area with medium brightness, similar to the level in the other image. That should give you an extra readout in the Info palette (#4 if you still have the three we used earlier in this chapter).

Next, click on the tiny triangle that shows up next to that new readout in the Info palette (**Figure 8.49**). Choose HSB from the menu, note the brightness (B) setting, and then set that menu back to RGB. Now, click on your foreground color to look at the color from the stock photo again. We want to use that basic color, but we don't want to change the brightness of our image much. To accomplish that, change the brightness (B) setting to what you saw in the photo you are attempting to color-correct and then write down the RGB numbers that show up in the Color Picker (**Figure 8.50**). That tells us how to use the color from the stock photo after changing its brightness to match the image we're going to apply it to.

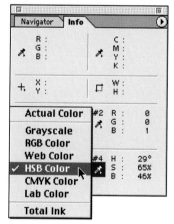

Figure 8.49 Note the brightness of the area you are working on.

Figure 8.50 Change the Brightness setting to find the perfect skin-tone setting.

Now it's time to adjust the skin tone in our image. Remember earlier when we used an adjustment layer to change the highlight, shadow, and gray areas? That adjustment layer should still be in the Layers palette, and we can use it to fine-tune our adjustment. Take a quick look at your image, and try to determine if the area of the skin that has a color sampler on it is brighter or darker than the gray area you adjusted earlier. If you didn't end

Figure 8.51 After adjusting for skin tones, the skin should look similar to the stock photo version. Compare to Figure 48.

up adjusting gray, then don't worry about that. Go ahead and double-click on the Curves icon to the left side of the adjustment layer to get back into the Curves dialog box. We'll add one more point to each of the red, green, and blue curves. You'll have to put this new point on either side of the point that you used to adjust gray (the one that's already in the middle). If the skin tone is darker than the gray area, then put it on the left of the gray point, because that's where darker stuff is in the gradient below; otherwise put it on the right. Now type in the number you see in the Info palette (the one on the left) and then type in the number we calculated a few minutes ago for the Output. Repeat the same steps for green and blue, and your skin tone should look much better (**Figure 8.51**).

The more you get used to using this technique, the less you'll have to rely on that catalog. You'll get used to knowing that the more red you pull out of your image, the more tan someone looks, and that the balance between green and blue determines the fairness of someone's skin.

If the skin-tone adjustment was a little too much for you to handle, then just start off by adjusting the highlight, shadow, and gray areas, and come back to this chapter after you've gotten comfortable with those. That might make it a little easier to understand and implement. The general concept is easy (and sneaky), but the execution isn't quite as simple as all that, because we have to make sure we don't mess up our earlier adjustments.

Specular Highlights

There's only one problem with the color-correction technique we just talked about. The brightest part of our image should be around 3% gray, which is perfect for reproducing most images. But if your image contains any bright, shiny objects, there will most likely be very bright reflections from the light source (also known as specular highlights). If we leave those areas at 3% gray, they will look rather dull and lifeless. Since those shiny spots don't usually contain detail, we can enhance them by making them brighter than 3% gray. To accomplish that, go back to the curves you used to color-correct your image and look at the area of the curve above white (**Figure 8.52**). You want that area to be all the way in the corner, so grab the Pencil tool and replace the flat part of the curve with a line that extends into the corner (**Figure 8.53**). Now those previously dull specular highlights will jump off the page and all your shiny objects will have much more life to them.

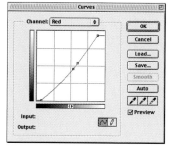

Figure 8.52 The flat part of the curve above the bright areas will make it so that no part of the image will be brighter than 3% gray.

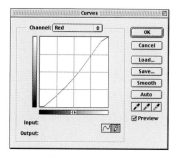

Figure 8.53 Use the Pencil tool to extend the curve all the way into the corner, which will allow reflections to be brighter than 3% gray.

It might have taken me over a dozen pages to describe how to color-correct an image; but the actual process, once you're used to it, should hardly ever take more than two minutes. Once you're happy with your colors and have removed any color casts, you'll most likely want to sharpen the image and possibly tweak the brightness, contrast, or saturation.

Further Brightness and Contrast Adjustments

The process we've gone through up until now was designed to correct the colors in the image. Now that the colors are better, you can also use all the ideas I showed you in the Curves chapter to further enhance the brightness and contrast of the image. Just be careful not to shift the colors of the image. (You can prevent that by setting the blending mode of all future curves adjustments to Luminosity, as was explained in the last chapter.)

But adjusting color, contrast, and brightness still can't guarantee that your images are as vivid as they could be. Following are two more techniques for making your images pop.

Optimize Saturation

Once you've adjusted your colors, you can choose Layer > New Adjustment Layer > Hue/Saturation and increase the Saturation setting. Choose View > Gamut Warning to see how you're doing; if no gray appears over your image, then you can keep increasing the saturation until you start seeing small areas of gray (**Figure 8.54**). You've gone too far if you see large, concentrated gray blobs on your image. After you've adjusted the image, you can get rid of those gray areas by turning off the Gamut Warning.

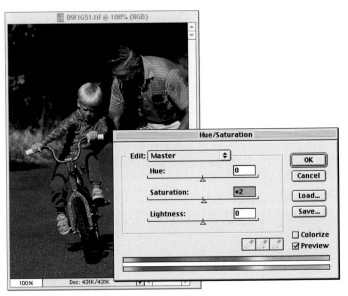

Figure 8.54 Keep increasing the saturation until a lot of gray shows up.

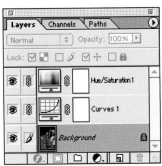

Figure 8.55 Merge the adjustment layers into the main image to simplify the document.

Once you've gotten to this point, you should simplify your document before you move on to sharpening the image. You can do that by clicking on the bottom layer (the one that contains your original image) and then clicking on the box that appears on the left side of each of the adjustment layers. Now you can choose Merge Linked from the side menu of the Layers palette to combine those adjustment layers with your image (**Figure 8.55**).

Sharpen the Image

I find that almost every image I work with can be improved by applying the Unsharp Mask filter. We dealt with that filter back in Chapter 6 when we talked about making grayscale images look good. When it comes to color images, you can use the same concepts we discussed in the Grayscale chapter, but you might find that the halos that show up after sharpening an image will be distracting. For instance, you might find that after sharpening an image of a pink dress, bright red halos appear around the edge of the dress.

To prevent off-color halos, you can use a special blending mode in Photoshop: choose Filter > Sharpen > Unsharp Mask and sharpen the image just like we did with a grayscale image. Once you are done sharpening the image, choose Edit > Fade, and then choose Luminosity from the blending mode pop-up menu (**Figure 8.56**). This will make it so that whatever you did last—in this case, sharpening—can only change the brightness of the image, but not the colors!

If you are *not* planning to print your image on a printing press, then you can sit back, smile, and skip the next step, because you are all done with color correction and can go ahead and save your image. And I really do mean a printing press; if your end result will be sent to a desktop color printer, the Internet, video, or a 35mm slide, you should leave your image in RGB mode. But if you're planning on printing your image on a real live printing press, then you need to know how to convert it to CMYK mode. Otherwise, your image might output as grayscale instead of color!

CMYK Issues

When you convert to CMYK mode, Photoshop uses the settings in the Edit > Color Settings dialog box (**Figure 8.57**) to figure out what type of paper and press you'll be using. If you don't set things up correctly in that dialog box before converting to CMYK mode, then you are really asking for trouble. For example, using the amount of ink that would

Note

In previous versions of Photoshop, the Fade command is found on the Filter menu.

Figure 8.56 Using the Luminosity blending mode prevents odd-colored halos.

be appropriate for a glossy brochure, but then printing the image in a newspaper, would be like taking a penicillin shot designed for a horse—it's way too much ink and would really mess up your printing job. So, let's see what we need to do.

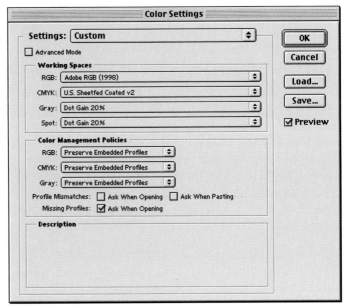

Figure 8.57 The settings in the Color Settings dialog box determine what happens during an RGB to CMYK mode change.

In order for Photoshop to correctly convert your image to CMYK mode, it will need a bunch of information about how the image will be reproduced. In the CMYK menu of the Color Settings dialog box, you'll find a whole slew of choices. The names listed in this menu are actually just profiles. Each profile contains information including the exact shades of cyan, magenta, yellow, and black ink that will be used to print your image; how much darker things will look when the ink absorbs into the paper; and more. A profile is really a convenient container of information that replaces Photoshop 5's CMYK Setup settings (**Figure 8.58**). You just have to make sure you have a profile selected that reflects the printing conditions that will be used to reproduce your image before you convert to CMYK mode. I'll attempt to translate their names and then show you how to get better results.

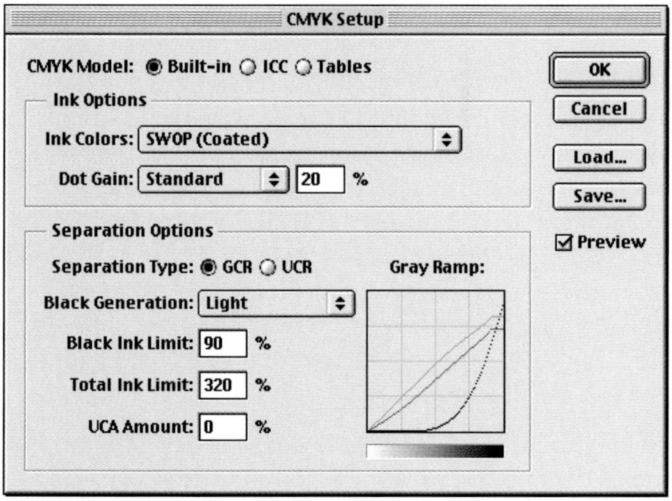

Figure 8.58 Photoshop 5's CMYK setup dialog box.

Here's the rundown on choosing stock for many standard publication types:

▶ Use U.S. Sheetfed Coated for glossy brochures.

▶ Use U.S. Sheetfed Uncoated for dull-finish brochures.

▶ Use U.S. Web Coated (SWOP) for magazines.

▶ Use U.S. Web Uncoated for dull-finish publications.

The profiles that come with Photoshop are making huge assumptions about the paper and inks that you are using. That means it's possible to get a much better result if you happened to have a custom profile created specifically for the paper and press you'll be printing on. And because every paper and ink set would need a different profile, you'd have to get each one from your printing company. The problem is that the majority of the printing companies out there don't have profiles available for their commercial presses, but it never hurts to ask. If you find that your printer doesn't have a custom profile available and you aren't getting acceptable results from the profiles I mentioned above, you might want to bypass profiles altogether and set up the CMYK conversion the traditional way. You'll find information about that on the CD at the back of this book.

Printing to a Desktop Color Printer

I've already mentioned that I usually work in RGB mode for as long as possible and only convert to CMYK mode when I consider my image complete, or when I need to do something that isn't possible in RGB. I also prefer to print to a desktop color printer from RGB mode, even if my end result will be sent to a printing press. The bottom line is, you don't *have* to convert just to print in-house, but there are a few settings you'll have to deal with to get the most accurate possible print.

When you choose File > Print, Photoshop will prompt you to make some choices (**Figure 8.59**). Let's take a look at them one by one. (To get to these settings, you might have to choose Adobe Photoshop 6.0 from a pop-up menu in the Print dialog box.) First, under the Source Space heading, choose Document if you'd like the printer to simulate what you saw on your screen, or choose Proof Setup if you'd like your desktop printer to simulate what your image will look like when printed on a printing press.

Second, in order for Photoshop to accurately simulate colors on your desktop printer, it has to know what colors of ink are built into that printer. All desktop printers use cyan, magenta, and yellow, but that doesn't mean they will all look the same. (Think about it; if you bought three different brands of red markers, you wouldn't expect all three to be the exact same shade of red, right?) So Photoshop reads a profile that describes the color of inks in your printer and a few other details (discussed a few paragraphs above). Most desktop color printers come with these profiles, but if you don't have one for yours, you should be able to download it off of the printer manufacturer's Web site. You need to be able to choose that from the Profile pop-up menu. If you don't have a profile, Photoshop has no idea what your results should look like, so you'd really be flying blind. Profiles are stored in the System Folder > Application Support > Adobe > Color > Profiles > Recommended (Mac) or Program Files > Common Files > Adobe > Color > Profiles > Recommended (Windows). If you get a custom profile for your printer, put it there.

Finally, you choose whether you'd like to simulate the paper color of a printing press. Choose Relative Colorimetric if you don't want to see the paper color or Absolute Colorimetric if you would like to simulate the paper stock (which might be a lot darker than the sheet of paper you have loaded into your desktop printer).

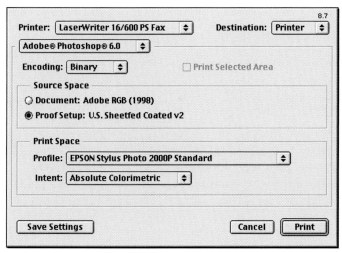

Figure 8.59 These settings determine what Photoshop will simulate when you print your image.

Closing Thoughts

There's no question that being introduced to color correction for the first time can be a little overwhelming. But look at it this way: if you were five years old and just learning how to write your name, the effort would seem Herculean. But by the time you're five and a half, writing your name is as easy as pie. So it will be with color correction after you've been through the process a few times. The techniques

Note

On the CD accompanying this book, you'll find a PDF file that supplements this chapter. The file, called "extras.pdf," contains the following topics related to CMYK color correction:

- Calculating highlight settings
- Calculating neutral grays
- Flesh tones
- Curves
- Traditional CMYK Setup settings

In the same file, you'll also find information about

- Correcting for scanner only
- Using unwanted colors
- Matching color between documents
- Enhancing blue skies
- Sharpening black channels

described in this chapter are the very same ones used by the high-paid color maestros who put out all of those ever-so-perfect glossy magazine ads. It will take you a while to really get the hang of these techniques, but once you do, it should take you less than two minutes to correct most images. And remember—you're infinitely better off if you can fix color problems at an early stage in the image creation process. And the more you understand about that process, the less fixing you'll have to do.

Here's one last bit of advice. Make sure to always correct your images separately before blending them together. That way, you will be able to maintain the color integrity of each component of your big picture.

Ben's Techno-Babble Decoder Ring

Neutral Gray—A pure gray that does not have any hint of color.

Specular Highlight—An intense reflection that contains little or no detail. You'll find specular highlights in jewelry, metallic objects, and very shiny surfaces.

Gamut—The range of colors that are reproducible on a particular device (monitor, printer, etc.).

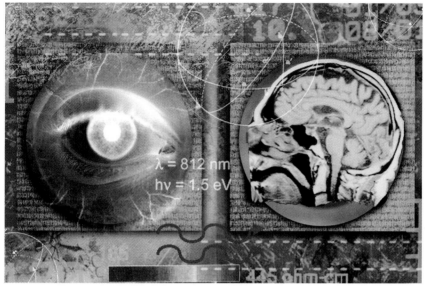

Courtesy of Naomi Shea, www.naomishea.com

Courtesy of Naomi Shea, www.naomishea.com

Courtesy of Stephen Wishny, www.portfolio.com/wishny

Courtesy of Stephen Wishny, www.portfolio.com/wishny

9 Channels

Why take the escalator when I have a perfectly good canoe right here?
–Austin Powers
in the movie "Austin Powers, International Man of Mystery"

Courtesy of Michael Slack, www.slackart.com

If you just did a double-take on the chapter quote and said, "huh, what?" then you reacted the same way that most people do the first time they hear about channels. Okay, at first glance, channels might be a little confusing. Let's just get that out in the open. But let's also not forget that confusion is not a fatal disease, and in this chapter, hopefully, you're going to get the cure. With the help of some plain, everyday language, we'll take a tour through channels, and you can see for yourself that there are no exotic mysteries, puzzles, or riddles about them.

To get to the root of all this confusion, you have to go back to when channels were first conceived and given their misbegotten name. The very name "channels" breeds confusion because it doesn't relate to anything in the real world, and so it doesn't mean anything to anybody. As a result, most people just give it a nickname. I've heard them called stencils, masks, friskets, rubyliths, and amberliths, to name a few. I don't know about you, but in the course of normal conversation (as opposed to Photoshop-speak), when I hear someone talk about channels, things like HBO, NBC, and CNN are the first ones that come to mind.

So, taking all of that into consideration, you might wonder what in blazes was Adobe thinking when they came up with that name? I can't answer that. But I can tell you that regardless of the hopeless misnomer, channels are absolutely essential to your work in Photoshop. Once you've mastered them, you will have one of Photoshop's most powerful tools at your beck and call.

Channels Are Worth the Pain!

To be fair, I have to tell you that a lot of people who try channels for the first time throw their hands in the air and give up. They convince themselves that they don't really need channels, and they learn how to patch things up in other ways. But I believe that if they really knew what they were missing, they'd take another crack at it.

Let's say you just met a secretary named Minnie. In her office there are two pieces of equipment: an old IBM Selectric typewriter and the best personal computer that money can buy. Whenever Minnie's boss gives her a memo to type, she immediately loads up the Selectric with a fresh piece of paper and starts rat-tatting away. "Minnie!" you ask, "Why don't you use the computer for that?" Minnie just gives you a dirty look over her bifocals. So you try to reason with her, "But, Minnie, what if you make a mistake, or the boss changes his mind? Wouldn't it be easier to have that memo stored in your computer?" Minnie lets out a long impatient sigh (the kind that only mothers can do justice to). Then she gives it to you straight: "Look, smartypants, maybe it *would* be easier, maybe it *wouldn't*, but whichever way you look at it, that thing is just too doggoned hard to learn." And with that, she swivels around, hunches over her beloved Selectric and finishes her memo.

Of course, everybody knows that Minnie is crazy as a loon not to use the computer. And anyone who uses a computer knows that, yes, it might have been a little challenging at first, but once you've learned it, how could you possibly live without it? That's exactly how it is with channels! Channels are so completely integrated into Photoshop that there's nothing you can do to your images without affecting the information that's stored in the Channels palette. And if they have that much influence on your images, wouldn't you want to know what they are all about? Of course you would.

Without channels, it would be impossible to save the shape of a selection so that you can get it back later. It would also be impossible to force a shadow to print with only black ink (which makes it look better). And you'd have terrible troubles working with metallic or fluorescent inks without the help of channels. So, let's take a headlong plunge into the not-so-mysterious world of channels. And for the purposes of this chapter, when we talk about them, we're going to be using just two terms: channels and masks.

Three Varieties of Channels

There are three varieties of channels: color channels, spot channels, and alpha channels (**Figure 9.1**). They all look about the same, but they perform completely different tasks. However, they do have some things in common: they have the same dimensions as the document that contains them; they can contain up to 256 shades of gray; and Photoshop treats them as if they were individual grayscale documents. Let's take a surface look at them; then we'll explore each one in depth.

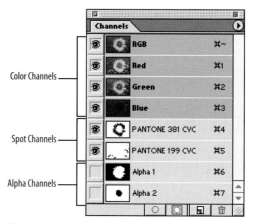

Figure 9.1 Channel types.

Color Channels

The topmost channels in the Channels palette are known as color channels because they keep track of all of the colors that will be printed and displayed. The names of these channels correspond to the mode your image is in (an RGB image will contain Red, Green, and Blue channels; a CMYK image will contain Cyan, Magenta, Yellow, and Black channels). So when you paint, edit, or apply a filter to your image, you're really changing the information in the color channels.

Sample Use: You've got an image taken by a digital camera. It's not just any image; it's your Granny blowing out candles on her ninetieth birthday. You know that pictures from digital cameras are notorious for looking "noisy," but this one takes the cake (so to speak). Your beloved Granny looks like her face is covered with blackheads. If you didn't know better, you'd probably just try to blur the image to get rid of the noise. But you *do* know better, because you've learned that if you did that, you'd end up removing the majority of the detail in the image. So instead, you switch over to color channels and start working on your image "under the hood." In just a few moments you've gotten rid of the noise and sharpened the overall image as well. Granny looks much better.

Spot Channels

Directly below the color channels are the spot channels. This type of channel is used in documents that will be printed using colors other than (or in addition to) cyan, magenta, yellow, and black. The name of a spot channel is usually the name of the ink that will be used (like PANTONE 185 CVC). Only documents that have been specifically set up for spot color work will contain this type of channel.

Sample Use: You're asked to create a "look" that resembles the cover of *Wired* magazine. You thumb through a few copies and notice that they go for the big eye-stopping colors: neon, fluorescent, metallic. You know—disco colors. You go to the standard Color Picker and choose a far-out shade of metallic purple not seen since the days of *Saturday Night Fever*. But you get flagged down by the CMYK Police: "Gamut Warning! Color Cannot Be Reproduced in CMYK, you idiot!" Nooo problem. Like a flash, you switch over to spot channels, where you confidently create your spaced-out color, knowing that you are also creating the necessary information needed by your printer to reproduce it accurately. Groovy.

Alpha Channels

Channels that appear at the bottom of the palette are called alpha channels. This is the real McCoy—the stuff people are usually talking about when they bring up channels, and the stuff they're most scared of. Alpha channels have user-defined names; or, if a name isn't supplied when a channel is created, Photoshop uses a generic name like

"Alpha 1." An alpha channel is a saved *selection*—it's that simple (well, almost that simple).

Sample use: You just spent the good part of an hour making an eye-straining selection of every curl and wisp of hair on a model who's got a mane bigger than Tina Turner's. You're doing this because your client requested a redhead when you only had a blonde, but you're on to this guy and justifiably suspicious that in the end he'll probably want a brunette. So, as usual, you outsmart him and save that selection as an alpha channel, knowing that you will be prepared for anything, even zebra stripes if necessary. (Then you have the option of charging the client for all the time you saved, or not.)

Navigating the Channels Palette

Okay, you've been briefly introduced to the channels family. You know their names (color, spot, and alpha); and you know, in the most general sense, what they're intended for. Before we look at them any more closely, let's take a moment and get familiar with their place of residence—the Channels palette.

If you've read the Layer Primer chapter (I hope you did) and now you're sitting there staring at the Channels palette, you'll probably notice that channels look almost identical to layers. Well, Adobe did this for a good reason. They want you to get used to one style of palette. They assumed that if you became comfortable with one kind of palette, you would quickly adapt to other palettes that were similar in design and function. So the Layers, Channels, and Paths palettes look almost identical (**Figures 9.2 to 9.4**). Just a few of the icons at the bottom of each palette are different. And even with these they tried to be consistent. For instance, the icon you use to create a new layer looks the same as the one you use to create a new channel or path.

As with layers, the eyeballs in the Channels palette control what is being displayed within the main image window. Just click in the column that contains the eyeballs to toggle them on or off. The channels that are active for editing are the ones that are highlighted. Click the name of a channel to make it active; to activate more than one channel at a time, Shift-click their names (I wish I could do that with layers). To change the stacking order of the channels, drag the name of a channel up or down within the stack (you can't change the order of the color channels). To create a new empty channel, click on the icon that resembles a piece of paper with a folded corner. To change the name of a channel, double-click on its name. Finally, to delete a channel, drag it to the trash can icon (**Figure 9.5**).

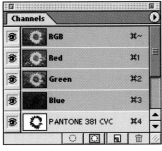

Figure 9.2 Channels palette.

Figure 9.3 Layers palette.

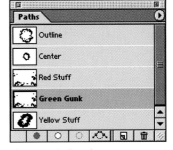

Figure 9.4 Paths palette.

Okay, that's enough for now. We'll cover the rest of the palette as we go through the different types of channels. So put on your thinking cap and let's get started.

Understanding Color Channels

Using color channels is like peeking behind the scenes and seeing how Photoshop is creating your image. You might think of color channels as the engine in your car: when you push the gas pedal, you are causing a whole chain reaction of events under the hood. In this case, while you are working in layers, the chain reaction is occurring in the color channels. They store up-to-the-minute information about RGB colors (red, green, and blue light), CMYK colors (cyan, magenta, yellow, and black ink), or any other color modes you are using. If you don't tamper with the channels, Photoshop will assume that whatever you're doing, you want it to affect all of the channels at the same time. But if you pop the hood and designate specific channels, you can do some very precise sculpting and manipulations that would be virtually impossible without using color channels.

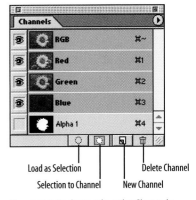

Figure 9.5 Understanding the Channels palette.

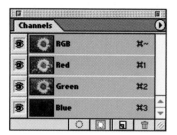

Figure 9.6 RGB channels.

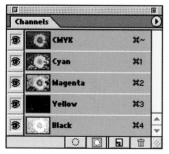

Figure 9.7 CMYK channels.

You'll need to choose a color mode to work in, but before you do, you might want to know a little something about your options.

Choosing a Color Mode

In RGB mode, Photoshop constructs your image out of red, green, and blue light (**Figure 9.6**). This is the mode most images start in, because all scanners and digital cameras use RGB light to capture images, and all computer monitors use RGB light to display images. Some fancy (and very expensive) high-end scanners might deliver a CMYK result, but that conversion occurs in software after the RGB scan. RGB mode is ideal for images that will be displayed using light (including those that will be used onscreen for multimedia or the Internet and those that will be output to video). You'll also want to use RGB mode when outputting images to 35mm slides, because the output device (a film recorder) will use RGB light to expose the photographic film. And since you view all your images on an RGB monitor while you are editing them, RGB turns out to be an excellent "working mode." Once you have finished editing the image, you can convert it to any mode you desire.

CMYK mode creates your image out of cyan, magenta, yellow, and black ink, also known as process colors (**Figure 9.7**). This is the mode that your image should end up in if your final destination is a printing press. When you convert an image to CMYK, Photoshop compensates for many factors (dot gain, total ink limit, etc.) that are specific to the type of paper and press that will be used. I recommend that you perform most editing and adjusting in RGB mode. This will allow you to adjust an image once and use it for multiple types of printing.

The Lab mode is a different animal. It separates your image into *lightness,* which means how bright or dark the image is, and two channels called A and B (**Figure 9.8**). The A and B channels are weird because they don't contain just one color. The A channel contains colors that are between green and red, and the B channel contains colors that are between blue and yellow. This makes it the only mode that separates how bright your image is from the color information, and that's what makes it so useful. Lab mode safeguards the brightness of your image so you can adjust the colors without shifting its brightness, whereas with RGB and CMYK mode, if you tried to do the same adjustments, the brightness would probably change. Lab mode is usually a temporary stop on your way to one of the other modes. It's not usually your final destination.

How Channels Relate to Layers

All of the information in the color channels is assembled from the elements in the Layers palette. If you view a single layer, the color channels display just that particular layer's content, as shown in **Figure 9.9**. If you view multiple layers, the color channels show the result of combining those layers, as shown in **Figure 9.10**. Because you can edit only one layer at a time, any changes made using the color channels will affect the currently active layer only.

Warning

Due to impurities in the CMYK inks, the CMYK mode cannot reproduce all the colors available in RGB mode. When using the Color Picker to choose a color, a small triangular warning symbol (known as the gamut warning) will appear next to the color you have chosen if it is one of the colors that are not reproducible in CMYK mode. Clicking on the triangle will give you the closest reproducible color.

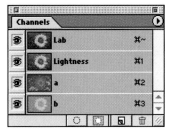

Figure 9.8 Lab channels.

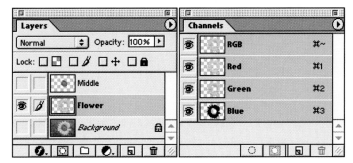

Figure 9.9 When a single layer is visible, the channels indicate what is contained in that layer.

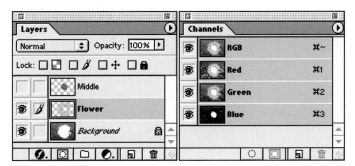

Figure 9.10 When multiple layers are visible, the channels reflect the combination of those layers.

The Composite Color Channel

If the image contains more than one color channel (RGB, CMYK, or Lab), then the topmost channel will be a special one known as the composite channel (**Figure 9.11**). This composite channel doesn't contain any information; it's just a shortcut to make all the color channels visible and active for editing, which is their default state if you haven't been editing the individual channels. So, in effect, this is how you get things back to normal after messing with the individual channels.

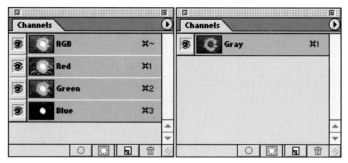

Figure 9.11 When multiple color channels are present, the topmost channel is known as the composite channel.

Viewing Channels in Color

When viewing a single-color channel (by clicking on its name in the Channels palette), it will appear as a grayscale image. This was done on purpose to make it easy for you to see exactly what the channel contains. If you view more than one color channel at a time (by turning on more eyeballs in the palette), the channels will appear in color.

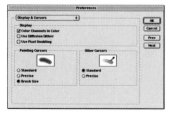

Figure 9.12 The Displays & Cursors dialog box.

You can force Photoshop to display individual channels in color (instead of grayscale) by choosing File > Preferences > Display & Cursors and turning on the Color Channels In Color checkbox (**Figure 9.12**). I don't find this all that useful because it becomes much harder to see exactly what is in each channel, especially when viewing the yellow channel of a CMYK image (it's just so light!). Go ahead and try it: open an image, convert it to CMYK mode, and take a peek at the yellow channel; then turn the preference on and off (**Figures 9.13 and 9.14**). Then you'll understand why they chose grayscale as the best way to view a channel.

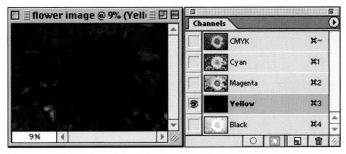

Figure 9.13 Color Channels In Color checkbox off. (© 1998 PhotoDisc)

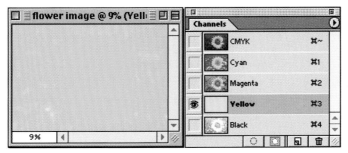

Figure 9.14 Color Channels In Color checkbox on.

Editing Multiple Channels

When you are adjusting an image using Levels or Curves, you'll notice a pop-up menu at the top of the dialog box, such as the one in **Figure 9.15**. This little menu determines which color channels you are editing (you can either edit a single channel or all of them).

But by using the Channels palette, you can force Levels or Curves (or any control, for that matter) to affect more than one channel at a time (**Figure 9.16**). Just click on the first channel you would like to change, and then Shift-click on another channel. Finally, turn on the eyeball of the composite channel (the topmost one) to make the rest of the color channels visible without making them all active. This can be

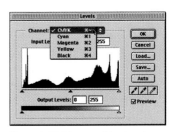

Figure 9.15 When applying Levels, you can either adjust a single color channel or all of them.

extremely useful when working on flesh tones, because they are mainly made from magenta and yellow ink.

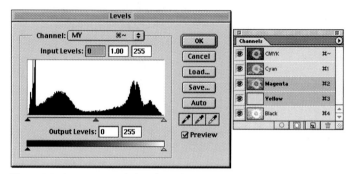

Figure 9.16 By messing with the Channels palette, you can get the Levels dialog box to affect the channels of your choice.

Applying a Filter to a Single Channel

Without using the Channels palette, it's impossible to get a filter to affect only one channel. When you don't use the Channels palette, a filter will always apply to all the color channels that are present in the document.

Images taken from digital cameras often appear noisy. If you blur the entire image to get rid of the noise, it usually looks terrible because you discard most of the important detail. But if you click through the channels, you might notice that the noise is most prominent in one channel (usually blue). By blurring just the blue channel, your image will look better without throwing away too much detail. To blur just the blue channel, click on its name in the Channels palette, and then apply the Blur filter (**Figures 9.17 and 9.18**). You might also try the Despeckle and Median filters. If you would like to see the image in full color, turn on the eyeball on the composite channel before applying the filter.

You can also improve the image by sharpening only those channels that don't contain a large amount of noise (usually the red and green channels), as shown in **Figures 9.19 and 9.20**.

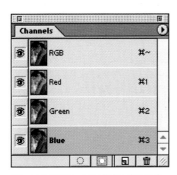

Figure 9.17 Viewing all the channels, but editing the blue channel only.

Figure 9.18 Apply the Gaussian Blur filter to remove noise.

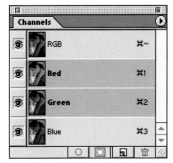

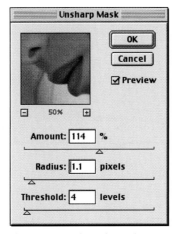

Figure 9.19 Viewing all the channels, but editing the red and green channels only.

Figure 9.20 Applying the Unsharp Mask filter to bring out detail.

Black-only Grayscale Images

Even with color images, there will be times when you want to force a portion of an image to black and white—for example, to make a color image pop all the more in contrast to a drab background. The most common way to force a portion of an image to black and white is to select the area and choose Image > Adjust > Desaturate. On screen, Desaturate will make it appear as if the image will be printed with black ink only. But if you open the Info palette and move your cursor over that now-black-and-white area, you'll notice that the image contains equal amounts of cyan, magenta, and yellow ink (**Figure 9.21**), which will look brown if you remember the basic concepts from the Color Correction chapter.

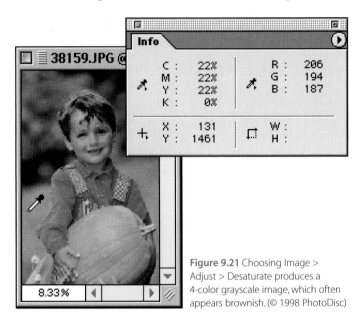

Figure 9.21 Choosing Image > Adjust > Desaturate produces a 4-color grayscale image, which often appears brownish. (© 1998 PhotoDisc)

To get the image to print with only black ink, you'll need to use the Channels palette. To begin, select the area you want to print with black ink, choose Edit > Copy, and then click on the black channel and choose Edit > Paste. That doesn't just paste the black channel information, but instead converts everything you copied to grayscale and then pastes the result into the black channel. But because you chose Copy instead of Cut, there will still be information left in the other channels, so click on each of the color channels (*except* black) and press the Delete (Macintosh) or Backspace (Windows) key to remove all information from those areas (**Figure 9.22**). Remember, only one layer can be active at a time, so pressing Delete or Backspace will only delete the channel information from the currently active layer.

You can get the same result by choosing Image > Adjust > Channel Mixer and turning on the Monochrome checkbox. You can even create a Channel Mixer adjustment layer—then Photoshop will force all the layers in the selected area to print with only black ink. Try it; it literally does all the work for you!

There are many more uses for the color channels, and we'll get to some of them in later chapters.

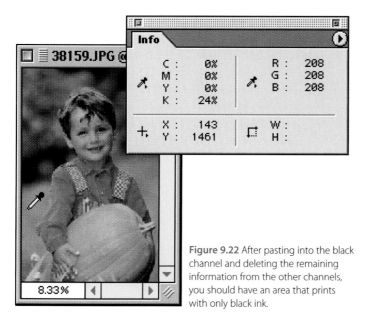

Figure 9.22 After pasting into the black channel and deleting the remaining information from the other channels, you should have an area that prints with only black ink.

Understanding Spot Channels

Remember when you got your first box of crayons? I'll bet you that it was the standard issue 8-color box from Crayola. I remember mine vividly. I thought it was great—that is, until the rich kid from across the street swaggered over and showed me his box. It was the gigantic 64-color model with the built-in sharpener. My box was limited to black, brown, blue, red, purple, orange, yellow, and green, which seemed adequate until I discovered Periwinkle,

Prussian Blue, and Raw Sienna in his huge set. Well, you can think of spot channels as a way to get all those colors that don't come in the standard (CMYK) box.

It all comes down to this. If you are planning on printing an image using inks other than (or in addition to) cyan, magenta, yellow, and black (such as fluorescent orange), you'll need to use one or more spot channels. These channels will allow you to paint with PANTONE colors (the most popular brand of spot color ink). Spot channels also allow your image to look correct on screen and print correctly from both Photoshop and your page layout program. But I should warn you before we get too far into this: if you are not actually purchasing a PANTONE ink, but would just like to simulate the look of PANTONE colors, then stay in RGB or CMYK mode and stay away from spot channels. Instead, just click on your foreground color and then click the Custom button to get to the PANTONE color picker. But beware that simulations are just that—the closest possible approximation—and they'll use a combination of the regular CMYK inks, which will cause those colors to look different than they do in a PANTONE swatchbook. But if you are really purchasing a PANTONE ink, then continue, and I'll show you how to get it set up.

No Layers Support

Just because Photoshop has direct support for spot colors doesn't mean it's easy to use them. The information you add to a spot channel will not appear on any layer—not even the background layer (**Figure 9.23**). It's as if the spot color information were sitting on an invisible overlay slapped on top of everything else. In fact, any information you put on a layer will be in the same mode as the document you're working on (RGB, CMYK, grayscale, etc.). That means that you can use layers, but none of the information on the layers will print using a spot color. If you'd like to strictly use PANTONE colors, start with a grayscale image and then choose Image > Mode > Multichannel. Then you can change the grayscale channel into a spot channel by double-clicking its name.

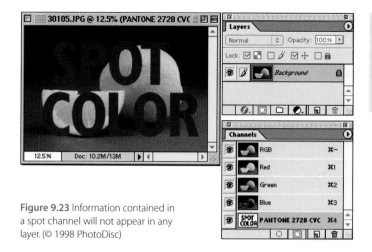

Figure 9.23 Information contained in a spot channel will not appear in any layer. (© 1998 PhotoDisc)

Creating Spot Channels

You'll need to create one spot channel for each PANTONE color you would like to use. To create one, choose New Spot Channel from the side menu of the Channels palette. A dialog box will appear, asking for the specific color you would like to use and its Solidity setting (**Figure 9.24**). To specify the color, click on the color swatch at the left of the dialog box. This will bring up a standard Color Picker dialog box. To get to PANTONE colors, click on the Custom button.

Unlike process colors, which are transparent, many PANTONE inks are almost completely opaque. Certain PANTONE colors (such as the metallic inks) will completely obstruct the view of colors that appear underneath them, while others will allow you to see a hint of the colors that are underneath. The Solidity setting controls how translucent these inks will appear on screen in Photoshop (**Figures 9.25 and 9.26**). Unfortunately, Photoshop doesn't automatically supply a setting for you, and there is no resource I can think of that will give you great settings. I contacted both Adobe and Pantone and neither of them could supply recommended settings. So, this is a setting you have to guess at unless you have a lot of experience with the inks you are using or have the time and money needed to perform a press check.

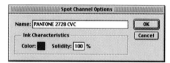

Figure 9.24 Spot Channel Options dialog box.

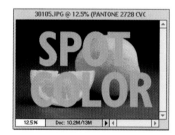

Figure 9.25 Solidity: 100%.

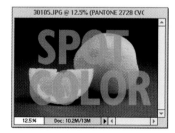

Figure 9.26 Solidity: 40%.

After you have created some spot channels, you can view those channels at the same time as the normal color channels by turning on the eyeball icon next to the composite channel as well as the ones next to each spot channel.

Painting with Spot Colors

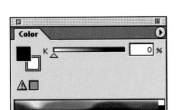

Figure 9.27 Color palette.

To paint with a spot color, you must first click on the name of the color you would like to use from the Channels palette. Next, open the Color palette and, from the grayscale slider, choose the percentage of this ink you would like to use (**Figure 9.27**), and then paint away. Photoshop acts as if you are working on a separate grayscale image when you paint in one of the spot channels. So if you attempt to paint with a color chosen from the Color Picker, Photoshop will convert it to a shade of gray when you are painting.

When you paint in a spot channel, Photoshop leaves the normal color channels unchanged (also known as over-printing). That means if you don't want the spot color you are painting with to print on top of the CMYK image (that is, if you want it to knock out as opposed to overprint), you'll have to manually switch to the color channels and delete the areas you painted across with the spot color. This can take a tremendous amount of time and isn't always the easiest thing to accomplish.

You can also paste images into the spot channels or apply any filter or adjustment that is available to grayscale images.

Proofing on a Desktop Printer

Most desktop printers aren't capable of printing an image that contains spot colors. The information in spot channels stays separate from the information in the RGB, CMYK, or grayscale channels, which are the ones your desktop printer uses to figure out what to print. That means you'll need to do a few things to get your image to print correctly on a desktop color printer (**Figure 9.28**). To start with, you don't want to mess up the document you've worked so hard creating, so choose Image > Duplicate to work on a duplicate image. Next, choose Image > Mode > RGB Color, click on one of the spot channels, and choose Merge Spot Channel from the side menu of the Channels palette (**Figure 9.29**). Repeat this process with all of the spot channels in your document. This will make your image printable on a desktop color printer by simulating the look of the spot colors using the normal RGB color channels. After the image has been printed, you can discard this file and go back to editing the original image.

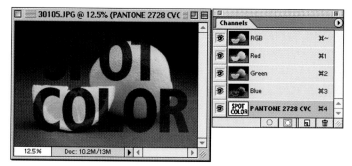

Figure 9.28 Information in the spot channels is difficult to print on desktop color printers.

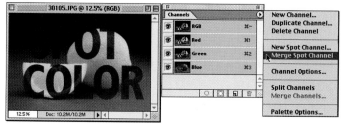

Figure 9.29 Merging the spot channels will simulate the look of spot colors in RGB mode.

Saving the Image

There are only two file formats that support spot channels: Photoshop and DCS 2.0 (DCS is short for Desktop Color Separations). Since most page layout programs can't deal with images in the Photoshop file format, you'll have to use DCS 2.0. The DCS file format is really part of the EPS file format, which is supported by most page layout programs. In order to be able to save your image in the DCS 2.0 format, the image must be in grayscale or CMYK mode.

When saving a DCS 2.0 file, you will be offered a bunch of options; unfortunately, most of them aren't all that straightforward. So let's take a peek at them (**Figure 9.30**).

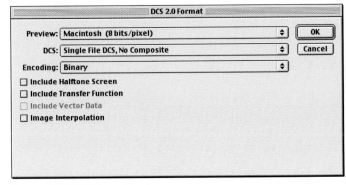

Figure 9.30 DCS 2.0 Save dialog box.

Figure 9.31 The DCS Preview choices (I think JPEG usually produces the best onscreen previews).

Figure 9.31a An 8-bit preview as seen in a page layout program.

Figure 9.31b A JPEG preview as seen in a page layout program.

The Preview menu (which pops up when you save your file in the DCS 2.0 format) determines what will be seen onscreen in your page layout program (**Figure 9.31**).

Why can't they use English! Let's try to decipher these choices. Use the TIFF options when the image will be used on the Windows platform, and use the Macintosh options for a Mac (duh). 1 bit/pixel means pure black and pure white (that looks terrible), 8 bits/pixel means 256 colors (that looks okay), and JPEG means full color (that looks great). See **Figures 9.31a and 9.31b**. Remember, these choices only affect the onscreen image that appears in other programs, not the printed version. No matter which option you choose, the printed version of the image will look great. So, what do I use? I always use the JPEG choice because it looks great and doesn't make the files overly large.

The DCS pop-up menu determines how many files you'll end up with (**Figure 9.32**). Unless you really know what you're doing and have a good reason to mess with this (some people can come up with one), leave it set to Single File With Color Composite. I haven't needed to use the other options for any of the files I've output.

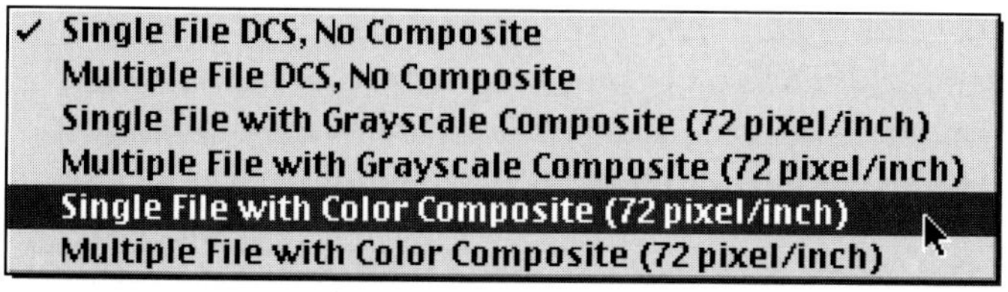

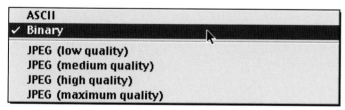

Figure 9.32 Single-file DCS documents are the easiest to keep track of.

The Encoding menu determines how the information that will be printed (as opposed to the onscreen preview) will be stored. Macintosh users should use the Binary option, and Windows users should use ASCII (**Figure 9.33**). Binary files are almost half the size of ASCII files, so if your printer can handle them, use them. Some really old Mac programs and printers cannot handle Binary files, so if you run into a problem, resave your image using ASCII encoding. The JPEG choices will degrade the quality of the printed image and deliver a dramatically smaller file. Use JPEG only if the image will not need to be resaved and if quality is not your first concern. (JPEG degrades the image more each time it is saved.)

Figure 9.33 Use Binary for Macs and ASCII for Windows.

If you you've added spot colors to a grayscale image and find that your printing company dislikes DCS files, you'll need to use CMYK mode in an unusual way. Start by choosing Image > Mode > Multichannel, and add empty channels until you have a total of four channels altogether. Arrange the channels so that Black is at the bottom and the other channels are organized by brightness (of the spot color, not the contents of the channel), darkest on top and lightest towards to bottom (**Figure 9.34**). If you're using a third ink, then put it right below the darkest spot channel. Finally, choose Image > Mode > CMYK Color and save your file (**Figure 9.35**). Now give that file to your printing company; tell them to only output the channels that contain information, and tell them which spot colors to substitute for the CMYK colors.

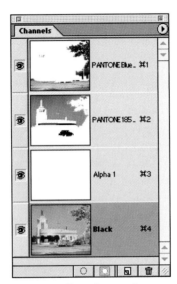

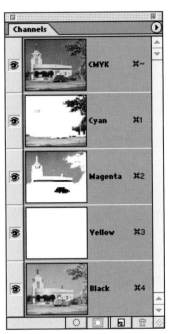

Figure 9.34 Channels set up for CMYK conversion.

Figure 9.35 Result of CMYK conversion.

Understanding Alpha Channels

Alpha channels are like big storage bins for selections. Whenever you spend more than a few minutes creating a selection and there's the remotest chance that you might need it again, you should transform it into an alpha channel for safekeeping. That way it will be available for you to use again and again. And the great thing about alpha channels is that they're not limited to being just a storage device; the channels are also malleable, like modeling clay, so that you can sculpt and manipulate your selections in ways that are not possible with mere mortal selection tools. Mastering alpha channels is the mark of a true Photoshop virtuoso.

Loading and Saving Selections

If you make a selection, and then choose Select > Save Selection, Photoshop will store the selection at the bottom of the Channels palette (**Figure 9.36**). Go ahead and try it. Make sure the Channels palette is open, so you can see what's going on. An alpha channel is a saved selection—it's that simple (well, almost).

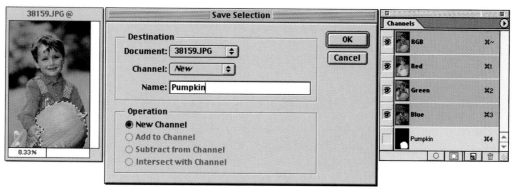

Figure 9.36 Choosing Select > Save Selection will produce a new alpha channel.

Now let's find out how to reload the selection you just saved. But first, choose Select > Deselect (or Command-D on the Mac, Ctrl-D in Windows) to get rid of the selection that is currently active. Good. Now, back to reloading: as long as you saved a selection, you should be able to get it back at any time by choosing Select > Load Selection (**Figure 9.37**). That won't bring the image back to what it looked like when you saved the channel; instead, it will just bring back the marching ants as if you created a selection from scratch.

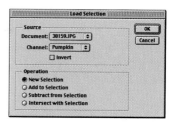

Figure 9.37 Choose Select > Load Selection to reload a saved selection.

Now let's try the same thing using the Channels palette. To save a selection, Option-click (Macintosh) or Alt-click (Windows) on the Save Selection icon at the bottom of the Channels palette (it's the second from the left). This accomplishes the same end result as choosing Select > Save Selection—a new channel (**Figure 9.38**). If you click on the Save Selection icon without holding down the Option or Alt key, Photoshop will assign the new channel a generic name such as "Alpha 1."

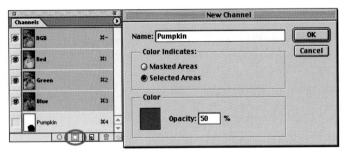

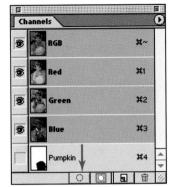

Figure 9.38 Option-clicking (Macintosh) or Alt-clicking (Windows) on the Save Selection icon is the same as choosing Select > Save Selection.

Figure 9.39 Dragging the name of a channel onto the Load Selection icon is the same as choosing Select > Load Selection.

Note

You can also Command-click (Macintosh) or Ctrl-click (Windows) on the name of a channel to load it as a selection.

To get the selection back, drag the name of the channel onto the far left icon at the bottom of the palette (**Figure 9.39**). That does the exact same thing as choosing Select > Load Selection. The advantage to using the Channels palette is that you get a visual preview of the shape of the selection.

Deleting Alpha Channels

There is no way to delete a saved selection (channel) when using the Select menu. Instead, you need to open the Channels palette and drag the name of a channel onto the rightmost icon (the one that looks like a little trash can).

Viewing Individual Channels

If you would like to see what a channel contains without loading it as a selection, you can simply click on the name of the channel in the Channels palette. This will display the channel in the main image window, as seen in **Figure 9.40**. White areas in the channel indicate areas that will be selected, and black areas indicate non-selected areas. After you're done looking at a channel, just click on the composite (topmost) channel to get back to editing all the color channels.

Figure 9.40 Click on the name of a channel to view it in the main image window.

New Channels

So far, all we've been doing is saving and reloading selections that we've made with the normal selection tools. But you can also create a selection by creating a brand new (empty) channel and editing the channel. Try this: click on the second icon from the right at the bottom of the Channels palette (the one that looks like a sheet of paper with a folded corner). This action will create a new empty channel and display it in the image window. Now change your foreground color to white, choose the Paintbrush tool and a hard-edged brush, and sign your name in the channel. If you're using a mouse (instead of a graphics tablet), it might not look exactly like your signature, but that's okay. Once you're finished, click on the topmost channel to get back to the main image, drag the name of the channel you were messing with to the Load Selection icon, and bingo! The shape of your signature is selected. Photoshop can't tell the difference between a channel that was created by saving a selection and one that was created from scratch (**Figure 9.41**). That means that you're no longer limited to creating selections with the Marquee, Lasso, and Magic Wand tools.

Figure 9.41 Result of painting in a new channel and then loading the channel as a selection.

Feathered Selections

Let's see what a feathered selection looks like when saved as a channel. Make a selection using the Lasso tool, and then save it as a channel. Next, choose Select > Feather and use a setting of 10, and then, again, save the selection as a channel. Now click on the name of the first channel and take a look at it, then click on the name of the second one to see the difference, as demonstrated in **Figures 9.42 and 9.43**. Feathered selections appear with blurry edges in the Channels palette. This happens because shades of gray in a channel indicate an area that is partially selected (50% gray means 50% selected). You can make the first channel look identical to the second by making it active and then choosing Filter > Blur > Gaussian Blur and use the same setting that was used to feather the other selection (10, in this case).

But when you look at the marching ants that appear after the channel has been loaded as a selection, they only show you where the selection is at least 50% selected. That isn't a very accurate picture of what the selection really looks like (**Figure 9.44**). But if you save the same selection as a channel, you can see exactly what is happening on its edge. So if you want to create a feathered selection when editing a channel, just choose a soft-edged brush to paint with.

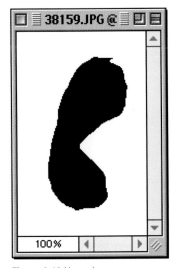

Figure 9.42 Normal.

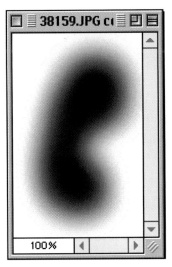

Figure 9.43 Feathered.

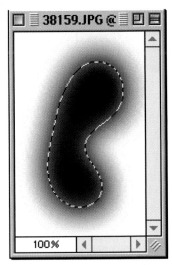

Figure 9.44 The marching ants show up where an area is at least 50% selected.

Shades of Gray

Try this out. Create a new channel. Paint in it with 20% gray, load that as a selection, and paint in the selected area with bright red. Now choose Select > Deselect, lower the opacity of the painting tool to 80%, and paint with bright red. They should look exactly the same. That's how Photoshop makes a selection fade out—by simply lowering the opacity of the tool you are using. The only problem is that the marching ants show up only where an image is at least 50% selected (that's 50% gray or brighter in a channel). So, try this one on for size. Create a new channel and paint with 49% gray, and paint in another area with 51%

gray. Then load the channel as a selection and paint across the area. Only the areas that are less than 50% gray in the channel show up, but the other areas are still selected (**Figure 9.45**). Try creating a channel and then paint with 55% gray. Now load that one and you'll even get a warning message, pictured in **Figure 9.46**.

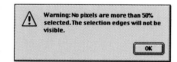

Figure 9.46 When you load a channel that does not contain any shades brighter than 50% gray, a warning will appear.

Figure 9.45 When painting in a channel, only the areas that contain less than 50% gray will be visible when the channel is loaded as a selection.

We really haven't done anything fancy with channels yet, so let's try something fun. To start with, you have to remember that when you are editing a channel, Photoshop treats it as if it is a grayscale image. That means you can use any tool that is available when working on grayscale images. So give this a try: Select an area using the Marquee tool, and save it in the Channels palette. View the channel, choose Filter > Distort > Ripple and mess with the settings until you've created something that looks a little kooky (**Figure 9.47**). Finally, click on the composite (topmost) channel and load that channel as a selection. You can create infinite varieties of fascinating selections with this simple technique.

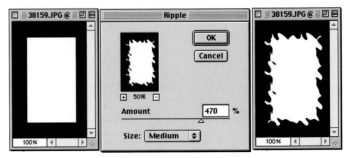

Figure 9.47 Applying the Ripple filter to a channel.

You can also "unfeather" a selection using the Channels palette (**Figure 9.48**). Remember, a feathered edge looks blurry when saved as a channel. Well, all you have to do to remove that blurry look is to save the selection as a channel, and then choose Image > Adjust > Threshold. This will give the channel a very crisp, and therefore unfeathered, edge.

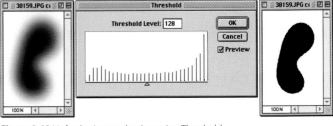

Figure 9.48 Unfeathering a selection using Threshold.

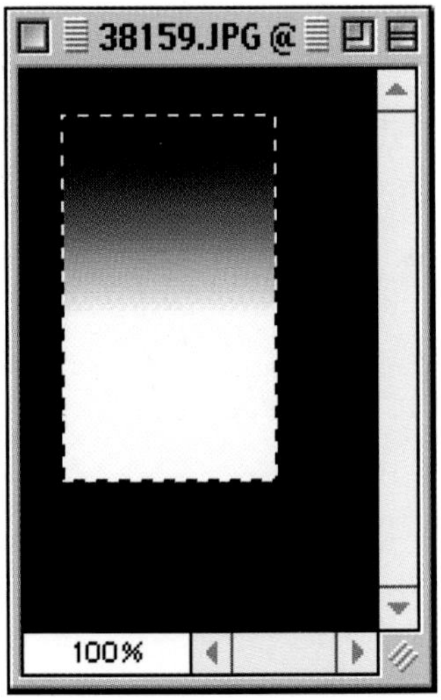

Selections Within Channels

You can even use a selection to isolate a particular area of a channel, as shown in **Figure 9.49**. A selection within a channel can help you create a selection that is only feathered on one side. To accomplish this, first create a new empty channel. Next, choose the Marquee tool and select an area. Now use the Gradient tool set to Black, White and create a gradient within the selected area. Once you're done, switch back to the main image (by clicking on the topmost channel) and load the channel you just created. To see exactly how this selection will affect the image, choose Image > Adjust > Levels and attempt to lighten that area by dragging the lower left slider.

Figure 9.49 Using a selection within a channel to restrict which areas can be edited.

View with the Image

We've covered some ideal uses for alpha channels, but their usefulness is very limited if you can't see how the channels line up with the main image. At any time, you can overlay a channel onto the main image by simply turning on the eyeball icon next to the composite (topmost) channel while you are editing an alpha channel (**Figure 9.50**). This enables you to see exactly which areas of the image will be selected. When you do this, the dark areas of the alpha channel will be overlaid onto the main image. (Photoshop substitutes a color for the shades of gray in a channel to make them easier to see.) You can change the color that is used by double-clicking on the name of the alpha channel (**Figure 9.51**). This setup is ideal when you need to create a selection that is feathered in one area and crisp edged in another. All you have to do is paint with a soft-edged brush for the feathered area, and then switch back to a crisp-edged brush for the rest.

Figure 9.50 Viewing a channel at the same time as the main image. (© 1998 PhotoSpin, www.photospin.com)

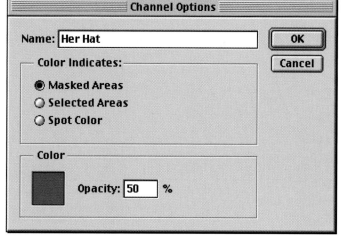

Figure 9.51 Channel Options settings used.

Photoshop also allows you to switch *where* the color shows up. You can specify whether you want the selected or unselected areas to show up. To change this setting, double-click on the name of the alpha channel and change the Color Indicates setting (**Figures 9.52 and 9.53**). Photoshop uses the term Masked Areas to describe areas that are *not* selected. Here's a way to help understand the reasoning of this. If you're painting a room in your house, what do you do to all the trim that you don't want to get paint on? You mask it off, right? Well, in Photoshop, you do the opposite—you select the areas you want to change, and the non-selected areas are the masked areas.

Figure 9.52 The Color Indicates setting changes where the color overlay appears.

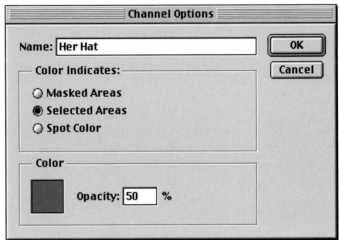

Figure 9.53 Channel Options settings used.

The Opacity setting determines how much you will be able to see through the overlaid channel. Viewing a channel at the same time as the main image is not a way to colorize your images. The channel that's being overlaid won't print that way; it's just a method for creating a selection, and nothing else. If you'd like to colorize an image, then check out Chapter 12 to find methods that are much easier than anything we're doing here.

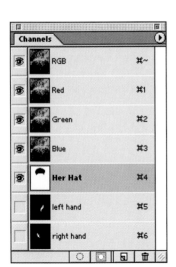

Figure 9.54 When viewing multiple channels, the channel or channels that are highlighted are the only ones being edited.

When you are viewing an alpha channel at the same time as the main image, you'll need to keep track of exactly what you are editing. The channel or channels that are highlighted in color are always the ones that you are currently editing, as shown in **Figure 9.54**. Other channels might be visible, but if they aren't highlighted, you won't be able to change them.

Saving Channels with Your Image

If you want to save your spot or alpha channels with your file, you'll have to use a file format that understands them. First of all, the Photoshop file format completely supports all kinds of channels, which makes it a great working file format. Unfortunately, most other programs can't understand images saved in the Photoshop format. The TIFF format also supports alpha channels, but it doesn't know the difference between spot and alpha channels, so it is not usually used for spot channels. The DCS 2.0 format supports spot channels and is compatible with the majority of publishing programs, so it is usually used for spot color work. Most of the other formats do not support alpha or spot channels, so they appear grayed out when attempting to save an image that contains those types of channels. If you need to save your image using a format that does not support spot or alpha channels, choose File > Save As when saving the file. This dialog box will automatically discard channels if the format you choose does not support them.

> **Note**
> In previous versions of Photoshop, you had to choose File > Save A Copy instead of File > Save As.

Use Extract to Select Complex Objects

In the previous edition of this book I demonstrated how to isolate a complex image from its background using alpha channels. It was a long and tedious process and involved a lot of guesswork. But now there's a marvelous feature that will save us all those headaches, so you can toss that old, hair-pulling technique in the trash as we explore one of Photoshop's newest and most welcome additions: the Extract command.

Before we start working with the tools in the Extract dialog box, let me give you an overview of what's needed to successfully extract an image from its background. First off, you'll need to highlight all the areas where the subject of the photo is intertwined with the background you'd like to remove. Not only that, but you'll also need to make it all the way around the object with your highlighting, except where the subject bumps into the edge of your document (this is going to show up in green). Next, you'll need to

Note

The Extract command will work on the entire image, unless a selection is active when you choose Image > Extract. In that case it would only work within the selected area.

fill (with blue) the area you'd like to keep (**Figure 9.55**). Then Photoshop will do all the work for you. It will keep all of the blue-covered areas, trash those that aren't covered in color, and then try to figure out what to do in the green transition areas, based on where all the highlighting is.

Start with the Highlighter

Go ahead and grab an image of someone with flyaway hair and then choose Image > Extract (**Figure 9.56**). Next, take a glance at the tools in the upper left of the dialog box; the Highlighter tool is active by default. Before you start tracing around the edge of your image, you should know that any areas that you cover with the Highlighter have the potential of being deleted, so be sure your highlighting overlaps both the subject and the background. That means if you're going to be sloppy, it's best to overspray onto the background because that area will be deleted anyway. But don't be too careful to avoid overspray on the subject; otherwise you'll end up leaving a tiny one-pixel speck of the background between your highlighting and the subject of the image. That tiny speck has the potential to confuse the Extract command, making it think that things similar to that speck should be kept instead of deleted. So, go forth and highlight the entire edge of the subject to show Photoshop which areas of the image contain a combination of background and subject (**Figure 9.57**).

Figure 9.55 An image complete with highlight and fill, ready to be extracted. (© 2001 StockByte, www.stockbyte.com)

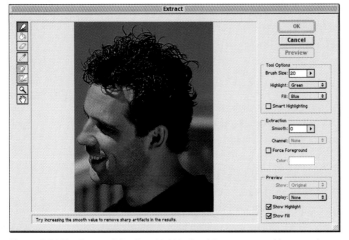

Figure 9.56 The Extract dialog box. (© 2001 StockByte, www.stockbyte.com)

Figure 9.57 The edge of the subject has been highlighted.

The Brush Size setting in the upper right of the Extract dialog box can be changed by pressing the bracket keys (][). If the area you are painting across has a very well-defined (non-blurry) edge, then you can turn on the Smart Highlighting checkbox to have Photoshop help you limit overspray onto the subject and background. But be sure that option is turned off when working on areas that have very soft or complex edges. You can also hold the Option key (Macintosh) or Alt key (Windows) to temporarily transform the highlighter into an eraser so you can remove overspray from your image. If you're working on a green object and you find that the green highlighting is too hard to see, then you can choose a different color from the Highlight pop-up menu in the upper right of your screen.

Fill with the Paint Bucket Tool

Once you've finished highlighting the edge of the image, choose the Paint Bucket tool and click in the middle of the subject of your photo. When you do that, the Paint Bucket tool will completely ignore the photograph you are working on and instead use the highlighting to determine which area should be filled. If, after clicking once with the Paint Bucket tool, the entire subject is not covered in blue, then click on additional areas of the subject that aren't yet covered (**Figure 9.58**). If you find that the entire image (minus the highlighting) is covered with blue, that means that your highlighting didn't make it all the way around the subject of the photograph, so go touch up the highlighting and then try to fill the subject again. (By the way, the paint bucket's official name is the Fill tool.)

Figure 9.58 The subject has been covered with the blue fill.

Keeping in mind that all areas that are covered with the blue highlighting will not be deleted, take a quick look to make sure no part of the background you are looking to delete is covered in blue. If you've messed up, then fine-tune your highlighting and refill the subject. If you find the blue is too difficult to see, you are welcome to choose another color from the Fill pop-up menu in the upper right of the dialog box. If you think that you have everything set up correctly, then click the Preview button to see what your extraction will look like.

Most of the time, the preview will look rather promising, but that's really deceptive because the checkerboard that appears can hide a lot of problems (**Figure 9.59**). I find it much more effective to replace the checkerboard with a solid color that contrasts with the subject by choosing Other from the Display pop-up menu in the lower right of the dialog box (**Figure 9.60**).

Figure 9.59 The checkerboard can hide many problems.

Figure 9.60 Replacing the checkerboard with a solid color will expose most of the problem areas you'll need to fix.

Zoom in and Fine Tune

Now it's time to use that Zoom tool to check things up close. Just remember that any area that's covered with the blue fill will not be deleted. So, scroll around your image and look for remnants of the old background (**Figure 9.61**). If you find any, then turn on the Show Fill checkbox and see if they become covered with blue (**Figure 9.62**). If they are, then grab the Highlighter tool and cover up those areas. Any time you use the Highlighter tool, the fill will disappear, so you'll need to use the Paint Bucket tool to refill the subject area and then re-preview the extraction.

After you've made sure that none of the background is visible, then switch gears and look for areas of the subject that might have been unintentionally deleted. You can do that by toggling back and forth between the Extracted and Original choices in the Show pop-up menu. If it looks like areas of the subject were deleted, then choose Original from the Show pop-up menu. Turn on the Show Highlight and Show Fill checkboxes and then search around your image for areas that contain the hints of the subject that aren't covered with highlight or fill (**Figure 9.63**). Remember, areas that do not have any color on them (either highlight or fill) will be deleted. So grab the Highlighter tool and cover up all those areas of the subject that don't have color on top of them. Now you'll need to refill the subject and re-preview the image.

Figure 9.61 Look for tiny remnants of the old background.

Figure 9.62 The background remnant was covered with the blue fill.

Figure 9.63 Look for areas of the subject that are not covered with color.

If just a tiny bit of the background is visible after previewing and most of the subject is intact, then start experimenting with the Smooth setting. As you raise the Smooth setting, the transition between the subject and the area that's been extracted should become softer (**Figure 9.64**). In order to see the effect of changing the Smooth setting, you'll need to re-preview the image.

Figure 9.64 Left: Smooth=0. Right: Smooth=100.

Figure 9.65 Use the Cleanup tool to rid your image of specks in the background.

Clean It Up

At this point, you can still refine the result, but let's get away from the Highlighter and Paint Bucket tools and take a look at the Cleanup and Edge Touchup tools. You can drag across your image using the Cleanup tool to slowly lower the opacity of an area. This can be useful when attempting to rid your image of specks that don't quite touch the subject of the photograph (**Figure 9.65**). Or, if you hold down the Option key (Macintosh) or Alt key (Windows), the Cleanup tool will increase the opacity of an area, which will allow you to bring back areas that should not have been deleted. Then, to clean up the areas that touch the subject of the Photo, use the Edge Touchup tool.

Use Force Foreground for Intricate Images

If the subject of your photo is too small or intricate to trace around and leave space for the fill in the middle (like a chain link fence), then cover the entire subject with the Highlighter tool (**Figures 9.66 and 9.67**). When it comes time to define the fill, turn on the Force Foreground checkbox and click on the color of the subject using the Eyedropper tool. That will make Photoshop look through the entire highlight area and attempt to keep things that are similar to the color you clicked on with the Eyedropper.

Once you click OK and exit the Extract dialog box, Photoshop will truly delete the background—as opposed to just selecting it—and will clean up any hint of the old background from the edge (**Figure 9.68**). If you'd rather get a selection out of the Extract command, then Command-click (Macintosh) or Ctrl-click (Windows) on the layer (after extracting it from its background) and then choose Select > Save Selection. Next, choose Select > Deselect, then View > Show History, and click in the indent to the left of the step listed before the Extract command. Finally, choose Edit > Fill and choose History from the Use pop-up menu. Now you should have the original image back and a saved selection which you can retrieve at any time by choosing Select > Load Selection.

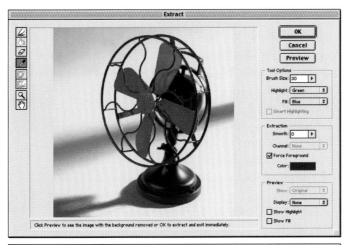

Figure 9.66 Original image. (© 2001 Stockbyte, www.stockbyte.com)

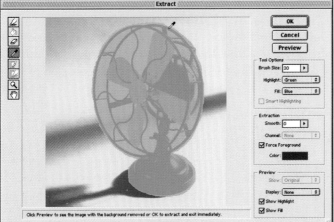

Figure 9.67 Covering the entire subject with a highlight, then checking Force Foreground and clicking the Eyedropper tool to find out what should be kept.

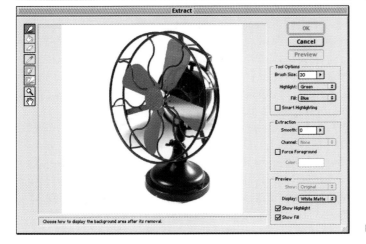

Figure 9.68 The extracted result.

Closing Thoughts

I truly hope that after going through this chapter you've come to terms with channels. They don't really deserve the mind-boggling reputation that seems to follow them. I like to think of them as three friendly little dogs: Spot, Color, and Alpha. They will be loyal to you throughout your lifetime as a Photoshopper and will take care of all sorts of special needs, especially when you're working with color or with complex selections (or, for that matter, *any* selection that you'd like to save for later). Likewise, the Extract command, once mastered, will save you hours of grief when it comes to removing backgrounds from complex images or making complex selections. So if for any reason you're still one of those people who want to throw their hands up in the air when the subject of channels comes up, think twice. It's worth the pain, and believe me when I tell you that the pain will turn into pure pleasure once you've realized what a gem the Channels palette is.

Ben's Techno-Babble Decoder Ring

Mask—Any time you view a selection as a grayscale image (as opposed to a "marching ants" selection), it is also called a mask. That means it's okay to call a channel a mask if you'd like. And when you see features like Quick Mask and Layer Masks mentioned in Photoshop, those are things that will also be stored in the Channels palette.

Bits—In Photoshop, 256 shades of gray is known as 8 bits. This describes how much memory Photoshop uses to keep track of all those shades. So if you find a setting in your scanning software that is called "8-bit grayscale," it just means a normal 256-shade grayscale scan. If you hear someone say, "I have a 24-bit color image," that means they have an image that is in RGB mode (RGB has three channels; each channel is 8 bits; 8 + 8 + 8 = 24). Or, if you hear about a 32-bit image, that just means the image contains four channels; they are either talking about an image that is in CMYK mode (4 channels) or an RGB image (three channels) plus one alpha channel (for a total of four channels).

Color Channel—When you edit an image in Photoshop, you are really editing the color channels. These channels break your image into one or more color components. The mode of the document will determine how many color channels will be present: RGB mode will have three channels (red, green, and blue), CMYK mode will have four channels (cyan, magenta, yellow, and black), and grayscale will contain only one channel (called black).

Spot Channel—Spot channels are a special variety of color channel that allow you to construct your image out of inks other than, or in addition to, cyan, magenta, yellow, and black. Spot channels are usually used when printing with PANTONE inks.

Alpha Channel—Alpha channels are basically saved selections. They do not affect how your image will be printed.

Composite Channel—The composite channel does not contain any information; in fact, it is simply a shortcut to view and edit all the color channels at the same time. This is often used to return the Channels palette back to its "normal" state after isolating a single channel for editing.

PANTONE—A brand of ink commonly used when printing with fewer than four inks, or when colors are needed that cannot be reproduced using CMYK inks (metallic colors, fluorescent colors, deep blues, and bright greens cannot be accurately simulated using CMYK inks). PANTONE inks are commonly referred to as Spot Color inks.

Gamut—A term used to describe the entire range of colors that is reproducible using a certain set of inks, dyes, or light. The gamut warning in Photoshop warns you that the currently chosen color is not reproducible using CMYK inks.

EPS—Encapsulated PostScript (EPS) is a file format used to transfer PostScript language page descriptions between programs and output devices. EPS files should be used only with PostScript-aware printers; otherwise, the resulting images will appear with a low-resolution "jaggy" appearance because they only print the onscreen preview.

DCS—Desktop Color Separation (DCS) is a special version of the EPS file format that comes in two versions, DCS 1.0 and DCS 2.0. You can think of DCS 1.0 as the old version of this file format because prior to Photoshop 5 it was the only version available in Photoshop; and it used to be integrated into the normal EPS save dialog box. DCS 1.0 files allow you to save a CMYK image and get five files total, one for each channel in the image, and one preview image. DCS 2.0 is new to Photoshop 5 and is special because it is the only file format (other than Photoshop's own format) that allows you to save spot channels in addition to the CMYK channels.

Keyboard Shortcuts

FUNCTION	MACINTOSH	WINDOWS
View composite	Command-~	Ctrl-~
View channel	Command-channel #	Ctrl-channel #
Load channel as a selection	Option-Command-channel #	Alt-Ctrl-channel #
Extract	Option-Command-X	Alt-Ctrl-X

© Nick Koudis, www.koudis.com

© Nick Koudis, www.koudis.com

Part III Creative Explorations

Courtesy of Alicia Buelow, www.aliciabuelow.com

10 Shadows

Between the idea
And the reality
Between the motion
And the act
Falls the Shadow.
–T. S. Eliot,
The Hollow Men, V

Photography: Howard Berman. Computer artist and landscape photographer: Robert Bowen.

What's New For 6.0

If you have been making your shadows based on the 5.0 version of this book, check out my simplified technique for creating cast shadows, as well as a new technique for making transparent shadows.

Go figure. You spend hours creating a great shadow. You sweat over the minutiae. You listen to an entire CD while you fuss over the tiniest details. And when you're done, nobody notices it…Good! You've got the right shadow.

Shadows can make or break an image. It's true. Even though we don't notice them, shadows help create a sense of solidness, of physical existence. Just try this: close your eyes and think about all the shadows that were present within your field of vision. You probably can't remember a single one. The presence of subtle shadows brings the illusion of substance to your digital images as well; remove the shadows and you remove the realism of the image. Shadowless images seem to float in thin air. On the occasions when anyone does happen to notice a shadow in your image, it's almost surely too dark.

How to Think About Shadows

Lay your hand on top of the desk you are sitting at (assuming you're not lounging on the sofa). Notice how dark the shadow below your hand appears. Now, slowly lift your hand above the surface and see what happens to the shadow. It should become lighter, and the edge should become softer. You might also notice that the shadow became larger—it's not always easy to see that happening, but it does. If there is more than one light source above your hand, you will most likely see multiple shadows. If you were to draw a line from one of the light sources to the middle of your hand, and then continue the line through your hand until it hits the desk, the line should be smack dab in the middle of the shadow.

Note

If you combine two images that have radically different light sources, it will be difficult to recreate realistic shadows. The dissimilar lighting of the subjects will not relate in a natural way to the new shadows you're creating, and your mind will know something is not right about the image.

But finding the light source in the real world is much easier than finding the light source in an image. If you can't see the light source in a photo (say, there's no lamp or ball of fiery sun), you can instead look at the part of the image that is darker than the rest. This will indicate from which direction the light was coming. Being aware of the source will really help you create natural-looking shadows.

Four Shadow Types

Ideally, when you want a shadowed image, you'd simply remove the background of the image and leave its shadow. This is possible if you happen to have a solid-colored background. But if the background is complicated, you'll have to resort to reconstructing a shadow that resembles the original. The farther you get from the original shadow, the less realistic the image will appear.

There are many techniques for creating great shadows; the complexity of the image will determine which technique you should use. The following four techniques will cover most all of the shadow situations you might encounter.

▶ **Natural Shadow**—Transforms an existing shadow into one that can be overlaid onto another image. Also removes any grays from beyond the edge of the shadow.

▶ **Reconstructed Shadow**—Replaces the original shadow with a new one so you can remove a complex background and still retain the basic shape of the original shadow.

▶ **Cast Shadow**—Exaggerates the height of an object. A cast shadow is based on the shape of the object that's doing the casting.

▶ **Drop Shadow**—A simple offset shadow that is the same shape as the object that is casting it.

Natural Shadows

Let's start with my favorite technique. We'll simply (well, not quite simply) slip the background out from beneath the original shadow, leaving just the shadow intact. Then we'll make this original shadow transparent so we can overlay it on any other image within Photoshop. This technique works when your image has a simple, low-contrast background; a white or gray background will give you the best results (**Figure 10.1**).

Figure 10.1 Here the shadow under the crab image was made transparent so it could be overlaid onto the two-dollar bill. (© 1998 PhotoDisc)

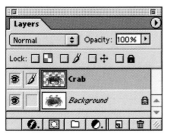

Figure 10.2 Isolate the subject onto its own layer.

Note

It is important to choose Layer Via Copy instead of Layer Via Cut in order to avoid getting a bright halo around your image. Halos are caused by replacing the underlying image with white, which happens when you cut the subject from its original layer. If you're curious, go ahead and try using Layer > New > Layer Via Cut and then look closely at the edge of the subject.

Isolate the Subject

The first thing you need to do is to get the subject of the photo (a crab, in this case) onto its own layer (**Figure 10.2**). That way you can isolate the shadow from its background without affecting the subject of the image. Do this by selecting the subject with any selection tool and then choosing Layer > New > Layer Via Copy. Or, if you have a complicated object, you can duplicate the layer and then use the Background Eraser or Extract command. This will leave you with two layers: one that contains the crab and the other that contains the crab and its shadow. To avoid confusion, whenever I mention the *subject* of the photo, I'm referring to the top layer (the one that contains only the crab); whenever I talk about the *shadow layer*, I mean the one that is under the subject (which contains both the crab and its shadow).

Now click on the shadow layer (the "Background" layer, in this example). This will allow you to modify the background layer of the image without messing up the subject of the image.

Find Edge of Shadow

Next, you'll want to locate the exact edge of the shadow and then force the rest of the background to white, leaving just the shadow visible. To do this, choose Layer > New Adjustment Layer > Threshold and move the slider all the way to the right. A good portion of your screen should now appear black, because the Threshold adjustment is exposing all areas that are darker than white. Now, click on the shadow layer, choose Image > Adjust > Levels, and move the upper right slider around until the shadow (which will appear as solid black) is as large as possible without bumping into the edge of the document. The black mass will indicate where the shadow ends and the background begins, as shown in **Figures 10.3 to 10.7**. After you've moved the slider a little, you can use the up arrow and down arrow keys on the keyboard to move the slider in small amounts. It's much too difficult to find the edge of a shadow with the naked eye, so you'll always want to use Threshold to help you.

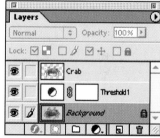

> **Note**
> If the background behind the image is not white or gray, then choose Image > Adjust > Desaturate before attempting to adjust the threshold.

Figure 10.3 Shadow is bumping into edge of the document.

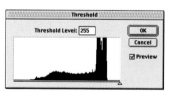

Figure 10.4 Move the Threshold slider all the way to the right.

Figure 10.5 Make sure you are working on the shadow layer before applying Levels.

Figure 10.6 Shadow is as large as possible without bumping into the edge of the document.

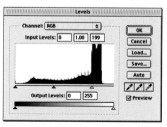

Figure 10.7 Move the upper right slider to change where the shadow stops fading out.

Clean Up Unwanted Grays

After getting the proper Levels settings, there might still be some unwanted shades of gray near the edge of the document (they would look like tiny black specks). Not all images will have the extra grays. To remove any specks, click on the shadow layer in the Layers palette and use the Eraser tool to brush over the "dirty" areas (you can see them in **Figures 10.6 and 10.8**). After you've gotten rid of all the extra grays, drag the Threshold adjustment layer to the trash icon at the bottom of the Layers palette.

Figure 10.8 Use the Eraser tool to clean up any stray specks.

Refine the Result

If you open the Levels dialog box a second time, you'll be able to control many aspects of the shadow's appearance. If you move the lower left slider, you will lighten the shadow (compare **Figures 10.9 and 10.10**). Remember to make your shadows a little lighter than you think they should be; otherwise, people might notice them, which would ruin the realism of the image. Also, if the image will be printed on a printing press, the image will appear darker than it does on screen.

Figure 10.9 Original shadow brightness.

Figure 10.10 Lightened by using Levels.

You can also control how the shadow fades out by moving the upper middle slider. If the shadow isn't dark enough, you can move the upper left slider over until it touches the beginning of the histogram.

Control the Shadow's Color

After applying Levels, you might notice some color in the shadow. Most of the time, the color will make the shadow appear more realistic. But sometimes the color is too intense. To adjust it, choose Image > Adjust > Hue/Saturation and move the Saturation slider (**Figure 10.11**). If you move the slider all the way to the left, there will be no hint of color in the shadow.

> **Note**
>
> If you can't tell if the shadow has color in it, just choose Image > Adjust > Desaturate to remove all the color from the shadow. Then choose Edit > Undo to see exactly how much color was in the shadow. Or if you want a shadow that has no hint of color, just choose Image > Adjust > Desaturate and don't choose Edit > Undo.

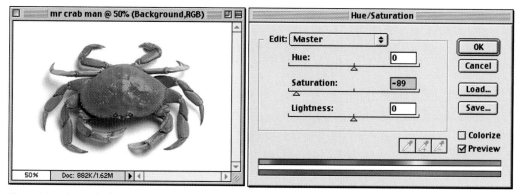

Figure 10.11 Lower the Saturation setting to reduce the amount of color that appears in the shadow.

On the other hand, if you would like to *add* color to the shadow, turn on the Colorize checkbox in the Hue/Saturation dialog box, move the Hue slider to pick the basic color, and adjust the saturation slider to change how intense it appears. This can be useful when you have a shiny object that should reflect some of its color into the shadow area.

Overprint the Shadow

Using the crab and the two-dollar bill images as an example, we'll overlay the crab's shadow on the money and then make that shadow print on top of the of the bill as if it were made out of ink. When you place the final image (in this case, the crab) on top of another, you might want its shadow to appear transparent so that the two images look like they belong together. To accomplish this integration, open the image upon which you want to cast the shadow (here, the two-dollar bill). Now, switch back to the image that contains the shadow (the crab) and link the layer that contains the subject to the layer that contains its shadow by clicking to the left of the layer in the Layers palette. A link symbol should appear, as shown in **Figure 10.12**. Now use the Move tool to drag the crab onto the second document. This should copy both layers into that document, as **Figure 10.13** depicts.

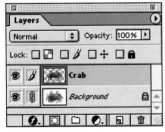

Figure 10.12 Link the layers by clicking to the left of the layer preview icon.

Figure 10.13 Using the Move tool, drag the image on top of another document.

To make the shadow transparent, be sure you are working on the shadow layer. Then, in the Layers palette, set its blending mode menu to Multiply, and bingo!—transparent shadow (**Figure 10.14**).

Figure 10.14 Use the Multiply blending mode to make the shadow transparent.

Creating a Truly Transparent Shadow

Using the Multiply blending mode to print the shadow on top of another image works great when you end up combining your shadow with an underlying image in Photoshop, as we did above. But what if you need to export your image and slide something under it in another program? I wouldn't suggest this for images destined for a printing press (the file formats we are forced to use don't support transparency), but sometimes you might need to do that when working with multimedia applications—for instance, when creating a video. Let's rewind our technique back to the point where we were about to drag the crab on top of the two-dollar bill.

To get true transparency out of our shadow, it must be the only thing visible. That means you'll have to Option-click (Macintosh) or Alt-click (Windows) on the eyeball icon for the shadow layer (that's a shortcut for hiding all the other layers). First I'm going to tell you to do a few steps without explaining what's going on behind the scenes. Then, after

Notes

You must drag from the image window to copy linked layers from one document to another. If you drag from the Layers palette, only one layer will be copied.

If the edge of the shadow is not soft enough, choose Filter > Blur > Gaussian Blur and use a very low setting, such as 1 or 2.

Warning

Multiply mode works best when your image is RGB. If you use it while in CMYK mode, you can easily get too much ink on the printing press. This happens when the shadow combines with the underlying image and, in effect, darkens it, producing excessive ink coverage. If you use Multiply before converting to CMYK, be sure to choose Flatten Image when converting, or use the black-only shadow technique described at the end of this chapter. For more information about potential CMYK problems, see Chapter 8, "Color Correction."

we get everything to look right, I'll clue you in on what you just did, OK?

Now that you only have one layer visible, type Option-Command-~ on the Macintosh or Alt-Ctrl-~ in Windows (the tilde "~" key is just to the left of the number "1" key), which should give you an unusual-looking selection (**Figure 10.15**). Choose Select > Inverse, create a new layer, and then fill that selection with black by typing D and then Option-Delete (Macintosh) or Alt-Backspace (Windows). Now, to finish the effect, throw away the old shadow layer, click on the crab layer, and choose Layer > Merge Down. You're done! (**Figure 10.16.**)

Figure 10.15 Option-Command-~ (Mac) or Alt-Ctrl-~ (Windows) will give you an unusual-looking selection.

Figure 10.16 When you're done, you'll have a truly transparent shadow.

Now that you have this wonderful looking transparent shadow, you might want to know how we accomplished that effect. The whole thing was possible because of that keyboard command we used (Option-Command-~ on the Macintosh, Alt-Ctrl-~ in Windows). Remember what was on your screen at the time you typed that command? Weren't you just looking at the shadow layer? Well, that command takes what's visible and selects all the areas that are pure white. It also partially selects shades of gray. For example, if there is an area that is 10% gray, it will become 90% selected. After we got that selection, we chose Select > Inverse, which gave us what we *really* needed—areas that used to be 10% gray became 10% selected, and areas that were 40% gray became 40% selected, etc. Then we created a new layer and filled our selection with black. That effectively took areas that used to be 10% gray and made them black with an opacity setting of 10%. This can be a difficult concept to grasp if you've never attempted it before, but actually the concept is simple—you are just translating brightness levels into opacity levels.

Reconstructed Shadows

If the background of an image is complex, then the natural shadow technique described above will not work. In addition to working only with simple, almost solid-colored backgrounds, the natural shadow technique will also get messed up if there is a wrinkle or crease in the background that runs directly under the shadow. If that's the case, I'd completely remove the background on the image and then attempt to recreate new shadows that resemble the originals (**Figures 10.17 to 10.19**).

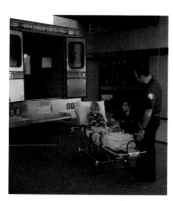

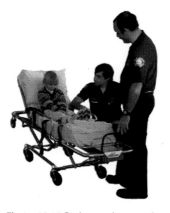

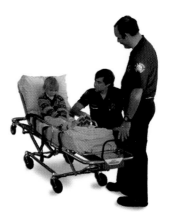

Figure 10.17 Original image. (© 1998 PhotoSpin, www.photospin.com)

Figure 10.18 Background removed.

Figure 10.19 Shadows added.

Isolate the Subject

As with natural shadows, the first thing you need to do is to get the subject of the photo onto its own layer, so you can create and edit shadows without changing the subject. Do this by selecting the subject with any selection tool and then choosing Layer > New > Layer Via Copy (**Figure 10.20**).

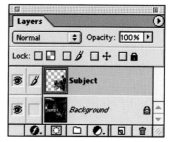

Figure 10.20 Isolate the subject onto its own layer.

Trace Shadow Edges

Before removing the layer that contains the shadows, it will be helpful if you trace the shape of the original shadows. That way, any new shadows you create can have the same shape and position. Use the Freeform Pen tool to trace around the edges of each shadow that appears in the image (**Figures 10.21 and 10.22**). Most images contain more than one shadow—maybe a hard-edged shadow on one object and a softer-edged shadow on another. You want to create a new path for each shadow (or small group of shadows) in the image. After you've done that, make a mental note about how soft the edges are and how dark the shadow is. Now you can finally delete the layer that contains the shadows.

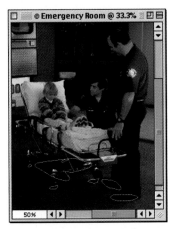

Figure 10.21 Use the Pen tool to trace the shadows

Figure 10.22 Each shadow has its own path.

Rebuilding the Shadows

To re-create the shadows, first create a new layer below the subject of the image. Now set your foreground color to black and drag the first path in the Paths palette to the first icon in the Paths palette. This should fill the shape of the path with your foreground color, which is black (**Figure 10.23**, where I've added a white background to make it easier to see what the end result will look like). The black shape should appear on the layer you just created. This shape represents one of the shadows. To lighten the shadow, just lower the opacity setting in the Layers palette (**Figure 10.24**). To make it look more realistic, choose Filter > Blur > Gaussian Blur and move the slider until the edge is as soft as the original, as shown in **Figure 10.25**. Repeat this process for each shadow in the image. It's a good idea to make a new layer for each shadow, so you can control each one separately.

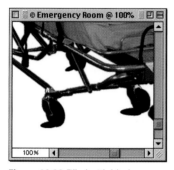

Figure 10.23 Filled with black.

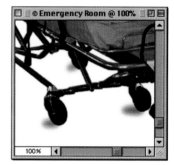

Figure 10.24 Opacity lowered.

Figure 10.25 Gaussian Blur applied.

To make the shadow fade out in a particular direction, drag the name of a path to the selection icon at the bottom of the Paths palette (it looks like a dotted circle). Choose Select > Feather to soften the edge, and then use the Linear Gradient tool (set to Foreground To Transparent) and drag across the selected area (**Figures 10.26 and 10.27**). Or, if you've already filled that area, you can make it fade out by choosing Filter > Blur > Motion Blur.

Once all your shadows look appropriate, link all the shadow layers together and then choose Layer > Merge Linked. This will create a single shadow layer.

Note

To quickly change the opacity of a layer, switch to the Move tool and press the number keys on your keyboard (1=10%, 3=30%, 35=35%, and so on).

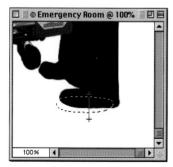

Figure 10.26 Selection.

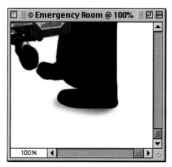

Figure 10.27 After gradient is applied.

Cast Shadows

To exaggerate the height of an object, you can create a shadow that falls at an angle away from the subject, also known as a cast shadow. The longer the shadow, the taller the object will appear. This will also make it appear as if the light source that's hitting the subject is coming from a specific direction (**Figures 10.28 and 10.29**).

Figure 10.28 The original file

Figure 10.29 Cast shadow added.

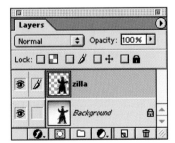

Figure 10.30 Isolate the subject onto its own layer.

Isolate the Subject

To create a cast shadow, you'll first need to get the subject of the photo onto its own layer (**Figure 10.30**). That way you can create a shadow without damaging the subject. Do this by selecting the subject with any selection tool, and then choosing Layer > New > Layer Via Copy.

Fill with a Gradient

Cast shadows are usually based on a blatant copy of the shape of the subject. To create such a shadow, Command-click (Macintosh) or Ctrl-click (Windows) on the layer in the Layers palette that contains the subject (not the background). This should give you a selection based on the information in that layer (**Figures 10.31 and 10.32**). Now, create a new layer and fill that selection with a gradient. Press D to reset your foreground color to black and then click on the Gradient tool. In the Options bar at the top of your screen, click on the triangle next to the gradient preview to get your drop-down presets palette. Choose Small List from the side menu of that drop-down palette. Now choose the preset that's called Foreground To Transparent (**Figure 10.33**). To fill the selection with a gradient, click on the bottom of the subject and drag to just above the top of the subject and then release the mouse button. Then get rid of the selection by choosing Select > Deselect.

Note

If you can't locate the "Foreground to Transparent" preset, then choose Reset Gradients from the side menu of the drop-down palette.

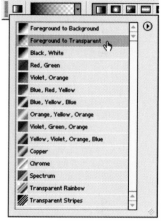

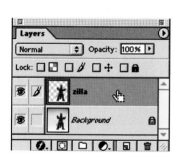

Figure 10.31 Command-click (Mac) or Ctrl-click (Windows) the subject layer.

Figure 10.32 The result of Command-clicking (Mac) or Ctrl-clicking (Windows) on the subject layer.

Figure 10.33 Choose Foreground To Transparent from the gradient drop-down menu in the Options bar.

Distort the Shadow Layer

Now you want to get the shadow to appear beneath the subject, so drag the shadow layer until it is below the subject layer in the Layers palette. To make the shadow fall at an angle, choose Edit > Transform > Distort; the transform bounding box will appear. Move the squares (or handles) on the upper corners of that box around until you have the desired angle, as in **Figure 10.34**.

Blur the Shadow

Now that we've applied a gradient and skewed the shadow layer, our shadow is fading out pretty nicely, but it still has a crisp edge. In the real world, shadows become more

Figure 10.34 Distorting the shadow by using Edit > Transform > Distort.

Notes

Instead of going up and choosing Blur each time, you can choose Command-F (Macintosh) or Ctrl-F (Windows) to reapply the last filter you used.

....

To create a more natural, less refined edge, choose Filter > Sylize > Diffuse and use the default settings. The Diffuse filter will add noise to the edge of the shadow, making it appear less man-made.

blurry as they get farther away from the subject of the photograph (or, in my case, the feet of 'Zilla). To get a natural-looking fade-out, choose the Marquee tool, then click and drag the selection from the upper-left corner of the image until the bottom of the marching ants slightly overlaps the topmost part of the shadow.

Next, choose Filter > Blur > Gaussian Blur and use a setting just high enough to slightly blur the shadow (**Figure 10.35**). Now move the selection down by typing Shift-down arrow a few times, and then blur the shadow again, using the same setting. Repeat this process until the selection is all the way at the bottom of the shadow (**Figure 10.36**).

Figure 10.35 Gaussian Blur filter.

Figure 10.36 The placement for the first blur. Move the selection down for each subsequent blur.

Achieve Proper Brightness

To brighten the shadow, adjust the Opacity setting of the shadow layer in the Layers palette (**Figures 10.37 and 10.38**). Make the shadow a little lighter than you think it should be; otherwise, people might notice it.

Figure 10.37 Shadow is too dark.

Figure 10.38 Shadow after lowering Opacity setting to 30%.

Simple Shadows

If you have a simple subject like a button, coin, or other relatively flat object, you can use Photoshop's Layer Styles feature to quickly add a drop shadow, as shown in **Figures 10.39 and 10.40**.

Note

Layer styles were known as layer effects in earlier versions of Photoshop and were found under the Layer > Effects menu.

Figure 10.39 Original image.

Figure 10.40 After a drop shadow has been applied.

First you must get the subject of the photo onto its own layer. (These steps should be starting to sound very familiar by now!) That way you can create and edit shadows without changing the subject. Do this by selecting the

307

subject with any selection tool and choosing Layer > New > Layer Via Copy (**Figure 10.41**). Now choose Layer > Layer Style > Drop Shadow and adjust the controls until the shadow looks appropriate (**Figure 10.42**).

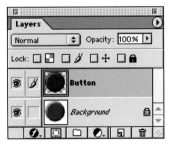

Figure 10.41 Isolate the subject onto its own layer.

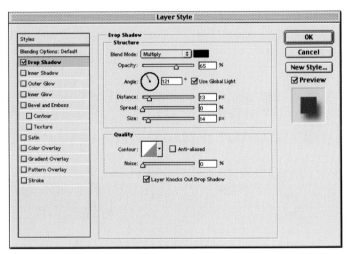

Figure 10.42 Apply a layer style to add a drop shadow.

Note

You can adjust the position of the shadow by clicking on the main image window and dragging the shadow while the Drop Shadow dialog box is still open.

Sometimes you might need to isolate the shadow onto its own layer so you can distort it using filters or place a layer between the subject and its shadow. You can do that by choosing Layer > Layer Styles > Create Layer. After getting the shadow onto an independent layer, I often distort it using the Ripple filter that's found in the Filter > Distort menu.

RGB versus CMYK

I usually create all my shadows while I'm in RGB mode, even if the end result will need to be in CMYK mode. Here are a few reasons I prefer to work in RGB mode:

▶ The natural shadow technique described earlier in this chapter will produce shadows that appear slightly brown if applied while in CMYK mode.

▶ The Multiply blending mode can cause problems with too much ink in an area if used in CMYK mode.

▶ File sizes remain smaller with RGB.

▶ All the filters work in RGB mode.

When you convert an image that contains layers to CMYK mode, a dialog box always appears asking if you would like to flatten the image. I usually choose to flatten it when converting; otherwise, I might run into problems with too much ink coverage (because I used the Multiply blending mode). The only time I don't flatten the image is when I'll be creating black-only shadows; there are no problems using the Multiply blending mode on these.

Closing Thoughts

If you feel funny taking so much time to perfect something that will never be noticed, you have two good reasons not to fret. First, shadows are every bit as important as light, but—strangely—the very best shadows are the ones that go undetected. Second, as with everything else in Photoshop, after you've test-driven them a few times, the techniques you learned in this chapter should take only a few minutes to perform. Isn't it worth a few minutes to get those subtle, flawless, ethereal shadows that no one will ever notice?

Note

On the accompanying CD, you'll find a PDF file that supplements this chapter. The file, called "extras.pdf," contains information about creating black-only shadows.

Ben's Techno-Babble Decoder Ring

Rosette—A pattern caused by printing four halftone screens at differing angles. You can see a similar effect by placing two bug screens together at different angles (you know, the kind you use in the screen door of your house).

Keyboard Shortcuts

FUNCTION	MACINTOSH	WINDOWS
New Layer Via Cut	Shift-Command-J	Shift-Ctrl-J
New Layer Via Copy	Command-J	Ctrl-J
Hue/Saturation	Command-U	Ctrl-U
Desaturate	Shift-Command-U	Shift-Ctrl-U
Levels	Command-L	Ctrl-L
Feather	Option-Command-D	Alt-Ctrl-D
Fill Dialog	Shift-Delete	Shift-Backspace
Toggle Preserve Transparency	/	/

Courtesy of Robert Bowen Studio. Photography by Eric Meola.
Art Director: Bronson Smith, Schieffelin & Somerset.

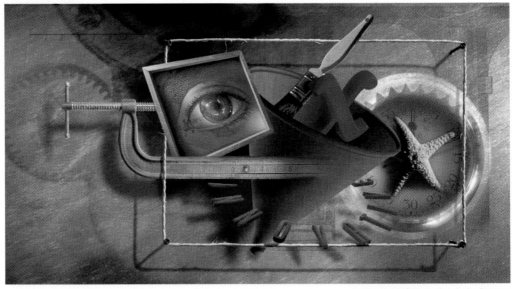

Courtesy of Chris Klimek, CK Creative

11 Image Blending

What you see on these screens up here is a fantasy; a computer-enhanced hallucination!
–Stephen Falken in "War Games"

Courtesy of Robert Bowen Studio, Sony Electronics, Inc., and Lowe & Partners/SMS. Photography by Howard Berman. Art Director: Maria Kostyk-Petro.

No matter how many times I see them, I'm always in awe of the amazing special effects you see in big-budget Hollywood flicks. I know it's all man-made digital voodoo, but I still get a thrill when the effects are done so well. Consider *Jurassic Park*, where they blended the computer-generated dinos with actors and live-action backgrounds—so incredibly lifelike that you wouldn't be surprised to find yourself standing behind a Velociraptor in the popcorn line.

In Photoshop you can create your own kind of movie magic by blending diverse visual elements into one big picture (the only difference is the picture doesn't move). Some people call this compositing or image blending. This is where Photoshop really gets to strut its stuff, and where you can put your creative agility to the test. The possibilities with compositing are truly boundless. Where else could you create a passionate embrace between an ugly, smelly, wrinkly bulldog and his arch-rival, a prim and proper kitty-cat? (Robert Bowen did it, and the piece won the Gold Lion Award in Cannes!) Where else could you put the face of a famous singer onto the body of a goldfish and have her swim around her own fishbowl? Certainly not in real life! But with Photoshop all you need is your imagination and a bag full of good blending techniques.

Four Ways to Blend

In this chapter we'll explore the features that allow you to blend multiple images into one seamless composite. We'll cover grouping layers, blending sliders, layer masks, and layer clipping paths. Once you've mastered all four, you'll be able to blend your images together like magic. But before we start blending some images, let's take an introductory look at how these features work.

Grouping Layers

When two layers are grouped together, the top layer will show up only in those places where there is information on the layer directly below it. This can be useful for simple effects like controlling where shadows fall or placing a photo inside of some text.

Sample Use: You've spent hours creating a big "retro" headline that could have come from the movie poster of *Creature from the Black Lagoon*. Your client—not exactly the king of good taste—calls and says he wants you to put flames inside the headline. You put aside your better judgment and agree to the flames, but only because he pays on time. Then he calls back; he's got some unresolved issues. He doesn't know whether he wants flames or hot lava inside the text, and he's also thinking about changing the headline altogether. He wonders out loud if it will take long or cost much more to do this? "Well," you say, "I think I could wrap this up in about three hours." Greatly relieved, he tells you you're a miracle worker and hangs up. Then you pop open the Layers palette, where you've grouped the headline and flames, and faster than you can say hocus pocus you've tweaked the text and swapped out some lava for the flames and are off to the beach for a three-hour (paid) vacation.

Blending Sliders

The blending sliders allow you to make certain areas of a layer disappear or show up based on how bright or dark they are. For example, it's very easy to make all of the dark parts of an object disappear.

Sample Use: A "big fish" prospect that you've been trying to snag for months finally throws you a bone. She's desperate because the super-swanky design studio she usually uses can't meet her deadline. You know she's just using you, but what the hey, it's a shot at a new client. She's given you some images that you've loaded into Photoshop. One is a photograph of some big, fat, billowy clouds; the other is of a bunch of whales. She wants you to make it look like the whales are swimming around in the clouds. In some places she wants the whales to replace the sky that is behind the clouds, but in other places she wants the whales to actually blend in with the clouds. Very surreal. She impatiently bites her nails and wants to know how many hours it will take to get the effect. You know you can nail this job in a jiffy with the blending sliders, so while your hands are busy with the mouse, you give her a fearless look and reply, "I'll do it while you wait." She frowns, "I can't just sit around here for hours!" You smile, "No problem, it's already done." The look on her face delivers the good news—you've got a client for life.

Layer Masks

I consider layer masks to be the most powerful blending function in Photoshop. With layer masks you can make any part of a layer disappear, and you can control exactly how much you'd like its edge to fade out. What you can do with layer masks is infinite.

Sample Use: You're waiting for your biggest client, a twenty-year-old creative genius with a ring in his nose. Although this is just a planning meeting, you know from experience that The Genius will want to see some action. Armed with your fastest computer and with Photoshop at the ready, you're not fazed when the kid comes in and starts throwing around madcap ideas like they're going out of style. Blending seems to be the theme of the day. First he wants something that looks like a skyscraper growing out of a pencil. Then he changes his mind and decides he wants to fuse together a hippopotamus and a ballerina. But then he gets a funny look on his face and says, "I know! Let's put Godzilla in an Elvis suit!" Ahhh, you think, a perfect day for layer masks. Without batting an eyelash, you go about the business of giving 'Zilla his new look. Six months later you almost choke on your coffee when you find out that your Elvis-Zilla ad got an award.

Layer Clipping Paths

Layer clipping paths allow you to attach a crisp-edged path to a layer; anything outside of the path will be hidden both on screen and when printed. This feature is special because the edge will remain smooth when printed to a PostScript printer, even if the pixels in the image are so large that the rest of the image appears jaggy.

Sample Use: You're doing a freebie brochure for your non-profit client, Defenders of the Naked Mole Rat. They want the rat to be the most noticeable image on the cover, so you make their logo small and place it in the corner so it doesn't distract from the lovely Rat. But at the last minute (of course!) your penniless client does an about-face and wants you to enlarge the logo to make it almost fill the page. You're tired of doing things for free and fed up with her endless requests, so you tell the client that scaling up the logo that large is a big request when it comes to Photoshop. You even demonstrate your point by scaling one of the photographic elements of the brochure up to a huge size, and of course it looks terrible, very blurry and jaggy. She squeezes out a few tears and gives you her song and dance about the plight of this dear little creature, and how crucial it is to have this brochure just right. You tell her that you'll work on it through the night, and send her on her way. The minute she's out the door, you scale up the logo in a millisecond, and because you used a layer clipping path, the edge remains perfectly crisp and will print that way as well. The job is done. The Naked Mole Rat lives on; unfortunately, since you're so good, the client will never go away.

Now that you have a feeling for the blending options that are available, let's get into the specifics of how this all works.

Grouping Layers

When you group multiple layers together, all the layers within the group will be visible only where there is informa-tion in the bottommost layer of the group (see **Figures 11.1 and 11.2**). When you group layers, Photoshop always groups the currently active layer to the one below it. You can group layers together by using any of the following techniques:

Figure 11.1 Result of grouping a photo with a type layer. (Original image © 1998 Adobe Systems, Inc.)

▶ Option-click (Macintosh) or Alt-click (Windows) between two layers in the Layers palette.

▶ Choose Layer > Group With Previous.

▶ Type Command-G (Macintosh) or Ctrl-G (Windows).

Changing the Stacking Order

Changing the stacking order of the layers may accidentally ungroup some layers, so you'll want to be careful. If you move one of the grouped layers above a layer that is not part of the group, you'll be ungrouping that layer. Or if you move an ungrouped layer between two layers that are grouped, then it will become part of that group. If you move the bottom layer of a group above or below a layer

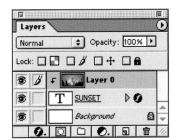

Figure 11.2 Layers palette view.

that is not part of the group, all the layers in the group will move with it.

Now that you know how to group your layers, let's take a look at a few of the things you can accomplish by doing that.

Adjustment Layers

Grouping layers can also be helpful when you're using adjustment layers. An adjustment layer allows you to apply an adjustment (like Levels, Curves, etc.) as a layer that affects all the layers that are below it. That's nice, because the change is not permanent—you can always trash that layer and the adjustment is no longer applied. By grouping an adjustment layer, you can force it to affect only the layers that are within the group. This can be extremely helpful when you want to brighten or darken a single layer and you don't want to make the change permanent (**Figures 11.3 to 11.6**).

Figure 11.3 Original image. (Courtesy of Chris Klimek)

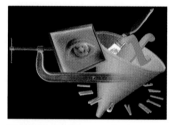

Figure 11.4 Adding an adjustment layer at the top of the layers stack affects the entire image.

Figure 11.5 Grouping the adjustment layer makes it apply only to the layers within the group.

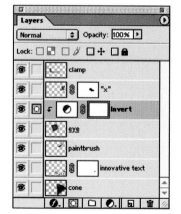

Figure 11.6 Layers palette view.

Limiting Shadows

I use grouping all the time when I'm creating shadows. Let's say you have some text, and underneath the text is an image of a piece of string, and you want the text to cast a shadow on the string. Once you create a layer that contains a shadow, all you need to do is group it with the string, and then the shadow will show up only where the string is (**Figures 11.7 to 11.9**).

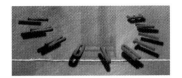

Figure 11.7 Original image.

Figure 11.8 Grouping the shadow to the string.

Stacking Order Tricks

Occasionally I use the grouping feature when I really don't want to restrict where a layer appears. That way I can fool Photoshop into doing some tricks. Here's an example: Ordinarily, you can only move one layer at a time up or down in the stack (unless you group some layers together). By grouping multiple layers, you can drag the bottom layer of the group (the one that's underlined) up or down in the stack; all of the layers within the group will also move (**Figures 11.10 and 11.11**). This can be immensely helpful when you are working on complicated images that contain dozens of layers.

Figure 11.9 Layers palette view.

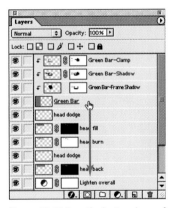

Figure 11.10 Drag the bottom layer of a group to change the stacking order of all the layers within the group.

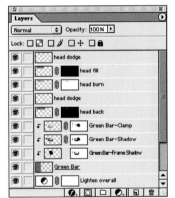

Figure 11.11 Result.

Once you have changed the stacking order, you'll probably need to ungroup the layers (that is, unless you really want to restrict where they are visible). To quickly ungroup a series of layers, click on the bottommost layer of the group and choose Layer > Ungroup.

The Magnifying Glass Trick

I travel all over the country presenting seminars and speaking at conferences, and I know I can always get people to ask questions by showing my magnifying glass trick. I start by opening what looks like a simple image of an ampersand (&). Then, as I move my cursor, a magnifying glass passes over the ampersand and it appears as if it's really magnifying the image! That's not really possible in Photoshop, of course, but I can still trick people into thinking that it's happening for a few seconds. Let's see how the magnifying glass trick works.

Start off by opening any image you'd like to work with. I use a simple one of a black ampersand on a white background. Next, you'll need an image of a magnifying glass or loupe that you can place on a layer above the ampersand (I've included two on the CD at the back of this book). Now select the background and the glass portion of the magnifying glass and press Delete (Macintosh) or Backspace (Windows) to remove those areas (**Figure 11.12**).

Note

If you're going to remove the background on the magnifying glass before dragging on top of another image, you should be aware that you can't remove a background layer. So, if that's what you have, double-click it to change its name and make it a normal layer.

Figure 11.12 Remove the background of the magnifying glass and place it on top of the image.

Figure 11.13 Make a drastic change to the duplicate layer using a filter.

Next, drag the name of the image you are using (not the magnifying glass) to the New Layer icon to duplicate it. Use a simple filter like Mosaic (choose Filter > Pixelate > Mosaic) to make an obvious change to the duplicate image (**Figure 11.13**).

Now let's get that modified image to only show up within the glass area of the magnifying glass. Grab the Elliptical Marquee tool and make a selection where the glass should be in the magnifying glass image. Make sure it lines up perfectly on all sides. Next, create a new empty layer and then type Option-Delete (Macintosh) or Alt-Delete (Windows) to fill that area with your foreground color and then choose Select > Deselect. Move the layer you just created so that it's positioned directly between the original image and the filtered version in the stacking order of the Layers palette (**Figure 11.14**).

Now, let's get the whole trick to work. Click on the layer directly above the one that contains the circle you just made, and then choose Layer > Group With Previous. Now click on the magnifying glass layer and link it to the circle layer by clicking just to the left of the circle layer's thumbnail image in the Layers palette. That'll make both layers move at the same time (**Figure 11.15**). To see if the trick is working, use the Move tool to drag around your screen. That should make it so the filtered image only shows up in the "magnified" area (**Figure 11.16**).

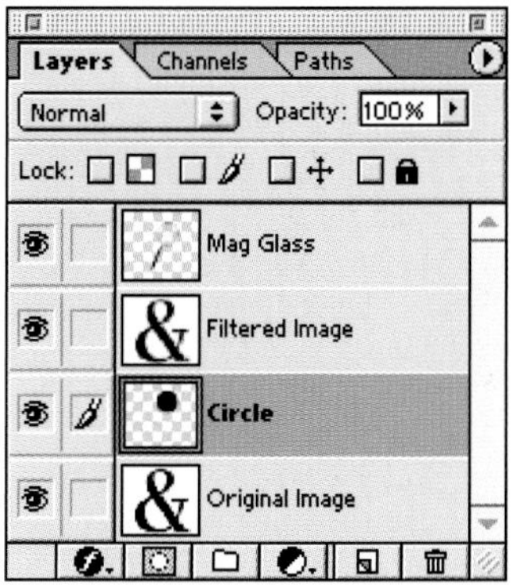

Note

When using the Marquee tool, you can press the spacebar to reposition the selection (but don't release the mouse button).

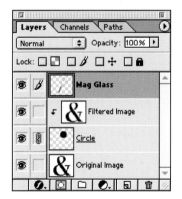

Figure 11.14 The new layer should be placed between the two image layers.

Figure 11.15 The final setup in the Layers palette.

Figure 11.16 The magnifying glass trick in action.

Blending Sliders

The blending sliders allow you to quickly make areas of a layer transparent, based on how bright or dark the image appears. You'll find the blending sliders by double-clicking the name of a layer (this will open the Layer Styles dialog box). The blending sliders are at the bottom of the Layer Style dialog box, shown in **Figure 11.17**. The first thing you'll notice is that there are two sets of sliders. One is labeled "This Layer" and the other is labeled "Underlying." The slider called This Layer will make areas of the active layer disappear. The slider labeled Underlying deals with all the layers underneath the layer that was double-clicked. This slider will make parts of the underlying image show up as if a hole has been punched through the active layer.

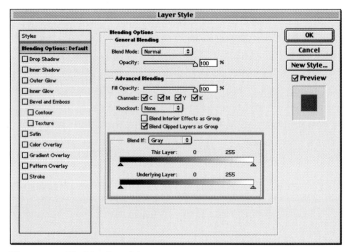

Figure 11.17 The blending sliders.

Figure 11.18 Original unblended image. (Fireworks image © 1998 Corel Corporation; lake image © 1998 Adobe Systems, Inc.)

"This Layer" Sliders

First, let's take a look at the topmost sliders. If you move the left slider towards the middle, the dark areas of the image (that is, all the shades that are to the left of the slider) will start to disappear. This slider can be a great help when you're trying to remove the background from fireworks or lightning. The only problem is, once you get the background to disappear, the edges of the fireworks will have hard, jagged edges (**Figures 11.18 to 11.20**).

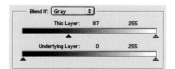

Figure 11.20 Moving the upper left slider makes the dark areas of the current layer disappear.

Figure 11.19 Removing the black sky from the fireworks image.

To remedy this situation, all you have to do is split the slider into two pieces by Option-dragging (Macintosh) or Alt-dragging (Windows) on its right edge. When this slider is split into two parts, the shades of gray that are between the halves will become partially transparent and blend into the underlying image (**Figures 11.21 and 11.22**). The shades close to the left half of the slider will be almost completely transparent, and the shades near the right half will be almost completely opaque.

Figure 11.22 Splitting a triangle into halves allows the image to smoothly blend into the underlying image.

Figure 11.21 The edges of the fireworks blend into the underlying image.

When you move the right slider, you will be making the bright areas of the image (all the shades of gray to the right of the slider) disappear. This slider can be useful when you come across a multi-colored logo that needs to be removed from its white background. Just like with the upper left slider, you can split this slider into two halves by Option-dragging (Macintosh) or Alt-dragging (Windows) its left edge (**Figures 11.23 to 11.25**).

Figure 11.23 Original image. (Courtesy of Nik Willmore)

Figure 11.24 Result of removing all white areas by using the blending sliders.

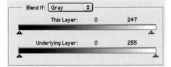

Figure 11.25 Moving the upper right sliders makes the bright areas of this layer disappear.

"Underlying" Sliders

By moving the two sliders on the Underlying bar, you'll be able to make areas of the underlying image show up as if they were creating a hole in the layer you double-clicked. These sliders are useful when you don't want a layer to completely obstruct the view of the underlying image. I might use this to reveal some of the texture in the underlying image. And, just like the top sliders, you can Option-click (Macintosh) or Alt-click (Windows) to separate the sliders into two parts (**Figures 11.26 to 11.28**).

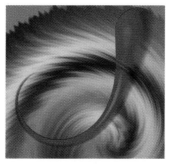

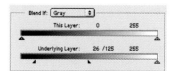

Figure 11.28 Moving the lower left slider makes the dark areas of the underlying image show up as if they are poking a hole in the active layer.

Figure 11.26 Original image.

Figure 11.27 Result of blending in the dark parts of the underlying image.

Understanding the Numbers

The numbers that appear above the sliders indicate the exact location of each slider. If you haven't split any of the sliders, then you should see a total of four numbers (one for each slider). When you split one of the sliders into two parts, you'll see one number for each half of the slider. These numbers use the same numbering system as the Levels dialog box (see Chapter 6, "Optimizing Grayscale Images," for a "Percentage to 0–255" conversion table).

If you move the upper left slider until its number changes to 166, for example, you'll have made all the shades darker than 35% gray on that layer disappear. It would be much easier if Adobe would allow us to switch between percentages and the 0–255 numbering system like you can when using the Curves dialog box.

Using Color Channels

If you leave the pop-up menu at the top of the blending slider area set to gray, then Photoshop will ignore the colors in your document and just analyze the brightness of the image (as if the image were in grayscale mode). By changing this menu, you will be telling Photoshop to look at the information in the individual color channels to determine which areas should be visible (**Figure 11.29**). For example, if you have a document that is in CMYK mode and you change the pop-up menu to cyan and move the upper right slider to 26, you'll make all areas of the layer that contain

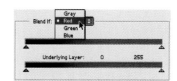

Figure 11.29 The Blend If pop-up menu in the Layer Styles dialog box determines which channels will be analyzed.

10% or less cyan disappear. This can be useful when you want to remove a background that contains one dominant color.

Choosing the best channel from this pop-up menu usually involves a lot of trial and error. I'll show you how I usually figure out which color would be most effective for different images.

First of all, if the color you would like to work with matches one of the components of your image (red, green, or blue in RGB mode), then the choice is pretty straightforward—to work on someone's blue eyes, just work on the blue channel. But what if you want to work on an area that is yellow and your image is in RGB mode? Well, to find out what to do, I usually hold down the Command key (Macintosh) or Ctrl key (Windows) and press the number keys on my keyboard (1–3 for RGB mode, 1–4 for CMYK mode); this will display the different color channels. You'll want to look for the channel that separates the area you're interested in from the areas surrounding it (**Figures 11.30 to 11.32**). When you find the one that looks best, choose its name from the Blend If pop-up menu in the Layer Style dialog box. Once you've found the best channel, glance up at the top of your document and you'll see the name of the channel you are viewing right next to the name of the document.

Now that you have a general feeling for how the blending sliders work, let's take a look at some of the things we can do with them.

Figure 11.30 Red channel. (© 1998 PhotoDisc)

Figure 11.31 Green channel.

Figure 11.32 Blue channel.

Enhancing Clouds

When you choose Filter > Render > Clouds, you'll get great-looking clouds, but there is one problem—you can't see through them. You'll probably want to see through the dark parts of the clouds, so double-click the name of the layer your clouds are on. By moving the upper left slider in, you're going to make the dark parts of the clouds disappear so you can see the underlying image. To make the edges of the clouds blend into the underlying image, hold down the Option key (Macintosh) or Alt key (Windows) and split the upper left slider into two parts. Now by experimenting with the halves of the slider, you'll be able to create the look of fog, faint clouds, or dense clouds (**Figures 11.33 to 11.36**). This technique also works great with photos of real clouds. You can even transform Photoshop's Clouds filter into a hurricane by applying the Twirl filter to it (Filter > Distort > Twirl).

Warning

If you've chosen a color from the pop-up menu before applying the blending sliders, be sure to flatten your image when converting it to another color mode (RGB to CMYK, for example). The appearance of unflattened layers will change because the blending settings will no longer affect the same color channels. If you apply the sliders to the red channel (first choice in the menu) and then convert the image to CMYK mode, the same slider settings will now be applied to the cyan channel (because it's the first choice in the menu). The image will not look the same because the cyan channel doesn't contain the same information that was in the red channel.

Figure 11.33 Original image.

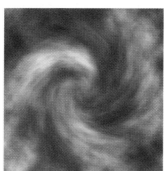

Figure 11.34 After creating a new layer and applying the Clouds and Twirl filters.

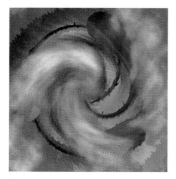

Figure 11.35 Result of discarding the dark area of the clouds by using the blending sliders.

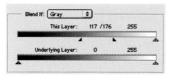

Figure 11.36 Settings used on preceding image.

Homemade Lightning

If you want to play Zeus and create your own lightning, you'll need to start with some clouds; so create a new layer, and then reset your foreground and background colors to their default colors (just press D). Next, choose Filter > Render > Clouds. This will give you clouds, but it won't look anything like lightning, as **Figure 11.37** reveals.

To get closer to something that resembles lightning, choose Filter > Render > Difference Clouds. Then go to the Image menu and choose Adjust > Invert. This should get you a little bit closer to lightning (**Figure 11.38**), but we still have a few steps before it looks electric.

If you remove all the dark information from this image, it might resemble lightning. So double-click the layer and pull in the upper left slider. You'll want to hold down the Option key (Macintosh) or Alt key (Windows) to split the slider into two pieces. Move the right half of the slider all the way to the right edge, as far as you can move it. Then grab the left edge of the slider and start moving it to the right until the lightning looks appropriate for the image, as in **Figure 11.39**. You'll have to move it almost all the way across.

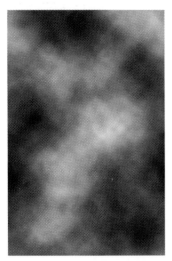

Figure 11.37 The Clouds filter is the starting point for creating artificial lightning.

Figure 11.38 Result of applying Difference Clouds and then inverting.

Figure 11.39 Result of removing all the dark information. (© 1998 PhotoDisc)

Making the Changes Permanent

The problem with the blending sliders is that they are just settings attached to a layer, and Photoshop doesn't provide an obvious way to permanently apply their effects. Well, if you've used only the top sliders, there is an easy way to get Photoshop to permanently delete the hidden areas. To do this, create a brand-new empty layer, and then move that empty layer underneath the layer that is using the blending sliders. Then all you have to do is merge those two layers. To do that, click on the layer that is using the blending sliders, go to the side menu on the Layers palette, and choose Merge Down. By doing this, Photoshop will permanently delete the areas that were transparent. This can be nice if your client requested the layered file, but you don't want them to know how you did it! (See **Figures 11.40 and 11.41**.)

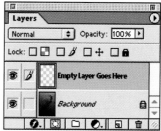

Figure 11.41 Result.

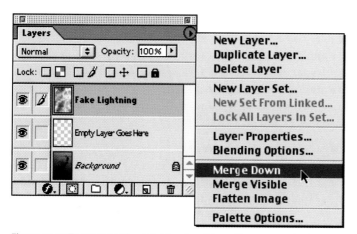

Figure 11.40 To permanently apply blending slider settings, merge the layer with an empty one.

Layer Masks

Now let's take a look at my favorite method for blending images together, layer masks. By adding a layer mask to a layer, you can control exactly where that layer is transparent and where it's opaque. You'll find that layer masks are used to create most high-end images—this feature really separates the beginners from the pros. But there's no reason why you can't be as adept at layer masks as the most seasoned veteran. It just takes a little time and sweat.

Creating a Layer Mask

Note

The only layer (active or otherwise) that you can't add a layer mask to is the background image. But you can change its name to make it become a regular layer (double-click to do this), and then add a layer mask.

Figure 11.42 The softness of your brush determines how soft the edge of the image will appear.

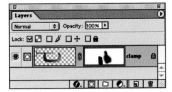

Figure 11.43 Layers palette view.

You can add a layer mask to the active layer by clicking on the icon second from the left at the bottom of the Layers palette (it looks like a rectangle with a circle inside it). Once you click this icon, you'll notice that the layer you're working on contains two thumbnail images in the palette. The one on the left is its normal preview thumbnail; the one on the right is the layer mask thumbnail. The layer mask is not empty (empty looks like a checkerboard, right?); instead, it's full of white. After adding a layer mask, you can edit it by painting across the image window with any painting tool. Even though this would usually change the image, you're really just editing the layer mask; it just isn't visible on the main screen. The color you paint with (which is really a shade of gray) determines what happens to the image. Painting with black will make areas disappear and painting with white will bring back the areas again. And remember, because you are using a painting tool you can choose a hard- or soft-edged brush to control what the edge looks like (**Figures 11.42 and 11.43**).

What's nice about a layer mask is that it doesn't permanently delete areas; it just makes them temporarily disappear. If you paint with white, you'll be able to bring back areas that are transparent. This can be helpful if you're doing a very quick job for a client who wants to see a general concept. You can do just a very crude job of getting rid of the backgrounds of images, and then later on go back in and refine that layer mask to get it to look just right.

Hiding Selected Areas

If a selection is present when adding a layer mask, Photoshop will automatically fill the nonselected areas of the layer mask with black so the image is visible in the selected area only (**Figures 11.44 and 11.45**). Or, if you'd like to hide the selected area and show the rest of the image, hold the Option key (Macintosh) or Alt key (Windows) when you click the layer mask icon. You can see exactly what Photoshop has done by glancing at the layer mask thumbnail in the Layers palette (**Figure 11.46**).

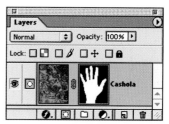

Figure 11.46 Layers palette view.

Figure 11.44 Make a selection before adding a layer mask. (© 1998 PhotoDisc)

Figure 11.45 Result of adding a layer mask.

If you choose Add Layer Mask from the Layer menu instead of just using the icon in the palette, you will be offered some choices:

▶ **Reveal Selection**—Hides the nonselected areas, giving you the same result as using the layer mask icon in the Layers palette.

▶ **Hide Selection**—Hides only the areas that are currently selected, leaving the non-selected areas visible.

▶ **Reveal All**—Does not hide any areas of the layer.

▶ **Hide All**—Hides the entire layer.

Paste Into

If there is a selection present when you're pasting an image into your document, you can choose Edit > Paste Into (instead of Edit > Paste) to automatically create a layer mask. This layer mask will make the image show up only in the area that was selected. You can also hold down the Option key (Macintosh) or Alt key (Windows) and

Notes

When a selection is present, you can Option-click (Macintosh) or Alt-click (Windows) the layer mask icon in the Layers palette to add a layer mask and hide the selected areas. If no selection is present, Option-click (Macintosh) or Alt-click (Windows) the icon to hide the entire image.

To quickly switch between editing the layer mask and editing the main image, use the following keyboard commands.
▶ Command-~ (Macintosh) or Ctrl-~ (Windows) to work on the image
▶ Command-\ (Macintosh) or Ctrl-\ (Windows) to work on the layer mask

choose Edit > Paste Into to hide the selected areas. If you choose Select > All before choosing Paste Into, Photoshop will create a layer mask and reveal the entire image. You can also hold down the Option key (Macintosh) or Alt key (Windows) and choose Paste Into to hide the entire image.

Disabling a Layer Mask

After you've created a layer mask, you can temporarily disable it by Shift-clicking its thumbnail in the Layers palette (**Figures 11.47 to 11.49**). With each click you will toggle the layer mask on or off. This is a great help when you want to see what the layer would look like if you didn't have a layer mask restricting where it shows up.

Figure 11.47 Layer mask active.

Figure 11.48 Layer mask disabled.

Figure 11.49 Layers palette view.

Switching Between the Layer Mask and the Image

Now that you have two thumbnails attached to a layer, you have to be able to determine if you are working on the layer mask or the main image. If you look at the layer mask icon right after you've created one, you'll notice an extra outline around its edge (**Figures 11.50 and 11.51**). That border indicates what you're working on. If you want to work on the main image instead of the layer mask, click the image thumbnail in the Layers palette. The outline will appear around the image thumbnail indicating that you are editing the main image instead of the layer mask. To work on the layer mask again, just click its icon and the outline will move.

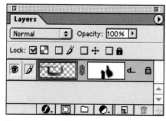

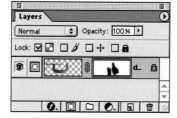

Figure 11.50 Editing the main image.   **Figure 11.51** Editing the layer mask.

There is another way to get a visual indication of whether you're working on the main image or the layer mask. If you look just to the left of the image thumbnail, you'll see a paintbrush icon if you are working on the main image, or the layer mask icon if you're working on a layer mask.

Viewing a Layer Mask

You can also view the layer mask in the main image window. To do this, hold down the Option key (Macintosh) or Alt key (Windows) and click on the layer mask thumbnail (**Figure 11.52**). You'll see it looks just like a grayscale image, and you can actually paint right on this image. I use this a lot when I get someone else's document, or when I open an old document I worked on months ago and can't remember exactly what I did in the layer mask. To stop viewing the layer mask, just Option-click (Macintosh) or Alt-click (Windows) its icon a second time.

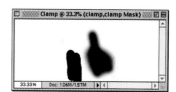

Figure 11.52 Viewing the layer mask in the main image window.

Shades of Gray

Photoshop treats a layer mask as if it were a grayscale document. That means that you can use any editing tool that is available to a grayscale image. Areas that are full of pure black will become transparent, pure white areas will be completely opaque, and areas that contain shades of gray will become partially transparent. Painting with 20% gray in a layer mask will lower the opacity of that area to 80%. So using a painting tool with an opacity setting of 80% will

> **Note**
> You can view a layer mask as a color overlay (just like Quick Mask mode) by Shift-Option-clicking (Macintosh) or Shift-Alt-clicking (Windows) on the layer mask icon, or by just typing \ (backslash).

produce the same result as painting with 100% opacity and then adding a layer mask that is full of 20% gray.

Filling Areas

Because Photoshop treats layer masks as if they are grayscale documents, you can create selections and fill those areas with white or black to hide or show the contents of a layer. To fill a selected area with the current foreground color (which is usually black), press Option-Delete (Macintosh) or Alt-Backspace (Windows). To fill a selected area with the current background color (usually white), press Command-Delete (Macintosh) or Ctrl-Backspace (Windows). This is nice because it frees you from having to use the painting tools.

Using Gradients

The most common way to make one image fade into another is to add a layer mask and then use the Gradient tool. In a layer mask, areas that are pure black become completely transparent and areas that are pure white are completely opaque. Shades of gray in a layer mask will make the image become partially transparent. So, if you would like one image to fade into another, apply a gradient to a layer mask with the Gradient tool set to Black, White (**Figures 11.53 to 11.55**).

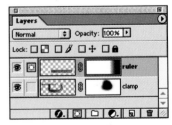

Figure 11.53 Image before adding a layer mask.

Figure 11.54 Result of applying a gradient to a layer mask.

Figure 11.55 Layers palette view.

If you try to apply the gradient a second time, you might run into a few problems. If you apply the gradient from right to left one time, and then immediately after that you apply a second gradient in the other direction, the second gradient will completely obstruct the first one. To combine two gradients, set the Gradient tool to Foreground To Transparent and make sure the foreground color is set to black. Then you should be able to apply the Gradient tool as many times as you want within a layer mask, and it simply adds to what was already in the layer mask (**Figures 11.56 to 11.59**).

Figure 11.56 First gradient.

Figure 11.57 Second gradient using Foreground To Background setting.

Figure 11.58 Second gradient using Foreground To Transparent setting.

Figure 11.59 Both ends of the ruler image blend into the underlying image because two gradients were used.

Applying Filters

After painting in a layer mask, you can enhance the result by applying filters to it (**Figures 11.60 to 11.63**). Choose Filter > Distort, and then select something like Ripple. Then, instead of having a really smooth transition, there will be some texture in it.

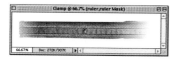

Figure 11.60 Original image.

Figure 11.61 Original layer mask.

Figure 11.62 Result of applying the Ripple filter to the layer mask.

Figure 11.63 Modified layer mask.

If you want the edge of an image to fade out slowly, you can choose Filter > Blur > Gaussian Blur. You can blur a layer mask as many times as you'd like; each time you blur it, the edge will become softer (**Figures 11.64 to 11.66**).

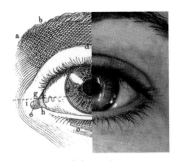

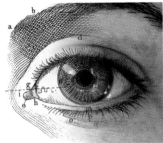

Figure 11.64 Color eye image contains a pure black and pure white layer mask. (Photo © 1998 PhotoDisc)

Figure 11.65 Apply the Gaussian Blur filter to a layer mask to give it softer edges.

Figure 11.66 Result of blurring the layer mask.

You can also expand or contract the areas that are transparent by choosing Minimum or Maximum from the Filter > Other menu (**Figures 11.67 to 11.69**). The Minimum filter will make more areas transparent, while the Maximum filter will make fewer areas transparent.

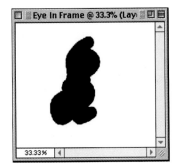

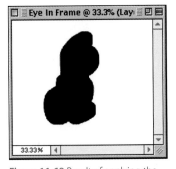

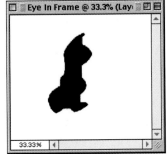

Figure 11.67 Original image.

Figure 11.68 Result of applying the Minimum filter.

Figure 11.69 Result of applying the Maximum filter.

Interesting Edges

To create a rippled-edge effect on your mask, try this out. Open the photograph you want to apply the effect to, and make a selection with the Marquee tool. Make sure your selection is a little inside the edge of the photograph (so there's room for our effect). To get the photograph to show up only where the rectangular selection is, click the layer mask icon at the bottom of the Layers palette.

Now you can distort the edge of the photo by using any filter you'd like (**Figures 11.70 to 11.72**). For now, just use one of the filters under the Filter > Distort menu, such as Ripple, Twirl, or Polar Coordinates.

Figure 11.70 Result of adding a layer mask to limit where the photo shows up. (© 2001 Stockbyte, www.stockbyte.com)

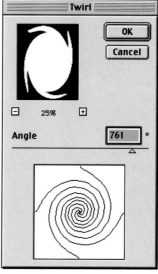

Figure 11.71 First apply the Twirl filter.

Once you're happy with how the edge looks, you might want to add some other effects, such as a black border around our shape. There's a trick for that, too. Choose Layer > Layer Style > Inner Glow (**Figures 11.73 and 11.74**). Now click on the color swatch to pick the color you would like to use and set the Mode pop-up menu to Normal. To get the color to appear around the edge of the image only, be sure Edge is chosen at the bottom of the dialog box. Now you can experiment with the Opacity, Size, and Choke settings to fine-tune the result. If you are having trouble getting the edge to completely show up, try increasing the Opacity and Choke settings. You don't have to restrict yourself to the Inner Glow effect, so experiment with the other layer styles until you find your favorite.

Figure 11.72 Then apply the Radial Blur filter.

Figure 11.73 Result of adding an Inner Glow layer effect.

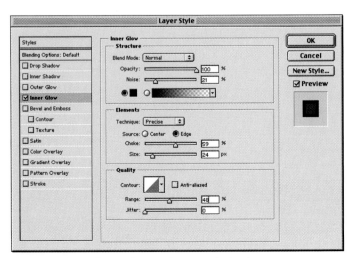

Figure 11.74 Inner Glow settings used to create the border.

Adjusting with Levels

You can also adjust the appearance of a layer mask (as long as it contains shades of gray) by choosing Image > Adjust > Levels. The sliders in the Levels dialog box (**Figure 11.75**) will do the following to your image:

▶ **Upper left slider**—Forces the darkest shades of gray to black, which will make more areas transparent.

▶ **Upper right slider**—Forces the brightest shades of gray to white, which will make more areas opaque.

▶ **Middle slider**—Changes the transition from black to white and, therefore changes the transition from opaque to transparent.

▶ **Lower left slider**—Lightens the dark shades of gray, which will make transparent areas appear more opaque.

▶ **Lower right slider**—Darkens the bright shades of gray, which will make opaque areas appear more transparent.

Image as Layer Mask

You can achieve interesting transition effects by pasting scanned images into a layer mask (**Figures 11.76 and 11.77**). I like to run off to the art supply store, purchase interesting

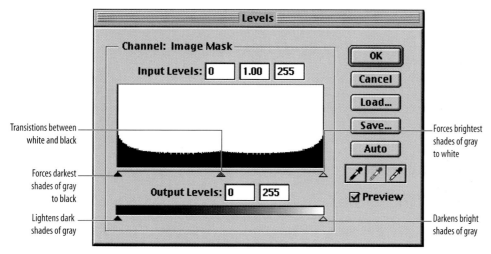

Figure 11.75 The Levels dialog box.

handmade papers, and spatter a bunch of ink on them using paintbrushes. Then, to get the image into a layer mask, I scan the paper, select the entire image by choosing Select > Select All, and then copy the image by choosing Edit > Copy. After I've done that, I close the scanned image and switch over to the image I would like to use it in. Next, I click on the layer I would like to work on and add a layer mask. In order to paste something into a layer mask, you must be viewing the layer mask. That means you must Option-click (Macintosh) or Alt-click (Windows) the layer mask before pasting something into it. To stop viewing the layer mask, just Option-click (Macintosh) or Alt-click (Windows) its thumbnail again.

Note

To quickly paste something into a layer mask, press the \ key to view the layer mask, type Command-V (Macintosh) or Ctrl-V (Windows) to paste the image, and finally type \ again to stop viewing the layer mask. This technique does not view the layer mask as it would normally appear; it shows up as a color overlay.

Figure 11.76 Scanned image to be used as a layer mask.

Figure 11.77 Two images blended together using scanned image as layer mask. (© 1998 PhotoDisc)

Using the Move Tool

After you have created the perfect layer mask, you might want to start rearranging your document by using the Move tool. You have three choices: you can move just the layer, just the layer mask, or both at the same time. The link symbol between the layer mask and image thumbnails determines what the Move tool will actually move. If the link symbol is present (that's the default), the layer and layer mask will move together (**Figures 11.78 to 11.80**).

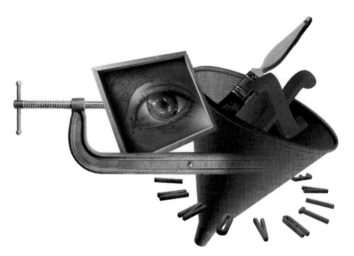

Figure 11.78 Original image.

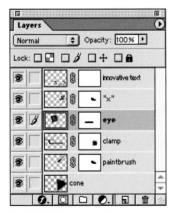

Figure 11.79 Layer and layer mask thumbnails linked together.

Figure 11.80 Eye layer and layer mask moved together.

If you turn off the link symbol (by clicking it), then you'll only be moving whatever has the extra-outline border around it. That means if the layer mask has it, you'll just be moving that around the screen. And if the main image has it, you'll move just the main image around the screen, leaving the layer mask in its original position (**Figures 11.81 and 11.82**). If part of the layer mask lines up with another part of the image, you'll want to move just the layer and not the layer mask (**Figures 11.83 and 11.84**).

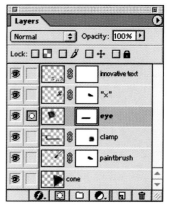

Figure 11.81 Moving just the layer mask, leaving the main image stationary.

Figure 11.82 When the link symbol is missing, the outlined border (layer mask) determines what will get moved.

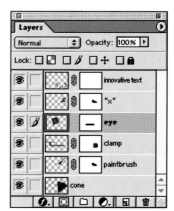

Figure 11.83 Moving the main image, leaving the layer mask stationary.

Figure 11.84 When the link symbol is missing, the outlined border (layer) determines what will get moved.

Load as Selection

Once you have perfected a layer mask, you might need to select the areas that are visible in order to add a border or perform another effect. You can do this in many ways. The fastest method is to Command-click (Macintosh) or Ctrl-click (Windows) the layer mask thumbnail, as demonstrated in **Figures 11.85 and 11.86**. If there is already a selection present, you can Shift-Command-click (Macintosh) or Shift-Ctrl-click (Windows) to add to the selection; Option-Command-click (Macintosh) or Alt-Ctrl-click (Windows) to subtract from it; or Shift-Option-Command-click (Macintosh) or Shift-Alt-Ctrl-click (Windows) to intersect the selection. Or, if you are not very good at remembering a bunch of keyboard commands, you can Control-click (Mac) or right-click (Windows) the layer mask thumbnail to get a menu of options.

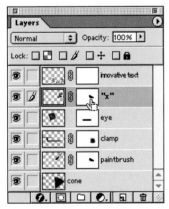

Figure 11.85 Command-click (Macintosh) or Ctrl-click (Windows) the layer mask thumbnail to select the areas that are visible.

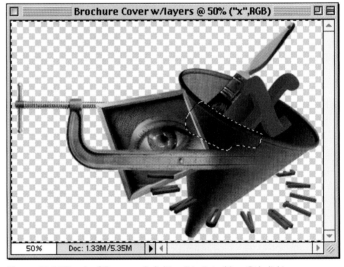

Figure 11.86 Result of Command-clicking (Macintosh) or Ctrl-clicking (Windows) on the "x" layer's layer mask thumbnail.

Converting the Blending Sliders into a Layer Mask

Earlier in this chapter we talked about making areas of a layer transparent using the blending sliders in the Layer Style dialog box. Occasionally, you might need to turn off the sliders and create a layer mask that produces the same result. (Why? You might want to be able to edit the layer mask using painting tools and filters instead of just the blending sliders.) To accomplish this, you'll need to go through a multi-step process.

First, create a new empty layer below the layer that is using the blending sliders. Next, click the layer above it (the one that uses the blending sliders) and type Option-Command-E (Macintosh) or Alt-Ctrl-E (Windows). This deposits information into the layer that does not use the blending sliders, but produces the same results (permanently deleting the transparent areas).

Now you can double-click the layer that uses the blending sliders and set all the sliders back to default positions so they are no longer affecting the layer. Then, to add a layer mask that produces the same result, Command-click (Macintosh) or Ctrl-click (Windows) the layer directly below the one that was using the sliders (to select its shape), and finally click the layer mask icon on the layer that used the sliders (**Figures 11.87 and 11.88**).

Figure 11.87 Result of typing Option-Command-E (Macintosh) or Alt-Ctrl-E (Windows) with an empty layer.

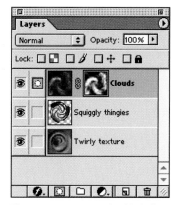

Figure 11.88 Layer mask added after Command-clicking (Mac) or Ctrl-clicking (Windows) the merged layer.

Remove Layer Mask

If you know you will no longer need to edit a layer mask and would like to permanently delete the areas that are transparent, you can choose one of the options from the

Note
A quick way to remove a layer mask is to drag its thumbnail to the trash can icon that appears in the Layers palette.

Layer > Remove Layer Mask menu (**Figures 11.89 and 11.90**). When you do this, you will be presented with two choices.

▶ **Apply**—Removes the layer mask and deletes all transparent areas.

▶ **Discard**—Removes the layer mask and brings the image back into full view.

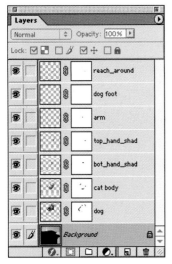

Figure 11.89 Simplified version of the "Dog & Cat" image shown at the beginning of this chapter. I removed over a dozen adjustment layers, all of which had layer masks attached to them.

Figure 11.90 Final "Dog & Cat" image.
Original image courtesy of Robert Bowen Studio, Sony Electronics, Inc., and Lowe & Partners/SMS. Photography by Howard Berman.

Layer Clipping Paths

Layer clipping paths allow you to control which area of a layer will be visible, by using an easily editable, smooth-shaped, crisp-edged path. This capability is brand new to Photoshop 6.0 and it represents a rather radical shift from what was possible in the past. Before 6.0, everything created in Photoshop was made out of pixels, where the resolution of the file determined how large the pixels would be when printed. If those pixels where large enough, then the image would appear jaggy when printed. But with layer clipping paths, you can create a very low resolution (read: jaggy) image and still get a smooth-shaped, crisp-edged transition between the content of a layer and the underlying image.

Adding a Layer Clipping Path

The simplest way to add a layer clipping path is to choose Layer > Add Layer Clipping Path > Reveal All. After you choose that option, the layer that is active will have two thumbnail images in the Layers palette (**Figure 11.91**). It should look like you just added a layer mask. The only difference is that with a layer mask, you paint with shades of gray to control which areas of a layer will be hidden or visible, whereas with a layer clipping path, you define the area that will be visible using a path.

The easiest way to define where the image should be visible is to use one of the shape tools. Before you start creating shapes, be sure to take a peek at the settings in the Options bar. You should find four options available on the left side of the Options bar when a layer that contains a layer clipping path is active. The leftmost choice allows you to create a shape to define where the image should be visible (**Figure 11.92**). The second choice will allow you to define a shape where the image should be hidden (**Figure 11.93**). The third choice will limit the areas that are already visible, so they only show up within the shape you draw (**Figure 11.94**). And the last choice will invert the visibility of the area inside the shape you draw, making visible areas hidden and hidden areas visible (**Figure 11.95**).

You can also use any of the Pen tools to create and modify a layer clipping path. If you're not already familiar with the Pen tools, then start out with the Freeform Pen tool because it allows you to create a path by drawing a freeform shape, much like the Lasso tool allows you to create a selection.

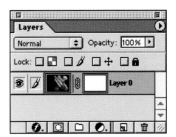

Figure 11.91 After adding a layer clipping path, you will see two thumbnail images in the Layers palette.

Note

To change the options for a shape, click on the shape with the solid-arrow tool and then change the settings that appear in the Options bar.

Figure 11.92 This shape defines where the image is visible.

Figure 11.93 The shape that was added is being used to hide part of the image.

Figure 11.94 The shape that was added is being used to limit where the image is visible.

Figure 11.95 The shape that was added is being used to invert the visibility of the image.

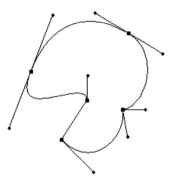

Figure 11.96 A path is made from many points and directional handles.

Figure 11.97 The curve of the handle changes from a tight curve to a more gradual one right where a point would be needed. (© 2001 Stockbyte, www.stockbyte.com)

Using the Pen Tool

The Pen tool can be a little tricky to learn because it does-n't work like anything else in Photoshop. Instead of creating shapes out of a grid of solid-colored squares (pixels), the Pen tool creates shapes from a collection of points and directional handles (**Figure 11.96**). If you've used Adobe Illustrator, then you might be familiar with paths, but just in case you're not, let's take a look at how they work.

First off, you'll need to think of the shape that you'd like to create as being made of a series of curves and straight lines that connect to one another. Visualize tracing around the shape and looking for transitions where one curve connects with another. That might be in an area where a very tight curve starts to become more gradual, like on some coffee cup handles (**Figure 11.97**). At each of these transitions, you'll want to click with the Pen tool to add a point.

When adding a point you'll need to click and drag if you are looking to create a smooth curve. If you don't drag, you'll end up with a sharp corner instead of a curve. When you click and drag, you'll add a point and pull a set of directional handles out of that point. The angle of the directional handles determines what direction the path will go when it leaves that handle, so make sure it points in the direction you want the curve to go in (**Figure 11.98**). I think of it as if you were walking around the edge of the shape using baby steps. Just think of what direction would you take for your first step—that's the same direction the directional handle should point when entering and exit-ing a point. When you first pull out a set of handles, they will both move at the same time and act a bit like a seesaw in that their angles will create a straight line that goes all the way through the point.

The lengths of the directional handles determine the over-all shape of the curve (**Figure 11.99**). Getting the length of the handles to be just right is difficult, because the curve won't show up until the next handle is made, and its han-dles will also influence the shape of the curve—so for now, keep your handles short.

Once you've added the next point and got the angle of the handle that points towards the last point positioned correctly, it'll be time to adjust the length of the handles. I find it easiest to adjust the handle lengths by holding the Command key (Macintosh) or Ctrl key (Windows) and dragging the middle of the curve that appears between the two points you just created (**Figure 11.100**). It's a little tricky, but by pulling on the middle of the curve, you should be able to get the curve to fit the shape you were attempting to create. If you find that you just can't get it to become what you need, then one of the directional handles must be pointing in the wrong direction. If you continue to hold down the Command key (Macintosh) or Ctrl key (Windows), then you should be able to reposition the directional handles as well.

On occasion, you'll find that you need one curve to abruptly change direction instead of smoothly flow into another curve. When that happens, remember that the directional handles determine which direction your path will go when it leaves a point. That means you'll need the two handles that come out of a point to be at radically different angles. You can accomplish that by holding the Option key (Macintosh) or Alt key (Windows) and dragging one of the handles that protrudes from the point you just created (**Figure 11.101**).

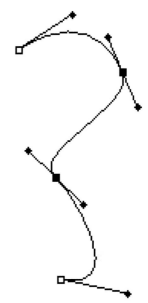

Figure 11.98 Click and drag to create a smooth curve.

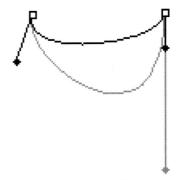

Figure 11.99 The length of the directional handles determine the overall shape of the curve.

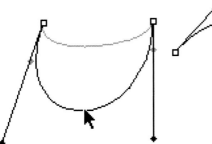

Figure 11.100 Hold Command or Ctrl and drag the curve to adjust the length of the directional handles.

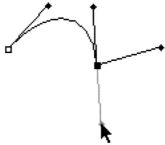

Figure 11.101 Hold Option or Alt to change the angle of one directional handle without affecting the other handle connected to that point.

Sometimes you will need to have a curve end at an abrupt corner, where the next portion of the shape will be a straight line. In that case, you'll need a handle on the side of the point that points towards the curve, and no handle on the side of the straight line. To accomplish that, right after adding the point and pulling out the handles, Option-click (Macintosh) or Alt-click (Windows) the point and Photoshop will retract the handle on the open end of the path (**Figure 11.102**).

Figure 11.102 A curve ending in an abrupt corner.

By combining these ideas you should be able to create just about any smooth shape you can think of. But since it's not an overly natural process, it might take you a while to master using the Pen tool. If you don't feel like tackling it right now, then stick with the shape tools and the Freeform Pen tool.

If you already have a path saved in your file (it will show up in the Paths palette), you can use it as a layer clipping path. Just make sure the layer you'd like to apply it to is active (you can't add one to the background layer), click on the name of the path in the Paths palette, and then choose Layer > Add Layer Clipping Path > Current Path. That will allow you to use any paths that are included with stock photos you have purchased.

Disabling the Layer Clipping Path

After you have created a layer clipping path, you can temporarily disable it by Shift-clicking its thumbnail in the Layers palette (**Figures 11.103 and 11.104**). With each click you will toggle the layer clipping path on and off. This is a great help when you want to see what a layer would look like if you didn't have a layer clipping path restricting where it shows up.

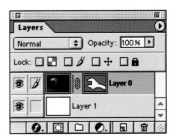

Figure 11.103 Layer clipping path active.

Using the Move Tool

When you use the Move tool to reposition a layer, you'll notice that the layer and the layer clipping path move together (**Figure 11.105 to 11.107**). If you turn off the link symbol (by clicking it), you'll leave the layer clipping path alone and just move the image (**Figure 11.108**).

If you'd like to move the layer clipping path and leave the image stationary, use the solid arrow tool that appears directly above the Pen tools (**Figure 11.109**).

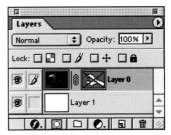

Figure 11.104 Layer clipping path disabled.

Figure 11.105 Original Image. (© 2001 Stockbyte, www.stockbyte.com)

Figure 11.106 Layer and layer clipping path moved together.

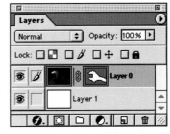

Figure 11.107 Layer and layer clipping path linked together.

Figure 11.108 Layer clipping path left stationary while the layer is repositioned.

Figure 11.109 Use the solid arrow tool to reposition a layer clipping path.

Transforming the Layer Clipping Path

The Edit > Transform commands are very useful when working on a layer clipping path. Since the path is made from a collection of points and directional handles (instead of pixels), scaling, rotating and other transformations will not degrade the quality of the shape. All you have to do is make sure the path is visible before you choose Transform Path from the Edit menu. You can toggle the visibility of a layer clipping path by clicking its thumbnail in the Layers palette.

Removing the Layer Clipping Path

If you find that you'd like to remove the layer clipping path from your image, just choose Layer > Delete Layer Clipping Path, or drag its thumbnail to the trash can that appears at the bottom of the Layers palette. You can also convert a layer clipping path into a layer mask by choosing Layer > Rasterize > Layer Clipping Path. But be aware that you'll lose the crisp-edged, smooth look of the path, and any transformations applied to the layer mask will cause it to appear blurry.

Saving Vector Data

If you plan on saving your image and using it in a page layout program (instead of using it for a Web site), then you'll need to be careful about how you save it; otherwise, the crisp edge of your path may be lost. Remember when I said that a path is different than pixels in that it's made out of points and directional handles? Well, technically, that's known as vector information, whereas images made from pixels are known as raster information. In order to maintain the crisp edges of your paths, you'll need to save your image in the EPS or PDF file formats (which support vector data). Not only that, but you'll have to turn on the Include Vector Data checkbox (**Figure 11.110**) when saving your file (this option only shows up *after* you click the Save button). There's one last thing: your paths will only print with crisp edges if you print to a PostScript output device like a $500+ laser printer. Most inkjet printers don't understand PostScript, so your image has the potential of appearing jaggy on those.

Note

You can print an image that contains vector data on a non-PostScript printer and maintain the crisp edges by saving it as a PDF file and printing it from Adobe Acrobat.

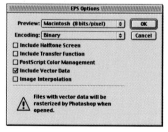

Figure 11.110 Turn on the Include Vector Data checkbox when saving your image for print-based publishing.

Image Clipping Path

You can also assign a path to a document, as opposed to a single layer. An image clipping path will limit which areas of an image will show up and print in a page layout program (**Figures 11.111 and 11.112**). These paths are simply known as clipping paths. To create one, use the Pen or a shape tool to create a path, and then choose Window > Show Paths to open the Paths palette. Next, double-click the name of the path and assign it a name. Then choose Clipping Path from the side menu of the Paths palette (**Figure 11.113**). When prompted, be sure to enter a Flatness setting. When the image is printed, it will be converted into a polygon made out of straight lines of identical length. The Flatness setting will determine the length of those lines. Low settings product short lines, which require more memory and processing time to output. If you use too low of a setting, then your printer might run out of memory when attempting to output your image. The more complex your path is (lots of points and directional handles), the higher a flatness setting is necessary to avoid printing problems. In general, I use a setting between 3 and 10 depending on the complexity of the path I'm using. After you've assigned a clipping path to an image, you'll need to save it in the TIFF or EPS file formats in order for it to be understood by a page layout program.

Figure 11.111 Image imported into a page layout program without a clipping path.

Figure 11.112 Image imported into a page layout program with clipping path.

Figure 11.113 Choose Clipping Path from the side menu of the Paths palette.

Closing Thoughts

I hope that you get as much of a kick out of blending images as I do. It's one of those things that never gets old; I can always count on another surprise waiting for me around the corner. We always have bets going on in our office about whether or not certain images have been "Photoshopped." That's how Robert Bowen's dog/cat piece for Sony found its way into this book. We saw the Sony ad in a magazine and had a day-long debate about whether or not you could actually get a dog and a cat to embrace like that. I lost the bet. Photoshop won.

I also hope that you'll devote some serious time to playing around with the three methods of blending (grouping layers, blending sliders, and layer masks), as well as learning how to use the layer clipping paths. Both separately and together, they will give you enormous amounts of freedom to do wondrous and strange things with your images. And besides all that, it can impress the heck out of your boss or next client.

The image of the dog and cat together on the sofa was created as an ad for a Sony video camera that has the capability of actually seeing in the dark. This picture is a composite created from several photographs that Howard Berman made of each animal. There were various heads, paws, tails, and body positions, which we brought together in Photoshop layers. These layers were then distorted and merged. The Shear filter was used to warp many of the elements. We studied the viewfinder of the actual video display and emulated the shadowing effect produced by the camera. We wanted the final image to appear both humorous and accurate to the technology it was representing.

—Robert Bowen

Courtesy of Robert Bowen Studio, Sony Electronics, Inc., and Lowe & Partners/SMS. Photography by Howard Berman. Art Director: Maria Kostyk-Petro.

Photography: Ryszard Horowitz. Computer artist: Robert Bowen

Courtesy of Louis Fishauf

Computer artist: Robert Bowen

© Bob Elsdale, www.bobelsdale.com

12 Enhancement

Elwood: *It's 106 miles
to Chicago, we've got a
full tank of gas, half
a pack of cigarettes,
it's dark, and we're
wearing sunglasses.*
Jake: *Hit it!*
–The Blues Brothers

Courtesy of Diane Fenster, www.dianefenster.com

To claim that I can teach you everything you need to know about enhancement is pure insanity. The potential is so vast that there really is no road map to guide us—only past experience. So use this chapter as your fueling stop, and then break loose and go looking for your own path. We'll fill up on a mixed bag of methods and techniques for enhancement—sort of a cookbook of digital recipes, taking what you've already learned from previous chapters and adding some interesting twists and embellishments (in this case, a lot of the twists have to do with blending modes). And if anyone tries to slow you down, just remember what Elwood Blues said to the policeman: "The light was yellow, sir."

Cooking With Pixels

As we get into each recipe, I will oftentimes show you multiple ways of accomplishing the same result. I do that on purpose. Sometimes you need the quick and easy method, and other times you will want to use the slow and more precise method, which gives you more control and flexibility. Instead of being limited to just one technique, you can glance through the different approaches and choose what you think might be best for your particular situation.

First, a little bit about how this chapter is organized. Many of the techniques I'm going to cover involve blending modes, so I've used blending modes as the underlying structure. I'll start with the top of the Blending Modes menu and work my way down (**Figure 12.1**). Each one of these modes will allow you to blend two images together in unique and unusual ways.

Dissolving Glows

Sometimes I find inspiration in the weirdest places. A friend of mine wanted to stop by a local Starbucks, and I obliged him, even though I can't stand the taste of coffee (and you don't want to see what happens to me when I have caffeine). I was sitting there right next to the checkout register when I spotted a bottled coffee drink called

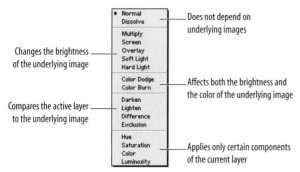

Figure 12.1 The Blending Modes menu is organized into five sections.

Frappuccino. And right at that moment I figured out a use for two unusual features in Photoshop. This might not sound all that exciting to you, but the more uses I can find for these things, the more I really understand them. So, I'll share with you what I came up with. The Frappuccino logo had an interesting two-color noisy glow behind the text, and I thought it might be fun to make it. And do you know what? It was (**Figure 12.2**). I'll walk you through what I did.

Figure 12.2 Example of Diffused Glow effect.

Create Glow Behind Text

First, scan in some black text (using a resolution of 300) and then remove the white background that always comes along for the ride. Press Option-Command-~ (Macintosh) or Alt-Ctrl-~ (Windows) to load the image as if it were a channel, and then choose Select > Inverse to produce a selection that is the same shape as the text. (It will even contain any shades of gray that were in the edge of the text. Thus, if there was 30% gray at the edge, now you have an area that is 30% selected.)

Now you want to fill this selection, so create a new layer, reset your foreground color to black by pressing D, and press Option-Delete (Macintosh) or Alt-Backspace (Windows) to fill it with black. You should now have a layer containing the text, sans the white background, so it's safe to get rid of the layer that contains the original scan. One word of caution at this point: When you typed the first keyboard command, Photoshop might have selected the exact opposite of what you were expecting (the background instead of the text). This can happen if you've messed with the settings in the Channels palette. But if that happened, it's no problem; all you have to do is choose Select > Inverse to fix things up.

Now that the background is gone, we can get on to our glow. You want to make sure the glow will be easy to see, so we'll doctor it up a little bit. Type Q to turn on Quick Mask mode, choose Filter > Other > Maximum, use a low number like 6, and then turn off Quick Mask mode by typing Q again. This will pull out the edges of the selection to make it larger. Next, you'll want to create a red blob, so make a new layer below the one that contains the text, change your foreground color to red, and press Option-Delete (Macintosh) or Alt-Backspace (Windows) to fill the selection (**Figure 12.3**).

> **Note**
>
> As an alternative to scanning in some text and removing the background, you can always enter your own text directly, using the Type tool. Once you've got the text, choose Layer > Rasterize > Type, and then Command-click (Macintosh) or Ctrl-click (Windows) the name of the layer. At this point, you'll be ready to make the glow.

Figure 12.3 The beginnings of a red glow.

Next, get rid of your selection by choosing Select > Deselect, and set the blending mode of the layer with the red glow to Dissolve (choose it from the pop-up menu at the top of the Layers palette). The Dissolve blending mode doesn't allow any pixels to be partially transparent; instead, it uses a pattern of noise to allow an area to blend into the underlying image. To transform your red blob into a dissolving glow, choose Filter > Blur > Gaussian Blur and experiment until you get just the right amount of glow. For this example I used a Radius of 5 (**Figure 12.4**).

Figure 12.4 Result of blurring a layer that is set to Dissolve.

This looks good, but the glow on the Frappuccino bottle contains two colors, so we still have some work to do. So, create a new layer directly above your red glow and set its mode to Dissolve as well. We want this second color to appear only where the original red glow was, so choose Layer > Group With Previous. (Grouping two layers forces the top one to show up only where the bottom layer contains information.) After you get all that put together, use the Lasso tool to select the bottom half of the red glow, type Q to turn on Quick Mask mode, choose Filter > Blur > Gaussian Blur, and use the same setting as when you blurred the original glow. Type Q again to turn off Quick Mask mode. Then, to fill the selected area, change your foreground color to green and press Option-Delete on the Macintosh or Alt-Backspace in Windows (**Figure 12.5**).

Figure 12.5 Filling the bottom of the glow with green.

Chunkify the Glow

After doing all that, I decided the glow didn't look chunky enough; the pixels were just too darn small. I decided to try something a little different. So, if you're still along for the ride, we will need to create a new document that is the

Figure 12.6 Link the glow layers and drag them to the new document.

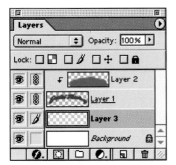

Figure 12.7 Create a new layer, and then merge the glow layers with it.

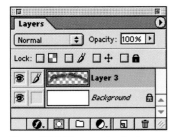

Figure 12.8 After merging the layers, the glow no longer uses the Dissolve blending mode.

same size as the one you were working on. Choose File > New and then, while the New dialog box is still open, choose the name of your "glow" document from the Window menu (that enters the width, height, and resolution of the document). Click OK to proceed with the new document. Next, you need to copy the two glow layers into that new document, so link the layers together and drag them (from the main image window, not the Layers palette) to the second document with the Move tool (**Figure 12.6**); hold down Shift to keep them in the same position.

Now we need to get the dots that make up the dissolved glow to change size. To do this, we're going to scale this new document down, mess with it, and then scale it back up. First, choose Image > Image Size, make sure the Resample Image and Constrain Proportions checkboxes are checked, and its menu is set to Bicubic (the default settings). Then change the Width pop-up menu to Percent, use 50%, and click OK.

Now we want to lock in the dots of the glow at their current size, which means that we don't want to use the Dissolve blending mode anymore. (When you use Dissolve, you cannot vary the size of the dots.) So to keep the same look and lock in the size of the dots, create a new layer, and position it below the two layers that make up the glow (**Figure 12.7**). Next, click on the layer that contains the green glow, unlink it from the red one, and then choose Layer > Merge Down, twice. This should cause the two glow layers to lose their blending mode setting (while keeping the same appearance), combine together, and appear on the new layer (**Figure 12.8**).

Now we just need to enlarge the pixels into squares and get them back into the original document. So choose Image > Image Size and again make sure Resample Image is turned on; but this time, set its pop-up menu to Nearest Neighbor. Most people think of this mode as almost useless because it just turns pixels into big squares, but in this case, it will be a big help. When we scaled down the image, we used 50%; so to get it back to its original dimensions, we'll have to use 200%.

To finish the effect, we'll need to get our modified glow back into the original document, so use the Move tool and drag the image back into the original document while pressing the Shift key. Now you will have two glows, so just throw away the two layers that made up the original glow and move the new glow so it is centered below the text (**Figure 12.9**).

Figure 12.9 After replacing the original glow, you should have the finished effect.

Colorizing Line Art

My brother is an artist in New York City. He does sketches with a fine ink pen, and his pieces always have lots of very intricate and involved detail—the kind of detail that you have to do a double or triple take on before you realize what's going on in the image. He likes to experiment with colors before he starts turning these images into paintings or other types of finished art. So he scans these black and white sketches and uses Photoshop to add color between all the black lines.

You, too, can do this very quickly in Photoshop, as long as you know about the Multiply blending mode (we've already used it once in Chapter 10, "Shadows"). The Multiply mode is like printing twice on the same sheet of paper. For instance, if you print an image that contains a black and white sketch and then you sent that sheet of paper back through your printer and printed another image that contained solid areas of color, the black lines of the sketch would completely obstruct your view of the colors (because transparent inks are used in CMYK printing), and the white areas of the first image would disappear, revealing the colors below. Using Multiply, you should be able to fill white areas in an image without having to worry about messing up the black lines of a sketch.

The way I'd do this would be to set the Paint Bucket tool's blending mode to Multiply and use a medium Tolerance setting (so it can get into any grays that are on the edge of the sketch). Then you click the Paint Bucket tool to fill in all the white areas of the sketch (**Figure 12.10**). After making your way across the entire image, you'll have a fully colorized image.

Figure 12.10 You can quickly colorize a line art image using the Paint Bucket tool and the Multiply blending mode. (Courtesy of Nik Willmore)

If you really want to see what Multiply does to an image, just open your favorite photo and create a new layer that's set to Multiply. Then use the Gradient tool set to Black, White, and drag across the entire width of the document. You should notice that white areas don't change the image at all, and shades of gray darken the image (**Figures 12.11 and 12.12**). You can also try placing two photographs one on top of the other, and setting the top one to Multiply (**Figures 12.13 and 12.14**).

Figure 12.11 Original image. (© 1998 Adobe Systems, Inc.)

Figure 12.12 Gradient set to Multiply.

Adding Density to Areas

Many of the images I'm asked to work with are less than ideal. Whenever the images don't originate from a professional photographer, I can always count on having to do a lot more color correction and making up for areas that are not properly exposed. But as long as there is still some detail in the under- and overexposed areas, I can usually fix them.

If you are crafty with blending modes, you can often perform miracles on these problematic images. There are two modes that will help you out: Multiply and Screen. I've already talked about Multiply in the chapter on shadows and in the technique previous to this one, so before we start repairing images, let's talk about Screen. If Multiply is like using ink to print two images on top of each other on the same sheet of paper, then Screen is the exact opposite. You might be thinking, "What could possibly be the opposite of that?" Well, all ink does is absorb some of the light that falls on a sheet of paper and let some of it reflect off the paper and into your eyes, right? Then the opposite of that would be to create your image using light! This time, think of projecting two images using a slide projector onto the same screen. Well, that's what Screen mode is like. The main thing to get out of this is that Multiply can only darken areas (like ink does), and Screen can only brighten them (like light does).

Try this simple experiment: Find some text or a simple sketch that contains black lines on a white background (you can scan it into Photoshop if you don't already have a file like this). Move that image on top of a photograph, and then set the blending mode at the top of the Layers palette to Multiply. That should cause the white areas of the black and white image to disappear, leaving just the black lines overprinting on the underlying image (**Figure 12.15**). If you're not sure why the white areas are gone, then just think about how Multiply mode is like using ink to print two images on top of each other. How do you print white? Don't you just leave the paper alone?

Figure 12.13 This image contains two layers. (© 1998 PhotoSpin, www.photospin.com)

Figure 12.14 The top layer of this document is set to Multiply.

Figure 12.15 Using Multiply to combine a sketch with a photo. (© 2001 Stockbyte, www.stockbyte.com)

Now that we've figured out a good use for Multiply, let's take a look at its opposite, Screen. If screen works like light, then all it can do is brighten things. One day I was at my brother's house in New York and he was having some big problems trying to create an image of a lamp he had just designed in his head. He attempted to create a photo-realistic image of it using a 3D program, but every time he attempted to make it look like he had turned on the light bulbs, the glass part of the bulb would completely obstruct the light. He could either have the glass of the bulbs, or just the filaments glowing, but not both (**Figure 12.16a and 12.16b**). I suggested that he save one image with the bulbs visible and the second with only the glowing filaments. After he did that, we just put the filaments on top of the other image and set its blending mode to Screen and bingo, he had what he had spent hours trying to perfect in his 3D program (**Figure 12.17**).

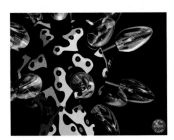

Figure 12.16a Image with bulbs visible.

Figure 12.16b Image with filaments visible.

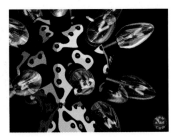

Figure 12.17 The result of setting the filaments layer to Screen.

Using One Image to Ghost Another

On occasion, I've needed to ghost (lighten) a photograph, using a second image to determine which areas will be lightened (**Figures 12.18** and **12.19**). I usually use the Screen blending mode to accomplish this (**Figure 12.20**). It works best when the underlying image is dark, so it won't look too washed out. But when you use blending modes on color images, they sometimes produce unusual and unwanted results, especially in CMYK mode. This problem occurs because the modes act on the individual channels of the image independently. This means that the information in the red channel only affects the red channel of the underlying image, which can cause the colors of an image to shift in an undesirable way.

In order to get an effect that applies evenly to all the channels (and therefore does not shift the colors), you'll have to desaturate the image before using a blending mode. By desaturating the image, you turn it into a grayscale image that contains only neutral grays. And, if you remember from Chapter 8, "Color Correction," you create a neutral gray by using equal amounts of red, green, and blue. By using equal amounts of red, green, and blue, you won't drastically shift the colors of the underlying image (assuming you're working in RGB mode).

Figure 12.18 The underlying image. (© 1998 PhotoSpin, www.photospin.com)

Figure 12.19 The active layer. (© 1998 PhotoSpin, www.photospin.com)

Figure 12.20 The topmost layer is using the Screen blending mode.

So, now that we have all that theory out of the way, let's figure out how to ghost an image based on the content of a second image. First, open the two images you would like to use. Combine them into a single document by dragging between documents using the Move tool. Be sure to place the image you want to ghost below (in the layer stack) the image you want to ghost it with. Then click on the top image and choose Image > Adjust > Desaturate to turn that layer into a grayscale image, as shown in **Figure 12.21**.

Next, set the blending modes of the top layer to Screen. This should lighten the underlying image, but may look overly complicated because all of the detail in the top layer is being used.

In Screen mode, areas that are filled with black do not affect the underlying image (**Figure 12.22**). That means you can simplify the image by adjusting it with Levels until the majority of the image becomes black and therefore disappears. So, choose Image > Adjust > Levels and move the upper left slider to force areas to black. You can also adjust the middle slider to brighten or darken the shades that remain (**Figure 12.23**).

Figure 12.21 To convert an image to shades of gray, choose Image > Adjust > Desaturate.

Figure 12.22 Grayscale images will not shift the color of the underlying image.

If you really want to see what Screen does to an image, just open your favorite photo and create a new layer that is set to Screen. Now use the Gradient tool set to Black, White and drag across the entire width of the document. You should notice that black areas don't change the image at all, and shades of gray (brighter than black) brighten the image.

Figure 12.23 Adjust the image with Levels to fine-tune the result.

Fixing the Emboss Filter

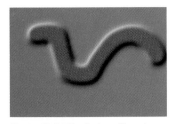

Figure 12.24 The Emboss filter always replaces the whole layer with 50% gray. Yuck!

I have a love/hate relationship with the Emboss filter: I love what it can do, but I hate the grays it leaves behind. If you want to see what I mean, just create a new layer, choose a soft-edged brush, and paint a few strokes across the image (use black paint). Now choose Filter > Stylize > Emboss and mess with the settings. Sure, you'll get an embossed effect (highlight and shadow), but you probably didn't want the filter to replace your entire layer with gray! (See **Figure 12.24**.)

Figure 12.25 In Hard Light mode, 50% gray areas disappear. (This divided image shows the original on top and the gradient-applied version at the bottom.) (© 1998 PhotoDisc)

There is a pretty easy fix for this problem, and guess what—it involves the blending modes (aren't they great?). But before we get to the fix, let's find out a little about the blending modes that will help us. Start out by opening any color photograph and creating a new layer. Next use the Gradient tool set to Black, White and drag across the full length of the image. Set that layer to Hard Light and see what happens. Areas that are 50% gray simply don't show up, areas that are brighter than 50% gray brighten the underlying image, and areas that are darker than 50% will darken the image (**Figure 12.25**). Hard Light is really a combination of the Multiply and Screen blending modes.

Now, let's figure out how this mode can help us get a good emboss. First of all, the grays that I so hate are always 50% if you work in RGB mode, and Hard Light mode makes areas that are 50% gray disappear, as seen in **Figure 12.26.** So, why not choose Undo to abort our first emboss attempt, and try again? This time, duplicate the layer that contains the black paint, set the duplicate layer to Hard Light, and then apply the Emboss filter. Go ahead, try it!

Figure 12.26 Hard Light can eliminate the 50% gray areas the Emboss filter always introduces.

That works great, but there is still one little problem. When you apply the Emboss filter to a color image, you don't just end up with grays; you often get some unwanted color remnants (**Figure 12.27**). You can solve that by choosing Image > Adjust > Desaturate before applying the Emboss filter. That way the layer will contain only grays and you will avoid the color remnants (**Figure 12.28**).

Figure 12.27 Embossing a color image always produces an unwanted color residue. (Original image © 1998 Adobe Systems, Inc.)

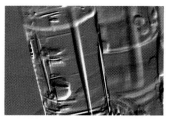

Figure 12.28 Embossing a grayscale image prevents color residue.

Fixing the Lens Flare Filter

I have an interesting relationship with the Lens Flare filter, too. In real life, lens flares are created when the sun interacts with the optics in a lens and produces an annoying flare. Most photographers go out of their way to avoid them. But I guess if you work for the *National Enquirer* or *Weekly World News,* you might want your image of an Alien Elvis Frog Baby to look more realistic, so you slap a lens flare on top of it. So I guess having the filter is okay, but what I don't like is that it can only brighten or darken the information in a single layer. That means I can't apply a lens flare and continue retouching the original image, because if I do, I'll mess up the flare.

Here's a way to work around that: Create a new layer, and then choose Filter > Render > Lens Flare. Lo and behold, you get the pesky "Could not complete the Lens Flare command because the selected area is empty" error. Right—since the layer you were working on was empty, there's nothing it can do. But the Hard Light mode can come to the rescue! Just think about it: Hard Light ignores areas that are 50% gray, brightens underlying areas that are brighter than 50%, and darkens areas that are darker than 50%. So, what if we created a new layer and filled it with 50% gray? Give it a try. Choose Layer > New and set the blending mode to Hard Light (**Figure 12.29**). Did you notice the checkbox that showed up? By turning on that checkbox, Photoshop will automatically fill the layer with 50% gray! So, do it.

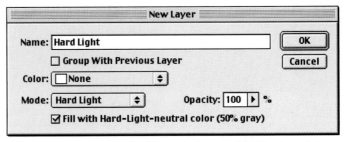

Figure 12.29 Turning on the checkbox at the bottom of the New Layer dialog box will fill the layer with 50% gray.

Note
You can use this same Hard Light trick to apply the Lighting Effects filter on an empty layer.

Because the layer is set to Hard Light and it is 50% gray, it shouldn't affect the underlying image at all. But try choosing Filter > Render > Lens Flare—it works! You've placed a lens flare on its own layer (**Figure 12.30**).

You're probably feeling pretty good about all of this, but there are still a couple of small problems. First of all, when you applied the filter, did you notice that the preview image was just full of gray? That made it so you couldn't see where the flare would appear relative to the image. To fix that, just apply the filter directly to the image first, and then choose Edit > Undo to remove the filter effect. Next, create your 50% gray layer and run the filter again; it will remember where you applied it the last time!

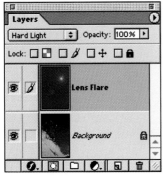

Figure 12.30 Lens Flare applied to a layer that contains 50% gray.

The other problem I have with this filter is that it's really hard to precisely position the lens flare; the preview is just too darned small. That's easy to fix as well. Before you apply the filter, move your cursor over the exact area where you would like the center of the flare to appear. Then write down the X and Y numbers (measured in pixels) out of the lower left corner of the Info Palette, as shown in **Figure 12.31**. Now choose Filter > Render > Lens Flare and Option-click (Macintosh) or Alt-click (Windows) on the little crosshair that determines where the flare is positioned. A dialog box will appear, allowing you to type in the exact position of the flare, using the numbers you wrote down (**Figure 12.32**).

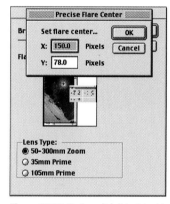

Figure 12.32 Option-click (Macintosh) or Alt-click (Windows) the crosshair to specify an exact position.

Figure 12.31 Use the Info palette to record the exact position where the Lens Flare should appear. (© 1998 Adobe Systems, Inc.)

Adding Contrast to an Image

If you ever run across a really flat-looking image (such as the one in **Figure 12.33**), it can be next to impossible to pull out detail without causing posterization. The Curves function just doesn't seem to do the job—that is, unless you couple Curves with Hard Light! Why not create a new Curves adjustment layer and set its blending modes to

Figure 12.33 Low contrast original image. (© 1998 PhotoSpin, www.photospin.com)

Figure 12.34 Result of applying a Curves adjustment layer using the Hard Light blending mode.

Note

Remember, you can always lower the opacity of a layer to lessen the effect. And you can also duplicate a layer to apply it twice as much!

Hard Light (**Figure 12.34**)? That will automatically give you more contrast. Then you can fine-tune the result by tweaking the settings in the Curves dialog box. This is just like the technique I showed you earlier in this chapter where we added density to a washed-out image.

Creating Reflections

Once upon a time, I was planning on building a house out here in Boulder, Colorado. I went as far as hiring an architect and getting some plans drawn up. My architect (hi, Tim, I know you are going to read this) even took hours, if not days, to create an incredible-looking wooden model. We thought it would be fun to scan a photo of the model and place it in a photograph of the land where it would be built. If you've ever attempted to do this, you know that it usually doesn't look very realistic, especially without reflections in the windows (compare **Figures 12.35 and 12.36**). But, as I learned with my house project, you can easily add your own reflections as long as you know about blending modes. The first thing you have to do is place the reflection image onto a layer above the object you would like to reflect it onto. Next, you'll want that reflection to be backwards. After all, when you look at text in a mirror, isn't it backwards? So click on that layer, and then choose Edit > Transform > Flip Horizontal.

Next, you will probably want to distort the image to match the perspective of the window, so choose Edit > Transform > Distort. Now you should be able to pull on the corners of the image to distort it to match the corners of the window you are reflecting it onto.

When you get it looking just right, press Enter to finalize the transformation. Now, to turn it into a reflection, change the blending modes of the reflection layer to Overlay, Soft Light, or Hard Light. One of those modes should do the trick nicely (after you use the Eraser tool to limit the reflections to the windows, that is).

You can use this same technique (minus the distortions) to apply textures to an image. But if you want to try that out, you should be reading Chapter 14, "Type and Background Effects," shouldn't you?

Figure 12.35 Windows without reflections appear flat and lifeless. (Courtesy of Tim Bjella…who's a very fine architect, by the way.)

Figure 12.36 Reflections add more realism to architectural models.

I always think of Overlay, Soft Light, and Hard Light as a group. I've already described Hard Light (back in the Emboss section of this chapter), so let's take a quick look at Soft Light and Overlay. Like Hard Light, they ignore 50% gray, but Overlay is the exact opposite of Hard Light, and you can think of Soft Light as being somewhere in between the other two. So, if Overlay is the opposite of Hard Light, it looks at the underlying image and appears to brighten and darken the *active* layer. But that's not how I think of it when I'm actually applying these modes. Hard Light always seems to make the active layer dominant, Overlay seems to make the underlying layer dominant, and Soft Light mixes them almost equally.

Note

If you are reading this chapter from start to finish, you've probably noticed that I've been pretty much going down the list of blending modes one at a time, in order. Well, now I'm going to skip two modes, Color Dodge and Color Burn, because they're discussed extensively in Chapter 13.

Better Blending

In Chapter 11 we talked about image blending. Now you can refine your blending techniques by supplementing them with blending modes. I'm sure you have run into those occasions when you apply clouds, or create lightning using the blending sliders from Chapter 11, and the result doesn't look quite right (**Figure 12.37**). Maybe the lightning you created looked perfect, but when you placed it on top of another photo, it appeared to be surrounded by a bunch of fog. This can happen because the lightning is not just brightening the underlying image; it might also be darkening it in certain areas. To prevent this, all you have to do is set the blending mode of the lightning layer to Screen (**Figure 12.38**). That way it won't be able to darken the underlying image.

Or let's say you wanted to blur the background of an image (**Figure 12.39**). Most of the time I think the blur filters produce very unnatural-looking results. They make it look like you smeared a thick coat of petroleum jelly on the surface of a camera lens.

Figure 12.37 Lightning layer set to normal. (© 1998 PhotoDisc)

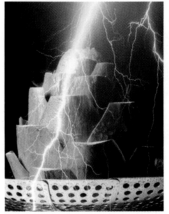

Figure 12.38 Setting a layer to Screen prevents it from darkening the underlying image.

Figure 12.39 The Gaussian Blur filter usually produces a very unnatural look.

To improve the look of the Gaussian Blur filter, you can choose Edit > Fade Gaussian Blur after applying the filter. By lowering the Opacity setting, you blend the blurry version of the image into the original and bring back some real detail (**Figures 12.40 and 12.41**). I think this looks much more natural.

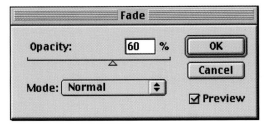

Figure 12.40 Choose Edit > Fade Gaussian Blur to blend the blurred image with the original sharp image.

You can enhance the result even more by changing the blending modes. Use Lighten if you want to brighten the photo, or Darken to darken it (**Figures 12.42 and 12.43**). These modes aren't quite as simple as they sound, though. Because a color image is made out of red, green, and blue channels, Photoshop applies these modes to the individual channels independently of each other. That means the red channel of one layer will affect only the red channel of the underlying image; the same goes for the green and blue channels. So you can't always predict what your result will look like unless you are working in grayscale mode, where there is only one channel for Photoshop to work with.

Figure 12.41 Fading the Gaussian Blur filter produces a more natural-looking blur effect.

Notes

If you would like the blurred area to slowly fade into the image, you can create a feathered selection using Quick Mask mode (see Chapter 2) before applying the Blur filter.

You can also refer to Chapter 6, "Optimizing Grayscale Images," for more uses of Lighten and Darken. There they are used to get more control over the sharpening process.

Figure 12.42 Fade using Lighten.

Figure 12.43 Fade using Darken.

Changing the Color of Objects

So you land a big project from a major toy manufacturer. Your mission: to produce their very expensive-looking annual report. You're feeling a little impish so you decide, why not make all the pie charts out of yo-yos? After all, it is a toy company. But there is just one minor problem; you have no idea how to do it! Well, all you have to know about is, guess what, another blending mode.

To start the project, open your yo-yo image, create a new layer, and make a wedge-shaped selection. Now, hoping to change the color of the yo-yo, you fill the selection with blue. But wait—the part of the yo-yo that's behind the wedge is completely obstructed by the new color. That's because Photoshop divides a color into three components: hue, saturation, and brightness (also known as lightness or luminosity). Hue is the basic color (red, for example), saturation is how vibrant the color appears (intense red, or light pink), and brightness is how bright or dark the color appears (**Figure 12.44**).

To fix the pie chart, you first have to think about what you want to accomplish. Do you want to brighten or darken the yo-yo? No. Do you want to change how vibrant the color is? No. Do you want to change the basic color of the yo-yo? Yes! That's it. All you have to do is change the blending mode of the layer to Hue (**Figure 12.45**). That way, Photoshop will ignore how saturated and how bright the color is and just change the basic color of the underlying image.

After you have finished adding colors to the yo-yo (**Figure 12.46**), you decide you'd rather have a more interesting transition between the colors. So you decide to start playing with filters. Your first choice turns out to be great; it's Filter > Distort > Ripple. Now you've got your interesting edge (**Figure 12.47**).

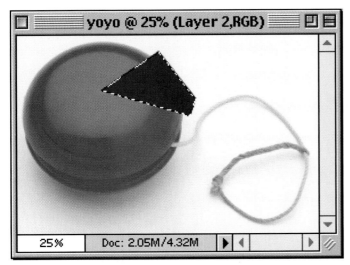

Figure 12.44 When a layer is set to Normal, Photoshop applies all three components of the color—hue, saturation, and brightness. (© 1998 PhotoDisc)

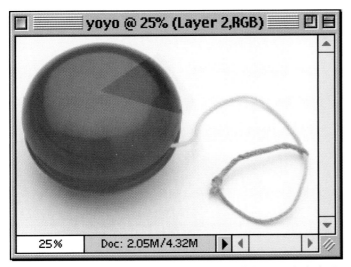

Figure 12.45 By setting the blending mode to Hue, you'll change only the basic color of the yo-yo.

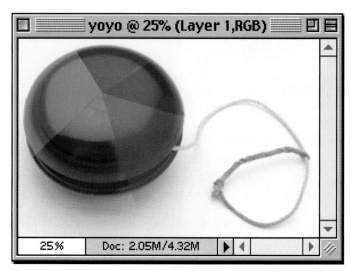

Figure 12.46 Result of applying multiple-colored wedges of color.

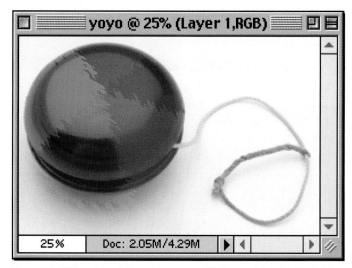

Figure 12.47 The edges of the color were modified by applying the Ripple filter.

But now you notice that the shadow under the yo-yo does not look right. You decide to try to remove any color from above the shadow. You use the Elliptical Marquee tool to select the basic shape of the yo-yo, Select > Inverse to get the background, and Delete (Macintosh) or Backspace (Windows) to remove excess color. But at this point, you notice that the shadow appears to be red (**Figure 12.48**).

Remembering that the original yo-yo was red, you figured that was normal, but now that you've changed the colors, it just doesn't look natural.

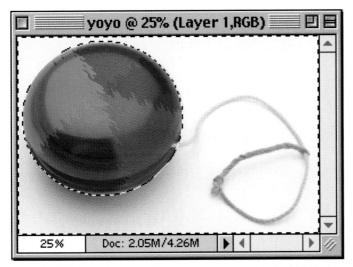

Figure 12.48 Deleting the excess color reveals the image's original reddish shadow.

With the background still selected, you decide to remove any hint of color from the underlying image. To accomplish this, you click on the layer that contains the yo-yo and choose Image > Adjust > Desaturate, and bingo! You're done (**Figure 12.49**).

Figure 12.49 After desaturating the shadow, the image looks more natural.

For your next chart you decide to change the color of half of the yo-yo. But you don't really want a crisp edge, so you decide to create a new layer and again set it to Hue. But instead of selecting an area, you decide to grab the Gradient tool and change its setting to Foreground To Transparent. Finally, you change your foreground color to blue and drag across the yo-yo, and it looks great! See **Figure 12.50.** (You even get visions of next year's report: a yo-yo with a flame job! No problem—all you need is a fancy selection and the Gradient tool.)

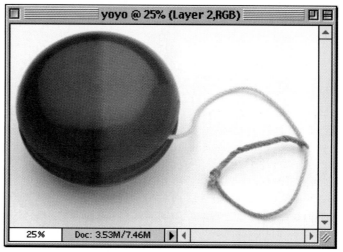

Figure 12.50 Result of applying the Gradient tool using the Foreground To Transparent setting.

Figure 12.51 The original image does not contain enough blue. (© 1998 PhotoSpin, www.photospin.com)

Shifting the Hue

Now you're ready to make the cover of the report, so you hire an artist to make a painterly background using brightly colored pastels (**Figure 12.51**). But after a week on the assignment, you get back something that's a little disappointing. The colors are all wrong! The company color is blue, and there is hardly any blue in the whole image.

So you decide to roll up your sleeves and fix it yourself. You choose Image > Adjust > Hue/Saturation and start tweaking the Hue setting, knowing that Hue refers to basic color (**Figure 12.52**). After a few minutes of tinkering, you end up with some nice blues, as shown in **Figure 12.53**.

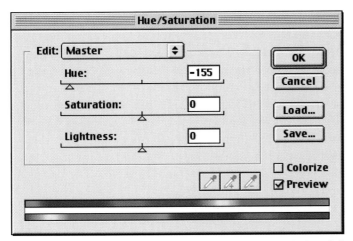

Figure 12.53 Result of shifting the hue to produce an overall blue theme.

Figure 12.52 The Hue/Saturation dialog box allows you to change the hue of all colors in a document.

That's better, but now you don't like a few of the other colors in the image. Maybe there is still too much green, so once again you're off to the Hue/Saturation dialog box. But this time you must figure out all the intricacies of this fine tool, so here's a little crash course. First, you can change the pop-up menu at the top of the dialog box to work on a preset range of colors (**Figure 12.54**). The top gradient (at the bottom of the dialog box) represents the colors as they would appear before making an adjustment; the bottom one shows you the result of your adjustment.

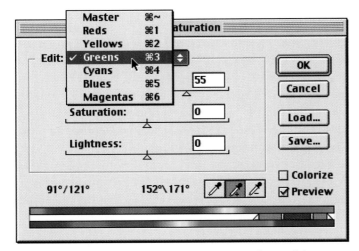

Figure 12.54 Choosing a color from the pop-up menu at the top of the Hue/Saturation dialog box allows you to adjust a narrow range of colors.

Since the choices under the pop-up menu are rather limited, you figured that you might have to fine-tune how it thinks about color. When you make a choice from that pop-up menu, a bunch of controls show up between the gradients at the bottom of the dialog box. These controls determine exactly which colors will be changed. The colors above the dark gray bar indicate which colors you are changing. The light gray bars determine how much the changes will blend into the surrounding colors. You can change these settings at any time. Here are some tips to navigate your custom changes:

▶ Drag the dark gray bar to move all the sliders as a group.

▶ Drag one of the light gray bars to move the sliders that appear on both sides of it.

▶ Drag the individual controls to move them independently.

▶ Click on the main image window to center the dark gray bar on a specific color from the image.

▶ Shift-click on the image to expand the dark gray bar to include more colors.

▶ Command-drag (Macintosh) or Ctrl-drag (Windows) the gradient to reposition the gradient and all the sliders at the same time.

So now you know how to focus on changing particular colors within an image. And just in time, too, because you find out that the client absolutely detests the color green, and wants even *more* blue. With a quick trip back to the dialog box, you choose Greens from the pop-up menu, move the left triangle that appears between the two gradients to the right so all the sliders smash together into one mass, and then click on the particular shade that you want to change in your image. Then, to make sure you're going to get all the greens, you hold down the Shift key and drag across all the greens while you watch the controls at the bottom of the dialog box following your every command. Once you have isolated the greens, a simple move of the Hue slider changes all those greens to the all-important company color, blue (**Figure 12.55**).

Figure 12.55 The greens have shifted to cyan.

Selective Black and White

Your next assignment is from a hat designer who brings you a nice image of one of her hats sitting on the beach. But your client is not happy. She thinks the hat does not stand out enough. So, you get the idea of making the background behind the hat grayscale; that way the hat will pop right out from it. Remembering back to how Photoshop deals with color (hue, saturation, and brightness), you decide that you don't want to change the color of the beach (that's hue), and you think the brightness looks just fine. So, what's left? Saturation! So you set a new layer to Saturation and start to experiment, first painting with a really bright green color. Actually, it doesn't matter what color you paint with. Photoshop will ignore the fact that you're painting with a specific color; instead, it just changes the saturation of the sand to match the saturation of the color you're painting with (**Figure 12.56**).

Figure 12.56 Using the Saturation blending mode causes the underlying image to match the saturation of the color that is being applied; I painted with green just above the hat. (© 1998 PhotoSpin, www.photospin.com)

So you think about it for a moment. What color should I be painting with to take away all the color from the underlying image? Why not a shade of gray? After all, grays don't contain a hint of color (**Figure 12.57**). To do this, you select the background, then type Option-Delete (Macintosh) or Alt-Backspace (Windows) to fill the area with the foreground color, black—the darkest shade of gray. But then you decide you want just a hint of color in the beach, so why not lower the opacity of the layer that contains the gray? Ahh...looks great (**Figures 12.58 and 12.59**).

Figure 12.57 Painting with a shade of gray will completely desaturate the image.

Figure 12.58 You can also select areas and fill them with gray.

Figure 12.59 Lowering the opacity of the layer will allow some of the underlying color to show through.

You don't have to limit yourself to the technique that was just described. The Saturation blend mode is great for changing the saturation of an area to match that of the color you are painting with. But what if you just wanted to *slightly* increase the saturation of an object? Well, you can use the Sponge tool. By painting across an area with this tool, you can increase or decrease the saturation by large or small amounts. All you have to do is adjust the pressure setting.

Colorizing Grayscale Images

If you are going to colorize grayscale images, you're in luck. Photoshop is a godsend when it comes to colorizing; in fact, it offers what might seem like an overabundance of colorizing features. Let's start off with a few blending modes, and then progress into more advanced methods. The first thing you'll have to do is change the mode of your grayscale image to RGB mode. Then, to colorize the image, you want to apply the hue and saturation of a color while leaving the brightness of the image unchanged (**Figure 12.60**). Photoshop offers you a mode that does exactly that; it's called Color. So give it a try: create a new

Note

I usually get good results by stealing colors from other documents. So, if you want a flesh tone, why try to create it from scratch? Instead you can open an image with a good color and use the Eyedropper tool to grab the correct color.

layer, set the layer's blending mode to Color, and start painting away.

If you like the color you are using, but feel you're changing the image a little too much, lower the opacity of the painting tool (**Figure 12.61**). You can change the opacity of your painting tool using the number keys on your keyboard (0=100%, 1=1%, 3=30%, 48=48%, and so on).

If you create a new layer for each area of the photo that you are colorizing (flesh tone, hair, clothes, and the like), then you can quickly adjust those colors by clicking on the layer you want to change and choosing Image > Adjust > Hue/Saturation. In this dialog box, you can change the Hue to alter the basic color, or mess with the Saturation to adjust the vibrancy of that color.

When you paint using the Color blending mode, you might find that, in certain areas, the color just seems to sit on top of the image and doesn't look integrated or natural. In those cases, you should switch over to the Color Burn blending mode. It will push the color into the image much more aggressively than Color ever would (**Figure 12.62**). Most of the time you'll need to lower the Opacity setting so that Color Burn won't overdo it.

Figure 12.60 Painting with the Color blending mode applies the hue and saturation without changing the brightness of the image. (© 2001 Stockbyte, www.stockbyte.com)

Figure 12.61 Left: 100% opacity. Middle: 70% opacity. Right: 30% opacity.

Figure 12.62 Color Burn mode will more aggressively apply color to the image.

Colorizing Selected Areas

You'll probably find that you don't always feel like painting to colorize an area, so I'll show you another method. You can select an area and then choose Image > Adjust > Hue/Saturation (or use an adjustment layer). Turn on the

Colorize checkbox in the lower right of the dialog box to get things started (**Figure 12.63**). Now you can change the Hue and Saturation settings until you get just the right color, as in **Figure 12.64**.

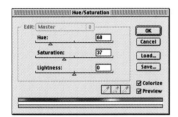

Figure 12.63 The Colorize checkbox allows you to apply color to a grayscale image that you've converted to RGB mode.

Figure 12.64 Background colorized using the Hue/Saturation dialog box.

Two-Tone Colorizing

Now let's look at some more methods of colorizing that are a little more out of the ordinary. First convert the image to RGB mode, create a new layer, fill it with the color you desire, and then set the blending modes of the layer to either Difference or Exclusion. This will give you a two-tone effect (**Figure 12.65**).

Another option is to choose Image > Mode > RGB and then choose Image > Adjust > Gradient Map (**Figure 12.66**). The Gradient Map dialog box allows you to replace all the shades of gray in your image with the colors that appear in a gradient (**Figure 12.67**). All you have to do is click on the down-pointing arrow to the right of the gradient and then choose from the same gradients that are available using the regular Gradient tool. Then, after you've chosen the gradient you'd like to use, click directly on the preview bar to fine-tune the gradient using the Gradient Editor dialog box.

Figure 12.65 The Difference blending mode will produce a two-tone effect.

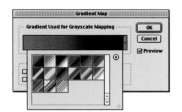

Figure 12.66 The Gradient Map dialog box.

Figure 12.67 The result of applying a Gradient Map.

I use this technique whenever I'm presented with a grayscale logo that needs to be colorized, or when I'm given scientific data (like weather maps or satellite images) that contains only shades of gray.

Using Lab Mode to Colorize

Now let's look at one more method of colorizing. This one will allow you to get a little more variation in your image without having to spend a lot of time painting. To get started, convert your image to Lab mode by choosing Image > Mode > Lab Color. Next, select one of the areas you'd like to colorize and then choose Edit > Copy. Now open the Channels palette and click on the "a" channel if you would like that area to appear cyan or magenta, or click on the "b" channel for blue or yellow. Now, to get some color, choose Edit > Paste (**Figure 12.68**).

If you don't like the color you've ended up with, you can choose Image > Adjust > Levels and change the Channel pop-up menu to the name of the channel you pasted the image into. Now you can adjust the top sliders to intensify the colors or change the overall look, or use the bottom sliders to lower the intensity of the colors (**Figures 12.69 and 12.70**).

Figure 12.68 Result of pasting a portion of the image into the "a" channel. (© 1998 PhotoDisc)

Figure 12.69 Result of applying Levels to the "a" channel.

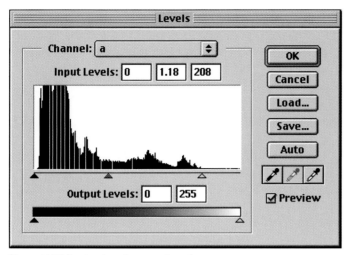

Figure 12.70 Use Levels to fine-tune the colors.

If you would like to use colors other than cyan, magenta, blue, or yellow, then you'll need to paste the image into both the "a" and "b" channels. Then, when adjusting the result with Levels, work on the "a" channel to shift the overall look towards cyan or magenta, and work on the "b" channel to shift it towards blue or yellow. I use this technique only when the others I've already mentioned don't give me the results I've been looking for; you can think of it as your last resort.

Adjusting Brightness Without Shifting Colors

Back in Chapter 7 we talked about brightening, darkening, and pulling out detail using the Curves dialog box. Although I really like using Curves, I run into a big problem when it comes to color images. Oftentimes, I'll just want to brighten up an image, but when I start to make the adjustment, the colors also start to shift, as demonstrated in **Figures 12.71 and 12.72**. This happens because Curves makes adjustments to all the color channels (RGB) in equal amounts.

You can fix this problem pretty quickly. If you are working with an adjustment layer, just set the blending modes of that layer to Luminosity (**Figure 12.73**). Or, if you applied Curves directly to the image, you can choose Edit > Fade Curves immediately after applying Curves.

Figure 12.71 Original image. (© 1998 PhotoSpin, www.photospin.com)

Figure 12.72 The colors of an image shift when applying a Curves adjustment.

Figure 12.73 Using the Luminosity blending mode will prevent adjustments from shifting the colors in an image.

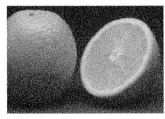

Figure 12.74 Applying filters to a color image often adds unwanted color variations. (© 2001 Stockbyte, www.stockbyte.com)

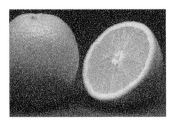

Figure 12.75 Blending the filtered layer into the underlying image using the Luminosity blending mode.

There is one more time when I find Luminosity helpful, and that's when I'm performing color correction. Occasionally, I'll have an image that has perfect brightness, but the colors aren't so hot. When I adjust the colors, I seem to screw up the brightness. Well, I can fix that quickly by duplicating the layer, setting it to Luminosity, and adjusting the colors of the layer directly under it. That way I can adjust the colors to my heart's content and, no matter what I do, I can't screw up the brightness of the image.

Adding Grain to an Image

Sometimes you get sick of normal crisp images and might want to create something a little more gritty—maybe give it that "homemade" feeling. I'll show you how to add noise to your images without changing the colors present in the image. If you attempt to do this by simply applying filters to the image, you'll find that the colors will shift (**Figure 12.74**). But if you first duplicate the layer and set the duplicate to Luminosity, the colors won't be able to change (**Figure 12.75**). Then you can experiment to your heart's content until you come up with a satisfactory result.

Special Filter Effects

Now we've made it through all the blending modes and are ready to move on to other nifty Photoshop features. To be honest, you can never really be "done" with blending modes. I learn something new about them almost every time I play with them. The more you use them, the more comfortable you'll get. So, keep playing and let me know when you come up with a new use for one of these modes. You can also find out what I've been doing with blending modes by checking out my Web site at www.digitalmastery.com. Whenever someone gives me a new idea, or I've got a new technique, that's the first place it goes.

You'll find the Blending Modes menu in so many places in Photoshop (painting tools, Edit > Fill, etc.) that it's often difficult to know which menu to use. An easy way of approaching this is to ask yourself if you want to affect *all* the underlying layers, or just the active layer. If the answer is "all the layers," then you'll have to use the menu attached to a layer. If the answer is "just the active layer," then you can grab the blending modes menu from anywhere in Photoshop.

Wrapping One Image Around Another

Let's say you've got a client who wants to have a wood texture bent to conform to the contours of someone's face and then permanently tattooed in that position. How much would you charge, and how long would it take? Well, if you knew how to use one of Photoshop's less-traveled filters, you could probably finish it up in about five minutes and charge the client as much as you'd like. The filter that will do the job is called Displace, and in order to use it you need to do some unusual things to your image. I find the results to be simply amazing. So let's give it a whirl.

To start out, I'm going to use a simple checkerboard image to show you what happens when you run the Displace filter; then I'll substitute some wood to get the effect we're looking for. The Displace filter is going to need some information to determine exactly how it should bend your image.

What it really needs is a grayscale image in which the dark areas will dictate where the image should be bent down and to the right, and bright areas will dictate where the image should be bent up and to the left. The good news is that you don't have to come up with a wild document to do this; a blurry grayscale version of your image will do just fine. So, choose Image > Duplicate to create an exact copy of your image (**Figure 12.76**).

Now choose Image > Mode > Grayscale to discard all the color information, and flatten the image while you're at it. This filter does not seem to like crisp edges, so choose Filter > Blur > Gaussian Blur and use a setting just high enough to soften the edges of any sharp areas (**Figure 12.77**).

Figure 12.76 Original. (Courtesy of Albert Sanchez (photographer), Ani Difranco, and Righteous Babe Records)

Figure 12.77 Blurred grayscale version of the file to be used with the Displace filter.

Next, you'll need to save this grayscale version of the image in the Photoshop file format and then close the grayscale image. Now go back to the original, full-color version of the face image (you can ignore the grayscale one until you're asked for it). Before you apply the filter, you'll want to use the Move tool and drag the wood image on top of the face, so it becomes the topmost layer of the face document. The Displace filter gets messed up if your image you're bending (the wood, in this case) extends beyond the document's bounds, so choose Select > All and then Image > Crop to rid yourself of any "big data."

Now you can choose Filter > Distort > Displace to bend the wood. During this process, you'll be prompted to open a file—use the grayscale replica of the face that's been waiting in the wings. The settings at the bottom of the Displace dialog box shouldn't apply to our image, because the grayscale face you created was exactly the same size as the face that is in your document. The only settings that matter are the Horizontal and Vertical Scale settings. You'll have to experiment with these settings. They determine how much bending or wrapping will occur; the higher the resolution of your document, the higher the setting you'll have to use. I usually start with the default settings, and then try others if the image doesn't look right. See **Figures 12.78 and 12.79** to see what would happen if you bent a simple grid instead of some wood.

Figure 12.78 Layer to be distorted.

Figure 12.79 Result of applying the Displace filter.

After you have a bent version of the wood, you can use a blending mode to apply it to the underlying face image. Because the image I used was so basic, Multiply should do the job (**Figure 12.80**). If you want the bent information to show up in certain areas only, you can either group it to the layer below or use a layer mask to hide areas.

Once you know how to apply the filter, you are free to experiment with different images, settings, and blending modes (**Figures 12.81 and 12.82**). Go have fun.

Figure 12.80 Checkerboard applied using the Multiply blending mode and grouped to the face layer to limit where it shows up.

Figure 12.81 Original wood texture after applying the Displace filter. (© 1998 PhotoSpin, www.photospin.com)

Figure 12.82 This wood texture was applied using the Color Burn blending mode and grouped to the face layer, so it only shows up where the face is.

Figure 12.83 Start with a grayscale image pasted into a layer mask.

Figure 12.84 End result of converting this photo into a drawing. (Original image © 1998 PhotoSpin, www.photospin.com)

Converting Photos into Drawings

All right, you want to change a photo into a drawing; let's find out how it's done. We're going to need to use a layer mask to accomplish this, but you can't add a layer mask to the background image. So, if you are working on the background image, give it a quick double-click in the Layers palette and change its name. Now you need to get a grayscale version of your image into the layer mask. I'll give you an odd but quick technique to do that. First press Option-Command-~ (Macintosh) or Alt-Ctrl-~ (Windows) to transform a grayscale version of the image into a selection as if it were a channel. Now choose Layer > Add Layer Mask > Reveal Selection. You should see a grayscale version of your image sitting in the layer mask (**Figure 12.83**), and the main image should look pretty strange.

To get just the edges to show up, choose Filter > Stylize > Find Edges and then choose Image > Adjust > Invert. Now you should be looking at the edges of the objects in your image. If the rest of your screen is full of a checkerboard pattern, then you'll want to add another layer underneath this one by creating an empty new layer and then choosing Layer > New > Background From Layer (**Figure 12.84**).

You can fine-tune the result by choosing Image > Adjust > Levels and playing with the top three sliders. Or, if you want to fill the lines with a solid color, click the image thumbnail (as opposed to the layer mask), change your foreground color, and then press Option-Delete (Macintosh) or Alt-Backspace (Windows) to fill the layer.

Painting with Filters

By using the History palette, you can turn any filter into a painting tool. The History palette is a feature you want to get very friendly with. Just briefly, it keeps track of all the changes you make to your image, and can get you back to any previous version with a simple click in the History palette. It takes a lot of the worry out of your work in Photoshop and gives you more freedom to experiment. In this section, we're going to be using the palette in conjunction with filters, but first let's take a quick look at how it works on its own (**Figure 12.85**).

Here are the History palette features:

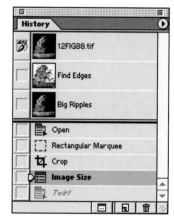

Figure 12.85 The History palette.

▶ Every time you make a modification to a document, your steps show up in the History palette.

▶ The steps are named after the tools and dialog boxes you use to modify your image.

▶ Only document-specific changes are recorded; program-wide changes are ignored.

▶ With default settings, the History palette will store the last 20 steps you performed (this can be increased to a maximum of 100 steps).

▶ The steps in the History palette are not saved with your file. So even if you save your document before you close it, you won't be able to use those steps again when you reopen the image.

▶ To revert to a previous step, just click the name of the step.

▶ If you change the image after clicking a step, all steps after that one will be deleted.

You can think of the History palette as multiple undo on steroids. To get back to a previous state of your image, all you have to do is click one of the steps listed in the palette. You can increase the total number of steps stored in the palette (maximum=100) by choosing Edit > Preferences > General (**Figure 12.86**). If you perform more steps on your image than the setting you used for History States, Photoshop will start discarding the oldest steps to make room for the ones you are currently performing.

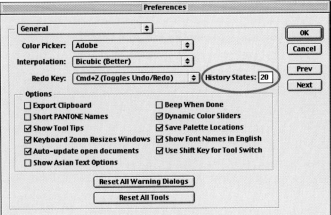

Figure 12.86 You can change your History States setting in the Preferences dialog box.

Because the steps are named after the tools and dialog boxes you used to modify the image, it can sometimes be tough to figure out exactly what a particular one was. If you really want to use this palette effectively, you can create snapshots of different document states. You can do this by choosing New Snapshot from the side menu of the palette. Snapshots work just like the normal steps in the History palette but they are stored at the top of the palette, they have user-defined names, and they display a preview thumbnail (**Figure 12.87**). Better still, unlike normal steps, they will not be removed when Photoshop runs out of space for steps.

When you create a snapshot, the options you specify will determine what you'll be able to do when you revert to

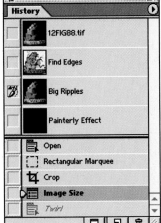

Figure 12.87 Snapshots appear at the top of the History palette.

that snapshot. Entire Document will record the current state of all layers in the document, and takes up the most memory. Current Layer will record only the state of the currently active layer, and takes up a lot less memory than the Entire Document setting. Merged Layers will record the visual look of the document as if all the layers were merged together; this can be useful if you want to use the History Brush on a different layer than the one that originally contained the information.

The History Brush

The History palette by itself is a great addition to Photoshop, but it becomes even more useful when you couple it with the History Brush. The History Brush will allow you to paint across a layer and bring it back to what it looked like in any previous state. All you have to do is specify which step in the History palette the brush should use as its guide. You do this by clicking just to the left of the name of one of the steps in the palette. Then, any time you use the History brush, it will paint using information from that step.

I use this all the time to trick Photoshop into converting a filter into a painting tool. Try this out: Open a color image and apply any filter to it. Now, to get back to the unmodified image, open the History palette and click the snapshot that appears at the top of the palette. This snapshot is automatically added and represents the original, unchanged document.

Now click just to the left of the bottom step in the History palette (it should be named after the filter you applied) to tell the History Brush which step to paint from. Then paint across your image. It should look like you're painting with a filter (**Figure 12.88**). If you want to paint with multiple filters, you'll want to create a new snapshot after applying each filter, and then choose Edit > Undo to get back to the original image before applying the next filter. That way you can have a whole pile of filter effects sitting at the top of the History palette, and all you have to do is set the History Brush to the one you want to use.

Figure 12.88 Using the History Brush to apply the Ripple filter to the edges of the artichoke leaves.

I use this technique to add the Motion Blur filter to the edge of objects (it usually applies across the entire image) or to add distortion to text (remember to rasterize the layer before you apply a filter).

Liquify

Adobe added an interesting new feature in Photoshop 6.0 called Liquify (yeah, I know it's misspelled), which lets you pull and push on your image as if it were printed on silly putty. When you choose Image > Liquify, you'll see a dialog box that absolutely dominates your screen (**Figure 12.89**).

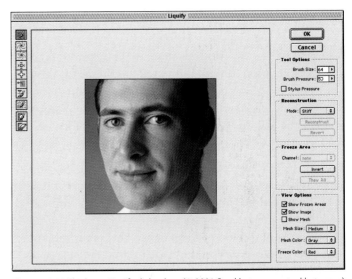

Figure 12.89 The large Liquify dialog box. (© 2001 Stockbyte, www.stockbyte.com)

Let's run down the tools that appear in the upper left of the dialog box.

At the top you'll find the Warp tool, which allows you to push the image in the direction that you drag (**Figure 12.90**). Next come the Twirl Clockwise and Twirl Counterclockwise tools, which slowly rotate the area inside your cursor (**Figure 12.91**). Under that you'll find the Pucker tool (tickly name, huh?), which allows you to pull the image in towards the center of your brush (**Figure 12.92**). Or, you can do the opposite of that by using the Bloat tool (no, girls, it's not about water weight) as shown in **Figure 12.93.** Below the Bloat tool is the Shift Pixels tool, which acts like the line you draw is a bulldozer, and pushes the image away from it on the left side (hold Option on the Mac or Alt in Windows to move the right side instead). See **Figure 12.94.** After that you'll find the Reflection tool, which will flip a portion of the image horizontally or vertically depending on the direction you drag. If you drag downward, then you'll be reflecting the area to the left of your cursor. Drag up and you'll reflect what's to the right (**Figure 12.95**). Drag right and you'll reflect the area below and drag left to reflect the area above.

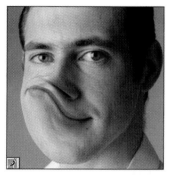

Figure 12.90 Result of applying the Warp tool.

Figure 12.91 Result of applying the Twirl tool.

Figure 12.92 Result of applying the Pucker tool.

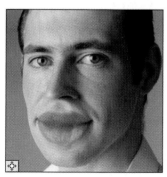

Figure 12.93 Result of applying the Bloat tool.

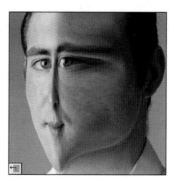

Figure 12.94 Result of applying the Shift Pixels tool.

Figure 12.95 Result of applying the Reflect tool.

There is no Brushes palette available to change the size of your brush in the Liquify dialog box. The size of your brush is determined by the number entered in the Brush Size field in the upper right of the dialog box. You can use the bracket keys (][) to change this setting in increments of one; I only wish you could change it in larger increments because you'll often have to press the bracket key 40 times to get the kind of change you were looking for.

For all of these tools, the Brush Pressure setting will determine how radical of a change you'll make when you paint across the image. If you have a pressure-sensitive graphics tablet, then you can turn on the Stylus Pressure checkbox to make Photoshop pay attention to how much pressure you're using with the pen. With that option turned on, the Brush Pressure setting will be determined by how hard you press down onto the graphics tablet with your pen.

If you find that you end up changing too much of the image, you can freeze an area to prevent it from changing. The Freeze tool will apply a red overlay on your image to indicate which areas have been frozen (**Figure 12.96**). The Freeze tool also uses the Brush Pressure setting, which means you can partially freeze an area to make it change less than the unfrozen areas (50% frozen areas will change half as much as unfrozen areas when painted across). Areas that are partially frozen will appear with a more transparent red overlay. If you'd rather not see the overlay, turn off the Show Frozen Areas checkbox. If you'd like to unfreeze an area, use the Thaw tool to remove some of the red overlay, or click Thaw All to unfreeze the entire image.

Once you're done manipulating your image, you might find that you went a little too far in a few areas. If that's the case, then grab the Reconstruct tool and paint across the area that you'd like to take back to normal (**Figure 12.97**). The more you paint across an area, the closer it will become to what the image looked like before applying the Liquify command.

After playing around in this dialog box, it's often difficult to determine the exact areas that have changed. You can see a different view of the changes you've made by turning on the Show Mesh checkbox (**Figure 12.98**). You might also want to turn off the Show Image checkbox, so you can get a clear view of the mesh (**Figure 12.99**). You can still use all the Liquify tools while the mesh is visible, which is often useful when using the Reconstruct tool so you can tell which areas still have a distortion applied.

Figure 12.96 The red overlay indicates an area that has been frozen.

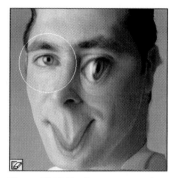

Figure 12.97 The Reconstruct tool will bring areas back to what they looked like prior to applying the Liquify command.

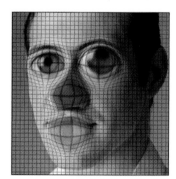

Figure 12.98 An image with the mesh visible.

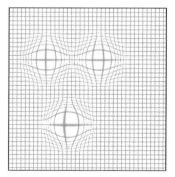

Figure 12.99 Viewing the mesh with the image hidden.

Closing Thoughts

If someone were to actually publish all of the great enhancement techniques out there, you'd be wading through a book ten times the size of *War and Peace*. With this chapter, I tried to give you some nice, tasty samples

Note

On the CD accompanying this book, you'll find a PDF file that supplements this chapter. The file, called "extras.pdf," contains the following topics:

▸ Creating a slide show
▸ Punching holes in a layer
▸ Inverted photo foolery
▸ Blending for better grays
▸ Creating distorted features
▸ Taking images into other programs using clipping paths

that would inspire you to go forth and try some more on your own. I hope you enjoyed it. This part of Photoshop is always a pure pleasure for me—I could do this stuff every day. (Wait a minute, I do!) The more you work with Photoshop, the more you'll be able to add to your own personal cookbook of enhancement recipes. The trick is to find the time to play. I used to stay at work until rush-hour traffic died down just so I could have more time to play with Photoshop. When I went to college, there weren't any Photoshop classes, so I'm self-taught, thanks to a lot of midnight jam sessions with the tunes cranked up and Photoshop glowing on my computer screen. And look at me, I got to write this book!

Ben's Techno-Babble Decoder Ring

Blending Modes—A function in Photoshop that alters the behavior of a layer or tool, allowing it to interact with the underlying image.

Snapshot—A user-created record of the current state of a document (content and order of layers, adjustment settings, and so forth).

Scratch Disk—The virtual memory scheme used by Photoshop. This allows Photoshop to create an invisible file on your hard drive that is used as a substitute for actual physical memory (RAM). That way Photoshop can manipulate files larger than could be opened in RAM.

RAM—Random Access Memory. The physical memory chips that are installed in your computer. (64MB of memory in your computer is called 64MB of RAM.)

Keyboard Shortcuts

The following keyboard commands change the blending mode of the current tool (if it supports blending modes); otherwise, they will change the blending mode of the currently active layer.

FUNCTION	MACINTOSH	WINDOWS
Previous blending mode	Shift-– (minus sign)	Shift-–
Next blending mode	Shift-+ (plus sign)	Shift-+
Normal	Shift-Option-N	Shift-Alt-N
Dissolve	Shift-Option-I	Shift-Alt-I
Behind	Shift-Option-Q	Shift-Alt-Q
Clear	Shift-Option-R	Shift-Alt-R
Multiply	Shift-Option-M	Shift-Alt-M
Screen	Shift-Option-S	Shift-Alt-S
Overlay	Shift-Option-O	Shift-Alt-O
Soft Light	Shift-Option-F	Shift-Alt-F
Hard Light	Shift-Option-H	Shift-Alt-H
Color Dodge	Shift-Option-D	Shift-Alt-D
Color Burn	Shift-Option-B	Shift-Alt-B
Darken	Shift-Option-K	Shift-Alt-K
Lighten	Shift-Option-G	Shift-Alt-G
Difference	Shift-Option-E	Shift-Alt-E
Exclusion	Shift-Option-X	Shift-Alt-X
Hue	Shift-Option-U	Shift-Alt-U
Saturation	Shift-Option-T	Shift-Alt-T
Color	Shift-Option-C	Shift-Alt-C
Luminosity	Shift-Option-Y	Shift-Alt-Y

Courtesy of Diane Fenster, www.dianefenster.com
From the Waste Land Series: Belladonna, the Lady of the Rocks, the Lady of Situations

Courtesy of Diane Fenster, www.dianefenster.com
From the Waste Land Series: The Drowned Phoenician Sailor, Those are Pearls that were his Eyes

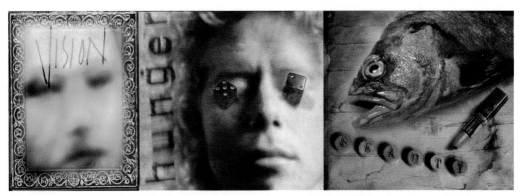

Courtesy of Diane Fenster, www.dianefenster.com

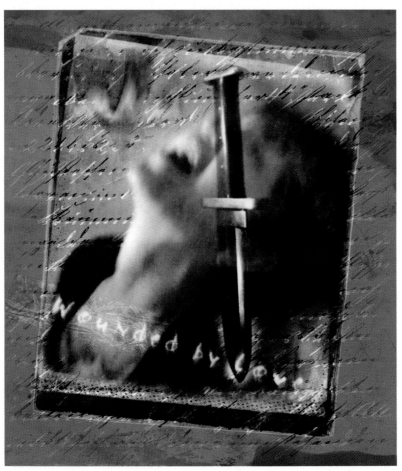

Courtesy of Diane Fenster, www.dianefenster.com

13 Retouching

A doctor can bury his mistakes, but an architect can only advise his clients to plant vines.
—Frank Lloyd Wright

Underwater Study #1647 from POOL LIGHT by Howard Schatz
© 1998 Schatz/Ornstein (Graphis Press, 1998)

The doctoring of photographs didn't begin with the advent of computers into magazine production departments. One of history's most notorious photograph "doctors" was Joseph Stalin, who used photo retouching as a way to manipulate the masses. People who vanished in real life, whether banished to the farthest reaches of the Soviet Union or eliminated by the secret police, vanished from photos as well, and even paintings. In many cases, they were airbrushed out completely; in others their faces were clumsily blacked out with ink.

And then there were the Hollywood photo doctors. They didn't want to get *rid* of anyone; they just wanted to make them look better. I think they actually coined the term "too good to be true." Think about it—did you ever see a photograph of a starlet with a blemish, or a wart, or bags under her eyes, or even the slightest indication that her skin actually had pores? Of course not!

If you look at it from these two extremes, you can appreciate why the subject of retouching is something of a, well, touchy subject. If you're brave enough to bring it up at a photographer's convention, you're likely to spark a pretty lively debate. A purist might tell you that every aspect of a photograph (including the flaws) is a perfect reflection of reality and should never be tampered with. Then again, a graphic artist, who makes a living from altering images, might tell you that an original photograph is just the foundation of an image, and that the so-called "tampering" is, in fact, a means of enhancing and improving upon it. Either way you look at it, you can't deny the fact that retouching photographs has become an everyday necessity for almost anyone who deals with graphic images. And when it comes to retouching, hands down, nothing does it better than Photoshop.

Photoshop packs an awesome arsenal of retouching tools. These include the Dodge and Burn tools, Blur and Sharpen tools, and the Rubber Stamp tool. We'll get to play with all of them, and for each one I'll also give you a little bag of tricks. You'll learn how to do all sorts of neat things like retouching old ripped photos, getting rid of those shiny spots on foreheads, and adding highlights to hair. Or, you can put yourself in the doctor's seat and give someone instant plastic surgery. Remove a few wrinkles, perform an eye-lift, reduce those dark rings around the eyes, and poof!—you've taken off ten years. So let's look at these tools one at a time, starting with what I consider to be the most important one.

Rubber Stamp Tool

The Rubber Stamp tool is often called the clone tool because that's what it does. (In fact, its "nickname" was such a good fit that in this version of Photoshop it's been officially renamed the Clone Stamp tool, but we all know the old name is better.) It copies information from one area of your image and applies it somewhere else. Before applying the Rubber Stamp tool, there is one thing you should know. All retouching tools use the Brushes palette, shown in **Figure 13.1**. So you have to decide if you want what you're about to apply to fade into the image or to have a distinct edge. For most applications it helps to have a soft edge on your brush so you can't see the exact edge of where you've stopped.

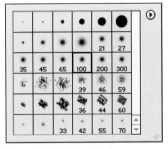

Figure 13.1 The brush that you choose determines how much your retouching work will blend into the underlying image.

I find that the default soft-edged brushes are often too soft, which can cause the area you retouch to look blurry compared to the rest of the image. To prevent that from happening, click on the brush preview in the Options bar and increase the Hardness setting. The default brushes have a hardness of either 100% (for hard-edged brushes) or 0% (for soft ones). I find a Hardness somewhere between 50% and 70% to be ideal for retouching with soft-edged brushes.

Cloning Around

After you've chosen your brush, you'll need to tell Photoshop exactly where you'd like to copy from. Do this by holding down the Option key (Macintosh) or Alt key (Windows) and clicking the mouse button. Then move to a different part of the image and click and drag the mouse. When you do, you'll notice two cursors (**Figure 13.2**). The first one is in the shape of a crosshair; it shows you the source of Photoshop's cloning. When you apply the Rubber

Figure 13.2 The Rubber Stamp tool copies from under the crosshair and pastes into the circle. (© 1998 PhotoDisc)

Stamp tool, there will be a second cursor—a circle showing you exactly where it's being applied (if the Caps Lock key is pressed, you may get a crosshair cursor). When you move your mouse around you'll notice both of the cursors moving in the same direction. As you drag, Photoshop is constantly copying from the crosshair and pasting into the circle.

Clone Aligned

The Rubber Stamp tool operates in two different modes: aligned and non-aligned (it's just a simple checkbox in the Options bar). In aligned mode, when you apply the Rubber Stamp tool, it doesn't matter if you let go of the mouse button and click again. Each time you let go and click again, the pieces that you're applying line up (**Figure 13.3**). It's as if you're putting together a puzzle: once you have all of the pieces together, it looks like a complete image.

Clone Non-Aligned

But if you turn off the Aligned checkbox, it's a different story. Then if you apply the tool and let go of the mouse button, the next time you click the mouse button it will reset itself, starting back at the original point from where it was cloning (**Figure 13.4**). So if you click in the middle of someone's nose, go up to the forehead, click and drag, you'll be planting a nose in the middle of the forehead. Then if you let go, move over a little bit, and click again, you'll add a second nose. But that would happen only if you have the Aligned checkbox off. For most retouching, leave the checkbox on (assume you'll need to have it turned on to follow the techniques I cover here, unless I specifically tell you to turn it off). That way you don't have to be careful with letting go of the mouse button.

Opacity Settings

Sometimes you don't want to completely cover something up; you may just want to lessen its impact (**Figure 13.5**). For example, you might want to completely wipe out a recognizable feature (like Gorbachev's birthmark) for fear that it'll be obvious the image was enhanced. To do this, lower the opacity on the Rubber Stamp tool (**Figure 13.6**). You can also press the number keys on your keyboard;

Figure 13.3 You can release the mouse button as many times as you want with the Align checkbox turned on because the pieces of the cloned image will line up to create a continuous image.

Figure 13.4 When the Aligned checkbox is turned off, the Rubber Stamp tool resets itself to the original starting point each time you release the mouse button.

pressing 1 will give you 10%, 2 will give you 20%, and so on. To get it all the way up to 100%, just type 0 (zero). This will allow you to paint over an area and partially replace it, so that the area you're applying blends with what used to be in that area.

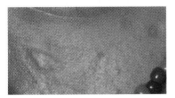

Figure 13.5 You might want to play down some recognizable feature.

Figure 13.6 By lowering the opacity of the Rubber Stamp Tool, you can reduce the impact of undesirable features.

Straight Lines

Have you ever seen a carpenter "snap a chalk line" to get a straight line over an area? There are occasions when I've been grateful to know how to do something similar in Photoshop. Let's say you've got an image with a few people walking on a sidewalk. You want to remove the people because you only need the sidewalk. That means you're going to have to replace them with a new chunk of sidewalk. In order to look realistic, of course, the new chunk of sidewalk will have to align perfectly with the rest of the sidewalk. When you get into this kind of situation, try this: Move your cursor until it's touching the original line (or edge of the sidewalk, in this case). When it's perfectly touching it, you'll want to Option-click (Macintosh) or Alt-click (Windows), as shown in **Figure 13.7**. Then go to the area where you want the new piece of sidewalk to appear and click right where you think it would naturally line up with the other part of the sidewalk. Then when you drag, your two cursors will line up just right, making the line look continuous and straight, as in **Figure 13.8**. You can even Shift-click in two spots and Photoshop will trace a straight line with the Rubber Stamp between those two areas. Other examples would be stairs, or a lamppost, or any object with straight lines that has been obstructed by another object.

Figure 13.7 When retouching straight lines, Option-click or Alt-click when your cursor touches the line, then click in another area that also touches the line. (© 1998 PhotoSpin, www.photospin.com)

Figure 13.8 If the cursors align, lines will remain nice and straight.

Layers

If you are using layers in your document, the Rubber Stamp tool will work on one layer at a time unless you turn on the Use All Layers checkbox located on the Options bar. With this option turned on, Photoshop will act as if your document has no layers at all. In other words, it will be able to take from any layer that is below your cursor, as if they were all combined. However, it will only apply, or deposit, the information you are cloning onto the currently active layer. That way, you can create a new empty layer, turn on the Use All Layers checkbox, and retouch your image (**Figure 13.9**). Don't worry if you mess up, because the information is sitting on its own layer, while the unretouched image is directly below it (**Figures 13.10 and 13.11**). This allows you to switch over to the Eraser tool and erase small areas of that layer, or do other things such as lowering the opacity of the layer.

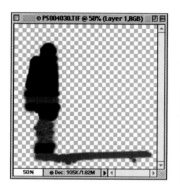

Figure 13.9 You can place your retouching on a new layer so it is isolated from the underlying image.

Figure 13.10 The underlying image will be untouched under the retouching layer.

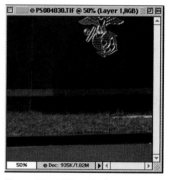

Figure 13.11 When the layers are viewed at the same time, you can see the complete retouched image.

Patch Work

Sampling from one area and applying it all over the place will make it look pretty obvious that you've cloned something. You'll start seeing repeated shapes. For instance, if there happened to be a little dark area in the image you were cloning from, you will see that same dark area in the image you've applied it to. And if you look at it closely enough, you will see the shape repeat itself, which can start to look like a pattern. (You've just been busted cloning!) Sometimes, though, you might want to do this just to fill in an area, but then go back and fix up the places that appear patterned. You can do this by Option-clicking (Macintosh) or Alt-clicking (Windows) a random area around the place you've retouched, and then applying it on top of one of the patterned areas. But watch out—Photoshop's round brushes can be a dead giveaway, because you can easily pick out the areas that you're trying to disguise. This is a great time to use one of the odd-shaped brushes that appear at the bottom of the Brushes palette. These will provide better cover for areas that look obviously cloned. Another trick is to apply some noise to the entire image, which will make any retouching you've performed blend right into the image. To accomplish that, choose Filter > Noise > Add Noise, use an amount somewhere around 3, set the Distribution to Uniform, and turn off the Monochromatic checkbox.

Let's see how this works in action. I'll show you how I reconstructed a forehead using the Rubber Stamp tool. **Figure 13.12** displays a photo of a man's face. I copied one side of his face, and chose Edit > Transform > Flip Horizontal to make it appear as a mirror image (**Figure 13.13**). However, the top of his head was cut off in the photograph, so I decided to put in a new one (forehead, that is). The first thing I did was clone the area directly below the part of his forehead that was missing (**Figure 13.14**). With the cloned forehead material, I filled in the missing part of his forehead, doing my best to make it even. After I applied several doses of forehead, it was obvious to me that I had cloned from one large area. So, I went in and touched up any repeated shapes to make it look more natural (**Figure 13.15**).

Now, however, if you look at the top of his head, there is a highlight on each edge that suddenly stops in the area I retouched. When I was filling up his forehead by clicking back and forth, I didn't get any of the highlights. So to add the highlight on the edge of his head, I grabbed from very small areas on other highlighted parts of his forehead and applied it right on the new edge (**Figure 13.16**).

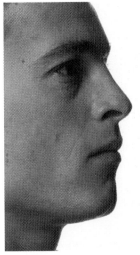

Figure 13.12 Original image. (© 1998 PhotoDisc)

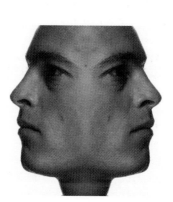
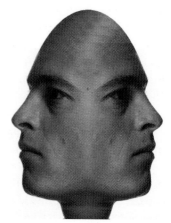

Figure 13.13 Two sides blended together, but missing a forehead.

Figure 13.14 Basic cloning to reconstruct forehead.

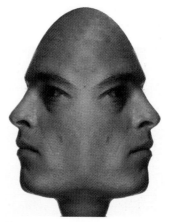
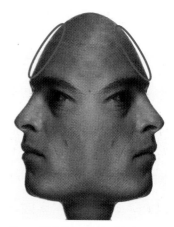

Figure 13.15 Repeated patterns retouched.

Figure 13.16 Highlight added to edge of forehead.

Lighten/Darken

It's easy to remove small scratches or little imperfections that are much brighter or much darker than the image that surrounds them; all you have to do is know a few little tricks. Let's say you have a background that has a scratch that is much brighter than the area around it. Naturally, you'll want to clone from the surrounding area; but before you do, you'll need to mess with the blending mode settings from the Options bar. (We talked about blending modes in Chapter 12, "Enhancement," so here we'll just look at what we need for the Rubber Stamp tool.) The Blending Mode pop-up menu in the Options bar is labeled Mode. The Lighten and Darken options are both very useful when retouching. If you set that menu to Darken, it will compare what you're about to apply to what the image looks like underneath, and it will only allow you to darken things. So let's say you had a light-colored scratch in the background of your image (**Figure 13.17**). You could clone from an area directly around it that is the correct brightness. But before you apply the cloned material to the scratch, you might want to set the blending mode to Darken (**Figure 13.18**). In Darken, all Photoshop can do is darken your picture. Under no circumstances will it be able to lighten it.

Figure 13.19 Image contains dark blotches in the background.

Figure 13.17 Original image.

Figure 13.18 Scratch retouched by using the Rubber Stamp tool set to Darken.

The Blending Mode menu can also be useful when you have a background with little bitty dark specks in it (**Figure 13.19**). To remove them, choose the Rubber Stamp tool and set the blending mode to Lighten (**Figure 13.20**). Then clone from the areas around the specks and cover up the dark specks. This will allow the retouched areas to blend into the image more so you don't see a big gob where you retouched the image.

Figure 13.20 Blotches removed by using the Rubber Stamp tool set to Lighten.

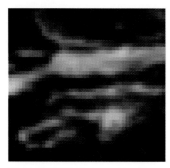

Figure 13.21 Unsharpened image.

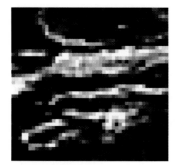

Figure 13.22 Image sharpened during scan.

Warning

In order to clone between two documents, both documents need to be in the same color mode. If one of the documents is in RGB and the other is in CMYK, Photoshop won't allow you to cross-clone.

Automatic Sharpening

The automatic sharpening function that's built into some scanners makes retouching much more difficult. If possible, turn off any sharpening settings in your scanning software (**Figures 13.21 and 13.22**).

Cloning Between Documents

With the Rubber Stamp tool, you're not limited to just cloning from what's in the active document. You can open a second image and clone from that image as well (**Figure 13.23**). All you have to do is move your cursor outside the current image window and on top of another open document. Now you can Option-click (Macintosh) or Alt-click (Windows) anywhere in that second document and apply it within the document you are working on. It will copy from one document and paste it into another.

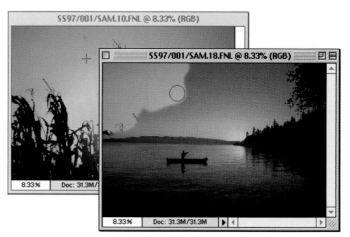

Figure 13.23 Cloning between two documents. (© 1998 Adobe Systems, Inc.)

The Dodge and Burn Tools

Now that we've had some fun with the Rubber Stamp tool, let's take a look at the Dodge and Burn tools. The words "dodge" and "burn" are taken from a traditional photographic darkroom. In a darkroom, an enlarger projects an image onto a sheet of photographic paper. While the image is being projected, you could put something in the way of the light source, which would obstruct the light in such a way that it would hit certain areas more than others—otherwise known as dodging the light. Or you could intensify the light by cupping your hands together, creating just a small hole in between them, and allowing the light to concentrate on a certain area more than others—otherwise known as burning. Using a combination of these two methods, you can brighten or darken your image. Photoshop reproduces these techniques with two tools: Dodge and Burn. If you look at the icons for these tools, you'll see that one of them looks like a hand; that would be for burning, allowing the light to go through the opening of your hand. The other one looks like (at least I think it looks like) a lollipop, which you can use for obstructing, or dodging, the light.

The Dodge Tool

Let's take a closer look at the Dodge tool. Because it can lighten your image, the Dodge tool comes in handy when you are working on people with dark shadows under their eyes. But before we get into cosmetic surgery, I'll introduce you to a very important pop-up menu, called the Range menu, which is associated with this tool. You'll find it in the Options bar at the top of your screen (**Figure 13.24**). The pop-up menu has three choices: Shadows, Midtones, and Highlights. This menu tells Photoshop which shades of gray it should concentrate on when you pan across your image.

> **Note**
> The spacing setting of your brush will also affect how much the image is changed when using the Dodge and Burn tools. Higher spacing settings will affect the image less.

Figure 13.24 Dodge tool Options bar.

If you use the Shadows setting, you will change mainly the dark part of your image. As you paint across your image, your brush will brighten the areas it touches. But as you get into the midtones of the image, it will apply it less and less. And if you paint over the light parts of the image, it won't change them much, if at all. The second choice is Midtones. If you use this setting, you will affect mainly the middle shades of gray in your image, or those areas that are about 25%–75% gray. It shouldn't change the shadows or highlights very much. They may change a little bit, but

Figure 13.25 Top: Shadows. Middle: Midtones. Bottom: Highlights.

only so they can blend into those areas. The third choice is Highlights. Highlights will mainly affect the lightest parts of your image and slowly blend into the middle tones of your image. You can see the effects of all of these settings in **Figure 13.25**.

Obviously, you'll need to decide exactly which setting would work best for your situation. If you don't do this before using the Dodge tool, you might cause yourself some grief. Let's say you're trying to fix dark areas around someone's eyes, but the Dodge tool doesn't seem to be doing the job (**Figure 13.26**). Then, after dozens of tries, you finally realize that the Range pop-up menu is set to Highlights instead of Midtones (look at the eyes in **Figures 13.27 and 13.28**).

Figure 13.26 Original image. (© 1998 PhotoDisc)

Figure 13.27 Dodge tool set to Highlights.

Figure 13.28 Dodge tool set to Midtones.

You also have an Exposure setting on the Options bar that controls how much brighter the image will become. As with most Photoshop tools, you can use the number keys on your keyboard to change this setting.

Color Images

The Dodge tool works exceptionally well on grayscale images. All you have to do is choose which part of the image you want to work on—Shadows, Midtones, or Highlights—and paint across an area. Unfortunately, it's not as slick with color images. If you use the Dodge tool on color, you'll find that it tends to wash out some of the colors and in some cases even change them (**Figures 13.29 and 13.30**).

One good solution is to duplicate the layer you're working on and set the blending mode of the duplicate to Luminosity before using the Dodge tool. That should maintain the original colors and limit your changes to the brightness of the image. Or, you can forego the Dodge tool and just use the Paintbrush tool. You can set your Paintbrush tool's blending mode to Color Dodge and choose white to paint with. But just going ahead and painting across an image will look rather ridiculous, because all it's doing is blowing out the detail (**Figure 13.31**).

Figure 13.29 Original image. (© 1998 PhotoDisc)

Figure 13.30 Eyes lightened by using the Dodge tool.

Figure 13.31 Painting with white by using the Color Dodge mode.

To get it to work correctly, just lower the Opacity setting on the tool to about 20% (**Figure 13.32**). This will allow you to create highlights or to brighten up areas. Sometimes this works a little bit better than the Dodge tool.

The Burn Tool

The Burn tool is designed for darkening areas of an image. Like the Dodge tool, it has Range options in its palette for Highlights, Midtones, and Shadows, as well as an Exposure setting. It, too, works great with grayscale images. So if you are ever dealing with a shiny spot on someone's (grayscale) forehead or nose because the light is reflecting off of it, you can go ahead and try to fix it with the Burn tool (compare **Figures 13.33 and 13.34**).

Figure 13.32 Eyes lightened by painting with white by using the Color Dodge blending mode and a low Opacity setting.

Figure 13.33 Original image. (© 1998 PhotoDisc)

Figure 13.34 Forehead darkened (subtly) by using the Burn tool.

Color Fixes

Just like with the Dodge tool, you'll start having problems when you use the Burn tool with a color image. Flesh tones are the worst—they just seem to look sunburned or turn black (**Figures 13.35 and 13.36**).

Figure 13.35 Face darkened by using the Burn tool set to Midtones.

Figure 13.36 Face darkened by using the Burn tool set to Highlights.

Let's say you're in CMYK mode. When you use the Burn tool, it's going to darken all of the different channels in your image (**Figure 13.37**). Remember, a CMYK image is made out of cyan, magenta, yellow, and black. Think about a face. Do you want very much black? Probably not. Do you want very much cyan? Maybe only a tiny bit. For the most part, Caucasian faces are mainly made up of magenta and yellow. (Black, Asian, and Hispanic faces might need a wee bit extra cyan; it makes the skin look tan.) Using the Burn tool, if you try to get rid of a bright spot on somebody's forehead and you're in CMYK mode, it's just going to make that forehead get darker and darker and, of course, look terrible. To overcome this, start out by setting the Range pop-up menu in the Options bar to Highlights, because you want to work on the light part of the image. Then isolate just the magenta and yellow channels by opening the Channels palette and clicking the magenta channel, and then Shift-clicking on the yellow channel (**Figures 13.38 and 13.39**).

Figure 13.37 Burning all the color channels.

Figure 13.38 Magenta and yellow channels visible.

Figure 13.39 Editing the magenta and yellow channels.

There's one more thing you might want to do, for your own convenience. If you look at the main image window, it will appear as if your entire image is made from just magenta and yellow. That makes it a little difficult to work with. Ideally, you'd want to view the image in full color, but still only work on magenta and yellow. To do this, turn on the eyeball on the topmost channel, which is the Composite channel (**Figure 13.40**). That will make it so you see all four channels of the image, but you're still editing magenta and yellow only.

Figure 13.40 Editing the magenta and yellow channels while viewing all the color channels.

Now you can go in and try to get rid of those bright spots on foreheads and noses (**Figure 13.41**). This should work quite nicely. If you are working in RGB mode, you can accomplish the same thing; you just want to work on the green and blue channels. You don't have to remember which specific channels to work on—instead, just click through the channels, look for where the problem area shows up, and fix only those channels.

One Last Step

Okay, you've retouched your image; now you have one very important bit of housekeeping to take care of. Remember when you clicked on the specific channels to isolate the colors? Well, if you leave the Channels palette as is, everything you do from now on will affect only those two channels. To remedy this, click the topmost channel in the Channels palette so that all the channels are highlighted and all the channels are visible for editing, as shown in **Figure 13.42.** Now you're ready to go.

Figure 13.41 Using the Burn tool on the magenta and yellow channels.

Figure 13.42 When you're finished, be sure to click the topmost channel to make all channels active for editing.

The Sponge Tool

Hiding in with the Dodge and Burn tools is the Sponge tool. It works as if you have a sponge full of bleach, where you can paint across your image and soak up the color. Or you can do the opposite and intensify the colors—it's all determined by what you choose from the Mode menu in the Options bar. If you choose Desaturate, then the Sponge tool will tone down the colors in the area you are painting. The more you paint across an area, the closer it will become to being grayscale. This can be useful when you'd like to make a product stand out from an otherwise distracting background (**Figure 13.43**). I also use it (with a very low Pressure setting) to minimize the yellow/orange color cast that usually shows up in the teeth of people who smoke or drink coffee a lot.

The Saturate setting will intensify the colors as you paint over them, which is great for giving people rosy cheeks (**Figure 13.44**). This can also be great for adding a bit more color to people's lips.

Figure 13.43 Some of the strawberries were desaturated to make the central one stand out. (© 2001 Stockbyte, www.stockbyte.com)

The Sharpen and Blur Tools

When you need to blur or sharpen an area, you have two choices: Select an area and apply a filter, or use the Blur and Sharpen tools. Using filters to blur and sharpen your image has a few advantages over using the tools. These include getting a preview of the image before you commit to the settings being used, and having the ability to apply the filter effect evenly to the area you are changing. But occasionally the Blur and Sharpen tools can really help when working on small areas, so let's take a look at how they work and when to use them.

Figure 13.44 The child's left cheek was enhanced using the Sponge tool set to Saturate.(© 2001 Stockbyte, www.stockbyte.com)

The Blur Tool

The Blur tool is pretty straightforward. You can paint across any part of your image and blur everything that your cursor passes over. In the Blur tool Options bar, you will find a pressure setting that determines how much you will blur the image; higher settings blur the image more. This can be useful if there are little, itty-bitty areas of detail obstructing your image. I generally prefer to use the Gaussian Blur filter instead of this Blur tool because it does a better job of evenly blurring an area.

Warning

Don't go over the image once with the Blur tool set to Lighten and then switch over to Darken and go over it again. That would be the same as leaving it set to normal, and you would be back to Vaseline face. So use it just once, with it set to either Lighten or Darken. Just think about what is most prominent in a wrinkle. Is it the light area of the wrinkle, or the dark area? That will indicate which setting you should use.

I like to use the Blur tool instead for reducing—not removing—wrinkles (**Figure 13.45**). If you turn the pressure way up on this tool and paint across a wrinkle a few times, you'll see it begin to disappear. But you'll also notice that it doesn't look very realistic. It might look as if you had smeared some Vaseline on the face. To really do a wrinkle justice, you have to take a closer look. Wrinkles are made out of two parts, a highlight and a shadow (light part and dark part). If you paint across that with the Blur tool, the darker part of the wrinkle will be lightened, while the lightest part will be darkened, so that they become more similar in shade (**Figure 13.46**).

To reduce the impact of a wrinkle without completely getting rid of it (if I wanted to get rid of it, I would use the Rubber Stamp tool), turn the pressure setting all the way up. Then change the blending mode to either Darken or Lighten. If the part that makes that wrinkle most prominent is the dark area, then set the blending mode menu to Lighten (**Figure 13.47**). Then when you paint across the area, the only thing it will be able to do is lighten that wrinkle. But because you are using the Blur tool, it's not going to completely lighten it and make it disappear. Instead, it will reduce the impact of it. You really have to try this to see how it looks.

Figure 13.45 Original image. (© 1998 PhotoSpin, www.photospin.com)

Figure 13.46 Forehead wrinkles blurred.

Figure 13.47 Forehead wrinkles lessened by using the Blur tool with a blending mode of Lighten.

Layers

When I'm retouching wrinkles, I usually create a brand-new, empty layer (**Figure 13.48**). Then, in order to be able to use the Blur tool, I have to turn on the Use All Layers checkbox in the Options bar (**Figure 13.49**). Otherwise, Photoshop can look at only one layer at a time, and it won't have any information to blur. By doing all these steps, I can easily delete areas or redo them without having to worry about permanently changing the original image. If you're attempting the wrinkle technique I mentioned earlier, then you'll need to set the blending mode of the layer to Lighten, and you might need to lower the pressure setting of the Blur tool.

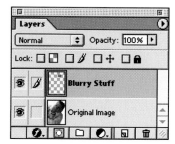

Figure 13.48 By creating a new layer before using the Blur tool, you can isolate the unretouched image.

Figure 13.49 The Blur tool will not be able to use information on other layers without turning on the Use All Layers checkbox.

The Sharpen Tool

The Sharpen tool works in a fashion similar to its relative the Sharpen filter. But with this tool you have to adjust the pressure setting in the Options bar to determine how much you want to sharpen the image. And you have to be careful: if you turn the pressure setting up too high or paint across an area too many times, you're going to get some really weird effects (**Figures 13.50 to 13.52**).

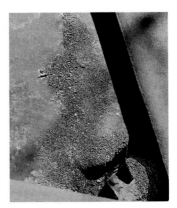

Figure 13.50 Original image. (© 1998 PhotoDisc)

Figure 13.51 Sharpened using the Sharpen tool with a medium pressure setting.

Figure 13.52 Sharpened using the Sharpen tool with a high pressure setting.

Figure 13.53 Original image. (© 2001 Stockbyte, www.stockbyte.com)

Figure 13.54 Metallic highlights sharpened.

Reflected Highlights

When you run across an image that contains glass, metal, or other shiny objects, it usually contains extremely bright highlights (known as specular highlights). This usually happens when light reflects off one of those very shiny areas, such as the edge of a glass. These extra-bright highlights often look rather flat and lifeless after being adjusted. This happens because whenever we adjust an image to perform color correction, or prepare it for printing or multimedia, the brightest areas of the image usually become 3% or 4% gray (instead of white). But if you sharpen those areas, you're going to brighten them up and make them pure white. This will make them jump off the page and look more like they do in real life. So this means any time you have jewelry, glassware, or reflected light in people's eyes, you'll want to use the Sharpen tool, bring down the pressure to about 30%, and go over those areas once. That will make them almost pure white; when you print them, they will almost jump off of the page, as they should (**Figures 13.53 and 13.54**).

Closing Thoughts

We've covered all the tools you'll need to become a bona fide "Photo Doctor." Bear in mind that you don't need to limit yourself to just photographs; the tools and techniques we've covered in this chapter can be used for non-photographic images as well. And, as with everything else in Photoshop, once you've gone around the block with these tools a few times, you'll probably think of a dozen other things you can do with them.

So, whether you're giving someone a facelift, removing your ex-boy/girlfriend from a photograph, or clear-cutting telephone poles from an otherwise perfect Kodak moment, just promise me that you won't do anything underhanded for some ethically challenged third-world dictator.

Ben's Techno-Babble Decoder Ring

Specular Highlight—An area that shines light directly into the camera lens, usually caused by a light source reflecting off the reflective surface of glass, metal, or other shiny objects. Specular highlights do not contain any detail and should be reproduced as solid white to maintain realism.

Keyboard Shortcuts

FUNCTION	MACINTOSH	WINDOWS
Next Brush	>	>
Previous Brush	<	<
First Brush	Shift-<	Shift-<
Last Brush	Shift->	Shift->
Tool opacity	0 through 9	0 through 9
Toning tool	O	O
Cycle through toning tools	Shift-O	Shift-O
Blur/Sharpen tools	R	R
Switch between Blur and Sharpen	Shift-R	Shift-R
Use Shadows	Shift-Option-S	Shift-Alt-S
Use Midtones	Shift-Option-M	Shift-Alt-M
Use Highlights	Shift-Option-H	Shift-Alt-H

© Nick Koudis, www.koudis.com

When ideas fail, words come in very handy.
—Goethe

In the 5.0 version of this book, I said "given Photoshop's past limitations with text, the new Type tool is nothing short of amazing." Well (I say with a red face), it seems I spoke too soon. It turns out that the 5.0 Type tool was actually a baby-step compared to the 6.0 model, which has been so completely revamped and improved, it's like a Ford Escort just morphed into a Ferrari. In a nutshell, we now have:

▶ Ability to create jaggy-free, object-based text

▶ Ability to flow your text into a resizable column that you've defined (finally!)

▶ Advanced typographic controls that act like those in a page layout program

▶ Warping effects that allow you to bend your text into different shapes

▶ Unbelievable special effects through the use of the new layer styles.

6.0 Banishes Jaggy Text

One of the main reasons for all this excessive enthusiasm has to do with the jaggies. Your text looks jaggy when the pixels in an image are big enough that you can easily see them when printed (**Figure 14.1**). They show up as rough, jagged edges on your printouts, and they are the cause of much hair-pulling and sudden bursts of profanity in the graphic arts industry.

Figure 14.1 Photoshop 5.5's text was pixel-based, which could cause it to appear jaggy.

In Photoshop 5, although we had a nice new feature called the Type layer, we still had jaggy text, because it was still just an image made up out of pixels. Photoshop's pixel-based text is great for the Web, but is less than ideal when you had to save the text in a file, use it in a page layout program, and send it off to the printer. Invariably you would get some degree of jagginess, which is why so many professional designers would bypass Photoshop and create text in their page layout program, or in Adobe Illustrator, where it would be object-based (also known as vector-based).

Stick with me on this. In the graphic arts industry, the distinction between object-based and pixel-based is an extremely important one, and understanding it will serve you well. Object-based simply means that the image is no longer made up of pixels; it's a single element that can be scaled up or down without losing the integrity of its shape. For example, if you import a photograph of a circular object into your page layout program and then try to scale it up, it doesn't make more pixels to accommodate the larger size. Instead, it simply makes each pixel larger to fill the space. Thus the jaggy look. Not so with object-based shapes! If you created that same circle in Adobe Illustrator (which creates strictly object-based images), you could do anything you want to that circle (make it bigger, smaller, oval, etc.), and it will always retain its smooth edge. That's why most logos are created in Illustrator. And now, with Photoshop 6.0, we can have object-based text (**Figure 14.2**).

But not everything is roses and chocolate. The one stipulation about the new object-based text is that it must be printed on a *PostScript printer*. Otherwise it will revert to being plain old pixel-based text again, and the jaggies you love to hate will be back staring you in the face. So if have a $200 inkjet printer, you're really no further ahead when it comes to the jaggies, unless your printer happens to have a PostScript RIP, which is usually a software accessory you can add to a low-end inkjet printer.

Am I in a Page Layout Program?

In addition to being able to create jaggy-free text, Adobe decided to bless us with a Type tool that no longer acts like the old Smith Corona typewriters. In Photoshop 5.0, when you were entering text, you had to hit Return (Macintosh) or Enter (Windows) to get to the next line, which made it quite clumsy when you were trying to type in a multi-line paragraph. Now, with 6.0, you can define a box that contains your text, and your text will wrap cleanly from one line to the next without having to use the "carriage return" (as we used to say in the old days). Also, there are a slew of new typographic controls, such as hyphenation and

Figure 14.2 In Photoshop 6.0, text is object-based, which allows it to stay crisp as long as it is printed on a PostScript printer.

Note
You can achieve crisp text on a non-PostScript printer by saving your image as a PDF file and printing it from Adobe Acrobat.

justification, first line indent, and Space Above and Space Below that are so useful and flexible, you might forget where you are and think you're in a page layout program. Don't get me wrong. It's no replacement for your page layout program. You still can't have multiple pages, there's no spell checker, no style sheets, and you can't flow text from one text box to another. But if you're doing a single-page poster or flyer and you're not dealing with excessive text, Photoshop will do an excellent job.

So, armed with our new toys, let's go cruising into the land of text and backgrounds, and see if the new type features are all they're cracked up to be.

Entering Text

This is going to be a short section, because all you have to do to lay down some text is click with the Type tool and start typing directly on your image. Photoshop will automatically create a new Type layer. If you want Photoshop 6.0 to act like previous versions—that is, where you have to press Return (Macintosh) or Enter (Windows) to create a new line—just click the mouse button without dragging, and begin typing. This is known as point text and is useful for creating headlines that you don't want to wrap onto multiple lines. But if you'd rather have Photoshop automatically wrap your text into a multi-line paragraph, then click and drag to create a rectangular box that will contain your text. Then you can enter your text and press Return (Macintosh) or Enter (Windows) whenever you need to create a new paragraph. Photoshop will do the rest, wrapping your text onto multiple lines based on the column width you define. While you are in the Type tool, you can always change the column width by dragging one of the side handles, and then the text will reflow.

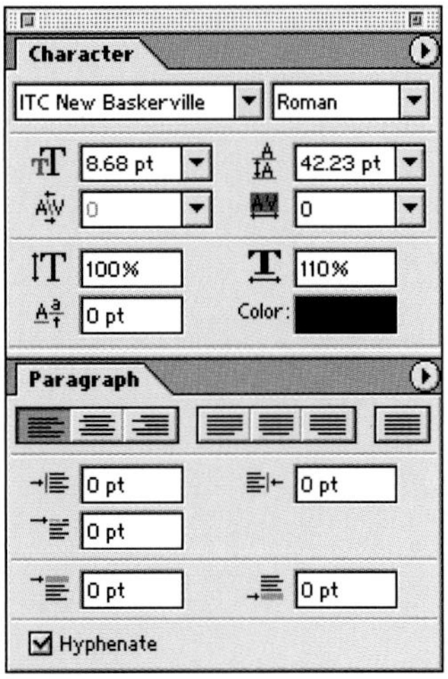

Editing Text

The Character and Paragraph palettes offer a wide range of choices for editing text (**Figure 14.3**). But before you start messing with these settings, you'll need to highlight the text you would like to edit. You can do this by dragging

Figure 14.3 The Character and Paragraph palettes.

across a range of text or by typing Command-A (Macintosh) or Ctrl-A (Windows) to select all the text. The Character palette will work exclusively on the text that is highlighted, whereas the Paragraph palette will work on entire paragraphs regardless of whether all the text is selected.

Some of you Photoshoppers may not have been steeped in desktop publishing, so here's a basic rundown of the typographical controls you're going to know and love.

Font—I like to click on the Font field and then use the up and down arrow keys to cycle through all the choices that appear in the list. You can also click on the Font field and start typing a font name, and Photoshop will move you to the first font that starts with those letters. Or, if you want to do it the traditional way, just click on the arrow to the right of the Font field and you'll be presented with a full font menu. If you have more than one version of the same font installed, then Photoshop will add (T1) next to the PostScript Type 1 version of the font, (TT) next to the TrueType version, or (OT) for an Open Type font.

Style—Once you've chosen the font family you'd like to use, you can find out which styles (bold, italic, etc.) are available by clicking on the Style menu. If you find that the font you want to use doesn't contain a bold or italic style, you can choose Faux Bold or Faux Italic from the side menu of the Character palette to have Photoshop thicken or slant the typeface.

Size—You can specify the measurement system that will be used to determine the size of your type by choosing Edit > Preferences > Units & Rulers. There are three ways to measure your text: in pixels, in millimeters, or in points. The pixels option is resolution-independent, meaning that the height of the text in pixels will be the same regardless of the resolution of your image. The only time I use the pixels option is when I need to match the height of some existing text that has already been measured in pixels. More often than not, I prefer to measure text in points because I can use the same setting in multiple documents and know that the text will appear the same size when printed regardless of the resolution of the file it is used in. It's also a system that's consistent with most publishing programs. I have never used the millimeters option because I don't know of any other program that uses that system to measure type.

To be honest, it isn't very often that I pay attention to the actual type-size settings. Instead, I eyeball it and compare the size of my text to the rest of the image. To quickly adjust the size of the text in increments of two, highlight the text and type Shift-Command-> or Shift-Command-< (Macintosh) or Shift-Ctrl-> or Shift-Ctrl-< (Windows). To change the size in increments of ten, just add the Option key (Macintosh) or the Alt key (Windows) to these keyboard commands. Also, you can scale text up or down using the Edit > Transform > Scale option; it won't harm your text.

Note

In earlier versions of Photoshop, the Auto Leading feature always used 120% and was chosen by leaving the Leading setting empty.

Leading—To change the vertical space between lines of text, you'll need to change the leading setting. If you leave it set to (Auto), then Photoshop will automatically calculate its own setting and keep it hidden from you (**Figure 14.4**). It does this by multiplying the size of the text by the percentage specified in the Justification dialog box that appears in the side menu of the Paragraph palette; the default setting is 120%. So 100-point text, for example, would have an automatic leading setting of 120. The Auto setting is useful if you know you'll be changing the size of the text later on, because the leading setting will change as you change the size of the text. If you don't like the Auto setting, you can type in your own setting (**Figure 14.5**). To quickly change the leading in increments of two, highlight the text, then type Option-up arrow and Option-down arrow (Macintosh) or Alt-up arrow and Alt-down arrow (Windows). To set the leading to Auto, either type (Auto) into the Leading field, or type Shift-Option-Command-A (Macintosh) or Shift-Alt-Ctrl-A (Windows).

Graphic Savage

Figure 14.4 Leading setting determined by Photoshop (auto).

Graphic Savage

Figure 14.5 Leading setting adjusted manually.

Kerning—If you need to tighten up or loosen the space between two letters, click between the letters, change the Kerning setting to increase (positive numbers) or decrease (negative numbers) the amount of space between those letters (**Figures 14.6 and 14.7**). Kerning is essential when working with numbers, because they are designed to line up in a spreadsheet program, which means the number 1 will always have a bunch of space around it to force it to take up as much space as the other numbers. To quickly change the Kerning setting in increments of 20, type Option-right arrow and Option-left arrow (Macintosh) or Alt-right arrow and Alt-left arrow (Windows). You can also add the Command key (Macintosh) or the Ctrl key (Windows) to these keyboard commands to increase the kerning setting in increments of 100. If you use the Metrics setting, then Photoshop will use the kerning settings that are built into the typeface.

> **Note**
>
> In earlier versions of Photoshop, you had to turn off the Auto Kern checkbox before you could change the kerning setting.

DAVE DAVE

Figure 14.6 Text entered with the Metrics kerning setting selected.

Figure 14.7 Manually kerned text.

Tracking—To add or remove space between all the letters in a range of text, highlight the text, and then change the tracking setting (compare **Figures 14.8 and 14.9**). Or type Option-right arrow (Macintosh) and Option-left arrow (Macintosh) or Alt-right arrow (Windows) and Alt-left arrow (Windows) to change the Tracking in increments of 20. To change the Tracking setting in increments of 100, just add the Command key (Macintosh) or Ctrl key (Windows) to these keyboard commands. To set the tracking to zero, just leave the Tracking field empty, or type Shift-Command-Q (Macintosh) or Shift-Ctrl-Q (Windows). I often use a negative tracking setting for headlines where I like the text to be nice and tight. I use positive tracking any time I have ALLCAPS text because it seems to make it easier to read.

Figure 14.8 Tracking: 0.

SPIFFY

Figure 14.9 Tracking: 260.

A solid foundation of knowledge is essential before attempting to understand Photoshop's more advanced features.

Figure 14.10 The initial capital in this paragraph was created by setting the Vertical and Horizontal Scale settings to 200%.

Vertical Scale—This setting allows you to stretch your text vertically without changing its width. I often do this when I want to create a raised capital at the beginning of a paragraph. I just set both the vertical and horizontal scale settings to an equal number, and then, when I change the size of the text, the raised cap will change along with it, as long as all the text is selected (**Figure 14.10**). To set the Vertical Scale to 100%, type Shift-Option-Command-X (Macintosh) or Shift-Alt-Ctrl-X (Windows).

Horizontal Scale—This setting allows you to stretch or compress your text horizontally without changing its height. I often lower this setting a small amount (like by 1%) to make a line of text take up less space and prevent it from overflowing the space I have allotted. The alternative would be to use tracking, which leaves the shape of the characters intact, and simply removes an equal amount of space between each letter. To set the Horizontal Scale to 100%, type Shift-Command-X (Macintosh) or Shift-Ctrl-X (Windows).

Baseline Shift—To shift one or more letters up or down, highlight the letters, and then change the Baseline Shift setting (**Figures 14.11 and 14.12**). This is very useful when working with symbols, where a parenthesis might appear to be too low compared to the text, or an equal sign needs to be shifted to make it look better. To change this setting in increments of two, type Shift-Option-up arrow and Shift-Option-down arrow (Macintosh) or Shift-Alt-up arrow and Shift-Alt-down arrow (Windows).

Figure 14.11 No baseline shift.

Figure 14.12 Equal sign and small 2 baseline shifted.

Color—To change the color of the text, click on the color swatch to bring up the standard Color Picker. To use your foreground color, type Option-Delete (Macintosh) or Alt-Backspace (Windows). To use your background color, type Command-Delete (Macintosh) or Ctrl-Backspace (Windows). In earlier versions of Photoshop, each Type layer could contain only one color, so for every color you wanted to use, you'd have to create another Type layer. You could cheat by placing some color on a layer above the text and then grouping that layer with the Type layer by typing Command-G (Macintosh) or Ctrl-G (Windows).

Alignment—The Alignment choices determine the method used to align multiple lines of text (**Figure 14.13**). Most of the time I use the flush left option because it seems to be the easiest to read. Type Shift-Command-L (Macintosh) or Shift-Ctrl-L (Windows) to specify flush left text. Centered is good for headlines; type Shift-Command-C (Macintosh) or Shift-Ctrl-C (Windows) to specify centered text. Flush right is often useful for numbers, because it will line up the decimal points. Type Shift-Command-R (Macintosh) or Shift-Ctrl-R (Windows) to specify flush right text. I only use the justified option when I'm using a rather long column width; otherwise it causes huge spaces between words. Type Shift-Command-J (Macintosh) or Shift-Ctrl-J (Windows) to specify justified text.

Left Indent—This setting is useful when you have a bulleted list that you want to set off from the main flow of text (**Figure 14.14**).

With a little practice, even the most complicated topics can be mastered including:

- Line Art Scanning
- Grayscale Adjustment
- Color Correction
- Understanding Levels and Curves

Figure 14.14 Bulleted list was set using a left indent of 12pts.

Right Indent—I often use this setting along with the left indent setting to make a long quotation stand out from the rest of the text (**Figure 14.15**). You can also make the quotation marks extend beyond the margins by choosing

Photoshop has keyboard shortcuts for just about everything. The key is to remember and use what's important to your particular workflow.

Photoshop has keyboard shortcuts for just about everything. The key is to remember and use what's important to your particular workflow.

Photoshop has keyboard shortcuts for just about everything. The key is to remember and use what's important to your particular workflow.

Photoshop has keyboard shortcuts for just about everything. The key is to remember   and   use

Figure 14.13 Paragraph alignment settings from top to bottom: Centered, Flush Left, Flush Right, Justified.

Note

On a Macintosh, type Option-8 to create a bullet; in Windows, type Alt-0149 on your numeric keypad.

Note

Did you know that the proper quote characters used by typography professionals are the curly ones, and not the straight ones (which are really inch and feet marks)? If you want to quote like a pro, you'll need to use the following key combinations:

▸ Macintosh: For a single opening quote, type Option-], and for a single closing quote use Shift-Option-]. For a double opening quote, type Option-[, and for a closing double quote use Shift-Option-[.

▸ Windows: For a single opening quote, type Alt-0145, and for a single closing quote, type Alt-0146. For a double opening quote, type Alt-0147, and for a double closing quote type Alt-0148. Use your numeric keypad, and make sure your NumLock key is on.

Unfortunately, the Hanging Roman Punctuation option does not recognize proper curly quotes.

Hanging Roman Punctuation from the side menu of the Paragraph palette.

It can be more pleasing when the flow of text is interrupted by other elements such as quotes and bullet points.

"This is a mighty fine example of a spiffy looking quote that is set off from the rest of the text"

Figure 14.15 Quote was set using a left indent of 24pts and a right indent of 30pts.

First Line Indent—This function indents the first line of each paragraph as if you pressed the Tab key on your keyboard. I also find this useful when I have a list of bulleted items that have more than one line each. I'll end up setting the Left Indent setting to something like 20pt and the First Line Indent setting to –20pt. That will force all the lines after the bulleted line to be indented (you may need to put some spaces after the bullet on the first line to make the text there line up with the lines below). Compare **Figures 14.16 and 14.17**. This technique is also useful when you want the first letter of a paragraph to extend into the margin.

Bulleted lists can pose many problems unless you are thoughtful when using Photoshop's settings.

• Some bulleted lists might extend to more than a single line, which can make them less than ideal for a simple left indent

• That's when you might want to consider using a negative first line intent setting along with a simple left indent to control the rest of the lines.

Figure 14.16 Bulleted list was set using a left indent of 12 points.

Bulleted lists can pose many problems unless you are thoughtful when using Photoshop's settings.

- Some bulleted lists might extend to more than a single line, which can make them less than ideal for a simple left indent
- That's when you might want to consider using a negative first line intent setting along with a simple left indent to control the rest of the lines.

Figure 14.17 Bulleted list was set with a left indent of 32pt and a first line indent of –20pts.

Space Above and Space Below—These settings are exactly what their names indicate. They control the space above and below your paragraph. I use Space Above as a substitute for indenting the first line of every paragraph (like all the paragraphs in this book). It is also useful when you have a bulleted list that contains more than one line per bullet point. I use Space Below to add a bit of extra space below the last line of a bulleted list so it doesn't look like it has melded with the paragraphs below it.

Hyphenate—This setting will use the settings in the Hyphenation dialog box (from the side menu of the Paragraph palette) to determine which words should break onto the next line of the text (**Figure 14.18**). Type Shift-Option-Command-H (Macintosh) or Shift-Alt-Ctrl-H (Windows) to toggle Hyphenation on and off. If you want to prevent a word from breaking, select the letters you'd like to keep together and then choose No Break from the side menu of the Character palette. The No Break feature is useful when you have initials, Web addresses, or company names that don't read well when broken onto multiple lines.

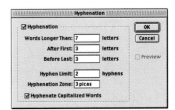

Figure 14.18 The Hyphenation dialog box.

You'll also find other useful options in the side menu of the Character and Paragraph palettes. Let's take a look at the choices in these side menus that we haven't covered already.

All Caps—Changes your text to all capital letters. This can be useful if, for example, you decide to make a few subheads uppercase after the text has been entered. (Remember that all-capped text is more difficult to read, so you may want to add some tracking, which can make reading a bit easier.) Type Shift-Command-K (Macintosh) or Shift-Ctrl-K (Windows) to specify All Caps type.

Small Caps—Changes all lower-case letters into smaller capital letters while the capital letters you entered remain full size. This is useful for headings (**Figure 14.19**). Type Shift-Command-H (Macintosh) or Shift-Ctrl-H (Windows) to specify Small Caps type.

The Small Caps style will convert your text into all capital letters, where the characters that were created using the shift key will be larger than the characters that were previously lowercase.

THE SMALL CAPS STYLE WILL CONVERT YOUR TEXT INTO ALL CAPITAL LETTERS, WHERE THE CHARACTERS THAT WERE CREATED USING THE SHIFT KEY WILL BE LARGER THAN THE CHARACTERS THAT WERE PREVIOUSLY LOWERCASE.

Figure 14.19 Top: type entered without formatting. Bottom: Small Caps style applied.

$\$20^{00}$

Figure 14.20 The dollar sign and last two numbers were set using the Superscript style.

H_2O

Figure 14.21 The 2 was set using the Subscript style.

Superscript—This will reduce the size of the selected text and move the characters above the baseline of the rest of the text. I use this all the time when I'm typesetting prices—I remove the decimal and then use this option for the dollar sign and cents (**Figure 14.20**). Type Shift-Command-+ (Macintosh) or Shift-Ctrl-+ (Windows) to specify Superscript type.

Subscript—This option will also make your text smaller, but will shift things downward. It's useful when entering scientific and chemical formulas (**Figure 14.21**). Type Shift-Option-Command-+ (Macintosh) or Shift-Alt-Ctrl-+ (Windows) to specify Subscript type.

Underline—This option will place a line under each letter of your text in the same color as the type. (You cannot control the placement or thickness of the underline.) This feature can be useful when you want to make a selection of text stand out, like a link on a Web page, or the cents in a price (**Figure 14.22**). Type Shift-Command-U (Mac) or Shift-Ctrl-U (Windows) to specify underlined type.

Strikethrough—This option will place a line through the center of the text using the same color as the type. (You cannot control the size or placement of the line.) This can be useful when advertising prices; you can cross out of the old price and place the new one right next to it. Type Shift-Command-/ (Macintosh) or Shift-Ctrl-/ (Windows) to specify Strikethrough type. I find that the Underline and Strikethrough options are usually too thin and often appear as semi-transparent lines on small text.

Ligatures—This option only works with Open Type fonts. It allows Photoshop to automatically replace certain combinations of characters (like "fi" and "fl") with a specially designed character that is a combination of those two, which makes them look more aesthetically pleasing (**Figure 14.23**).

fitness flex fitness flex

Figure 14.23 Left: text as entered with no formatting applied. Right: text with ligatures applied.

Old Style—This option only works with Open Type fonts. It tells Photoshop to use an alternative set of numerals that are smaller than the standard ones (**Figure 14.24**).

Fractional Widths—When this option is turned off, it forces Photoshop to use full pixels for spacing between words. This is useful for Web graphics where your text can be extra small and you want to prevent your text from smashing together (**Figure 14.25**).

Reset Character—This option will reset all the Character palette settings to their defaults. This can be useful when

$371⁵⁰

Figure 14.22 The last two digits were set with both the Superscript and Underline styles.

2929 2929

Figure 14.24 Left: text entered with no formatting applied. Right: text with Old Style applied (it only affects the numerals).

1111111   1111111

Figure 14.25 Left: Fractional Widths turned on. Right: Fractional Widths turned off.

you've just finished messing with a bunch of options and need to get back to setting some normal type.

Adobe Single-line Composer—This option is best when you want to "massage" type by hand and want to precisely control character and word spacing by manually kerning and tracking the characters.

Adobe Every-line Composer—This option will evaluate an entire paragraph to determine where each line of text should break. That means that the upper lines in a paragraph might suddenly change as you continue to add text to the bottom of a paragraph. This option usually gives you the best-looking text, but makes it a bit more difficult to manually tweak everything. Type Shift-Option-Command-T (Macintosh) or Shift-Alt-Ctrl-T (Windows) to toggle between the Single-Line and Every-Line Composer settings.

Reset Paragraph—This option will reset all the Paragraph palette settings back to their defaults. But be careful using it, because it will also reset all the settings in the Hyphenation and Justification dialog boxes.

The Options bar at the top of your screen contains the most commonly used choices from the Character and Paragraph palettes, along with a few options that can't be found in the other palettes. Let's take look at the options that are exclusive to this palette (**Figure 14.26**).

Figure 14.26 Photoshop 6.0's Options bar for typographical controls.

Note

In order to use the Type Mask or Vertical Type setting from the Type tool Options bar, you must choose those options before you click on your image to add text.

Type Mask—This option will deliver a selection shaped like text, instead of an actual Type layer. While you are entering your text, you will see a colored overlay that represents the bounds of the text. Once you finalize the text, it will create a selection. Just beware that you will not be able to edit the text after it has become a selection. If you're worried that you might find a typo later, then use the normal Type tool, and once you're done editing the text,

Command-click (Macintosh) or Ctrl-click (Windows) on the name of the layer to get a selection.

Vertical Type—This option will allow your text to run vertically, with each letter appearing below the previous one. This can be useful when setting type for the spine of a book, or when using Asian typefaces (**Figure 14.27**).

Anti-aliased—You'll find four options in this pop-up menu; None, Crisp, Strong, and Smooth (**Figure 14.28**). Using anything other than None will cause the pixels on the edge of the text to blend into the image and create a smooth edge. Crisp will make the edges appear sharper than the other choices, Strong will make the text look a little bolder, and Smooth with make the edges appear softer. These options are great when creating small text that will be used on the Web. I suggest experimenting with each setting until you think the text looks its best. You can also use the Strong setting when creating text that will be printed, because it can help disguise the jaggies that appear on non-PostScript printers.

Warp—This option is simply a shortcut for choosing Layer > Type > Warp Text. Either one will bring up the Type Warp dialog box, which we will cover later in this chapter.

Palettes—The Palettes button will open the Character and Paragraph palettes. This allows you to close those two palettes (which I usually have stacked together as shown in Chapter 1) to avoid screen clutter and then quickly make them available with a single click.

Type Layers

After you add text to your image, the text will appear on a Type layer (indicated by a T where there would usually be a preview thumbnail in the Layers palette). This layer is special because you can edit the text at any time by using the Type tool and clicking within the text. If a yellow warning triangle appears along with the T that designates a Type layer, that's an indication that the typeface you've

Figure 14.27 Text set using the Vertical Type option.

Figure 14.28 Anti-aliased settings from top to bottom: None, Crisp, Strong, Smooth.

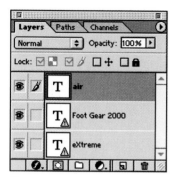

Figure 14.29 The Type layer's warning triangles.

chosen is not currently installed in your operating system (**Figure 14.29**). When a font is missing, you will not be able to edit the text without having Photoshop substitute a different typeface. You might also run into a gray warning triangle on a Type layer. That's an indication that the text will be reflowed if it is edited; that might change the way the paragraph breaks into multiple lines. You'll get that symbol any time you open an image that was created in a previous version of Photoshop.

A Type layer is also special because when you print your image on a PostScript printer, your text will appear crisp, even if the pixels in your image are large enough to make the rest of the image appear jaggy. That's because the text is object-based, instead of being made out of pixels. Photoshop will not convert the text to pixels unless you choose Layer > Rasterize > Type or merge a Type layer with another layer. Not only that, but Photoshop allows you to do a whole bunch of stuff to the Type layers without having to permanently convert them to pixels. Let's take a quick look at your choices. You can:

▶ Apply any of the choices in the Layer > Type > Warp Text dialog box.

▶ Apply most of the Edit > Transform functions.

▶ Add layer styles.

▶ Add a layer mask.

Before you can apply a filter or perform adjustments to the text, you have to convert the Type layer into a normal layer by choosing Layer > Rasterize > Type. That will convert the text from being object-based to being pixel-based. Once you've done that, you'll no longer be able to edit the text (Photoshop will treat it as a scanned image instead) and the text will no longer print with an absolutely crisp edge. If you don't rasterize, and you attempt to apply a filter to your text, Photoshop will warn you and then offer to rasterize the text for you.

Now that you've seen the options that are available when creating text, let's get into the juicy stuff and start creating type effects. I'll break the effects into three sections: effects that use type warping; layer styles (which are especially wonderful because they are the only effects that allow the text to be edited); and finally "photo-realistic filter effects," where we will use filters to their full advantage and create some awesome and tricky-looking effects. So without further ado, let's get started.

Type Warping

Let's begin by choosing Layer > Type > Warp Text. You'll find 15 different warping effects you can use to contort your text into numerous shapes (**Figure 14.30**). Remember, this is a layer-based feature, so you can't warp only a part of a layer, or just a few words on a layer.

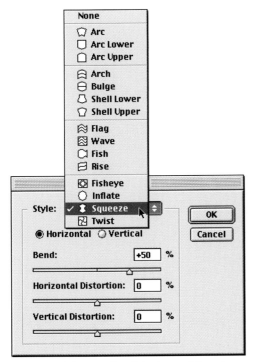

Figure 14.30 The Warp Text dialog box and the styles available on its drop-down menu.

The Bend setting determines how dramatically your text will change (**Figure 14.31**). The Horizontal and Vertical Distortion settings can make it look as if your text is being viewed from different 3D angles (**Figure 14.32**).

Figure 14.31 Bend settings from top to bottom: -50%, -25%, 0, +25, +50 (with the Arc effect).

Figure 14.32 Top: Horizontal and Vertical Distortion set to zero. Bottom: Horizontal Distortion of 85% and Vertical Distortion of 50%.

Warning

If you find that the Warp option is grayed out, then you most likely have used the Faux Bold style from the side menu of the Character palette. Unfortunately, warping doesn't work when that style is applied.

After you've warped your type, you'll notice that a curve has been added below the T in the Layers palette. That signifies that the layer is a Type layer with warping applied, but you can still edit the text by using the Type tool and clicking within the text. The warp function is also great for creating animations in ImageReady, which we'll explore in a later chapter.

Layer Effects

Okay, you've got your text formatted just the way you want it—you've typed and kerned and aligned and warped into wildness. Now you can rub your hands together and get ready for a thrill, because it's time to explore the type Styles dialog box (which is ground zero for creating type effects). Why the excitement? Because you'll be able to add a multitude of effects and still be able to edit your text! And because the effects are made by using layer styles, they won't require much memory (they are just simple settings applied to a layer) and should not increase the file size of your image too much. That means you can go crazy creating some great effects such as edge embossing, extruded or indented type, shadows, and beveled type, and you don't have to worry about bloating your file size. There are four ways to access the Layer Style dialog box:

▶ Double-click any layer name in the Layers palette.

▶ Choose one of the options from the Layer > Layer Styles menu.

▶ Choose one of the options from the Layer Style menu at the bottom of the Layers palette (it's the black circle with the "f" inside).

▶ Choose Blending Options from the side menu of the Layers palette.

Once you've made it into the Layer Styles dialog box, you can click on the name of any style listed on the left side of the dialog box to turn on that style and view its options. If you just click the checkbox next to a style's name, you will toggle that style on or off, but you will not view its settings—you have to click its name for that.

Layer styles determine their shape based on the contents of the layer that they are applied to. Typically, the entire

Notes

In order to add a layer style to the Background image, you must first change its name (by double-clicking on it) to convert it into a normal layer.

....

In previous version of Photoshop, layer styles were known as layer effects and were found under the Layer > Effects menu.

content of a layer is fully visible, and an effect adds dimension on top of, or a shadow underneath, that content. It doesn't have to be that way. Sometimes you might want just the *effect* to be in the shape of a letter or word, but you don't want the original solid text to be visible. In that case, you have the option of tricking Photoshop into hiding the solid text that's in the Type layer. That will allow you to just use the shape of the text to figure out where to apply the layer style. To accomplish that, click on the Blending Options choice in the upper left of the Layer Style dialog box, and then set the Fill Opacity (in the Advanced Blending section) to zero (**Figure 14.33**). That should make the contents of the layer disappear, but will not affect any of the layer styles applied to the layer.

Figure 14.33 Top: Fill Opacity 100%. Bottom: Fill Opacity 0% (© 2001 Stockbyte, www.stockbyte.com)

Shadow Type

Back in Chapter 10 we talked about how to create many kinds of shadows, but there was one thing we didn't get to. What if you want an entire layer to be completely defined by a shadow alone, without the text showing up at all? Well, the first thing you'd want to do is double-click on the name of the Type layer to get to the Layer Styles dialog box, where you can mess with the Blending Options for that layer. To make the text disappear, lower the Fill Opacity setting to zero. That should make the layer completely disappear. Now let's add a shadow so you can see the shape of what's hidden. Click on the Drop Shadow choice in the left of the Layer Style dialog box and you should suddenly see the shape of your type. Next, make sure the Layer Knocks Out Drop Shadow option is turned on (you have to highlight the words Drop Shadow in the menu, not just check the checkbox, to see this); otherwise the drop shadow will show up under the contents of the layer instead of just beyond its edge (**Figure 14.34**).

Figure 14.34 The top half of this image shows what a shadow looks like with the Layer Knocks Out Drop Shadow checkbox off; the bottom shows the shadow with that option turned on. (© 2001 Stockbyte, www.stockbyte.com)

Punch Out Type

With this effect we'll make it look as if you cut a hole in a photo and placed a piece of colored paper just below the hole. You can do that by adding the Inner Shadow layer style to your Type layer. The Size setting will determine how soft the edge appears (**Figure 14.35**). You can also

Figure 14.35 Inner Shadow layer style.

click on your image and drag to reposition the shadow while you're in the dialog box.

Indented Type

Now let's transform that Punch Out type effect into one that looks as if the text indents slightly below the surface of the image. You'll want to start out with a simple Inner Shadow layer style. Then, to get rid of the colored-paper look, click on the Blending Options choice and set the Fill Opacity to zero. Next, add a Color Overlay layer style, and set the color to black and the opacity to somewhere around 30% (**Figure 14.36**).

Figure 14.36 The Indented Type effect created by adding an Inner Shadow layer style. (© 2001 Stockbyte, www.stockbyte.com)

Multicolored Glows

Previous versions of Photoshop allowed you to add a simple glow to your type, but the options in Photoshop 6.0 have gone a step further. Start by adding an Outer Glow layer style, and then change from the solid-colored option to the gradient option by clicking on the radio button next to the gradient. Now you can create a multicolored glow by clicking on the arrow next to the gradient and choosing a multicolored gradient. If the glow seems to be a little weak, you might need to change the Blend Mode setting to normal and increase the Opacity setting (**Figure 14.37**).

Figure 14.37 A multicolored glow using the gradient option in the Outer Glow layer style. (© 2001 Stockbyte, www.stockbyte.com)

Embossed Type

The Bevel And Emboss layer style is my absolute favorite, because it allows me to quickly add dimension to any object. The Style pop-up menu makes the biggest difference in what your emboss effect looks like (you've got to click the name of the blending option in the dialog box—enabling the checkbox is not enough). The Inner Bevel choice will make the 3D effect happen only on the inside of the text. The Outer Bevel choice will do the opposite, adding the 3D effect just outside the shape of the text. The Emboss choice will combine those last two choices to create a 3D look that starts inside the text and extends beyond the edge of the type and onto the underlying image. Pillow Emboss will create a crater effect where the type will appear to raise above the image and then fall again inside the type shape (**Figure 14.38**).

Figure 14.38 From top to bottom: Inner Bevel, Outer Bevel, Emboss, Pillow Emboss. (© 2001 Stockbyte, www.stockbyte.com)

Water Droplets

Let's look at a simple method for simulating water droplets. Start by choosing a hard-edged brush, create a new layer, and then click to create a round shape. Now, double-click the name of that layer and turn the Fill Opacity setting all the way down to zero. Next, add a Drop Shadow style with the Layer Knocks Out Drop Shadow checkbox turned on, and an Inner Glow using white. To add the 3D look, add a Bevel And Emboss style using the Inner Bevel setting, and choose Smooth from the Technique pop-up menu. Finally, add a Color Overlay style, set the color to a very light gray, and set the mode to Color Burn (**Figure 14.39**).

Figure 14.39 A water droplet created using the Drop Shadow, Inner Glow, and Bevel And Emboss styles. (© 2001 Stockbyte, www.stockbyte.com)

Dimensional Stroke

Now let's figure out how to add a line around our text that has a 3D look. After entering your text, you want to be able to concentrate on the effects without being distracted by the color of the text, so lower the Fill Opacity to zero. Next, add a Stroke style and make sure the Size setting is high enough so that it's easy to see the stroke. Add a Bevel And Emboss style, choose Stroke Emboss from the Style pop-up menu, set the Technique pop-up to Chisel Hard, and then experiment with the stroke's Size slider until the 3D effect is big enough to cover the entire stroke. To finish the effect, add an Inner Shadow style (**Figure 14.40**).

Figure 14.40 A dimensional stroke effect created using the Stroke and Bevel And Emboss styles. (© 2001 Stockbyte, www.stockbyte.com)

Wild Type

We've created some pretty cool effects, but we've really only scratched the surface of what's possible. What's exciting is that you can combine as many of these layer styles as you'd like to create some truly eye-popping effects. In **Figure 14.41**, I've used the following styles: Pattern Overlay, Gradient Overlay (set to Hard Light), Stroke (with the Gradient setting), Bevel And Emboss (using the Stroke Emboss option), Inner Shadow, Drop Shadow, and an Inner Glow!

Figure 14.41 An example of what can be accomplished by combining many layer styles. (© 2001 Stockbyte, www.stockbyte.com)

The Styles Palette

If it feels like it took too darn much time to create these effects, then you can take comfort in knowing that

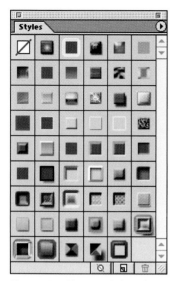

Figure 14.42 The Layer Styles palette (with a lot of my own styles added).

Photoshop 6.0's new Styles palette allows you to store a collection of layer styles so they can be applied over and over again. To save a style, just make sure the layer with the style(s) applied is active and then click the New Style icon at the bottom of the Styles palette (**Figure 14.42**). Your style should appear at the bottom of the palette. To apply that style to another layer, just make that layer active and then click on the style you created in the Styles palette. (Or you can choose Layer > Layer Style > Copy Style, click on the layer you'd like to apply it to, and then choose Paste Style from the same menu.) That's all there is to it! You can also remove all the styles applied to a layer by clicking on the No Style icon at the bottom of the Styles palette. The styles that appear in this palette will stay there (available in any document) until you decide to change them.

Now, this is significant, so please pay close attention. *With all the effects we just created, you have the freedom to edit the text and the effects will update.* That's a giant stride towards creative freedom. But not *all* effects out there in Photoshop allow you to edit the text. From this point on, the effects in this chapter will be a little more involved, and will not leave the text open to further editing after they're applied.

Photo-realistic Effects

We are now moving away from layer styles (where text is editable) and entering the fascinating world of filters (where the text is not editable). I've accepted this tradeoff; the upside of losing the editing flexibility is the chance to create an infinite variety of type effects by using Photoshop's filters (there are about 100 of them).

Here's a quick tour of how filters affect your text. Once you've applied a filter, your text will be rasterized, which will remove its editability and transform it from object-based to pixel-based text. After rasterizing a Type layer, you're no longer limited to using layer styles and warping, so you'll be able to achieve more radical results. The steps used to create these effects may not always seem logical, but stick with me until you see the result. I came up with them after many hours of experimentation. If you would like to create your own type effects, I suggest you start by getting a basic understanding of what each of the filters in Photoshop does. Each one applies its own unique brand of magic, and once you're on familiar terms with the filters, you might be able to think of the perfect filter to enhance the end result. The way I got used to the filters was to commit to experimenting with one side menu each day (Distort, Pixelate, and so on). I did this day after day until I could actually predict the result I'd get from most of the filters. Now I can create some interesting effects without having to go through the time-consuming task of randomly applying filters.

In short, my advice to you is that the best way to familiarize yourself with the filters is to just dive in and experiment to your heart's content. I'll give you a few to get you started.

3D Type

To create 3D type, you're going to use the Emboss filter. And since the Emboss filter produces weird color artifacts when you work on color originals, we'll just use shades of gray, and colorize them later.

The first thing you need to do is use the Type tool to create some black text. Then, because we're going to distort this text in ways that aren't possible with a Type layer, you'll need to choose Layer > Rasterize > Type. Next, open the Layers palette and turn on the Lock Transparency checkbox to make sure we don't end up with any residue around the edges. Lock Transparency will prevent you from modifying the empty—aka transparent—areas of the layer. Now, Command-click (Macintosh) or Ctrl-click (Windows) the name of the layer to select everything on it (**Figure 14.43**).

Figure 14.43 Command-click (Macintosh) or Ctrl-Click (Windows) the layer that contains the text.

Next, we need to add a light-gray rim around the edge of the text. To accomplish this, change your foreground color to a light gray (I used 125R 125G 125B). You don't have to be too particular when picking the gray—just make sure it's not really dark. We need to have the gray rim slowly blend into the text, so choose Select > Feather and use a setting of seven (any number between one and ten will work, I'm just picking a number off the top of my head). To add the gray rim, choose Edit > Stroke, set the

Width to the same setting you used when feathering the selection (seven, in my case), and set the Location to Inside. This should add a nice light-gray, soft-edged line around the edge of the text, as in **Figure 14.44**.

Now, to get the 3D look, all we have to do is choose Filter > Stylize > Emboss and mess with some settings. When the Emboss dialog box appears, type Command-H (Macintosh) or Ctrl-H (Windows) to hide the edges of the selection so you get a clear view of the result. The Angle setting determines which direction the light source is coming from, so click and drag the line until it matches the angle of the light that is hitting the image you are placing the text on top of (if applicable). If you're creating the image from scratch, I'd choose an angle of 135 because most light sources are above the objects they illuminate. The Height setting determines how much space the 3D edge takes up. This setting is dependent on the previous steps, so set it to twice what was used when you feathered the selection (7x2=14, in my case). The Amount setting determines how much contrast you'll end up with. Move this slider around until you have as much contrast as you can get without making the brightest areas pure white (I used 95%). The result is shown in **Figure 14.45**. Once you are done embossing the image, you can choose Select > Deselect because you shouldn't need the selection anymore.

Figure 14.44 Result of adding gray rim to the text.

Figure 14.45 After applying the Emboss filter.

Figure 14.46 The Hue/Saturation dialog box.

Figure 14.47 Result of colorizing.

Coloring 3D Type

Now that you have some 3D type, you might want to add a bit of color. (Hopefully, you're already in RGB mode even though you've been working with grays.) Let's explore a couple of options. The easiest way to colorize your text is to choose Image > Adjust > Hue/Saturation and turn on the Colorize checkbox (**Figure 14.46**). By moving the Hue slider, you can change the basic color of the text. Moving the Saturation slider will change how vivid the color appears (from gray to a very vibrant color). You'll also need to adjust the Lightness slider a wee bit, occasionally, to tweak the brightness of the text (**Figure 14.47**).

If you would rather have some two-tone 3D type, don't use the Hue/Saturation method I just showed you; instead, change your foreground color to one of your desired colors, and then choose Edit > Fill. In the Fill dialog box, choose Foreground Color from the Contents pop-up menu, change the blending mode to Difference, and turn on the Preserve Transparency checkbox. The result will include the color you chose and its exact opposite, just as if you chose Image > Adjust > Invert (**Figure 14.48**).

Multicolored Effect

We could go on for days (literally) about colorizing text, but I'll just throw in one more interesting technique. This one gives you multicolored text. First, make sure you are working on the layer that contains the text and the Lock Transparency checkbox is turned on (this will make sure you don't color outside the lines). Next, choose the Paintbrush tool and set its blending mode to Difference in the Options bar. Now, choose a really bright, intense color and paint across the text. Repeat this process using different bright, intense colors until you get an interesting result (**Figure 14.49**).

Chroming Your 3D Type

Before creating chrome, you'll need to create some 3D type by using the technique you just learned. After you've created 3D type, be sure to choose Select > Deselect to make sure you're working on the entire layer, and then choose Image > Adjust > Curves. We're going to create a pretty weird curve, so click on the Pencil icon at the bottom of the Curves dialog box and start scribbling in the grid area. By drawing different shapes, you'll end up with different types of metal (aluminum, chrome, pewter, and so on) or plastic-looking type. To create chrome, you usually need to create either a big W or a big M (**Figures 14.50 to 14.53**).

After you have a result that you're happy with, you can click the Smooth button to smooth out the shape you drew, and then click the Curve icon (right next to the Pencil icon) to convert your curve into a normal curve. To fine-tune the curve, move your cursor out of the Curves dialog box (but don't click OK yet) and click any area of the image that you don't like. A circle should appear on the curve in the Curves dialog box indicating the area of the curve that would

Figure 14.48 Two-tone colorizing using the Difference color mode.

Figure 14.49 Wild colorizing effect.

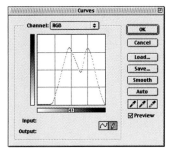

Figure 14.50 Experimenting with the curve.

Figure 14.51 Result of applying the curve from Figure 14.50.

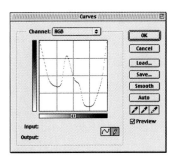

Figure 14.52 Creating a large W shape.

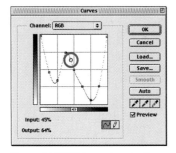

Figure 14.53 Result of applying the curve from Figure 14.52.

Figure 14.54 Click anywhere in the image window to find out which part of the curve is affecting that area.

Figure 14.55 Chrome type colorized to add a little blue to the image.

Figure 14.56 Liquid type effect.

Figure 14.57 Apply the Plastic Wrap filter a second time for an extra-ripply liquid type effect.

need to be changed to affect that area (**Figure 14.54**). Once you've got the shape to your liking, be sure to click the Save button and give that setting a name. That way, the next time you create 3D type, you'll be able to turn it into chrome in no time by choosing Image > Adjust > Curves, then clicking on the Load button.

After applying curves, you should end up with something that resembles chrome. To add even more realism, you might want to add a little bit of color to the type. To accomplish this, choose Image > Adjust > Hue/Saturation and turn on the Colorize checkbox. Adjust the Hue slider until the text appears light blue, and then move the Saturation slider to the left until you can barely see the blue. You want to keep the barest hint of color to establish the chrome look (**Figure 14.55**).

Liquid Type

To create liquid type, you'll need to start with 3D type. After you've created your 3D type (using the technique shown in the previous section), apply the Emboss filter a second time using the same settings used to create the 3D type. Then choose Filter > Artistic > Plastic Wrap. You can experiment with the settings, but I usually set the Highlight Strength to 5, the Detail to 15, and the Smoothness to 15 (**Figure 14.56**).

If you want the liquid to look a little more ripply, just apply the Plastic Wrap filter multiple times (**Figure 14.57**). After you've achieved the look you want, you can add some color by choosing Image > Adjust > Hue/Saturation and turning on the Colorize checkbox (**Figure 14.58**).

Intertwined Type

All of the effects we've just tried out can be a little more interesting if you make the letters of your type interact with each other. To do that, right after entering your text, choose Layer > Type > Convert To Shape. Next, grab the solid arrow tool that appears directly above the Pen tool and drag the individual letters around your screen. (You can drag a box around multiple adjacent letters to move them as a group.) To create holes where the letters overlap, click on the rightmost icon of the four that appear in the Options bar (**Figure 14.59**). You'll need to do that to each letter in order to get all of them to work that way. Finally, you'll need to choose Layer > Rasterize > Shape before you attempt to create any of the photo-realistic effects we've been talking about. I used this technique to create the art that appears in **Figure 14.60**.

Figure 14.58 Result of colorizing by using the Hue/Saturation dialog box.

Figure 14.59 Click the rightmost shape-area icon to make the letters punch out where they overlap.

Figure 14.60 End result of applying the liquid effect to the intertwined type.

Backgrounds & Textures

Backgrounds and textures might not be something that you'd think you want to spend a lot of time learning about. But if you look around at what's considered "high art" in the world of print, and especially on the Web, you'll notice that a skilled hand with backgrounds and textures can make the difference between elegance and clunkiness. In this section I'll show you how to create some background effects that I find interesting, and in the making you should be able to gain the skills you need to create your own elegant inventions. The first ones will be simple black and white textures that can be applied to photographs or colorized using the techniques described in Chapter 12, "Enhancement."

In general, we'll be starting with some raw material and then we'll enhance it to turn it into a texture. Most of Photoshop's filters require a detailed image in order to produce a noticeable result, but there is a select group of filters that can create something out of nothing.

Filters That Can Create Something out of Nothing

▶ Artistic > Sponge

▶ Noise > Add Noise

▶ Pixelate > Mezzotint

▶ Pixelate > Pointillize

▶ Render > Clouds

▶ Sketch > Halftone Pattern

▶ Sketch > Note Paper

▶ Sketch > Reticulation

▶ Stylize > Extrude

▶ Stylize > Tiles

▶ All filters in the Texturize menu

We'll walk through two of these raw-material filters to give you some ideas. Then you'll be free to go off and play with your new filter toys and come up with your own uniquely wonderful backgrounds.

Stone

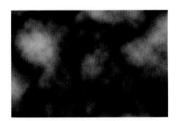

Figure 14.61 The Clouds filter supplies the raw material needed to create stone.

To create a simple stone background, create a new layer and reset your foreground and background colors to their default colors by pressing D. Next, choose Filter > Render > Clouds to add some texture to your image, and then choose Filter > Render > Difference Clouds to get more variation in the texture (**Figure 14.61**).

Now, choose Filter > Stylize > Emboss and mess with all the settings until you like the result. I used Angle: 135, Height: 3 pixels, and Amount: 500% (**Figure 14.62**). As with the other textures that use the Emboss filter, you can colorize the result using any of the techniques described in the Enhancement chapter.

Figure 14.62 Final stone effect.

Cloth

To create cloth, you'll first need some random information to distort. One way to fill your screen with random dots is to choose Filter > Noise > Add Noise. This filter doesn't work if an empty layer is active, so most of the time I fill the layer with white by typing D (to reset the foreground and background colors) and then Command-Delete on the Macintosh or Ctrl-Backspace in Windows (to fill the layer with the background color). If you know you are going to use the Emboss filter (we are), then you'll want to turn on the Monochromatic checkbox when applying the Add Noise filter (**Figure 14.63**). That's because if you emboss a color image, you'll get unpleasant color residue after applying the filter.

Now that you have some raw material, you're ready to stretch it into thread. So, choose Filter > Blur > Motion Blur, set the angle to 0° and use a Distance setting that still shows a little bit of variation in the image (**Figure 14.64**).

Now to weave the cloth, apply the Motion blur filter again using an angle of -90° and the same distance setting as before. The result should look like a blurry blob of gray junk, but don't fret; we're still in the "raw materials" stage (**Figure 14.65**).

To add some dimension to your faux fabric, choose Filter > Stylize > Emboss. A Height setting between 1 and 3 and an Amount of 500% usually produce the best result (**Figure 14.66**). The result should appear dark, and with little contrast. Before we brighten this up, you'll want to crop off the edges of the image because they contain areas that do not look woven. To do this, select the areas you would like to keep (using the Marquee tool) and then choose Image > Crop (**Figure 14.67**). To brighten the image, choose Image > Adjust > Levels and move in the upper right and upper left sliders until they touch the edge of the histogram (**Figures 14.68 and 14.69**).

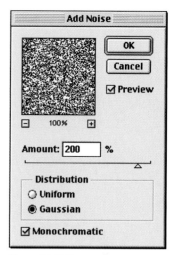

Figure 14.63 Turn on the Monochromatic checkbox when applying the Add Noise filter.

Figure 14.64 Result of applying the Motion Blur filter.

Figure 14.65 Apply the Motion Blur filter a second time with a different angle.

Figure 14.66 Apply the Emboss filter with a low Height setting.

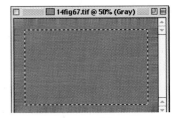

Figure 14.67 Crop off the non-woven area.

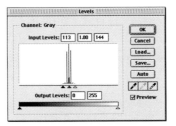

Figure 14.68 Apply Levels and pull in the upper left and upper right sliders.

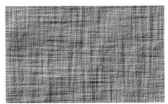

Figure 14.69 End result.

Simulated Leather

Now let's try to create the texture that is applied to the plastic dashboard of most cars (do they honestly think you'll be fooled into thinking you have a real leather dash?). We'll need to start with some random info, so type D to reset your foreground and background colors and choose Filter > Render > Clouds (**Figure 14.70**). To turn these clouds into something a little more interesting, choose Filter > Stylize > Find Edges (**Figure 14.71**).

Figure 14.70 Result of applying the Clouds filter.

Figure 14.71 Result of applying the Find Edges filter.

To add a little dimension to the result, choose Filter > Stylize > Emboss, set the angle to -48, use a low Height setting, and move the Amount slider all the way to the right (**Figure 14.72**). If you would rather end up with a more fiber-like result, use an angle of 135°.

Figure 14.72 Result of applying the Emboss filter.

Finally, to brighten up the result, choose Image > Adjust > Levels and move the upper right and upper left sliders until they touch the histogram.

Now I'd like to show you how I create color backgrounds. By varying the filters used in these effects, you should be able to come up with a wide variety of them.

Painted Backgrounds

Here is a technique you can use to simulate a painted background. Create a new layer, and change your foreground and background colors to two bright, intense colors. Next, choose Filter > Render > Clouds, then Filter > Blur > Motion Blur, pick an angle at random, and set the distance to around 100 (**Figure 14.73**). You can experiment with different distance settings to get different results.

Figure 14.73 Result of applying Clouds and Motion Blur filters.

Now create another new layer and pick two more bright, intense colors. Repeat the steps you did earlier (Filter > Render > Clouds, then Filter > Blur > Motion Blur), but use different angle settings. Once you're finished, set the blending mode of the layer to Difference (**Figure 14.74**). Repeat this process multiple times until you have an interesting collection of colors. You don't have to worry about the specific colors—you just want to get a good distribution of colors. After you have achieved that, link all the cloud layers together by dragging down the column just to the left of the preview thumbnails in the Layers palette, and then choose Merge Linked from the side menu of the Layers palette, as shown in **Figure 14.75**. If you don't like the overall color scheme, you can choose Image > Adjust > Hue/Saturation and move the Hue slider around until you get a pleasing result.

Figure 14.74 Result of applying Clouds and Motion Blur multiple times.

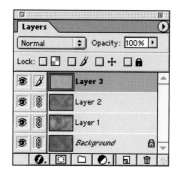

Figure 14.75 Once you have a good distribution of colors, merge the layers together.

Figure 14.76 Result of applying Polar Coordinates and Ripple.

Figure 14.77 Result of applying the Emboss filter.

Figure 14.78 Result of applying Colored Pencil filter.

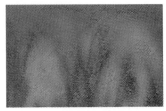

Figure 14.79 Adding a little dimension by applying the Emboss filter.

To vary the distribution of the colors, choose Filter > Distort > Polar Coordinates, and use the Polar To Rectangular setting. Then Choose Filter > Distort > Ripple and use an Amount of 200 and a Size of Medium (**Figure 14.76**). Now apply the filter a second time by pressing Command-F (Macintosh) or Ctrl-F (Windows).

To bring out more texture in the image, choose Filter > Stylize > Emboss, set the Angle to 135, the Height to 6, and the Amount to 275. Then choose Edit > Fade Emboss and set the blending mode to Hard Light (**Figure 14.77**).

To add a brushed look, choose the Eyedropper tool and Option-click (Macintosh) or Alt-click (Windows) one of the brighter colors in the image (this will change your background color). Then choose Filter > Artistic > Colored Pencil; set the Pencil Width to 4, the Stroke Pressure to 8, and the Paper Brightness to 25 (different settings will result in different painterly effects), as shown in **Figure 14.78**. Now blend this into the image by choosing Edit > Fade Colored Pencil and set the blending mode to Luminosity.

Finally, to add a little dimension to the image, duplicate the layer you've been working on and choose Image > Adjust > Desaturate to remove any hint of color. Next, set the blending mode of the duplicate layer to Hard Light in the Layers palette, and then choose Filter > Stylize > Emboss (**Figure 14.79**). I usually set the Height to 1 or 2, and just play around with the Amount and Angle settings until the image looks good. To finalize the effect, choose Merge Down from the side menu of the Layers palette.

Car Wash Foam

Let's try to create that foam they spray all over your car when you send it through a car wash. First, you want to start with a screenful of black and white noise. To do this, create a new layer and fill it with white by pressing D, then Command-Delete (Macintosh) or Ctrl-Backspace (Windows). Next, choose Filter > Noise > Add Noise, set the Amount to 400, the Distribution to Uniform, and turn on the Monochromatic checkbox.

Now let's distort that noise to get something a little more useful. Choose Filter > Distort > Spherize, set the Amount to 100% and the Mode to Normal. Next, choose Filter > Pixelate > Pointillize and use a Cell Size of three. Now, choose Filter > Distort > Polar Coordinates and use the Polar To Rectangular setting (**Figure 14.80**).

Finally, to turn this image into foam, choose Filter > Sketch > Plaster, set the Image Balance to 38, the Smoothness slider to 1, and the Smoothness drop-down menu to Top. Your result should look something like **Figure 14.81**. (That bottom menu should be called Light Position!) Then choose Image > Adjust > Invert. If you want to add a little color, choose Image > Adjust > Hue/Saturation and turn on the Colorize checkbox. I usually move the Hue slider around until I find a nice cyan-ish blue, then lower the Saturation setting until there is just a hint of color visible (**Figure 14.82**).

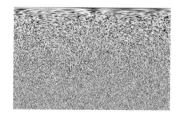

Figure 14.80 Result of applying Spherize, Pointillize, and Polar Coordinates.

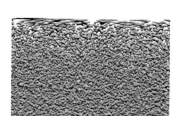

Figure 14.81 Result of applying Plaster filter.

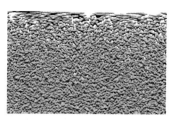

Figure 14.82 Result of colorizing the image.

Now that you've seen what we can do using just two "raw material" filters, imagine what you can do when you start to explore the full range of filters.

Repeating Patterns

Try this out: choose Edit > Fill and set the Use pop-up menu to Pattern. Then take a look at the preset custom patterns. These patterns are actually tiny images repeated over and over (like tiles on a bathroom wall). If you stood back, they would appear to be one large image instead of what they were—a bunch of small repeating images with their edges lined up with each other. These default patterns are all right for adding interest to simple shapes; but this is Photoshop, which means we're not stuck using plain old vanilla defaults. We can create our own exquisitely unique patterns! They can be used in many situations, especially when it comes to producing graphics for the Web. So, let's dive in and see what we can come up with.

There are two general methods I use to create a seamless pattern. The first one involves using filters that produce tile-able results. Then, after using a combination of filters, we'll find the smallest tile-able area and turn that into a pattern. The second method is to take an image that is not tile-able and to retouch the areas that would appear as seams.

Using Tileable Filters

Let's start with a pattern that is tileable from the beginning. We can use that small image to fill a larger area without it looking like the simple repeating image that it really is. First, create a new document in grayscale mode. Next, choose a light shade of gray and then type Option-Delete (Macintosh) or Alt-Backspace (Windows) to fill the image with that color. Now, choose Filter > Pixelate > Color Halftone, set the Max. Radius to 14, and set all the angles to 45. That should produce a bunch of circles on a grid (**Figure 14.83**). Next, let's add some dimension by choosing Filter > Stylize > Emboss; set the Angle to 135, the Height to 1, and the Amount to 75 (**Figure 14.84**).

Now that we've got something that is seamless, let's find the smallest area that can be tiled. That way, the pattern won't take up memory and our file size can stay small when we apply the pattern using layer styles and pattern layers. Use the Marquee tool to select a relatively small but wide selection near the top of the image. Next, choose View > Show Rulers, click on the top ruler and drag down a guide until it snaps to the top of the selection you just made (**Figure 14.85**).

Now you want to find out whether the information you just selected is used elsewhere in the image, and if so, where. We'll use an odd little technique to do that. Choose Layer > New > Layer Via Copy to place a copy

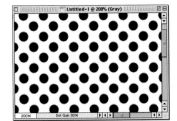

Figure 14.83 Result of applying the Color Halftone filter.

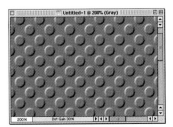

Figure 14.84 Result of applying the Emboss filter.

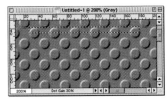

Figure 14.85 Drag a guide down until it snaps to the edge of your selection.

462

of the currently selected area onto a brand-spankin'-new layer. Next, change the blending mode of that layer (at the top of the Layers palette) to Difference. That mode will compare the layer that is active to the one below it, and will show you where the two layers are different. Since both layers are identical in that area, it should appear black. Now change to the Move tool and use the down-arrow key to nudge the layer one pixel at a time. As you move it down, the black area should change to indicate that the information no longer lines up with what's underneath it. You'll want to continue to nudge it down until that area becomes black again. Once that happens, drag out another guide and let it snap to the top edge of that layer (**Figure 14.86**).

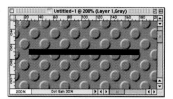

Figure 14.86 When the layer turns black again, add a guide that lines up with the top of that layer.

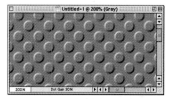

Figure 14.87 Repeat the process using a vertical selection.

Now you'll want to trash the layer you've been working with and repeat the exact same process using a vertical selection. So, make a tall, skinny selection, pull out a guide, and snap it to the left side of the marching ants. Then choose Layer > New > Layer Via Copy, set the blending mode to Difference, and then nudge that layer (using the Move tool) until it becomes black again. Finally, pull out another guide, snap it to the left edge of that layer, and then trash the layer (**Figure 14.87**).

You should end up with a total of four guides that define the smallest tileable area of the image. To turn that area into a pattern, use the Marquee tool to select the area defined by the guides, and then choose Edit > Define Pattern. Finally, test your pattern by creating a new document, choosing Edit > Fill, and selecting Pattern from the Use pop-up menu. You should find your pattern listed at the bottom of the pattern pop-up list.

The process of finding the smallest tileable area can be difficult if you are working on a very low-contrast pattern. If that's the case, choose Layer > Duplicate Layer and then choose Image > Adjust > Auto Levels to exaggerate the contrast in that new layer. Then go through the exact steps mentioned earlier for finding the smallest tileable area. Once you have all four guides placed, just trash the high-contrast layer so you'll end up with your original image and the four guides you need to create a pattern.

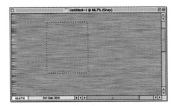

Figure 14.88 Cropping the image down to the area you'd like to use as a pattern.

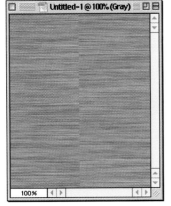

Figure 14.89 The Offset filter will expose the seams in your pattern.

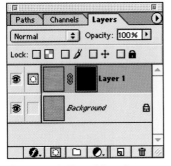

Figure 14.90 After adding a layer mask, the layer should contain two thumbnail images.

Create Your Own Pattern

Now that you've seen how to create a tileable pattern from scratch, let's see how we can produce one from an existing image (like a photograph or one of the textures we created earlier). Since we are striving for "seamless," we will first expose the seams of our image, and then retouch them to make them disappear. For this example, let's create a brushed-metal effect and transform it into a seamless tile. To create the metal look, create a new grayscale image and then choose Filter > Noise > Add Noise (I used Amount=400%, Distribution=Uniform, and I turned on the Monochromatic checkbox). Then choose Filter > Blur > Motion Blur (I used Angle=0 and Distance=60). You can see resulting brushed-metal look in **Figure 14.88**. Once you have the texture made (or you have the photo you'd like to work with), choose Select > All, and then Edit > Copy (though you won't be pasting for a while). Use the Crop tool to select the area you'd like to use for your pattern and then press Return or Enter to crop it (**Figure 14.88**). Now let's expose the seams that would show up if we used that image as a pattern. To accomplish that, choose Filter > Other > Offset and set the Vertical and Horizontal offset settings to approximately half the width of your image (**Figure 14.89**).

Now that we can see the seams that prevent our image from being a seamless tile, all we have to do is retouch them to make them disappear. If you are working with a photographic image, you'll most likely want to use the Rubber Stamp tool, but since we copied our full-size original to start with, we can take advantage of a different approach. Choose Edit > Paste to create a new layer (assuming you haven't copied something else in the meantime) and fill it with part of the original image. Next, choose Layer > Add Layer Mask > Hide All. Now you should notice two thumbnail images for the currently active layer (**Figure 14.90**). Next, choose the Paintbrush tool, choose white to paint with, and choose a very large, soft-edged brush (one that's about ⅓ of the width of your image). Use that large brush to cover up the seam by painting over it vertically. That should make the pasted image show up over the seam and blend into the rest of the image, resulting in a seamless pattern. To define your pattern, choose

Layer > Merge Down, Select > All, and then Edit > Define Pattern. Now you should be able to create a new, large document and choose Edit > Fill to apply your pattern (**Figure 14.91**).

Applying Dimension to a Photo

So, you've made a perfectly wonderful texture and it looks great. Now what do you do with it? Well, one thing that textures are especially good for is adding dimension to photographs. Of course, with Photoshop, there are many ways to do this, but all we need to do is explore a few methods, and that should give you what you need to branch out on your own.

Blending Modes

You can apply any of the grayscale textures described at the beginning of the Backgrounds & Textures section by using one of three blending modes. Place the texture you would like to apply on a layer above the image. Change the blending mode of the texture layer to Overlay, Soft Light, or Hard Light (**Figure 14.92**). If the effect is too strong, lower the Opacity setting of that layer. If you would like to intensify the effect, just duplicate the texture layer. You can also remove the texture from certain areas of the image by applying the Eraser tool to the texture layer (**Figure 14.93**).

Figure 14.91 The pattern applied to a large area.

Figure 14.92 Apply a texture using the Hard Light blending mode. (Original image © 1998 PhotoDisc)

Figure 14.93 After using the Eraser tool to remove some of the texture.

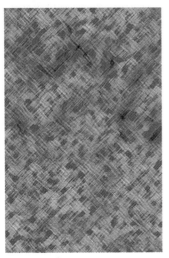

Figure 14.94 Texture to be applied to the photograph.

Lighting Effects

Using the Lighting Effects filter is a little more sophisticated than the last technique we covered. It also takes more time because you have to experiment with all the settings that come along with this filter. But hang on for the ride; it's worth the trouble.

To get started, open the Channels palette and create a new channel by clicking on the New Channel icon (the one that looks like a sheet of paper). Now you need to create a texture in that new channel. You can use any method you'd like, but just for kicks, I'll create one we haven't made before. Reset your foreground and background colors by typing D, and then choose Filter > Render > Clouds. Now choose Filter > Stylize > Find Edges, and then Image > Adjust > Levels, and pull in the upper right and left sliders until they touch the histogram. You'll see this will add contrast to the image. To finish the texture off, choose Filter > Artistic > Colored Pencils, set the Pencil Width to 18, the Stroke Pressure to 4, and the Paper Brightness to 25 (**Figure 14.94**).

Now, to apply the texture to the photo, click on the topmost (Composite) channel and then open the Layers palette. Click the name of the layer to which you would like to add texture, and choose Filter > Render > Lighting Effects. At the bottom of the Lighting Effects dialog box, you should see a pop-up menu called Texture Channel. From this menu, select the name of the channel you created earlier (it should be the bottom choice). Then adjust the Height slider to change how obvious the texture is (**Figure 14.95**).

To remove the texture from areas of the image, open the History palette and click just to the left of the step that is directly above the Lighting Effects step (**Figure 14.96**). Then use the History Brush to remove the texture from areas of the image (**Figure 14.97**). I usually use a really soft-edged brush to do this, so the texture blends smoothly into the image.

Figure 14.95 Result of applying the Lighting Effects filter by using a texture channel. (Original image © 1998 PhotoDisc)

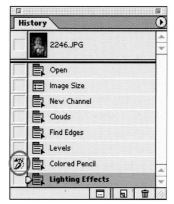

Figure 14.96 Set the History palette to the second to the last step.

Figure 14.97 Apply the History brush to remove the texture from areas of the image.

Closing Thoughts

With almost 100 filters, and the idea that you can throw them together in any combination, it's probably safe to say that you will be well into retirement before you could exhaust the supply of unique text and background effects that can be produced in Photoshop. That makes your job both challenging and exhilarating. Never stop testing the limits; never stop playing. And if you run out of ideas, do what I do—read through your favorite magazines for interesting looking text and backgrounds, rip out the pages with the best ones, and then try to reproduce them on your own.

Ben's Techno-Babble Decoder Ring

Point—A unit of measurement, used in the publishing industry, that is $1/72$ of an inch (there are 12 points to a pica, and 6 picas per inch). Most programs measure text in point sizes because it is much more friendly than using fractions of an inch. But there is very little consistency in the size of text. For example, 12-point Times is taller than 12-point Helvetica, so you can think of the point size as a general (not exact) measure of the size of your text.

Baseline—The invisible rule that a line of text sits on. Letters that drop below the baseline (such as lower case j, g, q, and y) are known as descenders.

Leading—The line spacing of a paragraph of text measured from one baseline to the next. It's named after the strips of lead that were used to increase line spacing in hot metal typography. In order to make sure the lines of text don't overlap, you'll usually want to use a leading setting larger than the point size of the text.

Kerning—The art (lost art, really) of removing space between letters to create consistent letter spacing. In Photoshop, the kerning increases (positive setting) or decreases (negative setting) the space between two letters.

Tracking—The act of increasing or reducing the space between all the letters in a range of text. Often used with upper case text to increase readability.

Courtesy of Jimmy Chen, www.typographic.com

Courtesy of David Bishop, www.dbsf.com

Part IV Web Graphics

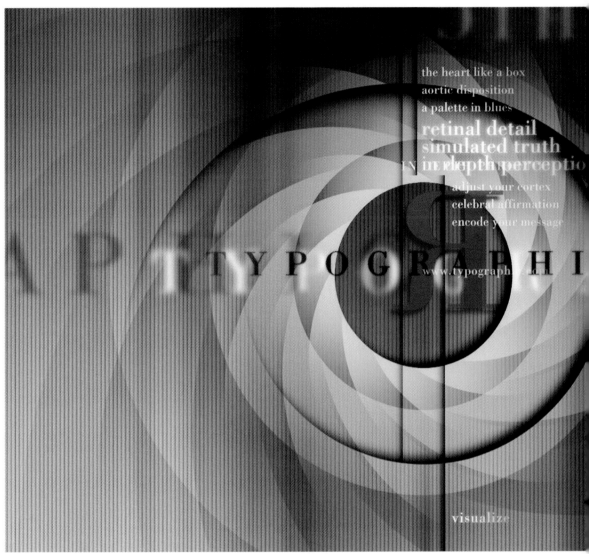

Courtesy of Jimmy Chen, www.typographic.com

15 Interface Design

Buckle your seatbelt,
Dorothy, 'cause Kansas
is going bye-bye.
Cypher, from "The Matrix"

Like the tornado that abducted Dorothy and spirited her away to the land of Oz, the World Wide Web is taking us by force and launching us into new orbits of digital reality. But this time around, *we* get to be the little man with the big mustache who hides behind the green curtain. If L. Frank Baum had been born in 2001, his Oz story might have more closely resembled *The Matrix*, and his wizard would have been an insomniac with an ergonomic chair, a high-speed data line, and a clutter of monitors and keyboards at his or her fingertips. In other words, someone just like you or me.

So, with Web-wizardry being a regular 9-to-5 job, and the competition between wizards becoming fierce, we are naturally motivated to keep up with the latest techniques that will keep our clients and bosses dazzled and bewitched. This chapter will help you toward that goal. It's where you can develop the understanding and skills needed to create highly professional looking interface elements for your Web site. For those of you who are new to the process of putting together a Web site, this chapter isn't about constructing your site, or about special effects like animation and sound. Instead, it's about creating the essential elements that help users navigate through your site.

The good news is that it doesn't matter whether you're the world's highest-paid designer doing graphics for BMW or you're just starting out with your first Web site on your home computer. You both use Photoshop, and there's nothing stopping you from creating stunning, Web-perfect interface elements that are worthy of any Fortune 500 company. This chapter will give you what you need to create your basic navigational elements, and once you've mastered that, you'll be ready to advance to the next chapters where you'll learn about optimizing your images and creating rollovers and animation.

Consistent Design Principles

This chapter isn't about "design," in the aesthetic sense, but there are some basic standards that are smart to follow to make it easy for all those people who are viewing your site on a variety of computer monitors. To get an idea of what I'm talking about, the next time you're browsing the Web, be sure to visit a few major corporate sites (like www.amazon.com and www.barnesandnoble.com) to see if you find any consistency between them. For instance, if you visit a bunch of major automobile manufacturers' sites, you might notice that they don't use the full width of your screen (**Figure 15.1**). On the day I wrote this chapter, the majority of people browsing the Web (52.6%) were using a monitor that displays 800x600 pixels. If you look at **Figure 15.1**, you'll notice that all the car sites I checked out limited the width of their sites to what is visible on an 800-pixel-wide screen. A few of the sites were even smart enough to leave space for the scroll bar that would usually appear on the right edge of the screen.

Figure 15.1 Major automobile manufacturer's Web sites. The red area indicates the area not visible on a 800x600 screen.

800x600 might be the norm, but currently 6.9% of viewers browse the Web using 640x480 screens. Sites designed for the widest audiences will often keep the most essential content within the width visible on this small screen (**Figure 15.2**). You might not think that 6.9% of viewers is a lot of people, but think of it this way: there are over 400 million users worldwide, and over 150 million users in the U.S. and

Canada alone. I know—counting Internet users is an inexact science at best, but even so, do the sloppy math, and you'll get an idea of the number of people who just might be browsing on a 640x480 screen (10.3 million in the U.S. and Canada, 27.6 million worldwide).

Figure 15.2 www.msnbc.com keeps the most essential information within the area visible on a 640x480 screen. The gray area indicates the edge of 640x480 and 800x600 pixel screens.

In browsing the Web, people are accustomed to scrolling vertically to see an entire site, but you still might want to keep the most important interface elements within the first screenful that would be visible on a small monitor. It's kind of like the fold in a newspaper—all the major story headlines always appear above the fold.

Your View of this Small World

If you're working on a large monitor, you'll most likely want to set up a special document that will remind you of what people with smaller screens will be able to view. To accomplish that, start by launching your browser. Turn on all the features that most people use (button bar, address bar, favorites bar, status bar), and then visit a popular site and expand your browser window to fill your screen. Now take a screen shot by typing Shift-Command-Control-3 (Macintosh) or Alt-Print Screen (Windows). Open Photoshop and choose File > New (use the default settings, which are based on whatever was copied last, which in this case is your screen shot). Next, choose Edit > Paste and then Layer > Merge Down. Now you'll want to add some guides that represent how much of your that browser would be visible on 640x480 and 800x600 screens. You'll need to choose View > New Guide a total of four times. First create a vertical guide at 640px, then create another at 800px. Finally, create two horizontal guides at 480px and 600px (**Figure 15.3**).

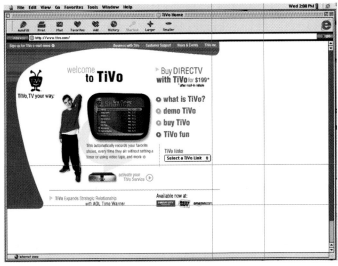

Figure 15.3 A screen shot of a Web browser with guides placed to represent 640x480 and 800x600 screens.

If you create all the graphics for your site within this document, you'll constantly be reminded of what the majority of your viewers will be able to see in one screenful. Try to keep all major navigation elements within the 640x480 space, and limit most of your content to what is visible in the width of an 800x600 screen.

Resolution and the Web

All documents that you work with in Photoshop have a resolution setting attached to them. That setting determines how large the pixels in the image will be (measured in pixels per inch, or ppi) if the image is printed. But when it comes to a Web browser, that setting is completely ignored. Why? Because your Web browser is not capable of changing the size of the pixels that make up your screen. In fact, you are the only one who is in control of that. The Monitors control panel setting (Macintosh) or Display control panel setting (Windows) determines how many pixels are displayed on your screen and therefore their size (**Figure 15.4**).

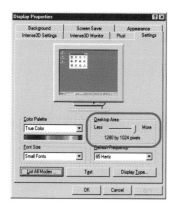
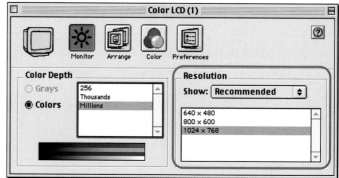

Figure 15.4 The system-level control panels (left: Windows, right: Macintosh) that determine how many pixels will be displayed on screen, and therefore how large the pixels will appear.

Note

To choose a resolution in Windows, go to the Display control panel, choose the Settings tab, and then drag the Desktop Area slider.

Since your browser can't change the size of the pixels, your Web browser simply uses as many screen pixels as your image requires, determined by its width and height in pixels. Most 15-inch monitors can display somewhere around 800x600 pixels total. There is no way a browser could display your images at a resolution of 300 ppi (the most popular scanning resolution)—that is, not unless you have a 15″ monitor that's capable of displaying 3600x2700 pixels!

So if your Web browser ignores the resolution setting, does it matter what setting you use when scanning an image? Yes! Your browser might ignore that setting, but your scanner uses it to determine how many pixels to create out of each inch of your original image. If you have a 3-inch-wide original and you scan with a resolution of 100 ppi, then you'll end up with 300 pixels in the width (3 inches x 100 pixels per inch = 300 pixels total). Scan the same image with a resolution of 72 ppi and you'll end up with only 216 pixels total in the width (3x72=216). Since your browser will ignore the resolution setting and just look at the width and height in pixels, the higher the resolution the image is scanned at, the larger it will appear in a browser (you simply get more pixels when you scan at higher resolutions). If you were to measure how many pixels fit in each inch of a typical computer monitor, you'd find that it's somewhere around 85. That means if you scan an image with a resolution of 85 ppi, then it should appear close to actual size in a Web browser.

But don't worry about scanning images with high-resolution settings, because you can always scale them down later. If you want to see how large an image will appear in a Web browser, then choose View > Actual Pixels when you're in Photoshop. If you find that's too big, then open the Navigator palette (View > Show Navigator) and move the slider at the bottom of the palette until the image is the size you'd like it to be in a browser. Next, choose Image > Image Size, turn on the Resample Image checkbox, change the Width pop-up menu to Percent, and then enter the percentage that shows up in the lower-left corner of your image. Now, if you choose View > Actual Pixels again, your image should appear at the size you'd like it to be in the browser.

Color on the Web

If you've already been creating graphics for the Web, you've probably had the painful experience of seeing one of your brilliantly colored images end up with a shade of color that doesn't even come close to your original creation when viewed online. Getting your colors consistent is another very important step towards achieving a professional looking Web site.

Most graphic designers have monitors that are capable of displaying millions of colors, but you might be surprised to learn that there are still some people out there who browse the Web using only 256 colors. That's right—5.3% of all your viewers will be using only 256 colors to browse your site (more than all the Mac users out there). Even those people who have a computer capable of displaying

> **Note**
> Did you know that the user interface that makes up your computer's operating system—icons, menu bars, dialog boxes, and so on—is completely designed using a special set of 256 colors (known as the system palette)? That's so that everyone has a consistent experience using the computer, no matter if their computer can display millions of colors or only 256.

millions of colors might, under certain conditions, end up seeing your site with only 256 colors. Just think about it for a moment. What if you start up your computer, then launch Photoshop, ImageReady, and GoLive so you are all set to create some Web graphics. Then you launch your e-mail program and decide you need to make a phone call, so you launch your contact management program. Then when you're on the phone, you have to check your calendar (another program) and then your buddy mentions a Web site for you to check out. With a total of six programs already running, do you think your Web browser will have much memory to work with? Well, when your browser is running out of memory, it takes some "conservation" measures to ration its use of memory. One of those measures might be to display all sites using only 256 colors. That means that even people with high-end computers might sometime end up seeing your site with only 256 colors.

So, what's your site going to look like with 256 colors? Well, any color used that isn't from that special set used for your computer interface will be simulated using two colors from the system palette. That means that a big blue logo might suddenly appear as blue with cyan specks sprinkled throughout it (the technical term for these specks is known as dithering). That's your browser's way of being able to simulate more than 256 colors. It's a good thing it can do that; otherwise photographs would look rather terrible (**Figure 15.5**). The only problem is that large areas of solid color don't look so hot when they are contaminated with specks of another color (**Figure 15.6**).

You can prevent areas from becoming dithered when viewed with 256 colors by creating your interface elements using the colors used in your system palette. That's easy enough to do, but (of course) there's a catch: the Mac and Windows operating systems use different system palettes. But if you were to compare the colors used in both operating systems, you'd find that there are 216 colors that are common to both. I call these the dither-free colors because they are the only ones I can use that guarantee I won't get specks showing up in areas that should be solid.

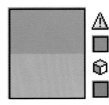

Figure 15.6 The left half of this image doesn't have dithering, the right half does.

Figure 15.5 Left: a photo without dithering. Right: the photo with dithering. (© 2001 Stockbyte, www.stockbyte.com)

But just because I like to call them dither-free colors doesn't mean everyone else uses that name. In fact, most people call them Web-safe colors. I hate that name, because many people think they must use those colors for *everything*, when they are really only useful in areas that should appear as a solid color. Dithering is not always a bad thing—it really helps on photographs and in graphics that contain gradients (**Figure 15.7**). You'll also find these special colors being called colors that are "within the color cube," which is what Photoshop uses as an icon to describe them (**Figure 15.8**).

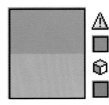

Figure 15.8 The cube icon is used to create dither-free colors.

Figure 15.7 From left to right: image viewed with millions of colors, 256 colors, and 256 colors with dithering. (© Derek Brigham)

Now that we know why these colors are so special, let's figure out how to use them in Photoshop. First off, when you're in the Color Picker dialog box, you could type in RGB numbers that are in increments of 51 and you'd be all set. But

Note

The concept of Web-safe colors is really simple, but the execution gets a little bit complicated. A Web-safe color is any color that is composed of red, green, and blue values in increments of 20%. That means if you have 0, 20, 40, 60, 80, or 100% of red, green or blue, you'd have a Web-safe color. But the RGB numbers in Photoshop are not measured in percentages. They range from 0–255. In that numbering system, 20% = 51. So as long as all your RGB numbers are divisible by 51, you've got Web-safe colors.

most people don't like having to think of those numbers. So, to make it easy, Photoshop provided us with a color cube icon that you can use to get your dither-free colors. After you've chosen a color, be sure to click that icon if you plan on using the color to fill a large solid area. Or, if you are picking a bunch of colors at once, you might want to turn on the Only Web Colors checkbox; then Photoshop will only display the dither-free colors (**Figure 15.9**).

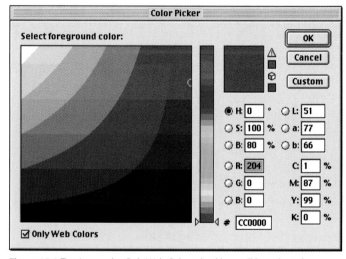

Figure 15.9 Turning on the Only Web Colors checkbox will limit the colors shown to the 216 dither-free colors.

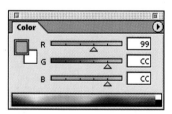

Figure 15.10 When using the Web Color Sliders, the tic marks indicate dither-free colors.

If you prefer to use the Color palette, you'll want to choose Web Color Sliders from the side menu of that palette. After you've chosen that feature, you'll find tic marks where the dither-free colors are (**Figure 15.10**). In order to have a Web-safe color, you have to get all three (RGB) sliders to point at those marks, but that's pretty easy, because the sliders snap to them. If you don't want a dither-free color, hold the Option key (Macintosh) or Alt key (Windows) to prevent the sliders from snapping to the tic marks.

You can also pick colors from the color bar that appears at the bottom of the Color palette. But be careful, because those colors aren't dither-free. If you choose Make Ramp Web Safe from the side menu of the Color palette, then all the colors within that color bar will be Web-safe.

Take a look at **Figure 15.11** and you'll see what a major news site looks like when viewed using 256 colors. Notice that most of the large areas of color are free from specks (dithering). As I've said before, dithering is useful on photographs, and you'll see it in all the photos on that site.

Figure 15.11 www.msnbc.com viewed with 256 colors.

Photoshop vs. the Browser:

Getting Consistent Color between the Two

You're probably champing at the bit and ready to start creating, but before we get down to business, we have to look at one more color issue that just can't be ignored. Often you'll find that the colors in your image will change (sometimes radically) when they are displayed in a Web browser. That's usually because Photoshop is taking steps to make sure the color in your image is accurate, but your browser is not taking those steps. To avoid this disparity between Photoshop and your browser, you can set up Photoshop to display things the way they will appear for the majority of people who browse the Web. Start by choosing Edit > Color Settings and choose Web Graphics Defaults from the pop-up menu at the top of the dialog box (see **Figure 15.12**). That will turn off the majority of Photoshop's color management features, which is a good thing, because your browser doesn't use that kind of stuff

Figure 15.12 Choose Web Graphics Defaults from the pop-up menu at the top of the Color Settings dialog box.

Notes

Over 96% of the people browsing the Web are using the Windows operating system, so that's what I use when designing my graphics.

....

Instead of switching between Proof Setups, you can leave the original at Windows RGB, choose New View, and set the new view's Proof Setup to Macintosh RGB. That way, when you make adjustments (such as a Curves adjustment layer), you can view Mac and Windows previews side by side.

to display your images. Next, choose View > Proof Colors (to enable that feature) and then choose View > Proof Setup > Windows RGB. (Windows monitors display images darker than Macintosh monitors, and when the Windows RGB option is checked, a Macintosh will display images as if viewed on a Windows machine.) Then, if I'm working on a critical area of the site, I'll switch Proof Setup back and forth between the Macintosh RGB and Windows RGB settings to make sure it will look good on both systems.

Creating Interface Elements

OK, you've got a veritable treasure trove of knowledge. You understand monitor size and screen resolution and how to deal with color. Now, using what we know, it's time to start learning how to create user interface elements. Bear in mind that there are literally hundreds of interface elements that can be created (as evidenced by a five-minute surf on the Web), and that this book can only dedicate so many pages to this subject. You can consider this chapter your starter kit. Try out my techniques, and then go off-leash and create your own interface masterpieces.

The Shape Tools

Photoshop 6.0's new shape tools are perfect for creating interface elements because you can makes changes to the elements later without lowering the quality of your imagery. We took a brief look at the shape tools in Chapter 1, but there's a lot more to know that will serve you well when creating interface elements. Before using the shape tools, be sure to check out the settings in the Options bar. You should see three choices in the far left of the bar (**Figure 15.13**). The leftmost choice is what you want; it's the one that creates a shape layer. Shape layers are special because you can scale, rotate, and manipulate them without degrading the quality of your image. If you find that the shape layer choice isn't available, then you are most likely already working on a shape layer, and Photoshop is assuming you would like to add to that layer. If that's the case, then press Return or Enter to tell Photoshop that you are done working on that shape layer and would like to start another one.

Figure 15.13 When you see three choices on the far left of the Options bar, choose the leftmost one to create a shape layer.

After you've created a shape layer, you'll see a new set of choices in the Options bar (**Figure 15.14**). The leftmost choice will allow you to add more shapes to the currently active layer. This choice is great when you want to create shapes that can be made from a combination of the shape tools (**Figure 15.15**). The second choice allows you to take away from the current shape using any shape tool (**Figure 15.16**). The third choice gives you just the areas where your next shape overlaps the current ones (**Figure 15.17**). And the fourth choice inverts what you have (**Figure 15.18**)

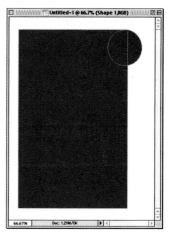

Figure 15.15 The leftmost choice in the Options bar allows you to add to the active shape layer.

Figure 15.14 The Options bar offers different choices when you're already working on a shape layer.

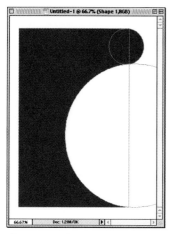

Figure 15.16 The second choice allows you to take away from the current shape layer.

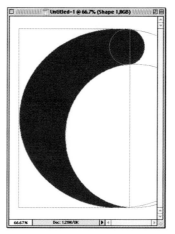

Figure 15.17 The third choice gives you the intersection between the current shape layer and the new shape you are creating.

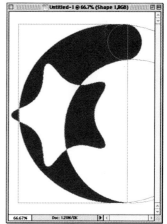

Figure 15.18 The last choice inverts the current shape layer in the area where you draw a new shape.

Using a combination of these features, you can create some rather sophisticated shapes. But you might find that once you've gotten the shape you'd like, your screen is littered with shapes that overlap each other (**Figure 15.19**). You can simplify the end result by switching to the solid arrow tool that's to the left of the Type tool in your Tools palette, and then clicking on the Combine button in the Options bar (**Figure 15.20**). This simplifies your shape down to a single outline instead of one that's created using a combination of shapes.

Figure 15.19 A sophisticated shape can be made from multiple shapes that overlap each other.

Figure 15.20 The Combine button will simplify a compound shape into a single element.

If you think you'll need to use that shape over and over, be sure to choose Edit > Define Custom Shape. That will make it available as a choice when you're using the Custom Shape tool (the rightmost of the shape tools in the Options bar). After you've chosen that tool, click on the shape preview in the Options bar and you should find your new shape (**Figure 15.21**).

Sometimes you'll find that you'd like to break an interesting shape into multiple pieces so they can be repositioned individually, or so they can be used as buttons on your Web site. You can accomplish that by adding shape layers on top of the shape you've already got (remember to press Enter to finish off each shape before attempting to add more shapes).

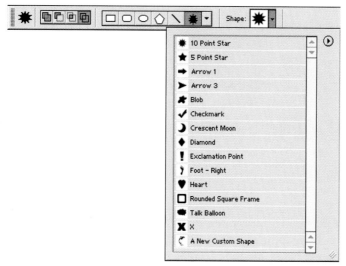

Figure 15.21 After you define a custom shape, it should show up at the bottom of the Shape Picker.

In **Figure 15.22** you'll see an example where I created a bunch of horizontal bars that cover an interesting shape; each bar is on its own layer. To divide the bottom shape into multiple pieces based on the other layers, I clicked on the shape thumbnail image in the bottom layer and chose Edit > Copy. Then, I clicked on one of the shape layers that define the horizontal bars and chose Edit > Paste. That added a path to that layer that is shaped like the bottom layer (**Figure 15.23**). (If you'd like to find out more about paths, check out the Layer Clipping Path section of Chapter 11.) Next, I clicked on the third choice from the left in the Options bar, which instructed Photoshop to use the shape I just pasted to transform this layer so that only the areas where the two shapes overlap are visible (**Figure 15.24**). Finally, I clicked on the solid arrow tool and then clicked the Combine button in the Options bar to simplify the shape. After repeating this process for each of the horizontal bars, I deleted the bottom layer and ended up with its shape divided into separate pieces

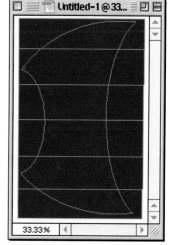

Figure 15.22 Multiple shape layers overlapping a central shape.

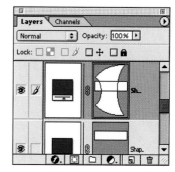

Figure 15.23 After pasting, you'll have two shapes on that layer.

that I could move around independently of each other (**Figure 15.25**).

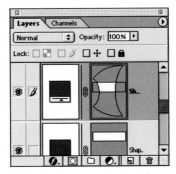

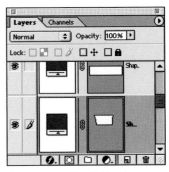

Figure 15.24 Clicking the third choice in the Options bar will use the pasted shape to limit where the other shape shows up.

Figure 15.25 After clicking the Combine button, you will end up with a simplified shape.

After you've created the shapes you need, you can scale and rotate them using a command from the Edit > Transform menu. Applying these commands (scale, rotate, etc.) will not lower the quality of the result at all.

If you have multiple shape layers that you need to align, click on the layer you'd like to align them with and then link all the other layers you'd like to work with (**Figure 15.26**). Then grab the Move tool and click on one of the alignment icons that appear in the Options bar (**Figure 15.27**).

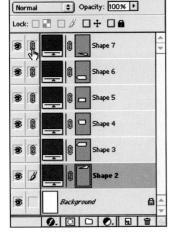

Figure 15.26 Link the layers you'd like to align.

Figure 15.27 The alignment icons in the Options bar.

Layer Styles

At this point, your button will look rather flat and boring, but we can quickly spice it up using a Layer Style. Make sure the layer you just created is active in the Layers palette, and then choose Bevel And Emboss from the Layer Style pop-up menu (it looks like a black circle with an "f" in it) at the bottom of the Layers palette (**Figure 15.28**).

In the Layer Style dialog box, you'll see lots of choices. But don't worry; we're just going to start with an easy one that'll work well with simple buttons: the Inner Bevel style. (You choose a style from the topmost drop-down menu.) The first decision you'll have to make for your Inner Bevel is what type of edge you'd like. The Smooth setting will give your button a rounded top look; Chisel Hard will give you a straight and sharp edge (**Figure 15.29**). Next, go to the Size setting and use the up and down arrow keys to adjust that setting until you think your button looks appropriate.

You can get much fancier than this by applying additional styles to your button. I occasionally use a drop shadow to simulate additional depth; a gradient fill can also give your buttons some extra life. I also like to vary the shape of the buttons; I might have rectangular ones in the middle and rounded corner buttons on the end of the button bar (**Figure 15.30**). It may seem like "perfecting" your button is taking a lot of time, but there's a payoff—you can save the style you're creating and easily apply it to other objects.

Figure 15.29 From left to right: original image, Inner Bevel with Chisel Hard style, Inner Bevel with Smooth style.

Figure 15.30 These buttons all have the following styles: Stroke, Bevel And Emboss, Gradient Overlay, Drop Shadow.

Once you have your button style complete, take a look in the Layers palette, where you'll find a list of the styles you used. You can experiment by turning on and off the eyeballs next to each style. Once you're sure it's what you want, just collapse the style by clicking on the arrow that appears within that layer. Now, let's save your style into the Styles palette, so we can easily apply it to other buttons. To accomplish that, click on the New Style icon (it looks like a sheet of paper) in the Styles palette, pictured in **Figure 15.31**. (You may have to choose Window > Show Styles to see the palette.) Now you should see a preview of your style at the bottom of the Styles palette. You can double-click on it to rename it.

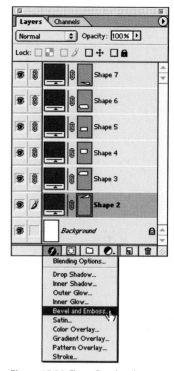

Figure 15.28 Chose Bevel and Emboss from the Layer Style pop-up menu at the bottom of the Layers palette to add a 3D look to your newly created button.

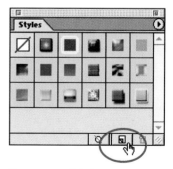

Figure 15.31 Click the New Style icon to save that collection of styles for later use.

With your style saved for future use, go back to the shape tool and look up at the Options bar. You should notice an area where you can specify a style, so choose the one you just created (**Figure 15.32**) and then continue making buttons until you have what you need. If the Style area isn't available, then press the Enter key to make sure Photoshop knows you don't want to add to the shape layer that is currently active. You'll have to press Return or Enter after each button you create, because you'll want each button to appear on its own layer—that will make it easier to add rollovers later. Now that you have everything set up, each time you create a button, Photoshop should automatically use the style you created. If you have trouble getting the buttons to line up, then turn on your rulers and pull out some guides. The guides will snap to the edges of the first button you created, which will make it easier to position future buttons. (Or, if each button is on its own layer, you could use the Alignment options that we talked about a few paragraphs ago.)

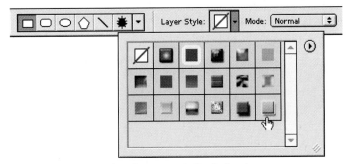

Figure 15.32 The Style drop-down menu in the Options bar.

Text for the Web

Once you have your buttons looking good, you can add some text to them. To accomplish that, first click on your foreground color and choose a Web-safe color, and then click in the center of your newly created button with the Type tool. If you have trouble finding the center of the button, try typing Command-T (Macintosh) or Ctrl-T (Windows), which should place a crosshair in the center of the button. Once you have your cursor positioned just right, press the Escape key to get rid of the crosshair and then click with the Type tool. Next, click on the centered text icon in the Options bar and then enter the label for this button. After you've gotten the text entered, type Command-A (Macintosh) or Ctrl-A (Windows) to select the full range of text, and then adjust its size by clicking on the size setting and using the up and down arrow keys on your keyboard. (Adding Shift to the arrow keys jumps the value up or down by 10.)

If you'd like to experiment with different typefaces, click on the name of the font in the Options bar and then use the up and down arrow keys to cycle through all the available fonts. If you need to kern any of the letters (change the spacing between individual pairs of letters), click an insertion point between two letters, click the Palettes button in the Options bar, click in the Kern option, and tweak away. Once everything fits the space and looks just about right, experiment with the Anti-aliased setting in the Options bar (it's the icon that looks like two lowercase A's). When you adjust this setting, make sure you are viewing your image at 100% because that's how the people viewing your Web site will see the text. You can do that by double-clicking on the Zoom tool or by choosing View > Actual Pixels. If you need to fine-tune the positioning of the entire text layer, switch to the Move tool and use the arrow keys to nudge the text one pixel at a time.

Using Lighting Effects For 3D Edges

If you'd like a more realistic 3D look for your button bars, try out the Lighting Effects filter, which lets you control the "source" of the light you're applying. First, choose the color, and then create a new layer and fill it with that color by typing Option-Delete (Macintosh) or Alt-Backspace (Windows). Now, make a selection in the shape you'd like your button bar to be. Type Q to turn on Quick Mask mode, which should turn your selection into a colored overlay. Choose Filter > Blur > Gaussian Blur; use a setting somewhere near 12. This should make the colored overlay fade out on the edges (**Figure 15.33**).

> **Notes**
>
> You can type Command-H (Macintosh) or Ctrl-H (Windows) to hide the selection box that appears after you drag across a range of text.
>
> ....
>
> When using the Type tool, you can hold the Command key (Macintosh) or Ctrl key (Windows) to temporarily access the Move tool.

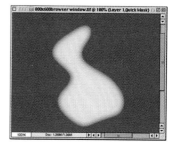

Figure 15.33 Use the Gaussian Blur filter to create a soft edge on the Quick Mask.

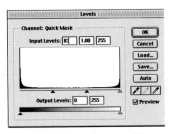

Figure 15.34 Move the upper left slider until it's at the end of the curved part of the left side of the bar chart.

Now, choose Image > Adjust > Levels, move the upper left slider in until it's at the end of the curved part of the left side of the bar chart (**Figure 15.34**) and then type Q to turn off Quick Mask mode. Choose Select > Save Selection and specify a memorable name. Now, to add the 3D look, choose Select > Deselect and then choose Filter > Render > Lighting Effects. At the bottom of the dialog box that appears, you'll find a pop-up menu called Texture Channel. Click on that menu and choose the name that you specified when you saved your selection (**Figure 15.35**). Now you can experiment with the controls in this dialog box until the button bar looks naturally 3D. If the end result has a stairstepped look, you can smooth it out with the Filter > Noise > Median filter.

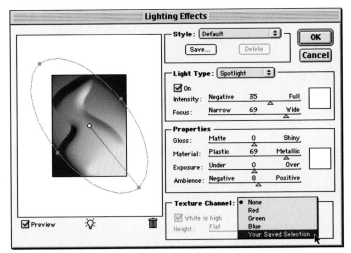

Figure 15.35 Choose the name of your selection from the Texture Channel pop-up menu.

Creating Smooth Shapes

If you're having trouble making really smooth shapes for your buttons, then you'll want to try these two tips. One method is to make a selection with the Lasso tool and then type Q to turn on Quick Mask mode. Then, to smooth the shape you've made, choose Filter > Noise > Median and play around with the slider until things look smooth (**Figure 15.36**). If the slider in the Median filter just can't go high enough for what you need to do, you can apply it more than once. This same technique can be used to round the corners on any polygon.

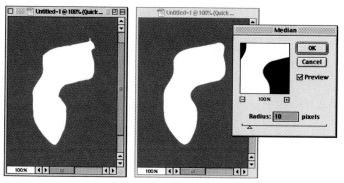

Figure 15.36 Left: original selection in Quick Mask mode. Right: result of applying the Median filter.

The other method is to use the Pen tool (which we talked about in Chapter 11) to draw a smooth shape. If you haven't mastered the Pen tool yet, then you might want to try out the Freeform Pen tool instead. It has a Curve Fit setting in the Options bar that allows you to control how much it will generalize the shape you make (**Figure 15.37**). After you've made a path, you can click on the name of the path in the Paths palette and choose Make Selection from the side menu of that palette.

Figure 15.37 The Curve Fit setting determines how smooth the path will be.

Multi-Colored Buttons

Let's try creating some interesting buttons using filters. Start off by creating a new layer and changing your foreground color to what you'd like to use as a starting point for your button (don't expect it to stay that color, though!). Now use the Rounded Corner rectangle tool to create a nicely shaped button. Be sure to use the far right choice in the Options bar (the one that just fills a specified area on a layer instead of creating a shape layer). Now type

Figure 15.38 You should end up with a selection in the same shape as the button.

Command-I (Macintosh) or Ctrl-I (Windows) to invert the color of the button...don't worry, it will come back to your original color in a few minutes. Next, hold down the Command key (Macintosh) or Ctrl key (Windows), click on the name of the layer in the Layers palette, and turn on the Lock Transparency checkbox (to the left of the tiny checkerboard at the top of the Layers palette). Now you should have a selection in the shape of the button (**Figure 15.38**).

Now let's add some dimension to our button. Choose Select > Feather and use a setting somewhere near 7 (use smaller numbers for smaller buttons). Type X to swap your foreground and background colors, which should move your original button color to the background. Click on the foreground color and make it a light shade of gray. Now choose Edit > Stroke, set the width to the same setting you used when you feathered your selection (7 in this case) and use the Inside setting. Next, choose Filter > Stylize > Emboss, set the Height to the same setting you used when you feathered the selection (7 in this case) and turn the amount all the way up (**Figure 15.39**).

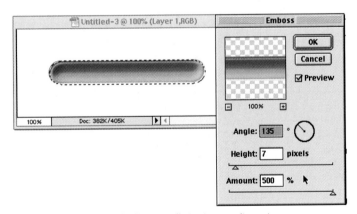

Figure 15.39 Embossing the button will give it some dimension.

You could stop here, or keep going; it's up to you. If you want a little more interesting looking button, choose Select > Deselect, and type X to swap your foreground and background colors. Now choose Filter > Sketch > Plaster and use the settings shown in **Figure 15.40**.

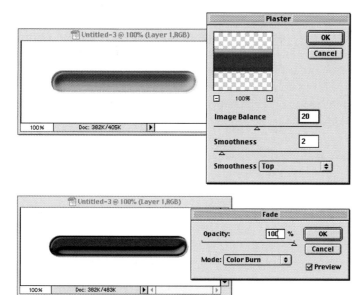

Figure 15.40 Use the settings shown here when applying the Plaster filter.

Finally, choose Edit > Fade and set the Blending Mode pop-up menu to Color Burn and your button is done!

Striped Graphics

I browse the Web every day, and I see a lot of graphics that contain really cool looking horizontal stripes. This effect is rather easy, and the GIF file format will make it so it your file size doesn't get much larger. Let's take a look at what it takes to make the striped look (**Figure 15.41**).

Figure 15.41 When I wrote this chapter, www.ibm.com featured a striped look.

Start by creating a new document that is one pixel wide, two pixels tall, and contains a transparent background. Next, grab the Pencil tool and fill in only the topmost pixel, leaving the bottom one empty. Choose Select > All and then Edit > Define Pattern. Photoshop will prompt you for a name, so use something like "horizontal stripes." Now open the image you would like to apply the stripes to, create a new layer, and then choose Edit > Fill. Set the Use pop-up menu to Pattern, click on the pattern square, and choose the pattern you just defined (you can use a selection if you don't want it to fill the entire screen). If you'd like the stripes to only apply to the layer below, then choose Layer > Group With Previous. Finally, if you'd like to use a different color for the stripes, turn on the Preserve Transparency checkbox at the top of the Layers palette (it looks like a checkerboard) and then paint away, or use the Gradient tool.

Wires

You can also use the Freeform Pen tool to simulate the look of wires. Start by drawing a line with the Freeform Pen tool. Now switch over to the Paintbrush tool and choose a hard-edged brush with the width you want for your wire. Next, create a new layer, pick the color for your wire, and press Return or Enter. That should make Photoshop trace the shape of the path using the tool that is currently active (also known as stroking). You can hide the path by clicking in the empty space below the path in the Paths palette. To add some dimension, add a Drop Shadow and Bevel And Emboss layer style (**Figure 15.42**).

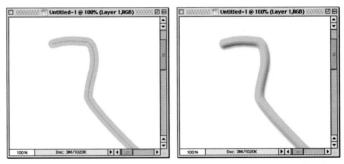

Figure 15.42 Left: stroking the path using the paintbrush. Right: result of applying two styles.

If you'd like to add the look of a copper core peeking out of your wire, then create a new layer and make a very small, short rectangular selection at the exposed end of the wire. Next, pick the Gradient tool and use the "copper" preset that comes with Photoshop. Click on the topmost area of the selection and drag to the bottom (**Figure 15.43**). Choose Select > Deselect, then Edit > Rotate, and adjust the angle until it looks appropriate. Finally, use the Move tool to put it in position, and the Eraser tool to remove any unwanted areas.

Screw Heads

This should be pretty simple. Go ahead and create a new document with a white background. Change your foreground color to a medium shade of gray, create a new layer, and then shift-drag with the Ellipse shape tool (not the Marquee tool) to create a round object (have it set to the rightmost setting so it doesn't create a path). Now add some dimension to the image by choosing Layer > Layer Style > Bevel And Emboss. Use the Smooth setting and experiment with the Size setting until the gray circle starts to resemble the head of a screw (a drop shadow can be another good addition to that layer). Now we just need to add the slot in the top and we'll be just about done. Create a new layer and use the Line tool (it's hidden in with the shape tools) and make a straight line across the screw head, making it extend beyond both edges. Type Command-G (Macintosh) or Ctrl-G (Windows) to group it with the image below, which should make it only show up where the screw head is. Change to the Move tool and link those two layers together by clicking the box at the left of the screw head layer in the Layers palette. Now click the Align Vertical Center and Align Horizontal Center buttons in the Options bar.

Our screw head is shaping up now, but that slot should look indented, right? So choose Layer > Layer Style > Bevel And Emboss, change the Technique to Chisel Hard, and click the Down radio button. You might also need to adjust the size setting until things look just right. If you think the result looks just a little too perfect, then click on the screw head layer (not the slot layer) and choose Filter > Texture > Texturizer. Use the Sandstone texture and turn the Relief setting way down (**Figure 15.44**).

Figure 15.43 Use the Gradient tool to add a copper wire.

Figure 15.44 The progression from simple circle to finished screw.

Drill Holes

Let's make some cool-looking indents that look like you drilled into a metal surface. Start by clicking on the new layer icon at the bottom of the Layers palette. Using the Elliptical marquee tool, go to one of the corners of the image and click and drag to create a circular selection about the size of the tip of your pinky (hold Shift to constrain it to a circle).

Figure 15.45 Set the Radial Blur filter to at least 35.

Now let's start to turn it into a drill hole. Choose Edit > Fill and select White from the Use pop-up menu (make sure the Preserve Transparency checkbox is turned off). Next, we'll need some random information to distort, so choose Filter > Noise > Add Noise and use a setting around 400%. Now, choose Filter > Blur > Radial Blur, set the amount to at least 35, and use the Spin setting (**Figure 15.45**).

Next we'll add a special gradient to help simulate lighting. Click on the Gradient tool and choose the third kind of gradient from the Options bar (known as the Angle gradient). After you've done that, choose Black, White from the gradient drop-down menu in the Options bar. Click directly on the gradient preview to edit the gradient and do the following: click on the white square on the far right of the gradient bar and then type 25% into the Location text field. Now hold down the Option key (Macintosh) or Alt key (Windows) and drag the white square towards the right—this will create a duplicate. To position this square in the correct location, enter 75% in the Location field. Now Option-drag (Macintosh) or Alt-drag (Windows) the black square to duplicate it and then enter 100% into the Location field, and then make one more black square for the 50% location. You should end up with something that looks like the dialog box below (**Figure 15.46**).

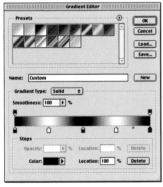

Figure 15.46 The finished gradient.

Now create a new layer above the layer that contains the circular object you made earlier. Choose Select > Deselect and then click in the center of the circle and drag until your cursor is at the upper right edge of the circle. Now you'll combine the gradient with the circle by choosing Layer > Group With Previous. Change the pop-up menu at the top of the Layers palette to Hard Light. You can also lower the opacity to let more of the circle texture show through (**Figure 15.47**).

One final touch: let's add an edge that will make the circle appear to be indented from the surface of the background. Click on the layer that contains the circle, choose Layer > Layer Style > Bevel And Emboss, and then choose Inner Bevel from the Style pop-up menu. To get the effect I have here, use the following settings: Highlight opacity 40%, Shadow opacity 87%, Angle 138°, Depth 70, Size 5, and I used the Down setting.

Figure 15.47 The progression from simple noise to a finished drill hole.

Closing Thoughts

Your interface design choices are truly unlimited when working in Photoshop. Once you're comfortable with the techniques covered in this chapter, you can start building your own inventory of fresh and fascinating interface elements. One good way to start is to go to your favorite Web site, look closely at the interface elements, and try to recreate them on your own. I'm not suggesting you steal ideas, but this is a great way to test out your skills.

Ben's Techno-Babble Decoder Ring

Dithering—The simulation (by placing small dots of color next to each other) of a greater range of colors than a given monitor can correctly display.

Web-safe Colors—A special set of 216 colors common to both the Macintosh and Windows operating systems that will not become dithered when viewed using 256-color displays.

Anti-aliasing—A technique that blurs lines slightly by mixing together the colors on both sides of a curved or a diagonal line (which may look jagged on your computer monitor, since it's made up of a grid of square pixels). Viewed from a distance, the anti-aliased line appears smooth.

8-bit Color—A technical term used to describe an image or computer that is displaying only 256 colors.

System Palette—A special set of colors that are used to create all the interface elements used in a computer operating system.

© 2001 Don Barnett, Nekton Inc., www.donbarnett.com

© 2001 Don Barnett, Nekton Inc., www.donbarnett.com

16 Slicing and Rollovers

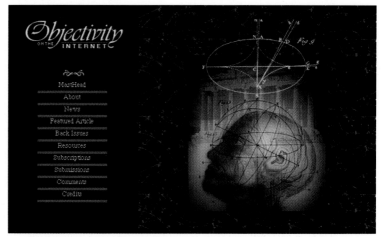

© 2001 Don Barnett, Nekton Inc., www.donbarnett.com

I invented the Internet.
–Al Gore

If Al Gore invented the Internet, I invented Spellcheck.
–Dan Quayle

In the last chapter we looked at techniques for creating the basic ingredients for your Web site, but now it's time to breathe some life into your design. In this chapter you'll learn how to set up your buttons so they send your audience to another Web page when you click on them. You'll also find out how to add interactivity to your site, so when a person moves their cursor over a button, it will change to indicate something's going to happen when they click it. This is known as a rollover. But before we get too far in our venture, we'll need to learn how to "slice" our image.

What does slicing mean, exactly? Well, imagine that you're a puzzle maker. You have a nice, big picture, and you're about to cut the shapes of the pieces into a puzzle. Your puzzle is going to be pretty simple—maybe you're doing Bambi and Thumper for the five-year-old crowd, and there are only going to be about ten pieces total. If everything goes well, any five-year-old should be able to reassemble those pieces and end up with the same image you started with. So, with that puzzle in mind, jump back to Photoshop. Like the puzzle maker, you "slice" your images into multiple pieces, and have Photoshop (instead of the five-year-old) do all the work needed to make sure the slices get put back together in your Web browser. (Unlike with a traditional jigsaw puzzle, the slices in a "Photoshopped" image are meant to be undetectable; no one browsing your site will ever know the image has been sliced.) Once you've sliced your image into rectangles, you can tell each piece how you want it to behave: you can choose an appropriate file format, prepare the image for a rollover, add HTML links, etc. So even though you've still got one big image in Photoshop, it's now made up of a bunch of little pieces (slices), each with its own set of behaviors.

The Slice Tool

Photoshop's Slice tool (just below the Magic Wand tool in Photoshop 6.0) allows you to slice your image into rectangular areas that will each get special treatment when you save your image. To create a slice, just grab the Slice tool and click and drag across your image. There are two types of slices: user slices and auto slices. A user slice is one that you've made; it appears with a blue background behind the slice number. Auto slices are the ones that are necessary to complete the rest of the image (and therefore filled in automatically), and appear with a gray background behind the slice number, as shown in **Figure 16.1**.

Note

You can hide the slices by choosing View > Show > Slices, or by typing Command-H (Macintosh) or Ctrl-H (Windows).

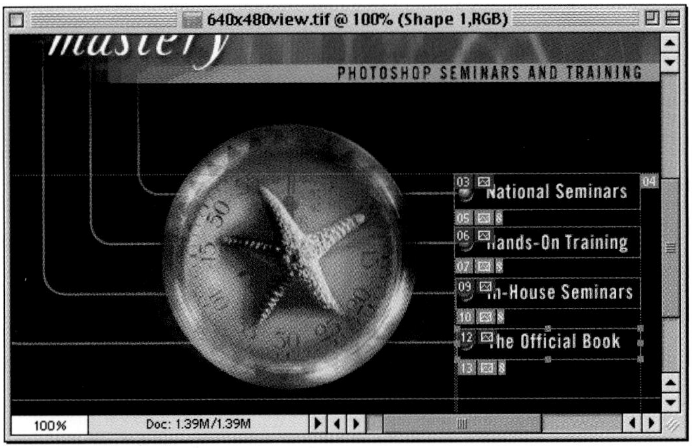

Figure 16.1 Slices show up as numbered rectangular boxes in Photoshop.

Once you have a few slices defined, you can click and hold on the Slice tool in the Tools palette to access the Slice Select tool (or just hold down the Command key on the Mac or the Ctrl key in Windows to temporarily access it while in the Slice tool). This tool allows you to resize and move slices that you've already created. Once you've gotten the size and position of a slice correct, double-click on the slice with the Slice Select tool to change the options for that slice (**Figure 16.2**).

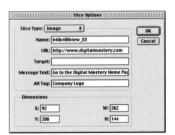

Figure 16.2 Double-click within a slice to access the Slice Options dialog box.

Let's take a look at the choices in the Slice Options dialog box. We'll start at the top and work our way down.

- The Name field determines the file name for the slice. Each slice name is based on the name of your Photoshop file and consists of the document name followed by an underscore and the slice number. Because of that, it's best to save your file so it's no longer called Untitled;

that way, all your slices won't end up with really unhelpful names like "Untitled_02."

▶ The URL field allows you to link to another Web page. You'll need to start the URL with http:// and then you can enter any Web address (like my site at www.digital-mastery.com). Once you have a URL assigned, clicking on that slice in a Web browser will send you to the Web site you entered in that field.

▶ The Target field is only used if you are using frames on your Web site. With frames, you can have multiple Web pages loaded into a single browser window that is divided into panes (also known as frames). The Target setting tells the Web browser which one of these panes you want to load for the Web page that you've listed in the URL field. If you've never dealt with frames before, then just leave that field empty.

▶ If you enter anything into the Message Text field, then that information will be displayed in the status bar at the bottom of a browser window when a user moves his cursor over this slice. If you leave that field empty, then the status bar in the Web browser will just list the URL you're linking to (**Figure 16.3**).

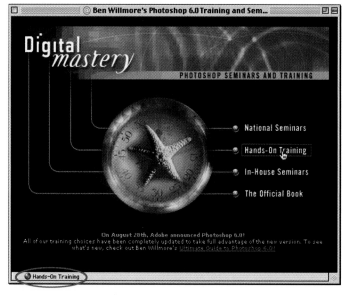

Figure 16.3 The Message Text field determines what will be shown in the Status bar of a Web browser.

▶ Finally, any text you put in the Alt Tag field will be displayed within a slice before the slice image loads. I usually enter a very short description (because it has to fit within the slice) of what the slice looks like. So if one of your slices contains your company logo, you might want to say something like "Digital Mastery Logo" in the Alt tag. That way people with slow Internet connections won't have to wait for the entire page to load before they have an idea of what's to come. (Plus, people who use text-only browsers will be able to see what the slice connects to, if it's a button.) If you have any button bars, I'd suggest you enter the text of each button into its Alt Tag field; that way, people can click on those buttons before the images load (**Figure 16.4**).

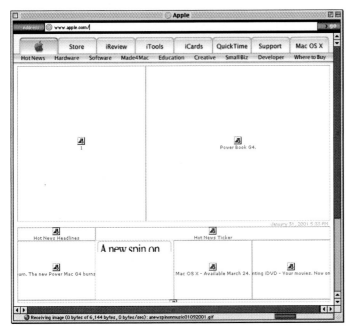

Figure 16.4 The Alt tags will appear within each slice before the images have had a chance to load.

You'll need one slice for each button that will contain a rollover, and one slice for each graphic that will contain a link or will be saved with different compression settings (we'll talk about compression settings in Chapter 18).

When you're adding slices to your image, you might have a crystal-clear vision of how those slices relate to the underlying image, but Photoshop isn't quite so smart. If you reposition a layer after you've put a slice around it, the slice won't be smart enough to know that it should move as well. This can create lots of problems if you suddenly want to make changes at the last minute (**Figure 16.5**), but there's a way to get around that.

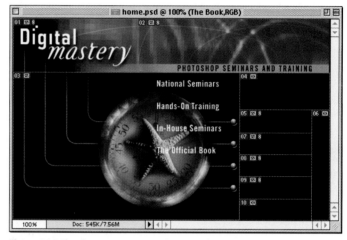

Figure 16.5 The slices you create won't move when you reposition a layer.

Layer-based slices can solve this problem. They give you the flexibility to rearrange, move, or edit buttons without having to redo any of your slicing. To create a layer-based slice, make sure the layer you are thinking about is active and then choose Layer > New Layer Based Slice. By doing that, Photoshop will create a slice that includes the entire contents of that layer (that way, if you move or resize that layer, the slice will update).

Layer-based slices are great when you create simple buttons, one per layer. You can even add a layer style (like a drop shadow) and the slice will expand to include the style. This makes slicing your images very quick and easy.

Creating Rollovers

Now that your image is sliced, you can set up a rollover that will make part of your image change when someone moves his or her cursor over a slice. But before you start

planning all your rollovers, you'll have to switch over to
ImageReady, because Photoshop isn't capable of creating
rollovers. ImageReady is loaded on your hard drive when
you install Photoshop, so even if you didn't know it existed,
it's there for you. ImageReady is designed for four functions: slicing, rollovers, animation, and optimization. For
now, let's stick to rollovers. To jump from Photoshop to
ImageReady, click on the arrow icon at the very bottom of
Photoshop's Tools palette.

ImageReady contains a lot of the same tools that are available in Photoshop (which therefore don't need much of an
introduction), but if you take a good look, you'll find that
ImageReady just isn't as powerful. I do most of my interface
design in Photoshop and then switch to ImageReady when I
need to do things that Photoshop can't (like rollovers and
animation). If you ever need to make a change to a slice
while you're in ImageReady, then click on a slice with the
Slice Select tool (just like you did in Photoshop). Change
the options in the Slice palette, which should be visible at
the bottom of your screen (**Figure 16.6**).

Figure 16.6 ImageReady's Slice palette.

> **Note**
>
> The Slices palette contains additional
> options (like Message Text and the Alt
> tag). To access them, click on the small
> arrows on the palette's name tab.

Now that you know a little about what ImageReady is
used for, let's explore the Rollover palette at the bottom
of the screen. It will most likely be blank when you first
open it, because a slice isn't selected. Grab the Slice Select
tool and click on one of the slices you created earlier. That
should make the Rollover palette come to life. To make the
image change when you move over that slice, you'll need
to add a *rollover state* to the slice. To do that, click the New
Rollover State icon (it looks like a piece of paper with the
corner turned over) and choose a rollover state from the
pop-up menu just above the new rollover state you created
(**Figure 16.7**).

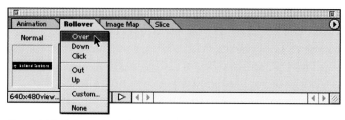

Figure 16.7 Click just above the thumbnail of your new rollover state to define the type of rollover you are creating.

Note
When you are creating rollovers, to select a slice you can either use the Slice Select tool or choose from the pop-up menu in the lower left of the Rollover palette (**Figure 16.8**).

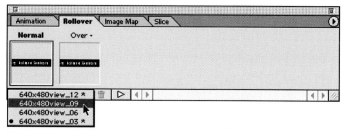

Figure 16.8 You can quickly select a specific slice by choosing its name from the pop-up menu in the lower left of the Rollover palette.

Here's what the rollover states do:

▶ **Normal**—controls what the slice looks like before the viewer has a chance to interact with it in any way.

▶ **Over**—controls what happens when the viewer moves the cursor over the slice, but does not press the mouse button.

▶ **Down**—controls what happens when the viewer presses the mouse button within the slice.

▶ **Click**—controls what happens when the mouse button is released after clicking on a slice.

▶ **Out**—controls what happens when the viewer moves the cursor outside of the slice. If an Out rollover state has not been defined, then the image will return to the Normal state.

▶ **Up**—controls what happens when the viewer releases the mouse button over the slice.

Each slice can have multiple rollover states attached to it. For example, you might have an image of a grayscale balloon; when you move your cursor over it (the Over state), it becomes a full-color balloon. When you press your mouse button over the image (the Down state), the balloon gets blown full of air (like it's about to burst). Then when you release the mouse button (the Click state), the balloon bursts and becomes a shriveled mess. Finally, when you move your mouse outside of the slice (the Out state), the deflated balloon becomes grayscale again. You can even make a rollover trigger an animation, so this whole thing could be pretty dramatic, but we'll hold off on animation until the next chapter. For now, let's concentrate on those rollovers.

Once you've created a new rollover state and have chosen the type of rollover you want, it's up to you to change the look of your image. When you're working with rollovers, you have to limit yourself to changing a simple setting that's attached to a layer. If you paint, run a filter, or do anything else that isn't a simple setting attached to a layer, then that change will happen in *all* of your rollover states (including the normal state). You can change the position, opacity, layer style settings, and visibility of individual layers to create different rollovers.

Simple Rollover Effects

The easiest way to create an interesting rollover is to click on one of ImageReady's preset styles (in the Styles palette) that contains a black triangle in the upper left corner; the triangle indicates that it contains a rollover (**Figure 16.9**). Or, you can choose one of the other styles, manually add a rollover, and modify the style settings on your own.

After you've made a change while one of the rollover states was active, you can preview the effect by clicking the Rollover Preview icon at the bottom of the Rollover palette (it looks like the Play button on a tape deck). When that mode is turned on, you can move your cursor over the slice in the image window to see exactly what the rollover looks like. I usually find the slice borders to be too distracting to get a good sense for what my rollover looks like. You can type Q to toggle the visibility of the slices. Once you're sure everything looks good, just click

Note

To work with layer styles in ImageReady (not the presets in the Style palette), choose an individual effect from the from the Layer Effects pop-up menu at the bottom of the Layers palette (it looks like a circle with the letter "f" in it). A Layer Options palette for that effect will appear.

Figure 16.9 Left: image in the Normal state. Right: the same image in the Over state. This is an example of an ImageReady layer style that includes a rollover.

that Rollover Preview icon a second time and you'll be back to normal.

If you manually created this rollover, you can now save it in the ImageReady Styles palette for later use. All you have to do is make sure that the correct layer is active and then click the New Style button at the bottom of the Styles palette. When you do, you'll be prompted for exactly what you'd like to save in the style (**Figure 16.10**). Just make sure the Include Rollover checkbox is turned on. The next time you'd like to apply that rollover style, just click on the layer you'd like to apply it to, and then click the style in the Styles palette. That's all there is to it!

Note

The Styles palette in ImageReady is independent of the one in Photoshop. Just because a style appears in Photoshop doesn't mean it will also appear in ImageReady. Also, ImageReady's Styles palette includes rollover information, which is not available in Photoshop."

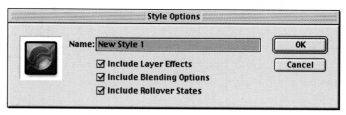

Figure 16.10 ImageReady's Style Options dialog box.

Sophisticated Rollover Effects

Our first rollover was pretty simple, so now let's create something that's a little more compelling. You can overcome the limitations I mentioned earlier (using only position, opacity, layer styles, etc.) by swapping the visibility of two layers that have been enhanced using filters or other effects. Here's how it works. First, click on the layer you'd like to work with to make it active. Next, choose Layer > New > Layer Via Copy, which should give you an exact duplicate of that layer. Hide the original layer, and then apply a filter to the duplicate layer (something like Filter > Blur > Radial Blur, which is what I used for the figure at left). Finally, create a slice and a rollover state for that area and then, in the Over rollover state, hide the dupe and show the original (**Figure 16.11**). You can use this technique to create just about any kind of rollover effect

Figure 16.11 Left: the Normal rollover state. Right: the Over rollover state. (© 2001 Stockbyte, www.stockbyte.com)

that you can imagine, because you're not limited to any particular tool.

The changes made to your image with a rollover don't have to be limited to the boundaries of the slice that triggers the rollover. The change can be anywhere in the image. That means you can have a rollover prompt a change in the central area of a Web page (**Figure 16.12**). You can even make a rollover trigger an animation, which we'll learn about in the next chapter.

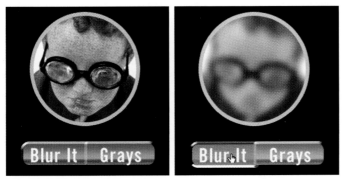

Figure 16.12 Left: the Normal state. Right: what happens when your cursor passes over one of the buttons at the bottom of the Web page. (© 2001 Stockbyte, www.stockbyte.com)

You have to be careful after you've created a rollover state; any changes to the position, opacity, layer style, or visibility will only affect that state, and not the others in the image. That means you can easily screw things up if you attempt to move your layers around later. If, after moving a layer, you find that you need it to be consistent across all the rollover states, then choose Match Layer Across States from the side menu of the Rollover palette. Or, if you need that layer to be consistent across all your slices and their rollovers, choose Match Layer Across All Rollovers.

Saving Your Image with Slices

Once you're done slicing your image and adding rollovers, you'll need to save your image in a special way so that the slices become individual images and so that the HTML code needed to make everything work is generated. You do that by choosing Save Optimized As from the File menu in ImageReady. In the Save dialog box, choose HTML And Images from the Format pop-up menu (**Figure 16.13**). After you save the file, you should end up with an HTML file and a folder full of images (**Figure 16.14**). If you look in the Images folder, you'll find one image for each slice that was in your image (both user and auto slices). You'll also find one image for each rollover your created.

Figure 16.13 Choose HTML And Images from the Format pop-up menu in the Save dialog box.

Figure 16.14 An example folder of images created from slices and rollovers.

Closing Thoughts

The majority of popular Web sites use slicing to make sure the graphics are optimized using the correct file formats (which we'll learn about in Chapter 18), and they use rollovers to enhance the user's navigational experience. If you work regularly with Web graphics, these techniques should become second nature to you, and even though this may not be the "fun" part of designing, the skills you gain from this chapter should be included in your inventory of essential tools for your Web work.

Ben's Techno-Babble Decoder Ring

Slice—A rectangular area of an image that will be saved as a separate file and can have special properties attached to it (HTML links, rollovers, etc.).

Rollover—A feature of JavaScript that allows a second image to be substituted for the original image when a user interacts with a slice.

JavaScript—A special programming language used to add features that make the Web page more interactive.

Frames—A method for loading multiple Web pages into a single browser window.

URL—An acronym that stands for Universal Resource Locator. Most URLs begin with either "http" or "ftp" and they direct a Web browser to a resource on the Internet (like a Web page or file server). Example: http://www.digitalmastery.com is the URL for the companion site to this book.

http—An acronym that stands for HyperText Transfer Protocol. Web browsers and the servers that house Web sites communicate using the http protocol.

ftp—An acronym that stands for File Transfer Protocol. Ftp is a very common method for transferring files over the Internet.

HTML—An acronym that stands for HyperText Markup Language. HTML is the programming language used to create Web pages.

17 Animation

> *A successful tool is one that was used to do something undreamed of by its author.*
> –S. C. Johnson

Courtesy of Jimmy Chen, www.typographic.com

In the last chapter we found out how to breathe life into our interface elements by adding HTML links and Java-Script rollovers. Now let's find out how to add even more energy to your graphics by exploring ImageReady's animation capabilities. (In case you didn't read the last chapter, ImageReady is a companion program for Photoshop that focuses on Web functions like rollovers and animation.) But first, a personal comment. Animation is fun and cool and can make for an exciting Web site. But this is one area where you really need to think about whether the animation adds or takes away from a good Web experience. In other words, will it slow your site down to the point that it's frustrating for users who have slower connections, or will it truly enhance the experience for your Web visitors? I think the trick is to always be able to answer this question honestly, and proceed accordingly. So, enough of my wet blanket, let's get on with the fun stuff.

ImageReady allows you to easily create layer-based animations. What do I mean by layer-based? It means you are limited to changing the position, opacity, visibility, or layer styles for a layer. If you paint, or apply a filter to, a layer, that effect will apply to the entire animation.

Once you have your animation created, you can save it as a GIF file that can be used on any Web page. You'll learn all about the GIF file format in the next chapter, but there's one thing you should know about it before you start creating your animations. GIF files are limited to 256 colors total. That means that photographic images will look a little less than ideal, and solid-colored graphics will look great.

Simple Animations

Let's start off with a simple example. Let's say you have a document that contains two layers; one contains a photo of the earth from space and the other contains an image of the moon. You want to make it look like the moon is moving back and forth across the earth. With the document open in ImageReady, you'd need to click on the New Frame icon (**Figure 17.1**) and then use the Move tool to reposition the moon. Now repeat that about a dozen times until you've completed the path that you'd like the moon to follow. Then, to preview your animation, click the Play button at the bottom of the Animation palette.

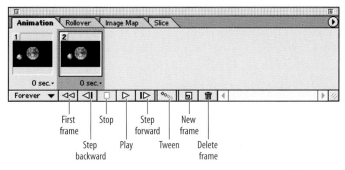

First frame — Stop — Step forward — New frame

Step backward — Play — Tween — Delete frame

Figure 17.1 Use the Animation palette to create and manipulate the frames of an animation. (© 2001 Stockbyte, www.stockbyte.com)

But what if you want to move the earth layer? Well, Photoshop only records the movement in the currently active frame of the animation (**Figure 17.2**). All the other frames still contain the original positioning of the earth. To change the position of the earth layer across all frames without animating it, you need to make sure the earth layer is active and then choose Match Layer Across Frames from the side menu of the Animation palette (**Figure 17.3**).

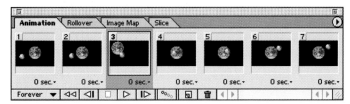

Figure 17.2 Moving a layer only affects the currently active frame.

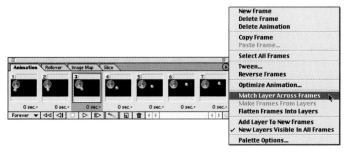

Figure 17.3 Choosing Match Layer Across Frames will make the currently active layer consistent across all the frames of the animation.

Tweening

The animation we just looked at could have been created much faster if we took advantage of ImageReady's Tween command. All you need to do is create the critical frames of the animation (called keyframes), and then Tween makes all the intermediate frames for you. So, in our example, you could create one frame with the moon at the bottom left of the image, another with it in the middle, and finally a third one with it at the top right (**Figure 17.4**).

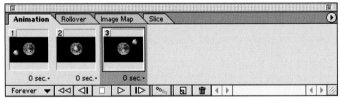

Figure 17.4 First create all the keyframes that you'll need.

Once you have the three keyframes, you can instruct ImageReady to create everything else. Start by clicking on the second frame. Then choose Tween from the side menu of the Animation palette and specify how many frames you'd like to have in the transition between the first two keyframes (**Figure 17.5**). Then repeat the process for the last frame of the animation and you'll be all done! (See **Figure 17.6**.)

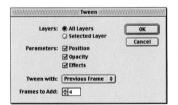

Figure 17.5 Choose Tween from the side menu of the Animation palette to instruct Photoshop to create all the frames needed for a transition.

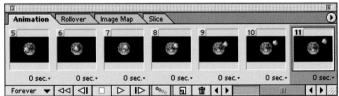

Figure 17.6 After creating the in between frames with tweening, you should have a full animation.

Oops, I think I spoke too soon. If you actually play this animation, you'd notice that the moon starts in the bottom left, smoothly moves to the middle, and then ends up at the top right. All that's fine, but once it's made that trip, then the animation starts over again—and the moon suddenly pops back to its original position. What we really need is to be able add a smooth transition from the end of the animation (as it stands right now) back to the beginning. Let's start by choosing Select All Frames from the side menu of the Animation palette. Next, choose Copy Frames, and then Paste Frames, from that same menu. When prompted, choose Paste After Selection so those frames will appear at the end of the animation (**Figure 17.7**). After doing that, you should end up with twice as many frames in your animation, and the frames you just pasted should appear at the end of the animation. You might need to use the scroll bar at the bottom of the Animation palette to see the new frames. Now all we have to do is choose Reverse Frames from the side menu of the palette to get all the frames in the correct order for a smoothly looping animation.

There's one final step. When we duplicated those frames and then reversed the order of the second half of the animation, we ended up with two frames that aren't needed. The starting and ending frame of our animation are identical, as are the middle two frames. So click on the last frame and then click the Delete button (trashcan), and get rid of one of the middle ones as well, and then everything should be perfect.

Changing Visibility

Now let's try something a little more complex. What if you want it to appear that the moon is orbiting around the earth in 3D space? If you just change the stacking order of the layers to put the moon behind the earth, then that change will happen across all the frames of the animation. That makes it impossible to accomplish this effect without an additional layer. But all you have to do is duplicate the moon layer and move one of them behind the earth. Then you can link them together so they move as a group (**Figure 17.8**).

Now you can go through the exact same steps as the last animation to create all the individual frames. To make it look like the moon is starting in front of the earth, and *then* slipping behind, you can click through the individual frames of the animation and turn off the eyeball icon for

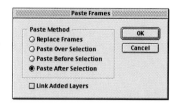

Figure 17.7 When you use Paste After Selection, all of the copied frames will be added into the palette, effectively duplicating your animation.

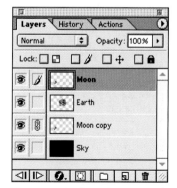

Figure 17.8 Duplicate the moon and move it behind the earth, and link the two moon layers together.

the top layer whenever the moon should be behind the earth. It's that easy! Well, if it doesn't feel easy yet, believe me, it will after you've done it a couple of times.

Text Warping

You can create some very interesting animations using Photoshop 6.0's Text Warping feature (which we talked about back in Chapter 14). Start with some text that has warping applied (you can do this in Photoshop or ImageReady). In ImageReady, create a new keyframe and adjust the warping settings by choosing Layer > Type > Warp Text (**Figure 17.9**). Then let ImageReady do all the work by tweening between those two frames! (See **Figure 17.10**.)

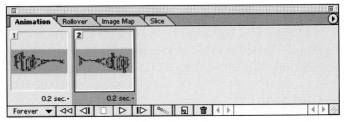

Figure 17.9 Start with two keyframes of warped text.

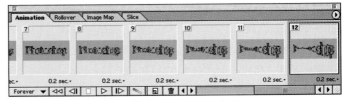

Figure 17.10 Use tweening to create the in-between frames.

Other Text Transformations

If you want your text to rotate and get larger or smaller as the animation progresses, you'll need to create a bunch of layers. But you have to remember that any change to the pixels in a layer (such as scaling) will affect all the frames of the animation. That means you'll need one layer for each frame! You can make this go much faster by using the Actions palette (and remember—in case you've been switching back and forth between programs—you need to record this one in ImageReady). You'll want your action to contain the following steps (**Figure 17.11**):

1. Create a new frame in the Animation palette.

2. Hide the layer you want to transform.

3. Duplicate that layer.

4. Make the duplicate layer visible.

5. Transform the layer using Edit > Transform > Numeric.

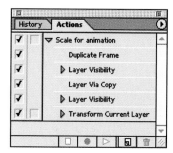

Figure 17.11 Use the Actions palette to automate the creation of rotational and zooming effects.

Unfortunately, there wasn't enough room in this book to include Actions, but this feature is actually very easy to use. Just go to the Window menu to activate (show) the Actions palette, and then you can use it to record the steps you take in Photoshop, and save them for later use.

When you do any scaling or other transformations, be sure to use percentages instead of exact measurements when you duplicate the layer. Otherwise the scaling will make all the scaled layers the same size, instead of progressively bigger. When you duplicate the layer, be sure to use the side menu of the Layers palette, so Photoshop doesn't keep track of the layer name (like it would if you just dragged that layer name to the duplicate icon). After you've created the action, just apply it over and over until you have the right number of frames for your animation.

After you've created all the frames you want, you can fine-tune the timing by changing the delay setting that appears below each frame. If you want to adjust the delay setting for more than one frame, just hold down the Shift key and click on more than one frame before changing the setting (**Figure 17.12**).

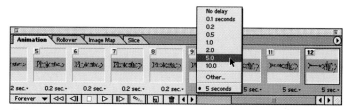

Figure 17.12 Select the frames you'd like to change and then click below one of the frames to specify the delay between frames.

Once you've got the timing just right, you should click in the lower left of the Animation palette to specify how many times the animation should repeat (**Figure 17.13**).

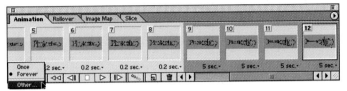

Figure 17.13 Click in the lower left of the Animation palette to choose how many times your animation will repeat itself.

Note

For more information about rollovers, check out Chapter 16,"Slicing and Rollovers."

Rollover Animations

Earlier in this chapter, we learned how to create a basic animation. You can go one step further and use a rollover to trigger an animation. All you have to do is create a rollover state in the Rollover palette, and then, when that state is active, create an animation. That will make it so the animation will play only when your cursor is over the slice that has the rollover assigned to it. Fun, yes?

Closing Thoughts

Animation can add quite a bit of spice to your Web site, but be careful, because animations can also distract your viewers from important content on your site. So use this powerful tool with caution. Otherwise, you might find people thinking your site looks cool, but they won't even know about the product or service you might be attempting to promote because the animation distracted them from your message. Or, if they suffer with (and from) a slow connection, they might have given up and gone looking for a faster site. So have your fun, but use your good judgement!

Ben's Techno-Babble Decoder Ring

Keyframes—The essential frames of an animation that are used to determine the important changes within the animation before using tweening to create intermediate, transitional frames.

Tweening—Creating a transition between two keyframes by making a number of intermediate keyframes, and automatically adjusting their settings so that the transition is smooth.

Courtesy of Jimmy Chen, www.typographic.com

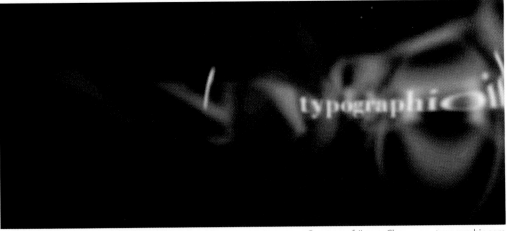

Courtesy of Jimmy Chen, www.typographic.com

18 Optimization

Courtesy of Jimmy Chen, www.typographic.com

Perfection is achieved, not when there is nothing left to add, but when there is nothing left to take away.
—Antoine de St. Exupery

What's New For 6.0

If you read the 5.0 version of this book, you'll see that this is another all-new chapter. We'll explore Photoshop 6.0's weighted optimization and slice optimization settings.

Have you ever stumbled onto some Web site where you felt like you could have gotten a haircut in the time it took for some huge image to appear on your screen? Did it make you want to do the primal scream? Well, if you want to do your part to keep the rest of the world sane, and make sure that your Web graphics look great, but are nimble and fleet of foot, you'll want to learn everything there is to know about optimizing your images. What does "optimizing" mean? Simple: it's all about effectively managing the balance between image quality and file size. That means understanding how to reduce the size, colors, and quality of the image to the exact point where the image still looks good but the file size is as small as possible.

A big part of optimizing is using the right compression methods. To do that, we have to know about the most commonly used Web file formats, how they compress your image, and which is optimal for your kind of image. We'll also venture into an exciting new feature known as weighted optimization, which allows you to set different optimization levels for various parts of your image. Once you've run your image through its "optimization paces," you'll be ready to incorporate all your graphics along with text in an HTML editing program like Adobe GoLive. But first, let's get down to the serious business of optimizing. There are two major methods for reducing the file size of an image: JPEG and GIF formats.

JPEG Compression

JPEG is an acronym that stands for Joint Photographic Experts Group. It's a file format that was designed to reduce the file size of photographic images. Let's take a look at the general idea behind it. First off, JPEG is known as a *lossy* file format because it degrades the quality of the image each time it is saved. So what exactly does JPEG do? It separates your image into color and brightness information, and then degrades the quality of the color information while maintaining the quality of the brightness information.

To get a sense for how this affects an image, open any full-color photograph and then choose Filter > Blur > Gaussian

Blur. Move the slider around and see how much you can blur (read: degrade) the image before you really notice it. It doesn't take much blurring before you can see a huge change in the image (**Figure 18.1**).

Now, click Cancel to get back to the original image. Duplicate the layer that contains the photo by dragging its name onto the New Layer icon (it looks like a piece of paper with the corner folded over). Next, choose Luminosity (another word for brightness) from the pop-up menu that appears at the top of the Layers palette (also known as the Blending Mode menu). That will make it so any changes you make to this layer will only change the brightness of the image and won't shift the colors. Now try your blur test again, seeing how much you can get away with before you really notice it (but ignore the preview window in the filter's dialog box and just look at the document window). It shouldn't be much different from our first try (**Figure 18.1**). Click Cancel again to return to the non-blurred version of the image.

So how is this going to show us how Photoshop can get away with making such small file sizes? Now you'll see: set the Blending Mode menu to Color and then try the blur test one last time. You should notice that you can blur the image like crazy and you won't see a large change in the image (**Figure 18.1**). The only areas that usually start to look terrible are the ones where you have large areas of solid colors touching each other (what I would call graphics, as opposed to photos). That's how JPEG gets away with compressing an image—it mainly degrades the quality of the color transitions, which are not very discernible by the human eye. That's why it's the preferred format for compressing photographic images.

Figure 18.1 From left to right: original image, full image blur=5, blur=5 on luminosity, blur=5 on color. (© 1998 Adobe Systems, Inc.)

GIF Compression

GIF is an acronym that stands for Graphics Interchange Format. It's a file format designed for saving images that contain large areas of solid color (what I call graphics). GIF achieves a small file size by dividing the image into one-pixel-tall horizontal strips. Then it analyzes those strips and looks to see if any adjacent colors are exactly the same. If it finds same-colored areas, it can compress them by describing them in a more efficient way. So, instead of describing every single pixel (red pixel, red pixel, red pixel, red pixel, red pixel), it can describe it as a solid colored line (red pixel x 5). This can save considerable space on your hard drive as long as there are lots of solid-colored areas in the image. In order to guarantee some file size savings, the GIF format limits your images to 256 colors or less (also known as indexed color mode). If you want to get a sense for how GIF thinks about your image, open the same image you blurred earlier, choose Image > Adjust > Posterize, and use a low number like 2 (**Figure 18.2**). This will reduce the number of colors in your image, and you should notice that more areas of solid color appear. You should also notice that photographic areas don't look so good, but graphical areas (logos, text, bar charts, etc.) generally look fine. So now you should be able to see why GIF is mainly used to compress graphics.

Figure 18.2 Left: original image. Right: posterized with a setting of 2.

Optimize in Photoshop or ImageReady?

In general, Photoshop is fine if all you want to do is slice and optimize a few images, but you'll need to optimize in ImageReady if you're working with rollovers or animation. The optimization features are almost identical between the two, but you'll find that they present the information differently. Let's take a tour and see what kind of options we have for optimizing our images.

To optimize an image in Photoshop, choose File > Save For Web. This will bring up a huge dialog box that will pretty much take over your screen (**Figure 18.3**). At the top, you can choose to view the original, the optimized version, or a combination of both. At the bottom of the image window, you'll find information about how small the file size has become and how long the image should take to download. To tell Photoshop what type of connection to think about when calculating file size, click on the small arrow in the upper right of the preview image window (**Figure 18.4**).

Next, let's look at the optimization settings in this dialog box. The first step to optimizing an image is to choose the file format you'd like to use (GIF for graphics and JPEG for photos). When you change file formats, the options in the optimization area will change to reflect what the selected format offers. If you'd like to use some preset optimization settings, choose one from the Settings pop-up menu.

Note

If your image is large enough that you can't see the whole thing at once, then press the spacebar to temporarily access the Hand tool (or just grab it from the Tools palette) and then scroll around your image.

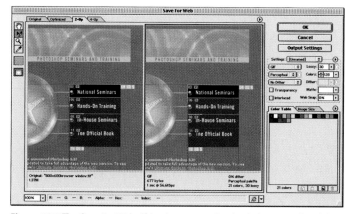

Figure 18.3 The Save For Web dialog box, set to view both the original and the optimized version of the image.

Note

If you find that the upper right area of the Save For Web dialog box is mostly empty, then you've probably got a sliced image and none of the slices are active, so grab the Slice Select tool from the upper left and click on the area you'd like to optimize.

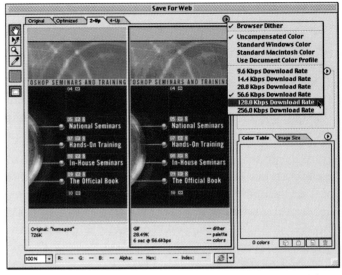

Figure 18.4 Changing the connection speed used to calculate download times.

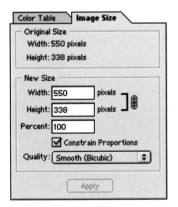

Figure 18.5 The Image Size area of the Save For Web dialog box.

Below the optimization area, you will find the Color Table (which works for GIF files only) and Image Size tabs. The Image Size area often comes in handy once you can see what your image will look like when it's optimized, because you can squeeze the file size further by reducing the dimendions of the image a small amount (**Figure 18.5**). If you need to scale an image down, just change the width (assuming the Constrain Proportions checkbox is on) and then click Apply.

That's how easy it is in Photoshop. Now let's look at how ImageReady organizes these same features into a collection of floating palettes (**Figure 18.6**).

At the top of the document window, you'll find the familiar tabs to determine what you'd like to view. The file size information is at the bottom as in Photoshop, but now you can also choose the connection speed from a pop-up menu at the bottom of the palette (**Figure 18.7**). The Optimization palette is in the upper right and the Color Table palette is directly below that. The Slice palette replaces Photoshop's Slice Options dialog box, and the slice tools are in the main Tools palette. So, as you can see, Photoshop and ImageReady are very similar. I use Photoshop if all I want is to slice and optimize a few images; I switch to ImageReady any time I need rollovers or animation.

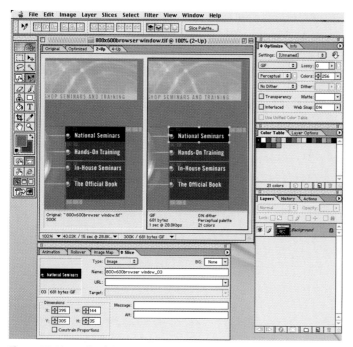

Figure 18.6 ImageReady's optimization tools.

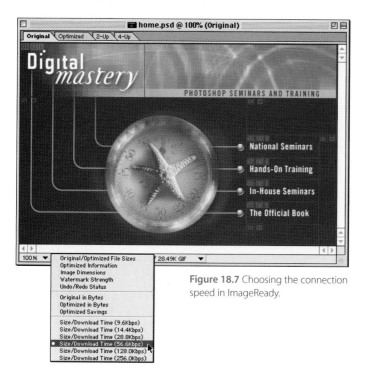

Figure 18.7 Choosing the connection speed in ImageReady.

Optimizing Photographs

Let's take a tour of the features needed to optimize a photographic image. (Remember, if you're in Photoshop, you're still in the Save For Web dialog box—this is "where is all happens" in terms of optimization.) First you'll need to set the Format pop-up menu to JPEG. Next, try to determine the best optimization setting (**Figure 18.8**). You can do that by watching the optimized view of your image while you choose a general setting from the Quality pop-up menu. After you've done that, you can fine-tune the setting by moving the Quality slider around (click on the triangle that appears next to the Quality number). I find that settings below 30 only work for images that don't contain much detail. I always leave the Optimized checkbox turned on because it will deliver a slightly smaller file size.

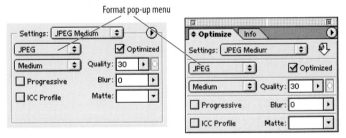

Figure 18.8 Left: Photoshop's JPEG compression options. Right: ImageReady's JPEG compression options.

The Progressive option makes it so that your image will display a low-resolution preview that slowly becomes more detailed as more of its data is downloaded to the Web browser (**Figure 18.9**). That's essential for large images in today's fast-paced world, where a five-second wait could mean the difference between someone who browses your site and one who leaves in a fit of impatience. If you have an image that is over 20K in size, you might want to consider using the Progressive checkbox in an attempt to entice viewers to wait for your graphic to load before moving on.

Figure 18.9 From top to bottom: the progression of an image being downloaded using the Progressive option. (© 2000 Stockbyte, www.stockbyte.com)

I do not suggest you use the ICC Profile feature unless you're producing a site that sells expensive clothing. An

ICC profile will attempt to make the colors in your image appear to be more accurate in a Web browser. That sounds like a great thing, but the profile is often much larger than the file you are attempting to optimize, and will therefore increase download times. Not only that, but the only people who will see an accurate image are those who have calibrated monitors and have a browser that understands profiles (not many do).

If you'd like to squeeze a few extra K out of your image, consider using the blur feature. Blurry images usually achieve better compression than overly sharp ones. Likewise, applying the Sharpen filter to any image saved as a JPEG file will increase its file size.

The JPEG file format does not support transparency. The color specified in the Matte field will replace all transparent areas (transparent=checkerboard in Photoshop) as shown in **Figure 18.10**. You can get the look of transparency by setting the Matte to the same color that will be used for the background of your Web page.

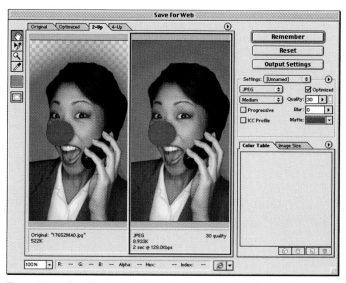

Figure 18.10 Photoshop's checkerboard will be replaced with the color specified in the Matte field. (© 2000 Stockbyte, www.stockbyte.com)

Optimizing Graphics

Graphics present a whole different set of challenges. The first thing you'll need to do is change the Format pop-up menu to GIF and then clear out any unusual settings (**Figure 18.11**). I always start with Lossy, Web Snap, and Dither set to zero. Then you can experiment with the Colors setting. I usually click on the pop-up menu just to the right of this setting (it looks like a tiny arrow pointing down), start with the lowest setting, and then increase it until the image has acceptable quality. Each time you change this setting, the program will double the number of colors used. Once the quality seems to be OK, try reducing the number of colors even more by clicking the down-pointing arrow directly to the left of the Colors setting, which will reduce the number of colors in increments of one. Next, try each of the choices in the pop-up menu that appears to the left of the Colors setting. This setting determines exactly which colors will be used. Finally, if the colors in your image slowly fade out (like a gradient), then you might want to experiment with the Dither setting as well (**Figure 18.12**). But be careful, because you can often get better results by leaving that feature off and just giving the image more colors instead. As you work through these options to figure what's going to work best for your image, keep your eye on the file size, which is displayed below the optimized image.

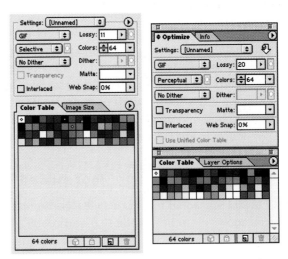

Figure 18.11 Left: Photoshop's GIF compression options. Right: ImageReady's GIF compression options.

Figure 18.12 Left: dither set to zero. Right: dither set to 60%.

The Interlaced checkbox allows your image to download a little at a time in a striped pattern (**Figure 18.13**). This allows someone to get a general sense of what the image looks like before the entire image loads. I usually reserve this feature for large images, where I need to supply a preview in order to entice viewers into waiting for the image to load. I also avoid it on normal-sized images because it will increase their file size. Interlacing a GIF image is the same concept as creating a progressive JPEG image, but the result looks a little different.

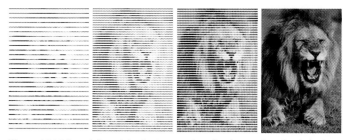

Figure 18.13 From left to right: the progression of an image downloaded using the Interlaced option. (© 1998 PhotoSpin, www.photospin.com)

The GIF file format supports transparency, but that doesn't mean that it can reproduce exactly what you see on screen. You know that in Photoshop, an image can contain very soft, subtle edges (like a drop shadow), but the GIF format only supports one level of transparency. That means an area can be either 100% transparent or 100% opaque, but nothing in between. It's almost like you are using a pair of scissors to cut out your image—and I don't have to tell you it's impossible to make soft edges using scissors. To enable transparency in a GIF image, just turn on the checkbox in the Optimization palette. The Matte color listed in the Optimization palette will be used to fill any partially transparent areas, so pick one that matches the background color of your Web page (**Figure 18.14**).

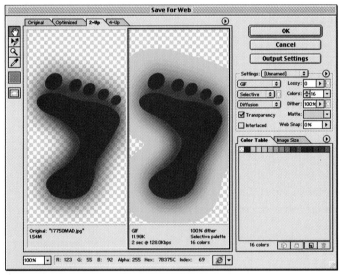

Figure 18.14 Partially transparent areas are filled with the Matte color.

Once you think you have your image perfected, you'll want to start thinking about what it will look like on monitors that display only 256 colors. (At the time I wrote this chapter, 6.7% of all the people browsing the Web were using computers limited to 256 colors.) You can do that by choosing Browser Dither from the View menu in ImageReady, or by clicking the triangle that appears in the upper right of

Photoshop's Save For Web dialog box. When you turn on Browser Dither, you'll suddenly start to see random specks in many areas of your image (**Figure 18.15**). This is also known as dithering. These dithered areas usually look good where one color fades into another, but not so good in areas that should appear as solid colors (like logos and text). But you can get rid of the dithered look. Look at your image with the Browser Dither feature turned on, and note which areas need to be changed. Then turn off the Browser Dither feature. Now, grab the Eyedropper tool and click on an area that was dithered (when the preview was on), but should now be filled with a solid color, and then click the cube icon at the bottom of the Color Table (**Figure 18.16**). If you find that the color used doesn't look good in the image, double-click the color in the Swatches area and choose an alternative color (just make sure it's a Web-safe color). Continue to do that with the rest of your image until you've fixed all the areas that didn't look good when the Browser Dither preview was on. Once that's set up, you can turn Browser Dither on again to check your work.

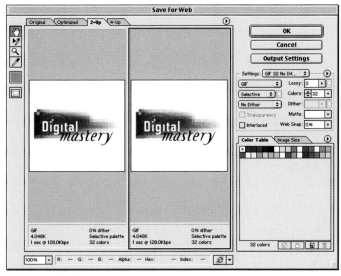

Figure 18.15 Left: image as shown using GIF compression. Right: image shown with Browser Dither preview turned on.

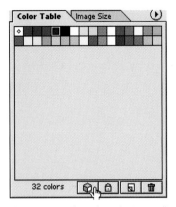

Figure 18.16 The color cube icon will convert the currently highlighted color to a Web-safe color so it won't dither.

Figure 18.17 When the Lossy option is set too high, you'll see noisy looking artifacts.

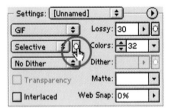

Figure 18.18 Clicking this symbol will allow you to use weighted optimization settings.

At this point you've taken advantage of a lot of GIF optimization features. But there is one more way to squeeze more out of your image. Click on the Lossy setting and play around with the up and down arrow keys while you stare at the image. Keep increasing the setting until you notice some noisy looking artifacts showing up (**Figure 18.17**), and then back off just enough to make the artifacts disappear. This feature will attempt to create more areas that contain solid color, but it does it in a very unusual way that often produces noise. It's kind of weird to find a Lossy option when saving a GIF file, because GIF is known as a lossless file format. Photoshop hasn't changed the way GIF files are saved; instead, they've just added a special feature that degrades the look of your image *before* it's saved.

Weighted Optimization

Weighted optimization is a new feature in Photoshop 6.0 that allows you to make one area of an image look better than the rest without slicing the image into multiple files. Here's how it works: You start by making a selection of the area that is most important to you. You can choose Select > Feather if you want a to have the quality slowly change over an area. Once you have a selection in place, choose Select > Save Selection and assign it a memorable name. Then, when you go to optimize your image, look for a small dotted-circle symbol (**Figure 18.18**) that will appear next to many of the optimization settings (Lossy, Dither, and Color for GIF files and Quality for JPEG). If you click on that symbol, then you'll get to a special dialog box where you can specify how you'd like Photoshop to use your selection (**Figure 18.19**). The white slider determines the setting for the area that was selected; the black slider determines which will be used in the area that was not selected. If the selection was feathered, then the settings will slowly change across the area that was feathered.

You've now learned how to use weighted optimization to influence where Photoshop will apply the highest Quality settings without slicing your image into multiple documents (**Figures 18.20 and 18.21**).

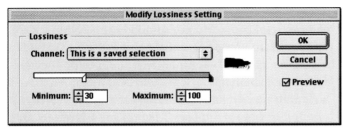

Figure 18.19 The Weighted Optimization dialog box. Depending on which feature you chose, it will reflect a different name, but it's always about modifying a setting.

Figure 18.20 Image before applying weighted optimization. (© 2000 Stockbyte, www.stockbyte.com)

Figure 18.21 The result of using weighted optimization.

Combo Images

So far, we've separated our images into two categories—graphics and photographs—but you'll often have an image that contains a combination of both. When that's the case, you'll have to make a compromise and decide which area is most important to the image. If it's the solid areas of color, then save it as a GIF file (**Figure 18.22**). On the other hand, if the photographic areas are more important, then use the JPEG file format (**Figure 18.23**). This can also be a great time to use the new weighted optimization feature that we just talked about, so you can use different settings for each area of the image (**Figure 18.24**). No matter what you choose, part of the combo image will look less than ideal, but that's the nature of combination images.

Figure 18.22 A combo image saved in the GIF file format. (© 2001 Stockbyte, www.stockbyte.com)

Figure 18.23 A combo image saved in the JPEG file format.

Figure 18.24 A combo image saved in the GIF file format with weighted optimization.

Slice Tricks

If your interface design contains many same-colored buttons, you might want to use the same optimization settings for all those buttons. You can accomplish that in ImageReady by Shift-clicking on each one of the slices when you're using the Slice Select tool. Next, choose Link Slices from the Slice menu. That will force all the buttons to use the same compression setting.

Optimizing Rollovers

If you have created rollovers in ImageReady, be sure to look at the optimized view of both rollover states. You can do that by turning on the Rollover Preview button in ImageReady, which looks like a hand with lines radiating from the fingers (it's near the bottom of the main Tools palette in ImageReady). With the preview turned on, you should be able to move your cursor around the screen and see how the optimization settings affect the look of the rollovers. Also, be sure to turn on the Browser Dither preview again to make sure your rollovers will look good in 256 colors. If you're in a multi-pane view (2-up, 4-up) this only works when the pane you're trying to preview is active.

Optimizing Animations

The JPEG format does not support animation, so you'll have to use GIF, even if your animation contains photographs. When optimizing an animation, be sure to click through all the frames of the animation, because some frames might contain more colors than others. And be extra careful when attempting to optimize an animation; it's really easy for an animation's file size to get out of hand. I often lower my image quality standards when working with animations, just so they load fast in a Web browser.

Saving Your Images

After you've chosen the optimization settings for each area of your image, it's time to save the resulting file. In Photoshop, that's a pretty simple affair. All you have to do is click the Save button in the Save For Web dialog box and assign a name to your image. But in ImageReady, you'll have to choose File > Save Optimized As and then choose HTML And Images for sliced images or Images Only for non-sliced images from the pop-up menu near the bottom of that dialog box. If your image contains slices, you'll end up with a folder that contains one image for each slice and another for each rollover. Animations will be saved as a single GIF file.

Closing Thoughts

When you save your graphics in the correct file format, and with appropriate settings, they will look better and load faster than what you'd get from any other file format. In fact, optimizing your images can often result in a Web site that loads twice as fast as most other sites. And you now know how to do all that, so you're all ready to load your images and HTML file into an HTML editing program like Adobe GoLive. So, go forward and optimize your Web world so everyone has a chance to see and enjoy it.

Ben's Techno-Babble Decoder Ring

GIF—An acronym that stands for Graphics Interchange Format. This lossless file format is limited to a maximum of 256 colors and is ideal for imagery that contains large areas of solid color.

JPEG—An acronym that stands for Joint Photographic Experts Group. This lossy file format achieves great levels of compression by generalizing the color information in the image, while maintaining most of the brightness information. It's ideal for images containing soft edges, gradations, or a wide range of color, such as photographs.

Lossless Compression—Any kind of compression that results in a lower quality image when compared to the original.

Lossy Compression—Any kind of compression that delivers an identical image when reopened.

Courtesy of Jimmy Chen, www.typographic.com

And the Beat Goes On

I'm terrible at goodbyes, and I'd like to think that our experience with Photoshop is a never-ending discovery. So, instead of saying adios, I'll leave you with a couple of thoughts that you can reflect on as you set off on your own flight into the upper atmosphere of Photoshop.

First off, there's no question that as soon as this book is printed, and no matter how exhaustive I think I've been, I'll have some new technique I wish I could have shared with you. There are hundreds of thousands of people out there trying out new stuff and doing their own experimentation (including yours truly). In the coming months I'll be presenting my Photoshop Mastery seminar and I always get challenged to solve a multitude of problems and come up with a new solution or technique. Whenever that happens, and I get something that I think is really juicy, I'll talk about it in my Tip of the Week, or I'll post it to my Web site. You can subscribe to my free Tip of the Week at **www.digitalmastery.com/tips**, or visit the book's companion Web site at **www.digitalmastery.com/companionsite**. I'd also love to see you at one of my seminars. To find out if I'm going to be visiting your area, please visit **www.digitalmastery.com**. Beyond that, I'd really like to hear from you. Any reaction you have to the book would be most welcome, as well as your own personal feedback and insights into Photoshop. You can write to me at **willmore@digitalmastery.com**.

And finally, if anyone ever tells you that Photoshop is too difficult, or you have any doubts about your abilities to master this program, throw them in the garbage instantly (the doubts *and* the negative person)! I can attest to you that I am the original poster child for the "Self-Taught Photoshopper." When I first played with Photoshop, there were no books, seminars, or CD-ROMs to show you what to do. The point is, anyone can learn Photoshop. All you need are a few ounces of patience, a little bit of faith, and a true desire to learn this amazing program. And never forget the words of the great Gordon MacKenzie, "Orville Wright did not have a pilot's license."

Index

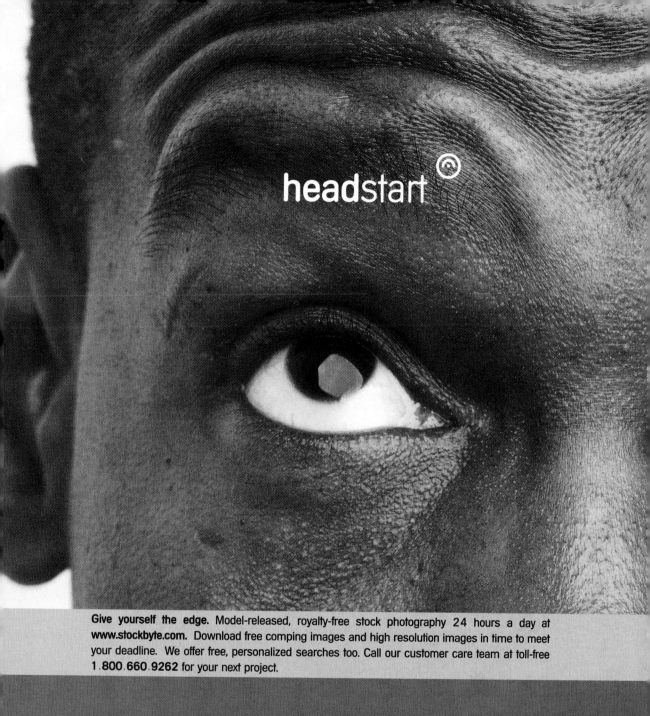

headstart

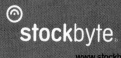

stockbyte

www.stockbyte.com

Licensing Agreement

By opening this package, you are agreeing to be bound by the following:

This software product is copyrighted, and all rights are reserved by the publisher and author(s). You are licensed to use this software on a single computer. You may copy and/or modify this software as needed to facilitate your use of it on a single computer. Making copies of this software for any other purpose is a violation of the United States copyright laws.

Please remember that existing artwork or images that you may want to include in your project may be protected under copyright law. The unauthorized incorporation of such material into your new work could be a violation of the rights of the copyright owner. Please be sure to obtain any permission required from the copyright owner.

This software is sold as is without warranty of any kind, either expressed or implied, including but not limited to the implied warranties of merchantability and fitness for a particular purpose. Neither the publisher nor its dealers or distributors assumes any liability for any alleged or actual damages arising from the use of this program. (Some states do not allow for the exclusion of implied warranties, so the exclusion may not apply to you.)

WARNING! The Stockbyte low-resolution (comping) images contained on the accompanying CD may not be used for any item which will be printed or published in any medium. Please carefully read the full text of your License Agreement, contained in the CD folder titled "Image Use Restrictions." By using the images you are consenting to the full terms of the license.